Where the Light Falls

A PORTRAIT OF EDWIN ARLINGTON ROBINSON

Edwin Arlington Robinson

CHARD POWERS SMITH

Where the Light Falls

Falls

A PORTRAIT OF EDWIN ARLINGTON ROBINSON

Where the Light falls, death falls;
And in the darkness comes the Light.

THE MACMILLAN COMPANY, NEW YORK
COLLIER-MACMILLAN LIMITED, LONDON

First Printing

The Macmillan Company, New York
Collier-Macmillan Canada Ltd., Toronto, Ontario
Library of Congress catalog card number: 65-11479

DESIGNED BY MARY A. BROWN

Printed in the United States of America

Acknowledgment is made to the following for permission to use copy-
righted materials:

Charles Scribner's Sons for quotations from *The Children of the Night*
and *The Town Down the River*. Columbia University Press for quotations
from *Philosophy in the Poetry of Edwin Arlington Robinson* by Estelle Kap-
lan, 1940. William Morrow and Company, Inc. for quotations from *Edwin
Arlington Robinson* by Emery Neff—copyright © William Sloane Associates,
Inc. 1948. Harvard University Press for quotations from *Untriangulated Stars:
Letters of Edwin Arlington Robinson to Harry de Forest Smith, 1890–1905*,
Denham Sutcliffe, ed. 1947, copyright © The President and Fellows of
Harvard College 1947. The Virginia Quarterly Review for quotations from
*Early Letters of Edwin Arlington Robinson, edited by Daniel Gregory
Mason*, Winter 1937 and *Letters of Edwin Arlington Robinson to Daniel
Gregory Mason, edited by Daniel Gregory Mason*, Spring 1937 copyright ©
The Virginia Quarterly Review 1937. Radcliffe College Alumnae Associa-
tion for quotations from *Edwin Arlington Robinson—A Musical Memoir*
by Mabel Daniel in the November 1962 Quarterly. University of California
Press for quotations from *The Literary Background of a Traditional Poet*
by Edwin S. Fussel, 1954. Colby College Press for quotations from *Edwin
Arlington Robinson and his Manuscripts* by Esther Willard Bates in Colby
College Library, 1944; from *Robinson's Notes to His Nieces* by Richard
Cary in The Colby Library Quarterly, December 1960; *Edwin Arlington
Robinson as Soothsayer* by Richard Cary in The Colby Library Quarterly,
June 1963. The Macmillan Company for extensive quotations from *Edwin
Arlington Robinson—A Biography*, by Hermann Hagedorn, 1938; *Edwin
Arlington Robinson: A Critical Study* by Ellsworth Barnard, 1952; *Selected
Letters of Edwin Arlington Robinson*, edited by Ridgely Torrence 1940, and
Collected Poems. Appleton-Century for quotations from *Next Door to a
Poet* by Rollo Walter Brown copyright © D. Appleton-Century Co., Inc.
1937.

To Eunice

Contents

ILLUSTRATIONS

Preface

IN TERMS OF BOTH style and substance, Robinson as poet was
a phenomenon of the scientific revolution of the late nineteenth
century that discarded the Fundamental Christian myth, from
Creation through Resurrection, together with the phantasma-
goria of Victorian manners and morals. It was a time when a
great culture was in final decay but had not yet collapsed; the
framework of society still held, but the intellectuals were released
from prejudice into free inquiry, and among the results was a
surge of literary production. Robinson was preceded by Poe, with
the dubious support of Emerson, in the repudiation of the Victorian moral standard of criticism with its limitation of "poetic subjects" to maidenly and sentimental ones. And he was preceded
by Whitman in the substitution of the vernacular for Victorian
"poetic language." But he was the first to dramatize common experience at once in the language of common speech and in the
standard verse forms. With Masters, both born in 1869, he was
senior among the poets whose maturity produced the polyphony
of the teens and twenties of this century. And he was preeminent
in that major group of them who were trying to discover a meaning of life to replace or revise the Judeo-Christian one which was
being denied along with the myth in which it had been articu-
lated.

In the population generally, there were three types of reaction to the scientific derogation of the myth in terms of which
the Western world had long conceived the human situation. One
group, calling themselves Fundamentalists, accredited the myth,
taken literally, as essential to the religion; wherefore they clung
to it and rejected science, denying that it took the angry old
Gentleman more than six turns of the earth to finish the job, or
that their ancestors might have had tails. A second group,
calling themselves Liberals and comprising most of the intellectuals, likewise identified religion with the myth read as literal
prose; wherefore, preferring the scientific account to the mytho-
logical one, they repudiated with the latter, not only Judeo-
Christian religion, but all religion. Any account of man other
than a materialistic one they were able to recognize as Funda-
mentalist superstition.

Between these two strong and extreme groups, a third and
smaller one distinguished between reality and its expression, between content and form. While discarding the literal myth under
the revelations of science, they did not thereby suppress the
intuition that there is some meaning of human life other than
material comfort and gratification. This group, since its dedication was to a reality more profound than the formulations of
conscious reason, we might call the Realists, or, as among intellectuals, the Moderates. They were mavericks, individuals,
independent of each other and of both the old-fashioned and new-
fashioned herds of sheep. Whenever one of them did come on a
central meaning of the cosmos, human life, or both, he spoke as
a prophet in the deepening wilderness.

Among the prophetic visions of the poets of the twenties, perhaps the humblest were those of Sandburg and Stephen Vincent
Benét, who saw human reality in terms of the old Westward
March, the romance of prairies and stars. More profound were
the romantic self-assertions against the dark, sometimes universal-
ized by pantheistic perception, on the part of Frost, Crane, William Rose Benét, Millay, William Carlos Williams, Jeffers, and
others. There were affirmations of beauty as ultimate reality by
Millay, LaFarge, Mr. Rorty, Mr. Holden, and others. There was
LaFarge's mystical perception of a merciful universe, and Mr.

Eliot's inclusive statements of time transcended. And more comprehensive humanly than any of these was Robinson's assertion
of a cosmic "scheme" whereby all persons will eventually find a
happy resolution for which the "hell" of this existence and the
loss of the self in its battle are "logical" prerequisites: altogether
a kind of abstract or unmythologized religious affirmation which
would fit Hinduism, Buddhism, basic or unpersonified Christianity, and all other religions or cults that recommend the subservi-
ence of the predatory outer self to the imagination. Yet it was not
for his larger affirmations that Robinson was acclaimed. If a poll
had been taken among poetry readers in the late twenties and
early thirties, he would surely have come off with a plurality as
the laureate of the day. But his reputation then, and such of it
as survives now, rested and rests almost exclusively on his relatively slight objective things, chiefly his dramatic portraits. To
this day his major prophecies have been little examined and less
understood.

Meanwhile, through the brief period of Robinson's popularity
the general trend against religion, or equivalent inclusive perception, was broadening in scope. Long before 1930, both home
and school had abandoned the ancient belief that there were
fixed verities that ought to be taught the young. The only recognized realities were the children themselves, each with his unique
bundle of potentials whose emergence without frustrating direction was the delicate and precious assignment of his mentors.
Truth was plural and relative. Religion, and with it all large ideas,
was repudiated by the intellectual world, not only as erroneous
but as evil, being identified with persecutions, inquisitions,
tortures, and the engaging new black myth about the American
Puritans and their fictitious moralism and "witch-burnings." By
1930 we had the strange phenomenon of educated people who
called themselves liberals, and were so in many respects, in-
trenched in an intolerance of metaphysical inquiry at least as
solid as the bigotry of the Fundamentalists.

After the economic debacle of '29-'30, three parallel trends
combined to put the final quietus on the prophets of fading truth.
The popular posture among the enlightened became that of "social consciousness," which held physical welfare and psychic

complacency to comprise the good life of man. Philosophy
plumped into Logical Positivism, denying the reality of all general principles, all alleged metaphysical truth, and in effect all
philosophy. In literature the New Criticism, which, at first identified with Mr. Eliot, had been a rising avant-garde trend through
the twenties, began to move into ascendance. Not content simply
to deny large content, it denied all content, limiting critical
standards to those of technique and "pure poetry," "the poem
itself." Not content to taboo the metaphysical imagination, it dis-
couraged all imagination and encouraged composition by careful,
conscious, rationalistic concoction. Soon after Robinson's death
in '35, the modern movement of artistry in poetry which he had
introduced denied him. By the beginning of the War, his prophetic affirmations were not only unread but unknown. Of his
great poems only the tragic negations *Eros Turannos* and *Mr.
Flood's Party* survived, and chiefly he was and is known for his
clever, thumbnail dramas such as *Richard Cory* and *Miniver
Cheevy*. No obliteration of a prophet could be more complete.

At some time in the fifties there seemed to be a slowing of
the pendulum in its swing into human vacuity, and a pause possibly portending a return towards fullness of life. There was the
over-bruited and now long overdue revival associated with an
increasing enrollment in the churches, probably panicky rather
than religious. The young novelists set up a fashion of wailing for
meaning in life, though without presuming to whisper an assertion
of one. Many of the younger poets, daring to break from the
esoteric emptiness of the New Criticism, began announcing fugi-
tive mystical hints of reality, what Robinson might have called
"gleams."

But none of this awakening curiosity, so far as I know, is yet
in sight of any kind of integrated understanding. In its way there
stand strong walls of taboo set up and buttressed by two generations. Recently, speaking to a prominent liberal critic, I happened to use the word "god." The critic knows me well, knows
that nothing could be farther from my mental landscape than any
of the anthropomorphic superstitions; yet he must inform me
impatiently, in Nietzsche's language, that "God is dead." Talking
with a young and tolerant professional philosopher, I referred to

the long-settled ban upon metaphysical gestures of the imagination. In his considered response he identified the latter, as matter
of course, with "anxiety," a maladjustment of the mind. It has
not occurred to our current intellectual leaders that the hunger
for truth could be anything but a sublimation of some frustrated
healthier impulse. It is incomprehensible to them that the normal
activity of all of the cells of the brain may be as basic as that of
the cells of the rest of the body, and that the frustration of the
imagination may be at least as unhealthy, the results at least as
psychotic, as the frustration of the sex glands. It does not occur
to them that the current universally recognized tensions of both
young and old may arise from anything as simple as the defeat of
the natural human desire to discover some reason for living.

And yet it may be that the very violence of the taboo upon
inquiry into "truth" and "reality," like that upon words of sex
sixty years ago, is some evidence of the strength of the impulse
repressed. It may be at any moment now that the young will
succumb to wonder again, will begin to demand prophets again,
and the fashion will turn. The whole herd of literary sheep—
writers, readers, critics, and publishers together—will go clatter-
ing back across the pasture to the former corner with its verdure
of large ideas and nourishing truth. There at night they will bleat
again at the old fixed stars whose American constellation includes
Whittier and Emerson, Whitman and Dickinson, with Robinson
and perhaps one or two more just appearing on the horizon.

When I attached the name "prophet" to poets crying for truth
in the humanist wilderness, I might as well have called them
"great" poets. For great poets are those inciting in the reader an
expansive movement of the imagination into identification with
some "great" or large percept. Like other quantitative terms, this
one is of course various in degree. It would include a spectacle of
the cosmos, as in *De Rerum Natura,* a vista of human life in its
generality, as in *Paradise Lost,* or simply, as in *Canterbury Tales,*
a large array of people composing a world. Any of these, and
others equivalent, may be great poems. And a poet who habitually
deals in such sizable goods becomes a great poet.

In contrast, a minor poet is one who incites the imagination

to relatively small perceptions, though they may be, and usually
are, more "purely" presented. Usually the minor poets are qualita-
tively better poets than the great ones, because their excellence
is their only credential and they are less bewildered by size and
complexity in their visions. Most of the great poets, like Milton
and Wordsworth, are guilty of appreciable passages of loose and
prosaic writing. But the high minor ones, like Herrick and
Marvell, Gray and Patmore and Housman, are almost without
flaw. In our time, the obvious contrast is between Robinson and
Frost. Frost was a far better poet, far "purer" in his saturation
of poetry; and, moreover, he achieved greatness in a few poems.
Robinson, on the other hand, while he probably has a larger
bulk of pure poetry than Frost, is, because of his voluminousness
in ideas and people, often blurred with obscurity, sometimes even
banality. And yet, in his *Collected Poems* we have a symphony
of large perceptions, involving a numerous population, which
reduces the sum of Frost's music to the sound of a delicate stream.

Robinson is great in two categories. Among the 208 titles he
finally preserved, there are—if we include the great passages in
the long works which are never read—well over thirty pieces that
belong in the world anthology of poems of large vision. Yet there
are eight or ten great poets in English whose record is in this respect at least as impressive. It is in the other category of greatness,
that of size of population, that Robinson is preeminent among
poets in English except those who wrote for the stage. His 233
fully drawn characters are approached only by Chaucer's 188—
the latter at a cursory count. Browning, with less than a hundred,
follows far off—as indeed do Goethe and Hugo, whose works are
notably populous in their respective off-stage poetic literatures.
In Robinson you are in the presence of a world which for size
and completeness of portraiture is hardly equaled elsewhere in
modern poetry except among the playwrights. In the double epic
Merlin and *Lancelot,* he gives us a general statement of the
meaning of life that will stand with those of Milton and Blake, of
Wordsworth and Shelley and Whitman. But in his presentation
of many people and their multitudinous dilemmas, he is almost
alone. The distinction between the greatnesses of idea and population may of course be more apparent than real. To portray many

people in detail may require as much sweep of imagination as the
perception and statement of one large and inclusive idea.

The original motive of this book was simply to write another
memoir of Robinson, another little volume to join the half dozen
already contributed by other friends, adding a few new anecdotes
and a few new interpretations of aspects of the character. When
I had finished a draft, I was satisfied with it as a report of my
acquaintance with him from 1924 till his death in '35. But in the
work I had developed an irresistible curiosity about the environment, vicissitudes, and decisions that had formed the man during
the fifty-four years of his life before I met him, matters which
seemed to me to be incompletely treated in Mr. Hagedorn's sympathetic and generally perceptive biography, and touched hardly
at all in Professor Neff's more austere work of scholarship. I was
curious about the family debacle, both financial and personal,
which sent Robinson away from home in the late nineties. I was
curious about the one principal love which Robinson had revealed to me positively but without specification. I was curious
above all about the apparent split in the personality between a
high degree of selflessness or saintliness and the necessary self-
centeredness of the artist. And, perhaps related to this split, I
was curious about the almost lifelong self-dissatisfaction which
seemed to resolve only at the end into the belief that he had done
what he had to do, that he had done well.

With these and other less fundamental objects in view, I began
to look into the sources, and presently found myself outlining a partial biography, partial in that it would be weighted on the side of
the matters that I thought had been previously underemphasized,
the aim being to provide the ultimate, definitive biographer with
a richer fund of material to draw upon, leaving the final balancing
and fitting to him. As I began drafting this second account of
Robinson I soon saw that I was actually transcribing a personal
drama strung along its emotional suspenses, climaxes, and reso-
lutions, and that any close analysis of Robinson's ideas or "philosophy" would be out of key. Wherefore, when I had finished
my personal story I wrote such an analysis, to comprise a third
and distinct part of the book. By a final readjustment, I divided

the original memoir into two parts at the critical year of 1927, interpolating the biographical and intellectual sections between them.

Thus I have combined under one title three different kinds of writing. Parts One and Four, the original memoir, attempt what Professor Edel in his classification calls "pictorial" biography or portraiture.[1] Part Two attempts what he calls "narrative-pictorial or novelistic" biography. And Part Three is not biography at all, but intellectual analysis. I have tried to integrate these disparate methods within a uniform, quasi-colloquial style, by much inter-reference, and by my own percept of Robinson.

Parts One and Four, the attempted portrait, pretend to no scholarship. The material comes almost exclusively from my memory, thirty to forty years after the events, and the memories of mutual friends of equivalent duration. The pretense is rather of a creative work of art, an all-round painting of the subject in which photographic details may be distorted and even improvised in order to emphasize the essentials of the personality. The charge of inaccuracy is the more plausibly invited by the fact that I never Boswellized Robinson, due to a seemingly decent instinct which was in fact hypocritical. Whenever I was impelled to set down some expression of his or some anecdote that revealed a facet of his character, I restrained myself on the ground that it would be shameful to capitalize on friendship. Yet at the same moment I deliberately and forcefully engraved the remark and its setting deep in my cortex, and proceeded systematically to keep it intact there by frequently repeating the exact words to myself and to others through the years. Furthermore, these significant expressions and scenes were usually fused into memory by some emotion or other. Robinson's expressions, where I have retained them verbatim, were funny, or they related to some emotionalized concern, either of his or of my own. Besides the incidents and comments I have recorded, I hold in presumptive memory many more which I have excluded, supposed phrases that do not always recur identically in my mind, supposed episodes whose physical setting is vague. Some of these I omit with extreme regret, for they recommend themselves as the solutions of important un-certainties in Robinson's life.

In view of the care I have taken to make these distinctions among my recollections, I dare assert that, in the memorial Parts One and Four, whatever I have set down as essential is true if ever memory can be true. "Essential," as I use it here, applies to any of three features in a given episode. Always Robinson's central statement, which is usually the point of the anecdote, is absolutely as he said it. Also, the locale is always right. And thirdly, any action of Robinson's that is unusual, un-Robinsonian, may be taken as part of the emotionalized imagery of the scene and so as essential—pulling down a shade, jumping up and pacing around the room, many other gestures which the reader, with a little familiarity, will recognize as atypical, unique.

Outside of these three categories—the articulate comment, the locale, and the unusual gesture—the array of Robinson's actions accompanying them in my account are inessential and from the factual point of view may be looked on with suspicion—the rocking a little forward and back, the expanding blast of cigarette smoke, the pursed lips, the upwrinkled forehead, or the long finger pressed into it. These were his common gestures, one or more of which probably punctuated every recorded episode. Yet I can never know certainly which ones occurred in any particular context. They are the work of imagination, not in its function of perceiving the essence of the material, but in its formulative function, its creativeness, its integration of a portrait. In each instance these details are recalled, not as of that particular time and place, but as of Robinson generally. They are real, not as fact, but as art. At all times they are facets of the personality and necessary to the completion of the form. If at any moment when I attributed these gestures to Robinson he did not in fact perform them, he should have!

Besides my reports of Robinson's incidental actions, there are also two whole scenes in Part One of the book where to some extent I used the method of factual essentials and typical details. These were my first two evenings at the MacDowell Colony in which, as a background of my first view of Robinson, I wanted to present the Colony as a whole, both physically and in personnel. Every act and speech that I there attribute to Robinson or to myself is true. But otherwise there is some generalization.

I am not at all certain of the list of colonists in that early June of 1924, and outside of specific actions in which I was involved, I merely present a typical array for any time during the mid-twenties. But for those two evenings, the scenes I report at the Colony are authentic, complete with personnel.

In Part Two, the biographical section recounting Robinson's life before I met him, there is of course no memory of mine involved. All facts asserted without qualification are properly documented, or they derive from one of two sources too copious to be cited in detail and only generally acknowledged.[2] All matters of inference, conjecture, and opinion are labeled as such.

The portrayer of a poet can hardly avoid involvement in the perennial debates over critical biography—the use of the poetry for the interpretation of the life—and biographical criticism—the use of the life for the interpretation of the poetry. Except in the effort to contribute to the revival of Robinson's reputation for greatness, as I have defined it, there is no criticism intended in this book. Especially, I have tried to avoid biographical criticism which, by explaining the poetry in terms of the life, tends to overshadow each with the other. If I were writing a criticism of Robinson's *Tristram* and interpolated that at least one important scene was autobiographical,[3] the reader's responsiveness to the poem thereafter would be to some extent perverted into curiosity for similar realism in other passages. Instead, I have tried to follow the method of critical biography. What I call the "Legend of Emma" contains much personal interpretation of Robinson's verse on the part of one who knew him intimately, and, following this lead, I have drawn some biographical inferences of my own. In such use the poetic evocations, the poetry proper, is not adulterated by its biographical source. It is simply neglected, unseen, never unwrapped. Accepting the report of the Legend that a particular scene in *Tristram* is autobiographical, I have combed the poem for other analogous revelations, ignoring the poetry in the search for prosaic confession or the pseudo poetry of unintended self-revelation. Except for the occasional celebrations of greatness in a passage or a poem, there is only one class of Robinson's verse in which I have let the biographical analysis reverse into implicit criticism. This is in that appreciable body of early, subjective work where the poetry is little objectified out of the poet's personal experience; here Robinson, like many young poets, is telling us principally about his feelings, wherefore any collateral knowledge of those feelings that we may bring to the reading will increase our capacity for the appreciation of the poem. *Luke Havergal, Credo, The Altar, Calvary, Two Sonnets,* the *Octaves,* and many others—we can understand these better as poems if we know something of the particular tortures Robinson was suffering when he wrote each of them. In these cases, while drawing biographical material from the poems, I have also not hesitated by implication to explain parts of the poem in terms of their vital background.

There remains to be said something about a few words in the vocabulary of this book, raising that semantic problem which we shall continue to have with us as long as our society and its language are in an unstable state of transition. Like most of the denizens of the twenties, I am habituated to bandying about psychoanalytical terms with only sub-amateurish knowledge of their meaning. Wherefore, I have eschewed them in this text, substituting my own naïve vocabulary of the "inner self," the "outer self," and a "subconscious" so comprehensive as to include, I am sure, half a dozen categories in the professional vocabulary. Similarly, although I have been forced to use the words "idealism" and "pantheism" because Robinson used them, and I have dared once or twice to use other philosophical terms in their common meanings, yet generally I have avoided philosophical vocabulary also. This would seem to be prudent in a time when American philosophy fashionably aims at no truth but merely at the creation of an esoteric vocabulary and neo-Socratic method for the sole purpose of breaking down any perceptions of truth, all presumptively foolish. In my critical vocabulary, involving words like "imagination," "fancy," and "reason," I speak with more assurance. I have defined these words elsewhere and use them as a professional—though, alas, other professionals sometimes use them differently!

All this self-consciousness in the use of language is, of course, a function, not only of social uncertainty, but even more surely of the increasing specialization of the age when there is hardly a field in which anyone can communicate with anyone but a colleague. Whether futilely or not, Robinson stood against all this. He spoke to everyone about everyone's experience. He knew that poetry would never be read except by a few. But this for him was an aspect, not of specialization, but of all and confused mankind.

An acknowledgment of the sources with comment on some of them will be found at the end of the text.

C. P. S.

Part I

FRAGMENT OF GOD'S HUMOR

There was that about him . . .
That made as many of us as had wits
More fond of all his easy distances
Than one another's noise and clap-your-shoulder.
                        —*Ben Jonson Entertains a Man from Stratford*

I

WHEN I came home from Italy, in April of 1924, bringing the body of my wife on the same ship, I was a badly broken boy. As an adolescent of twenty-nine, I had need of a father, of God. I had need of Him in bereavement and grief—although I was already helping myself in this respect by pouring out the elegiac sonnets that became the body of my first book. I had need of Him as a teacher to explain to me a state of things in which an exceptionally brilliant and loving young woman should suffer for months and die. I needed Him as a guide to help me in the practical decision I was facing, whether I should continue in the career of a poet, which represented my desire and in which my wife had encouraged and helped me, or whether I should return to the practice of law.

To encourage me in the more attractive calling, which I had in fact been following for about a year, I had already achieved publication in two or three poetry magazines—momentous endorsement for a frightened novice in the aesthetic world of 1924! Yet I needed further assurance in my dilemma, for I had no doubt that the fate of the world hung on the direction my very great genius might take. I still needed a word from God. At the outset His avatar bore the name Robert Frost, somebody who was older, had gained the heights of two or three slim volumes, had been reviewed by the pantheon of celestial critics, and whom in the main I could read. On landing I wrote him a brave letter in Amherst, not doubting that he would grasp the cultural importance of the crisis. He never acknowledged my letter. (I hasten to interpolate that years later Mr. Frost made me a kindly gesture which may have been intended as restitution for this discourtesy.)

My literary acquaintances in New York included John Erskine, then president of the Poetry Society of America, and Lloyd Morris, whose *The Poetry of Edwin Arlington Robinson*—the first book on that poet—had appeared recently. Mr. Erskine told me with his wide, wise, motherly chuckle that Mr. Frost, who was a close friend of his, never answered letters from strangers. He assured me that the place for me was the MacDowell Colony,

3

ideal retreat for impecunious genius, of which he was a director. Lloyd, who had been a colonist, supported the opinion of Semi-God, and by dint of I know not what diplomacy they got me in for early July. I went as a fledgling poet, one or two of whom were usually among the elect of the Colony, youngsters who had unimpressive publication but impressive introductions—though for my own part, I assumed that my appearance in the most elevated and esoteric little periodicals was of the essence. Lloyd said he would write E. A. Robinson about me, and told me to introduce myself to him on arrival. Further, he asked me a number of un-aesthetic and trivial questions about my customary diversions, especially indoor diversions, including anagrams and pool.

Lloyd's letter, which I never saw, was surely a turning point in my career. As for Robinson, I had in fact considered him against Frost for the office of God, and had turned him down because I had trouble reading him. Also, he was suspect of respectability —why Frost wasn't I don't know. Above all, he was paralyzingly grand for having won the Pulitzer prize last year. I bought his current book, *The Man Who Died Twice*, and read most of the words several times.

On the designated afternoon early in July I proceeded north-ward on the local train from Worcester, and never doubted that the railroad officials were aware of the high consummation they were privileged to assist. I had a moment's misgiving when the conductor stopped the train at no station in order that the passengers might descend and pick strawberries; but I took it with regal tolerance for the pleasures of the poor. At Peterborough I got off the train and whispered the name of Heaven to the local taxi driver. When we had climbed the village hill and were in the country, we passed on the right a small green sign with arrow at a break in a hedge, bearing in black the phrase "To the Grave"— the grave of Edward MacDowell, as I learned presently. My Dantesque contemplations inspired by the sign were shortly dissipated by our entrance between two ugly, rustic gateposts of field stone, each capped by a large ovoid stone like a dinosaur egg.

Swirling round the circular drive with a flower bed in the middle, the driver stopped and discharged me in front of the clapboarded, white, former cow and hay barn known as Colony

Hall. In the office in the wing attached I got my keys and directions from Mary Tonieri, the Irish cook and wife of Emil (pronounced like Evil) Tonieri, the caretaker. Returning to the circular drive, I passed before the red, saltbox farmhouse, now serving as a dormitory for women and known as "The Eaves," and proceeded to my room in "Pan's Cottage"—in 1924 rustic Victoria was still dominant over much of MacDowell Colonial nomenclature and architecture.

Before I was well stowed in my room, the frightening dinner bell clanged from the peak of the shed behind "The Eaves," and through nervousness I was a few seconds late in returning to Colony Hall. Hurrying through the former barn with its posts hideously cased halfway up in stained boards, its pool table, huge rustic fireplace, bookcases, and commonplace appointments, I slowed up in awe at the two swinging doors with short passage between them that led to the dining room. Softly I edged through and entered the banquet hall of the gods. Everybody was seated around the four tables for six each. They were all colonists of a month's standing, so a newcomer drew glances from twenty-odd pairs of imperious eyes. Immediately on the right as I entered there was an empty seat at the nearest table, in front of the now unlighted stone fireplace, rustic of course, a happily placed seat that faced the other tables and the windows on two sides of the big square room. Five ladies occupied the other chairs at the table and four of them united in a gentle gasp as I included them all in an inquiring bow and pulled out the chair to sit down. But at the same time they observed that I was new, about thirty, nicely tweeded, not unseemly of feature, and I had easy bearing. Nancy Byrd Turner, of Virginia tradition and sitting at what would be my right, first smiled out of the general gasp, introduced herself and presented me to the rest. There was stately dramatist and librarian Elizabeth Marsh, who had stated when she came to the Colony that it was the first time she had ever traveled without a maid. There were poet Leonora Speyer, magnificent and friendly, composer Mabel Daniels, critical and consciously broad-minded, and on my left dramatist Esther Bates, who alone hadn't gasped and was now smiling to herself—I learned presently that she typed Robinson's manuscripts. As for the two poets Nancy

Byrd and Leonora, I recognized them at once as of highest Parnassus! Here I was! Arrived! I sat down and relaxed into my best social manner.

Even before I sat down I had of course surveyed the room apprehensively, expecting to see very God. I was sure he wasn't there, and I was relieved. But the moment I was seated everybody seemed remarkably aware of me, giving me little smirks, poking neighbors with their backs to me, causing them to turn around, glance at me, and smirk likewise. First, my social self-consciousness wondered what was amiss. I touched my tie, my hair, under the table my fly. All in order. Then, in a flash I realized that naturally all geniuses knew about each other! Of course they had all seen my distinguished publications in *Contemporary Verse, Poetry, Voices,* and the *Saturday Review of Literature!* My gentle breeding laid its wings of modesty over me, and my graciousness increased. In my fatuous moment a door opened beyond the fireplace, and God of the frontispiece of the Pulitzer-prize-winning *Collected Poems* entered from his room upstairs, clad in an undistinguished business suit.

For a moment he stared at me out of enormous dark eyes, a tall and lean, vertical, moustached, fifty-five-year-old dragonfly, his brittle wings quivering indecisively while all the room rustled. Then he glanced at an empty seat the other side of the room, gave a little jump of decision, and climbed to it with the longest strides of the longest legs I ever saw. Several vulgar people looked at me and laughed out loud. I smiled magnanimously at whatever it was I didn't know.

Once or twice during the meal I caught E.A. looking at me, and instantly his big brown eyes would drop to the table. I saw his beautiful, large head, delicate as eggshell, the more beautiful for the slight retreat of the dark hair from the brow. Even at twenty feet remove, I noticed his hands, the longest and leanest fingers I ever saw on a man, yet a large and strong hand, a masculine hand.[1] And I noticed his precise daintiness in eating, sawing his meat into tiny cubes like parcheesi dice, spearing them one at a time with his fork like a finch's bill and chewing them with satisfaction, his moustache wiggling.

So passed my first meal in Heaven. The courteous ladies at my table spared me until coffee. Then Esther Bates leaned forward, chuckling, and said softly, "You are bound to learn soon, so I may as well tell you that you took Mr. Robinson's chair, the only seat reserved for anybody. I assure you he'll like you for it." This broke my aplomb. I smiled nauseously at my five ladies, excused myself and left the dining room, fled through Colony Hall, out through the little screen porch, letting the door slam, past The Eaves, and secreted my agony in Pan's Cottage. Far from hurting me with E.A., this was, as Esther said, an ingratiating *faux pas*. It was one of his little hypocrisies to pretend that he didn't have any special seat, that he always took the nearest one. My mistake would amuse him, and his acceptance of it would strengthen him in this shameless lie.

The next morning, no doubt under subconscious direction, I just got inside the 8:30 last bell for breakfast, and through the French doors at the back of the dining room saw E.A.'s tall, narrow back and legs, under the little white canvas hat, swinging off down the western road through the meadow towards the pines and distant Monadnock, one long arm flailing his stick to decapitate weeds, the other holding a book close up to his side. It was a quality of E.A. that, while there wasn't much he could do in the physical world, what he did do he did gracefully. Thirty years before, he had written to a friend, "I was born awkward"; [2] yet it was perfectionism, not awkwardness, that limited him. To the same friend he had written of his enjoyment in sawing wood and trimming trees. These were things he learned to do. Every gesture of life, external or internal, he addressed with hesitant gravity, considering what might be the best, and therefore the only, way of doing it. When he had mastered the inward idea, the truth of it, he essayed the material application in the outer world. And the result, while not always externally efficacious, was a work of art; it had a special, finely rhythmed beauty of its own. Like the precise way I had seen him cutting up his meat and feeding himself one tiny piece at a time. Like his manipulation of table accouterments generally. Like his minute, perfect, and sometimes legible writing on a small pad, and his deliberate selection of words in speech. Like his poetry which was the one steady activity in the external world which, by dint of hard work, he could perform almost to his satisfaction. Like his walk alone to his studio in the morning—graceful, not in the common athletic, cross-country or tramping sense but in a unique way of his own. His long strides cleared fences, mountains, and all other worldly obstacles. Though he had a writer's stoop when standing—partly because he had to look down at almost everybody—when he walked he threw his head back, swung his stick, and you could imagine him singing the "Pilgrims' Chorus." He was bound somewhere.

That morning Emil Tonieri, of Scotch accent, handsome Italian face, and infinite wisdom, drove me in the pickup Ford truck to my studio, the Chapman, which was the farthest Thule of the eighteen studios then finished in the Colony—a few colonists worked in their rooms. Over the next thirty years it became my favorite spot in the world. Stretching away in front of it was a cloister of full-grown birches, ice-bowed to meet in a gothic roof. Beyond them was the overgrown, ferny sheep pasture which was the reputed place for colonists to get engaged. The nearest other studios were the Wood, a quarter mile back on the road through the then prehurricane pines, and, invisible at the same distance across a deep, wooded ravine, the Adams and the Veltin, which latter was E.A.'s rustic stone-and-log castle with its vista of Monadnock cut through the trees. That first morning I was able to squander two or three hours exploring, building a need-less fire in my fireplace, arranging my books and papers on the big worktable, and sharpening dozens of pencils, until the pickup truck came again with my basket lunch. Then I got down to my sonnets to my wife and the accompanying luxury of tears.

I knew I would be in for it at dinner. I couldn't avoid pre-senting myself to God as Lloyd Morris had commanded. I went over to Colony Hall promptly at the dinner bell, passed the gath-ering geniuses at the pool table, the fire, the meager bookcases, and entered the dining room among the first. I went to the far-thest table, where E.A. had gone last night, and, as the auspices continued to have it, found earlier birds located, so I had to choose between sitting with my back to the room or taking the chair E.A. had been forced into by my *faux pas*. I took the chair E.A. had had, and in the jolly introductions noted that I was a famous character. The rest poured into the room, all passing the holy "siege perilous" by the swinging door. When they were settling down, E.A. came as before through the door from his upper eyrie, paused a moment, glanced at me—making my stomach turn over—puckered his lips, and surveyed the room with a pretense of searching for any vacant chair. As if by surprise, he discovered the reserved one, gave his little jump, strode to it and, as if apologetically, drew it out, considered it and the waiting ladies, and sat down. The supercourteous old humbug!

After the introductory jollification at my table, it was an uncomfortable meal, as if I were going to make a speech. Tennessee Anderson, sculptor, recently divorced wife of Sherwood, was there. She was large-featured and hearty, always wore a peacock feather in professed defiance of hard luck in catching another husband (a few years later she died alone in a small room in Chicago). Now she said to me, "I can see you won't be long for this boarding school!" The remark did not draw me out. I was embarrassed at being accredited with a sophistication I lacked. The Colums were there, greatly beloved little Padraic in one of his silent moods, solemn in his pixiesque way. Mollie sat opposite me and frequently stared me down with her self-assured arrogance, probably seeing through me for the spoiled innocent I was. Sometimes I stole glances at E.A., and once or twice caught the final fleck of a glance at me swinging quickly up, his busy, small, strong chin raised, chewing, apparently seeing nothing. Again I observed his precision in dissecting his roast beef, and I noticed besides his air of satisfaction as he consumed one piece at a time, looking round the room as if proud of his social feat, chewing like a kind of nervous ruminant, not with the slow, rotary assurance of a cow but with quick little chops like a llama. Also, he was relishing Mary Tonieri's excellent cooking. I never observed any confirmation of his reputation for being a gourmet in any esoteric sense. He merely liked to eat, and he liked especially to eat sumptuous, conventional food, substantial New England cooking such as he had grown up on. He liked rich gravy and desserts, but had no use for tasteless things—"Who ever decreed that carrots were edible?" [3]

My memory is blank for the middle portion of that banquet

of torture, that murderer's last meal. By the time Maud, the pretty, English waitress, was clearing tables for dessert, I was in paralyzed panic—'How do you do, Mr. Robinson—my name is Chard Smith . . .' 'How do you do, Mr. Robinson—Lloyd Morris said I might introduce myself' . . . 'How do you do, Mr. Robinson—I wanted to tell you how much I admire . . .' 'How do you do, Mr. Robinson—Of course you never heard of me, but . . .' My mind rolled round and round through banalities, trying to refine them so as to impress God, all my frightened snobbery cringing, sometimes straightening up and trying to swagger before itself. After all, had I not—in *Poetry*—and the *Saturday Review*? . . . But the Pulitzer prize! . . . And the new book that I couldn't read! . . . 'What in God's name am I doing here? I'll leave tomorrow and go back to Rochester and law practice where I belong. . . .'

Maud and Trudie, the sprightly, redheaded second waitress, got the rice pudding around rapidly, the little pitchers of light cream, and immediately the coffee. Certain high gourmets began to get up and saunter out of the dining room—no rice pudding for them! I didn't touch mine, didn't know it was there. Why didn't I get up and go out? But I'd have to pass close to him—that chair where I had sat! Why, for the love of God, didn't *he* go? He reached out and tinkled the little bell on the table, and when redheaded Trudie came running he ordered a *second rice pudding!* What should I do? Order a second too? I began pecking at my first—taking it dry—forgetting the cream.

They were almost all gone! DuBose and Dorothy Heyward, respectively poet and playwright, stopped to chat gaily with God, who looked up at them with his big woodchuck smile, wiped his mouth and, out of deference to Dorothy, gave a correctly fake hunch in his chair as if to rise. Beautiful DuBose and Dorothy— both semicrippled, he by polio, she by arthritis—had been married in Mrs. MacDowell's "Hillcrest" last year—they were the only couple I know to have confessed that they actually did get engaged in the sheep pasture.

Thornton Wilder came up to them and stood twittering, smirking, bowing right and left to people and shadows—"Good evening, good evening." Elinor Wylie, who hated E.A. for hav-

ing advised her to wait before publishing *Black Armour*, sailed
magnificently by, Constance Rourke, essayist and critic, classi-
cally lovely with pink dress and pure white hair, drifted up and
paused, smiling at Thornton who told her an engaging confidence,
and chuckled. DuBose, Dorothy, Thornton, and Constance went
out through the swinging door. At the royal table the last of the
waiting women, Mabel Daniels and Leonora Speyer, rose and did
each other the excessive civilities at the door. The room was almost empty. Poet Bill Benét and artist Grant Reynard went out
together, Bill pausing to whisper to E.A., who nodded. Then he
went on mouthing rice pudding with great comfort, pursing his
lips around each mouthful, sometimes scowling at the table, then
inspecting the ceiling, obviously unaware of me. From a distant
corner Frances Patterson, movie critic, walked out purposefully,
twiddling two fingers at God as she passed, and he glanced up
and nodded. The swing door slapped behind Frances. But for
Trudie flitting out with the trays of empty dishes, we were alone!

I'm not sure there was ever such a crisis in the affairs of men.
There was I, frozen, drained of intelligence, almost of consciousness, shy to the point of faintness, also snobbish, genius-struck,
aware of God who controlled my future and was surely going to
strike me down. And there was He, in still greater throes—if
only I had known it—under the compulsion of Lloyd's letter, the
necessity of making a social gesture toward a stranger! I had my
standardized social manner which *in extremis* would work auto-
matically. He had no such resource. With his "skin on inside out,"
he had to consider, select, and adapt perfectly every word and
movement to each particular case. My agony was partly meretri-
cious. I had something to gain. His was selfless, absolute and unrelieved.

There we sat twenty feet apart, each pretending not to know
the other was there. Out across the meadow westward the sun
had only a few minutes to drop before it touched Monadnock,
where ten years before it had framed *The Man Against the Sky*.
E.A. looked out there through the French windows to his left,
and I looked out through the sash window at my right. At the
same moment we both looked back into the immediate, confined
scene, but our eye-lines carefully didn't cross. Why in hell didn't

he go? This was his joint, not mine! It was up to him to move first.
I nibbled at my rice pudding again. He did the same. I took a
letter out of my pocket and seemed to reread it—holding it
upside down. He also took a letter out of his pocket and considered it carefully, the grave look, the lips puckered under the
moustache, the fate of the world under consideration. I put the
letter back in my pocket. He restored his, took a sip of coffee.
. . .

Years passed. . . . Why, oh, why didn't he go? What was he
up to? A thought crossed my mind—Did he have a date with one
of the waitresses? Was I spoiling his show? This made me look
straight at him, probably with an analytical scowl. For a flash our
eyes met, then he quickly averted his and focussed on a point on
his table, his lips sticking out extremely, his round eyes enlarging,
and the skin on his high, china-like brow drawing upward as in
amazement. It was a characteristic expression that meant the
still vague perception of another unresolved incongruity between
the inner and outer worlds; as I learned later, it expressed suspension and might resolve in any direction.

Now, I understood none of that. I only knew that either I was
gumming up some game of his or he was being discourteous to
me, making me uncomfortable in what was the same as his house.
To hell with him! I'd go right out past him and not make a sign
unless he did! I sat up, scraped my chair back, looking at him.
Instantly his brow rose higher in a million little wrinkles—it was
his look of ultimate panic. I relaxed. After all, it wouldn't do to be
rude to the old boy. I slumped back again. The wrinkles smoothed
from his forehead. He considered the table again. I did likewise.
I thought it couldn't be that he had a date with a waitress. He was
about my father's age, they about twenty. His reputation of being
a cold fish . . .

For more centuries we both sat in stone. . . . (Perhaps in
all, five minutes had passed since Frances Patterson went out.)
Suddenly we both looked up to a sound like a soft wooden blow.
The kitchen swing door had opened, and Trudie came in again,
wondering if we wanted anything. We both looked at her. I
smiled and she smiled back. She fetched me back to sanity. I felt

my absurdity—after all, hadn't I been around? What was to prevent my leaving the room, and doing whatever seemed right as I
came alongside him? So, still looking at the pretty redhead, I stood
up and started across for the door. . . .

And as I came on something happened in the universe. With
his slow precision, God uncoiled out of his chair to his narrow six-
feet-two of height, calculated the line of my approach, side-
stepped, and stood glaring in my path. My social reflexes took
over and I advanced jovially, extending my hand. He made his
one effeminate gesture, holding his hand up and dangling it in
front of his chest, as if he were afraid to let it go. I seized its limp-
ness and said, "How do you do, Mr. Robinson, I'm——"

He interrupted me, speaking with precision—"I hear you like
to play pool."

Our eyes met and for an instant the universe hung suspended.
The film cleared from our eyes and we were unembarrassed. I
smiled and he smiled his rabbit smile. We saw each other in our
dualisms that were the same, the inner world of reality where we
both lived, and the outer world of appearance that had just now
so absurdly confused us. It was a little sudden, and for a moment
I withdrew shyly behind my eyes, but without averting them.
E.A. did not withdraw, his big round brown eyes remaining
clear and loving. I did not know that he had a motive for accepting me that was more profound than a moment's perception.
I did not know he had taken me on before I came because Lloyd
Morris had written him that my wife had died abroad, that I was
in pain. I was one of the baffled duffers who were his world, the
hurt and the broken who had "borne the day's load," marching
on the road "to the town down the river," "like a stairway to the
sea where down the blind are driven." I was a mild case of those
in the human procession whom, as E.A. had said to Esther Bates,
he avoided if he could because to see them made him suffer more
than he could bear. But—what he hadn't told anyone and perhaps
didn't know himself—once he took them on, nothing could make
him abandon them, no misfortune of his, no misconduct of theirs.
They became people in his inner world, his cosmos of humility
and compassion. People with their sacred privacy and their never

fully comprehended motives. He saw them, and they existed, they and their inexplicable, individual fates. Whatever they might do was as it was, as it had to be.

I said, "I'll bet Lloyd Morris told you I liked to play pool. It was nice of him. I'm not very good." E.A. half smiled and said, savoring the words, "We'll make mincemeat of you"—I thought of the little cubes of beef. He stepped over to the swing door and put his hand on it. My own sensitiveness rushed up and displaced my self-consciousness. I saw what he wanted to do, stepped over to the door, gave him room to push it open and hold it for me, felt his gratitude and his pride in doing something worldly. I was ahead of him in the short narrow passage between the two doors. It would have been awkward to change places. So I jumped on, pushed through the second door and held it for him, feigning confusion. Trying to look casual, he came on, and as he was passing me he hesitated, looked straight at me again and beamed his fronttoothy smile. I smiled back in my best spontaneous, comprehending fashion. We were agreeing what asses we were with all this shyness and evasion and pretense, how absurd mankind is. It was only a moment, but it was outside of time and completed our introduction. E.A. passed me and strode freely over to the pool table under its floodlight, ignoring the crowd by the fire where Nancy Byrd Turner and Thornton Wilder were pouring out anagrams onto a card table.

Bill Benét and Grant Reynard were fooling around with the four cowboy-pool balls, waiting for E.A. and any fourth. When I followed him up to them he stood embarrassed and pressed a long finger against his forehead in his usual gesture of registering thought. Perhaps he'd forgotten the names of one or both of them, or of me. More likely he'd forgotten what you did at such a juncture. Anyway, he gave up with a resigned sigh, waved at me, and said with his slow exactness, enjoying the sibilants, "This— is—Mister—Smith." Bill and Grant introduced themselves cheerfully. E.A. said, "He's a—champeen—pool player." "Fine!" "Fine!" "Come on!" E.A. and I walked to the cue rack. The more shameless in his female retinue came over from the July fire and womaned the grandstand of two or three chairs on each side of the table. Two of them had other than shameless motives. Both

Mrs. H. H. Beach, composer, whose husband had been a distinguished billiard player, and Esther Bates understood cowboy pool and liked to watch it, Esther smiling at the gravity of the males, Mrs. Beach sighing with Victorian rapture when a ball clicked, sped, and chunked into a pocket. Little Rose Cohen, author of a currently successful autobiography, came over with her bouncing steps and sat down, exuding tenderness. Strong-faced Mabel Daniels took with dignity the round-armed wicker chair, as if it were a box seat at the opera, and as before, surveyed me judicially. Bill Benét said to E.A., "Suppose Grant and I take on you and the champion." My ego surged. The partner of E. A. Robinson! I wondered if the weekly paper in the village reported the pool games!

In the dining room I had seen a glimpse of the inner landscape of E.A. At the first swinging door I had seen his rudimentary, wistful outer self that wanted to make proper gestures in the world. And at the second swinging door I had caught his humor that delighted in the incongruity between the two worlds. Now, at the pool table, I saw again the desire to be like other men, to be in the crowd, not now the tired and heavy laden but the world's crowd, the late Victorian crowd of his childhood whose initiates could make the correct, late Victorian gestures, could dress smartly and say funny things that made people laugh. At pool E.A. had vanity. Since it was part of the outer world, he didn't expect to win, but he wanted to do well and have it observed. He looked around, disgruntled, if his audience didn't assemble, and he was chagrined as a boy if no one noticed when he did well. Esther Bates told me that once after she had been looking elsewhere when he made a good shot he sidled over to her and confided that she knew nothing about cowboy pool. When she explained it to him in detail, he still grunted with superiority.

Outside of discussing literature or music and holding his liquor, pool was, I think, E.A.'s only fully developed, conventional social exercise—though even so, he never initiated a game but would merely stand at the table, looking silently receptive, till someone else proposed it. What everyone liked to watch was his beautiful long left hand on the table, the care with which he placed it and shifted it minutely this way and that, aiming, then paused and essayed the stroke. Sometimes he made it, and then he raised his head and walked proudly round for the next shot, glancing at the female gallery. But usually he missed it, and where another man, wanting to do well and not a great player, would have snapped his fingers or cursed or stamped over to a window and back, E.A. would make a single tiny sideways shake of his head, then would step back, lower the butt of his cue soundlessly to the floor or the toe of his black shoe, hold it near the tip with both hands and stand staring at the table, not even lifting his forehead or puckering his lips, just staring at nothing, while all the knitting women loved him. He had a unique way of chalking his cue. Instead of scrubbing the tip with the green, concaved cube as others did, he first considered both the tip and the cube, then applied the latter to the former in dainty dabs till he was satisfied that it was all covered. Then he set down the chalk and looked, not inordinately, but moderately self-satisfied. And in such moments of fatuous detachment he sometimes had to be reminded of his turn. I remember an occasion, probably in that summer of '24, when he was preparing to try a thin billiard and Bill Benét said, "Kiss it, E.A., kiss it gently as you would your sister." E.A. scowled, grumbled, "But I haven't got a sister," and resumed adjusting for the shot. There was a possible reference in the remark that we didn't understand, then.

I don't remember who won the two or three strings we played that first night, but E.A. and I probably did. For, as of that quadrumvirate, I was indeed the champeen, having cut my ivories with a high school gang in a pool room, and E.A. was no worse than Bill and Grant. I remember his watching my shots with timid, not quite humorous, admiration. I think we won and my newcomer's reputation was further enhanced. I had not only bearded God, I had assisted Him. Not a knitting woman was sure she had done so much.

II

Through July I played pool every evening, E.A. usually in the game, and after a string or two we would join the crowd in the village and essay prohibition near-beer in the Monadnock Café. E.A. loathed it and would leave it barely sipped. To the best of my recollection, that month comprised one of his occasional excursions on the wagon. But it may have been simply that he hadn't yet received me so far as to share with me whatever he had in his room. When the crowd came back from the village, we always went out to the pantry where Mary left us many quarts of milk in the icebox, and sometimes a pan of cake on the kitchen table.

Meanwhile I was turning out my sonnets and getting genuinely devoted to E.A. Often I would shoulder out a waiting woman from his table, and after dinner we would sit there over coffee, my Luckies, and his Sweet Caporals, postponing pool while we explored our respective pantheisms. Or I would edify him with plans for my epic whose composition would be my life's aim if I finally quit law for poetry. He would listen with judicial solemnity, staring at a crumb on the table, sometimes lifting an abandoned piece of cutlery, inspecting it, and replacing it. Often he would hold for a long time his blank, startled expression, the forehead upwrinkled a little, the lips slightly protruded under the moustache, the big brown eyes expanded but apparently seeing nothing. I came to understand its premonitory significance, and it would almost stop my flow of wisdom. It meant generic emotion, as yet unspecified, creation in abeyance while chaos awaited formation into a concept. To be in the presence of it was a little like being a wounded gladiator in the Colosseum awaiting Caesar's thumb. The suspense might break in any direction: into terror and flight; into the faint smile, even the chuckle; into the contracting little scowl and extremely protruding lips meaning deep concern or tentative disapproval, further emphasized, if the inward passion was great, by two or three long fingers drumming twice on the tablecloth, followed by a shift of position. Sometimes in these periods of suspense I would be able to change my base and inject a genuine witticism, thus directing the resolution gratefully into the smile, the chuckle, even the gasping laugh which, until you got accustomed to it, was itself a little awesome. It was not, as with most people, a series of coughs on a single exhalation, but each cough had its own separate intake and outgo, just as every word in a poem should be separate with a life of its own. This full laugh, whether at his own or another's brilliance, was hearty and almost free, expressing his nearest rapport with the environment when he was cold sober. I watched his every gesture with loving voracity. My chirography, my facial expressions, even my accent, began to reflect his.

Hilarious and grim were the minor expressions of his great chilvalry towards women. He had learned how to hold a lady's coat, if ever he could find it in the closet in Colony Hall—not very effectively, to be sure, for he tended to lift it too high for her, and he grasped it with both hands at the middle of the collar so she had a job finding a sleeve, let alone two. But the initiates knew the trick. More excruciating was his pushing of ladies' chairs at the table, something he seemed always bound to do. As far as his own chair went, he drew it out just the right distance, considered it for a few seconds to be sure it was indeed a chair and properly placed, then stepped one to the left, one forward, one to the right, and sat down. He tried an equivalent technique with ladies. He would draw the chair out while the assisted one waited, but he never grasped the truth that he should draw it out farther than for himself if she were going to step in while still standing upright. So, when he had studied its location and approved it, he would turn to the lady with brows lifted in invitation. She struggled in, trying not to capsize the table, while E.A., sensing that something was amiss, held the chair firmly and fiercely, not pushing it in or drawing it out, till at last the lady got down, smiled up at him over her shoulder, and hunched herself into place.

And once he and the cohort of five were settled, the ballet of serving him was never-ending and never the same. When he wanted something he assumed his brow-stretching, puckering stare, not knowing what it was. All the ladies were at once in agitation, all trying to be specific: "Would you like the salt, Mr. Robinson?"—"Would you like the water, Mr. Robinson?"— "Would you like the bread, Mr. Robinson?"—"The butter?"— "The cake?"—"The chocolate sauce?" All the condiments would pile around him while he stared . . . till at last he saw the right one or heard it named. He gave his little jump out of his trance, expressed thanks, and helped himself or was helped.

Sartorially E.A. was of his culture, an old-time combination of rusticity and courtliness. By 1924, having emerged, by dint of one Pulitzer prize and another forthcoming, from almost complete dependence on patronage, he was beginning to indulge a long-suppressed desire to look respectable as he had in his youth, as his friends Isaacs and Ledoux and Hagedorn did now. He had bought at least one good and expensive business suit. It fitted him but didn't become him. It looked borrowed. Yet, one evening when he was going out in the world and came downstairs in a tuxedo, it suited him, was part of him. Like every other Yankee from way back, he was at home in bare suspenders, and he was equally at home dressed up—black tie, white tie, or cutaway. But nothing between. No citified nonsense. No Racquet Club. No boards-of-directors meetings.

Dressed up or not, he always loathed large gatherings because of the "dilution" of intelligence they involved. He loved people individually, wanted to establish real rapport, mutual perception with each one separately, and this was impossible in a cackling atmosphere. Agonizing were his ordeals at parties in Colony Hall for the outer world, when the ladies of Peterborough, Hancock, Dublin, and farther horizons were sure to lionize him above all other geniuses. There was a balcony around the inside of the old barn, and some of us wicked youngsters used to escape up there with our cake, our Sunday-school punch and any drug-store alcohol of the prohibitionist twenties that we might have on our hips. Down in the jolly gathering E.A. would be suffering at some point where the pack had run him to bay—usually with his back against one of the old barn posts. Rarely he sprang and escaped through the swing doors into the dining room and so up to his room where he may have had a bottle of something un-palatable in his bureau. From the balcony I once overheard a passage that led to such a departure. One costly lady alone—in hunting terms, an old tufter of the pack—had him flattened against a post. "Oh, Mr. Robinson, you remind me so much of one of your characters." "Which one?" said E.A., whistling the "ch" through his teeth. "Miniver Cheevy," said the doting enthusiast. It was then the stag leapt and vanished, shaking his antlers. (*Miniver Cheevy* is indeed in some respects a self-satire.)

There are many such anecdotes in the record. High among
them is the one Rollo Walter Brown recorded. It was at the Nu-
bansit Tea Barn where the colonists dined once a week, in order
to give a night off to the staff at Colony Hall. A committee of
ladies from New Jersey or Kansas cornered E.A. in what he had
thought would be a hiding place by the stairway. In Mr. Brown's
account, one of them assured him, " 'I just adore your poetry, . . .
in fact we all do. But it is so hard to understand. I wish you could
tell us of some easy way.' His face expressed greater helplessness
than ever, but he did manage to reply: 'I don't know that there is
any, except just to read it, one word after another.' " [4] Actually,
E. A. usually held his ground and stood these tortures manfully.
For he took very seriously his responsibility to the Colony and
Mrs. MacDowell, and he knew that these levees might mean
handsome checks, perhaps a new studio, perhaps a new truck or
other needed machinery.

Toward the end of July, I gave E.A. the typescript of my proposed first book, most of it the elegiac sonnets to my wife. As
always, he accepted graciously this assignment from a tyro. From
the late eighties when he had been one himself, there is no evidence that he ever ducked a candid literary, or allegedly literary,
request, ever failed to acknowledge fan mail unless it was face-
tious, even though after '27 this duty might call for over a
thousand of his little notes for a single book. But while he was
gracious in undertaking to advise an applicant, he was graciously
ruthless in giving his opinions. Even when he liked a manuscript
he usually advised the aspirant gravely to wait a couple of years
before publishing. The story of Elinor Wylie's tantrum when he
advised her to delay publishing *Black Armour* is now legend—
beautiful Elinor, who was not restrained in her requirements of
obeisance.

One evening following pool, not long after I gave him my
dossier, he invited me to come up to his room over the dining
room. He motioned me to a straight chair, himself took the high-
backed rocker, and sat for a moment with one long finger pressed
against his brow, as if to push a secret button and release thought.
I put in my journal the pronouncement of Fate that ensued: "I
like your sonnets, all except two which need more work," and he

added, with his appalling humility, "or so it seems to me." Pause, as he rocked two inches each way—a sign of emotion. "Some of them I like very much."

He got the typescript, I stood by his chair, and we went through it. Besides the two he didn't like, he had indicated bad spots in half a dozen others, and he explained them. If he hadn't pointed out the flaws I should not have noticed them, for his marks were pencil dots in the margins, hardly visible—of course he wouldn't presume to deface anybody's manuscript! Somewhere I have that typescript with its half-dozen dots. It would be hard for me to persuade a bibliographer that these were the corrections of Edwin Arlington Robinson!

Having made his comment, he handed me the black binder, and I, reeling with humility from the Lord's pronouncement in the Temple, sat down. Then he spoke again: "If you will fix those two sonnets, I see no reason why you shouldn't go ahead and publish." I stared at him and was probably pale. He raised his forehead and widened his eyes in generic impulse to action, rose, fished in his bottom bureau drawer, and produced a pint. I stopped him at a third of a tumbler, went into the bathroom and watered it. When I came back he had poured himself a full tumbler straight and was fingering it impatiently on the arm of his chair. I divined that he wanted to propose a toast and didn't know how. So I raised my glass, and he lifted his an inch or two, looking at it fiercely as if he hoped it wouldn't get away. He drank along with me, and when I refused a second, poured himself another half-tumbler. "I don't drink for the taste," he said, "but for the effect," biting off the stops with delight.

And so it seemed that in my callowness I had come into the good graces of the great E.A. I shall never know whether he passed unbiased judgment on those twenty-five sonnets, whether he liked them on account of me, or liked me on account of them, or liked either or both because I was a human being who had been hurt by the world. For whatever reason, he kept them by him. That first book of mine, published a year later, was, at least until my last call at his room in the fall of '34, the only slim volume of a youngster of an age to have been his child which he kept always in the three-by-four bookshelf in New York that was his library. It was, I think, the only volume by a youngster which he never relegated to the huge wooden box by his door where he piled his presentation copies to use as gifts for callers. Perhaps he liked it for itself, or for the gallant character of my wife which it portrayed. Or perhaps he knew I saw it there, year after year, and, being an abject coward before the possibility of hurting a friend, didn't dare remove it from my occasional sight!

Through the rest of that summer of 1924 at the Colony, I sometimes sat with E.A. in his room in the evening, and he gave me two further signs of the accolade of friendship. One was that he usually received me in his suspenders, and the other was that our communication was increasingly in the idiom of silence. It was real. Out of the silence one of us, almost always E.A., would say something, framing a thought that usually spoke to the thoughts of the other. I can now remember only one of those silent exchanges at that time, psychologically a simple one but the substance of great importance to me. Long before, I had told E.A. of my major problem whether to go on with poetry as a profession or to return to law, as my father, a year older than E.A., was begging me to do in every letter. On this occasion, one evening in September, I sat down in his room, and after some triviality we fell silent for what in that early stage of our friendship was a long time, perhaps two minutes. Toward the end of the silence he lowered his head so he could press the tips of two long fingers against his brow while resting his elbow on the arm of the rocker. Then he broke the mutual reverie: "I may be wrong, but I think you've got it." (He enjoyed saying "got it," both as sound and as impropriety.) "I starved twenty years, and in my opinion no one should write poetry unless he is willing to starve for it." Pause. "I think you will probably have to wait longer than I did for recognition." He was trying to rationalize me into the category of the people who mattered most to him in the world, namely the hurt and defeated, the external failures. Knowing that I had a small competence, he wanted to find for me a substitute for his only sure qualification for inner success, namely a period of starvation. From that moment I chose him for my mentor in all things in place of my natural father. And I think he accepted the nomination.

Meanwhile, people had left and had been replaced at the Colony. Douglas Moore and beautiful Emily had a house outside and were with us at Colony functions. Margaret MacLean, prodigious young composer, stayed briefly. Motherly, poetic Muna Lee was there. And Margaret Widdemer, not long divorced from Bob Schauffler, poet, very prim and beribboned and Victorian, in more or less open competition with Tennessee Anderson for the retinue of unattached males. Of permanent residents, these included Bob MacBlair, bald and charming writer for the slicks; Fritz Day, shaggy-eyebrowed dramatist; a young, sparkling- and innocent-eyed poet whom I shall call X— he was my neighbor in Pan's Cottage and I had grown fond of him. It had been a good summer for production, although E.A.'s major contribution was *Dionysus in Doubt,* the title poem one of his least. Thornton Wilder finished *The Bridge.* DuBose Heyward went through a metamorphosis. Having frail Dorothy for wife of a year, and brand new baby Jennifer, he suffered comprehensible doubt that poetry would support them. He set out to try a novel, and occasionally had some of us—I remember Constance Rourke and Rose Cohen—down to their duplex Barnard studio to hear his experiments in prose. He plied us with personal charm, orange juice and so-called gin, but to small purpose. We all agreed that the story of the little crippled Negro was atrocious, and that he and Dorothy and Jennifer would be wiser to starve for poetry. But DuBose finished the thing in spite of us, took it to New York when the Colony closed on October first, and showed it to John Farrar. He instantly accepted it. It was called *Porgy.*

Just before that, I gave the farewell colonial party, and grazed manslaughter. An ulterior object was to get assembled advice for my young friend X, who was in a typical poet's dilemma. For a year before coming to the Colony he had been a guest in the house in Chicago of Mrs. William Vaughn Moody, widow of E.A.'s Harvard friend and hostess to much indigent genius. The question was whether he should return to sponging there and write verse, or accept a respectable job and write no verse. Latterly, I had been moved from the Chapman Studio to a ten-by-ten room in an upper corner of Colony Hall, its walls immaculate in white plaster. It was the only "studio" in the Colony not in the woods and so exempted from the prohibition upon night use—allegedly because of the danger of inorganic fire. It was, therefore, a good place to assemble the authorities in the evening when they could give unhurried attention to X's problem.

On the afternoon before the farewell party, I provided myself with the requisite can of alchohol and the juniper drops from the amenable local druggist, and so repaired to my little upstairs laboratory for the chemical experiments. My incidental equipment, obtained from the kitchen, was an empty quart ginger-ale bottle, two pitchers, divers funnels, a milk bottle of orange juice, and a dozen or so tumblers. My method would be to fill the quart bottle with grain alcohol, fill the quart pitcher with water duly impregnated with the juniper drops, then pour them together loftily into the large pitcher, thus aerating—allegedly purifying—them and mingling them together.

For what reason I can't recall, E.A. came up my stairs during the process and stood fascinated, eyeing the mysterious proceedings on the table with extremely pursed lips and brown eyes darkened and expanded in their widest, most enchanted stare. When I reached the penultimate phase when the alcohol was in the ginger-ale bottle, and the water and drops were in the pitcher, he conceived that the experiment was successfully completed, stepped forward, picked up the bottle of pure alcohol, lifted it to his lips, and, being an experienced beer drinker, forewent the amateurish restraint of swallowing and started pouring the contents down his throat—glub—glub—glub. I lost seconds in a spasm of terror, then grabbed the bottle, held up to his mouth and poured in the pitcher of water, slopping it over him. Fortunately he caught with atypical speed the notion that something in the outer world was amiss, and he did not resist. He himself took the pitcher in both hands and hastened the dilution. Finally he lowered it and regarded me. His face was putty gray, but the color soon began returning. His lips began to pucker normally, and his eyes to shine. As soon as he could he rasped, "Thank you very much."

For the party after dinner I had to move out the table to make room for the dozen people who were left in the Colony. E.A. alone had a seat, a rocker I found and set in the midst. Everybody else sat on the floor around the walls. I dispensed the simple fare, Bob MacBlair assisting. Those present were Bob, E.A., Doug Moore (Emily baby-sitting), Thornton Wilder, shiny-eyed little X, DuBose Heyward (Dorothy baby-sitting), Margaret Widdemer, Constance Rourke, Muna Lee, and Tennessee Anderson.

The party was soon animated, and I directed the conversation early to the dilemma of X, a dilemma which all had at some time and in some degree faced. The debate was passionate and polyphonic, none but myself, X, and E.A. wasting time and great ideas to listen to the rest. Tennessee Anderson, I recall, captured Thornton early, sat him down beside her on the floor, and got a strong sculptress's arm around him to prevent escape. Thornton, unconscious of his toils, spoke steadily and with stammering and supersonic speed, waggling his finger at all, sundry, and nobody in particular, and two or three times breaking away from Tennessee only to be snatched back, still orating, not skipping a syllable. Doug Moore and Bob MacBlair, both normally the mildest of gentlemen, got swept far into rage, not at each other but at mankind, and each had a voice louder than Thornton's. Margaret, Muna, and Constance, being perfect ladies, sat side by side and discussed the crisis earnestly and inaudibly—even to each other. DuBose got periodically into convulsions of laughter at the show, and between times tried seriously to advise X, sitting beside him. Poor X himself sat with beautiful eyes and saintly smile raised to heaven, apparently understanding, profiting by, and grateful for all.

Throughout the medley E.A. sat absolutely silent in his chair, not rocking a millimeter, he alone requiring that his "gin" be unviolated by orange juice, he alone taking it by the tumbler, slowly and sedately, putting away three undiluted tumblers during the brief festivities, always looking straight before him, beaming contentedly, blowing out periodic volcanoes of Sweet Caporal smoke through rounded lips, sometimes twitching a smile at some salvo of wisdom. At the end of the rendition, when all had to go home to pack, everybody had expanded into abstraction far beyond concrete X, but they recovered enough to shake his hand warmly and to wish him the very best of luck. During the departure there was a good deal of autographing called for, and the pen produced was reluctant. Bob MacBlair found to his amusement that by shaking it horizontally at the white plaster wall it could be persuaded to work for a signature's length of time. So he obliged for those involved, one after the other, and my wall took on an interesting abstract mural in a somber palette.

At last everyone was gone but E.A. I was drunk, disappointed, and mad at him. "For God's sake, E.A.," I said—using the familiar for the first time—"why didn't you say something to X? The whole point of the party was to get you to help him." E.A. put on his best, unimpressed pucker and little smile, and rocked a half-inch forward and back. Then he got off, now for the second time to me, one of his private clichés: "I never advise anybody to write poetry unless they're willing to starve for it." So, ultimately, the only significance of the party was that I joined the multitude of the elect, including most of the waiting women, who called E.A. by his initials. In contrast, even among his oldest friends I never knew a man—and knew only two women—whom he addressed otherwise than by their surnames, the ladies of course with their formal prefixes.

After a visit to my home town, I came down to New York in December for the winter. E.A. was established in his upper back room in sculptor James Fraser's house in the first block of West Eighth Street, and I called him at once and invited him to dinner and the theater. It was snowing soggily when I came for him, and after the Frasers' maid had buzzed warning, I climbed the three flights, entered his open door, and stood in my overcoat, at first powdered, and presently dripping. I was impatient and self-conscious for not having left enough time for leisurely dinner before the show whose tickets I had in my pocket.

E.A. was in his suspenders as usual, and for the first time in our still brief acquaintance he didn't greet me. When I entered he first stood up, and after a moment's appraisal seemed satisfied with my identity. Then he grew unusually animated, hastened into the bathroom and emerged with a straight chair, which he set against the radiator under one of the room's two windows. Mounting it, he captured the shade which was wound all the way up and, clasping the middle of the bar between thumb and first finger, drew it down slowly all the way, getting off the chair adroitly near the end of the process and experimenting with the

shade to be sure it would stay. Then he carried the chair to the
other window and repeated the exercise. Meanwhile I stood there
dripping audibly, not wanting to lose time by taking off my coat,
wishing he'd come along and stop worrying about the people in
the backs of the Washington Square houses looking into his room
when he would be out of it. Having completed his double acro-
batic stunt, he stood for a moment surveying the results with
satisfaction. Then he picked up the chair carefully, returned it
to the bathroom, emerged, looked at me, and said cheerfully,
"Hello." I responded, and he looked puzzled for a moment,
probably considering the problem of my coat. Then he grinned
his big rodent grin and said, "This afternoon I went up to Vern
Hackett's bookshop, and he asked me to write my name in a
book. So I did. He gave me a bottle of whiskey. Thought we might
drink it."

Being glad enough to substitute real whiskey for dinner, I
carried my coat into the bathroom, left it draining in the tub, came
back and sat down on one side of the round table. He got the
full quart of real Haig & Haig out of his usual cache in his bureau,
fetched two tumblers, gave me a whopping drink, told me to help
myself to water in the bathroom, poured himself a full tumbler,
stood the bottle between us on the table, and sat down.

The upshot was that we did as he had "thought we might" do.
We drank the bottle. Rather he did, I assisting with five or six
drinks over a period of five hours. Somewhere along in his second
half-pint he began to read me Wordsworth, probably the first
among his three favorite non-dramatic poets, the realistic, rustic
triumvirate that included Crabbe and Hardy. I suppose others
heard him read, but I suspect my experience was unique in duration and in the alcohol-released naturalness of his technique. To
call it bad reading was to misconstrue it. It was not reading at
all. Rather it was the delighted, voluptuous ejaculation of one
word and then another, with rhythmless pauses between in which
he would look across at me with challenging eyes—"Get that?
Get that?" And once he added, "You're too damned young to get
that!"

So he read me "one word after another," emphasizing the key
sounds of each, ignoring utterly the meter, the line structure, and
the cadence. Perhaps the point was that the verse rhythms, in-

cluding the interwoven cadences, were easy—anyone with an ear could hear them; but the possible nuances in the stark words, both as meaning and as sound, were infinite, and each use was always new. I think I saw the unique phonetic and semantic foundation of Robinson the poet, the exacting, perfectionist labor that went into both his packed single words and his elaborate circumlocutions. I understood how it was that in an age that, following him, was emphasizing conscious craftsmanship, he remained preeminent.

At this remove, I can't remember much that he read. He brushed aside most of the popular things, though lingering on the "Intimations" and the "Lucy" poems for several analytical rereadings. (What a bore it would have been for a non-objective self-expressionist!) Meanwhile, I had long abandoned hope of dinner, and when at length, like an orchestra moving without pause into the main theme, he started on *The Prelude*, I abandoned the theater as well. About midnight, while neither Wordsworth nor his interpreter gave out, the liquor did, and we sallied forth. The snow had stopped and we took a few blocks of air up and down the Avenue, returning to enter the closing Brevoort and to demand both scrambled eggs, which we got, and more liquor, which occasioned a demurrer. I mounted into eloquence, first in my bad French, then in my worse Italian, celebrating for the assembled waiters the privilege they had to serve *"il grande poet, il piu grande poeta dopo il Dante divino."* Meanwhile E.A. beamed at his most eager, his most boyish, his most released, as he never could do when he was sober. Perhaps it was because he had a Dante story, but he didn't tell it to me then. At length my eloquence got us several cups of "tea," very sour and the color of "dago red." I don't recall how extreme were my matinal regrets after that evening. In those first years I assumed, perhaps erroneously, that E.A. never had any.

III

From then on I was one of the beneficiaries of E.A.'s combination of realism, sensitivity, humor, and loyalty which comprised his one social genius, that for male friendship. I don't mean that I stood in his affections alongside his old friends, his contemporaries. Certainly I was at that time too far gone in the swinish "philosophy" of the twenties to appreciate his greatness as a person, the selflessness more nearly absolute than I have known in another man, coupled with the unqualified passion for truth. I could hardly then have understood his having his "skin put on inside out," [5] or his statement to Esther Bates, "It is because I am too completely at the mercy of people that I find I have to keep away from them." [6] And yet E.A. tolerated me. For one thing, I had social ease, which he liked to have around him, so long as it was not exercised in a fashion to humiliate him. For another and more important thing, I was beginning to appreciate his great poetry, whereas most people never read it. He let me waste hours of his time arguing that *Merlin* was his greatest poem, greater than *Lancelot* because it was more "real." And in spite of my elaborate, metaphysical rationalizations, what I of the self-expressionistic, Freudian twenties then meant by "real" was simply that the lady and gentleman involved did then and there, in the presence of the reader, healthily go to bed together. And E.A. would smile his unconvinced half-smile and remark, "But in *Lancelot* I said what I have to say."

In the late spring of '25, after E.A. had left New York for Boston and Peterborough, the Frasers moved from Eighth Street to far East Forty-second, and in the fall they installed him on the whole top floor, two big rooms and bath. By that time I was doing a little growing up, beginning to understand his pool of hypersensitivity to disrespect for what he considered his awkward bearing in the world. With expert, junior sycophancy, I learned how not to stir it up, while at the same time trafficking in naughty irreverences that skirted his touchiness and hit his humor, laughing at external mannerisms without implying his essential absurdity. Ridgely Torrence was one of the first of his old friends to accept me, and we became a team for imitating him, both to his face and for the edification of others. We would sit together in deep thought, scowling profoundly, pressing our relatively stubby fingers against our foreheads, and would eventually come forth with hesitant and qualified banalities, delivering them slowly, one word after another, getting full phonetic value out of every letter. E. A. would usually approve with his second-grade chuckle, the entirely inner one that shook a little but made no sound and, but for the sparkle of the eyes, left the facial expression unchanged.

The intimate idiom of communication with E.A., especially when you were alone with him, was, as I said before, silence. Inner world to inner world. Mood adjusting to mood, unsymbolized, direct and clear. It was like poetry. The whole truth could only be intimated, the actual perception necessarily left to the imagination in silence. In her book Miss Bates says ". . . it was as if he liked to leave the enigma undisturbed, when brought face to face with it. Something was lost in the process of elucidation." [7] Barnard refers critically to his "reluctance to come to the point" in his dramatic verse, and, in a different connection, to his lack of pretense of knowing everything about people, his leaving to each of his characters an "area of privacy" in which, as in actual life, no one can fully understand these matters. One day he appeared in Ridgely Torrence's apartment in New York in high dudgeon. "A man just called on me," he said, "who wanted to tell me the whole truth! He ought to be killed."

In New York, beginning in the winter of '25–'26, I went up to see him in the late afternoon every week or two, either to take him out to dinner and the theater or just to sit. I usually called him before coming, thinking it less trouble for him to go down three flights to the basement phone than it would be to have me interrupt something. When you went up, duly announced on the house phone by the Frasers' maid, you normally would find him sitting in his suspenders in his rocker in the back room beside the round table, his back to the door. Here he faced the left of the room's two windows that looked southward, with the three-by-four bookcase between them. Farther to the right the rest of the room was mostly occupied by a large Victorian bed, the guest bed, where you threw your hat and coat. Between this bed and the second window was the visitor's chair, another mission rocker. Opposite the door from the hall and beside the door to the front room was his bureau, where an ancient, paintless, wooden hairbrush was the only implement I remember. Immediately to your right as you came in, partly blocking your entrance, was the enormous wooden box where he piled his presentation copies, though never until he had read them, or in them, and acknowledged them.

When you came up E.A. would have been adding methodically to his thousands of correct little acknowledgments in his microsopic writing on a microscopic pad, and when you entered he would be setting the breadboard that was his desk off the arms of his rocker onto the round table. Sometimes he would get up and say, "Hello." Sometimes he would just look up and say it. Sometimes, if he had something weighty on his mind, he wouldn't greet you at all. In this case he would be rocking a little in emotion. You could measure the strength of it by the length of the rocks. An arc of six inches forward and six inches back was maximum.

You took the visitor's rocker, and, after preliminary mumbles or smirks back and forth, settled into the ritual of silence, each of you gazing ahead and down. His Sweet Caporal would be smoking up a fast, blue column in his hand or in the ashtray, and in the silence it would quiet down and sometimes out. Occasionally E.A.'s forehead would lift, his eyes expand and his lips purse, showing that a thought was taking form. The silence was the most comfortable social communication possible. No physical imperfections to interfere with the ideas, especially that of the fundamental relationship, that were the reality. It would last from a minute or two up to a quarter of an hour. But after all, we were materially embodied and imperfect. Eventually the silence must end. Almost always I waited for E.A. to break it and address the meeting. And almost always he would speak to the condition of my thought then current. Sometimes he spoke to some notion I had formulated but had not expressed, saying, "Yes, I believe so," or "No, I don't think so." But usually he got off a complete statement that was germane to the general subject I was thinking about. I have confirmed this apparent telepathy of E.A.'s with others of his friends. Doubtless it would be possible in every case to trace a common line of association from some notion mutually familiar. The phenomenon is not rare. But we all agreed that in his case it was extreme.

I wish I had Boswellized those eruptions out of prolonged silence, for I remember with certainty only four or five of them, only two or three from this early period. One, though striking as an aphorism, was obvious enough in association, for it dealt with the hope of doing something immortal, which was never far from our thoughts. On this day, after we had sat a few minutes in silence, he gave two or three little rocks and said, "Most men are born, live, die, and are *ab-so-lute-ly* forgotten." (He loved to say, *"ab-so-lute-ly."*)

I suppose that one thing E.A. liked about me was that I never asked favors of him except to read my manuscripts. I never asked for letters of introduction, recommendations, and all that. Not that he didn't want to do good turns for his friends, but just as he had "little stomach for breathing on the boots of publishers" [8] in his own interest, so he didn't understand just what you did to grease the practical wheels for somebody else. A case of his telepathy rose out of an exception to this general, unworldly helplessness; and I'm sure it was not consciously precipitated by me. Among the young geniuses of my acquaintance in the Village there was a good deal of weighty snobbery about *Who's Who*, a little sense of caste between those who were in it and those who weren't. One day,—probably a year or two after the period 1924–27 now being considered,—I came up to E.A.'s room in a sour mood. I had been seeing editors about the treatise on poetry which I was writing, and I had struck no spark. Without any preamble of silence, I announced with sophomoric finality, "The whole publishing world makes me sick! I go in to an editor's office and there on the top of his desk sits *Who's Who*. I know that the second I'm on the elevator he'll have it down and, since he won't find me in it, that will be the end of me!" I finished my sputter and we passed on to sounder topics. A few days later I came in again, and we fell at once into our Quaker silence. I remembered my recent vulgar explosion and was thinking up a way of telling E.A. I was ashamed of it. The silence didn't last very long. I caught him looking at me with his mildly entertained smile. He gave a little rock and said, "I wrote a hot letter to *Who's Who*." His smile became the lapin one, showing his front teeth.

Though he wasn't of much use in practical affairs, he was a great bulwark to his friends personally, endlessly patient with your whimperings of discouragement. One afternoon I sat there complaining because my epic poem wasn't going, and when E.A. wouldn't rise I asked directly, "E.A., do you think I'll ever finish that damned thing?" This angered him and he rocked full quota forward and back, blew a Sweet Caporal volcano at me, and said, "I know you will." Like his earlier statement that had settled me in the career of poetry, this of course dropped me into an oubliette of humility and became a milepost for me. We settled into a long silence. After a few minutes he exploded, "For seven years I had *ab-so-lute-ly* nothing but the bottle."

E.A. was unique among drinkers in that he had the greatest capacity anyone ever heard of, and yet he never became an alcoholic. With one, two, or three friends, he would drink along with them, glass for glass, but with the difference that their portions would be highballs with an ounce or two of whiskey, while his would be a glass of straight whiskey—and not always the best whiskey—at least four times theirs. Yet the only effect was to make him beam his "sunny" smile at the ridiculous world, to sprout a small rose in the center of each long cheek, and sometimes, though not always, to make him talk freely; and when he talked freely he talked very well. He had a countryman's suspicion of wine—probably would give you the sour stomach. He loved liquor, even hooch, took it "not for the taste but for the effect," and yet, at least during my eleven years' acquaintance with him, he could do without it any time. He never drank before dinner time, and he took frequent, considerable jaunts on the wagon. It seemed as though, while he was slow in making up his mind, when he did make it up there was never any question but that the "idea" was stronger than any other impulse involved.

As far as he himself was concerned, he never had any doubt of his self-control. In 1924, writing to Laura Richards about Prohibition, he said: "All human beings who are not made of putty are going to stimulate themselves in one way or another; and alcohol, in spite of its dangers, is the least harmful of all the more active demons. Everything is dangerous that is worth having. For example, think of poetry and music, not to mention fried onions and cucumbers." [9] One evening at Peterborough, some years later, we were walking down to the village, and I complimented him on having just quit liquor on the doctor's orders, with no visible distress. He walked along, swinging his stick, taking his long, free strides, looking now up, now down. When we were passing the firehouse he said, "When I was young there was a devil in all of my family. But I knew that liquor was not the devil that would get me. Poetry was the devil that would get me." We walked on, and presently he added, "I never could have done anything but write poetry." [10] It wasn't until much later, when he was dying, that this statement became something other than an apology.

Possibly the almost lifelong self-doubt that E.A. suffered over being nothing but a poet contributed to his affectionate curiosity about all and sundry and his maintenance of an enormous, miscellaneous acquaintance. Basic to this catholicity was, of course, his very nearly limitless human tolerance. He never passed final negative judgment on anybody, but when impelled to do so he instinctively transferred the impulse into a search for something in him or in his experience which he had not understood. Corollary to this respect for everybody was his loyalty, his reluctance to let a person go once he had accepted him. And an aspect of it that was a fault, and eventually contributed to much unpleasantness and one major tragedy, was his inability to complain of and try to correct mistakes and flaws of character in even his closest intimates. Always the friend was somebody else, with a different background, a different karma, and the right to privacy in it. Who was he to intrude? Related to his tolerant curiosity about all people was his preference for seeing them singly and giving himself completely to each in turn. Even with two people, unless they were independently good friends of each other, he was at a loss. And here also there was a fault that was counterpart of the virtue. His habit of compartmenting his friends, in effect keeping them ignorant of each other, tended to make each feel that he was unique in intimacy. And this led to suspicion between them, or groups of them, and eventually to some costly misunderstanding.

By voluminous epistolary effort, most of it in brief, perfunctory notes, E.A. kept all of the different-toned tops of his acquaintanceship spinning. The wide discrepancy between the economic extremes of his association earned him some whispers of hypocrisy, and even occasional twinges of self-suspicion. Certainly his fundamental prejudice was for the broken and defeated of mankind, among whom he reckoned himself until after '27, and in some degree always. And yet, he seemed just as devoted to his cultivated, rich friends whom we used to see with their chauffeurs and furs, coming to carry him off from the Colony; and furthermore, as will appear later, he believed they represented the highest level of civilization that modern man had attained. Because of this devotion and this illusion, his considerable sojourns in their houses comprised virtually the only domestic happiness he ever knew. Until a few years before I met him, he had lived, since about 1905, almost entirely on patronage. Besides the long visits spring and fall he paid to friends in their country and suburban houses, he had four months a year also free at the MacDowell Colony, his year-round apartment at the Frasers' in New York— either free or for nominal rent—and an anonymous subsidy of $1,200 a year, while Esther Bates did his typing for minute fees, sometimes as low as a dinner and theater for the transcription of the year's output. And even while he accepted and returned affectionate loyalty for all this help and support, he was restive under it, for he never soothed himself with the notion that as a poet society "owed him a living." It was not until the very end of his life that he entirely outgrew his shame for his long period of indigence.

Among E.A.'s friends my active acquaintance was on the side of a few of the unfortunates, those who had "borne the day's load" and were not, as he had said of the rich when he was at his own economic nadir, the "victims of good luck." By '24, handsome big Percy MacKaye was a success, but he had done his apprenticeship of starvation. Lovable, devoted Stanley Braithwaite, literary editor of the old *Boston Transcript*, editor of the Brimmer Press, and famous anthologist, was one of the people E.A. always stopped in Boston to see, spring and fall; he was not a failure in external terms, but his life was uncomfortable because, as he was a quadroon, Boston over-patronized him in official respects, ignored him unofficially, and ignored his wife always. This subhumanity eventually drove him out of Boston into teaching, and so out of the active literary world.

E.A.'s busiest relationships that I saw much of were with the triumvirate Ridgely Torrence, George Burnham, and Carty Ranck, three originals who, outside of being intellectuals and failures, could hardly have had less in common. Ridgely was an elegant minor poet, utterly charming, witty, and worldly, all qualities which E.A., lacking them, greatly enjoyed and admired in others. As Ridgely provided animated entertainment for him, so he always delighted Ridgely with his solemn, deliberate, but withal solemnly humorous carriage. Unlike E.A., Ridgely had a specific social concern, devoting much of his dramatic writing to the Negro cause. Twice E.A. thought he would get the Pulitzer prize for poetry, but his work got little attention and eventually passed entirely out of notice.

George Burnham was a pure spirit who reinforced the mystical side of E.A. At seventeen he had run away from home and progressed around the West from frontier job to frontier job, until one January night in Wyoming, having taken the wrong road, he had both feet frozen, crawled into a settlement, declared that he was not going to die, and presently had them amputated. As a cripple with two wooden legs he had returned East to study law at Harvard while E.A. was a student there in the early nineties. They became close friends and roommates, both then and later in New York, where Burnham practiced law until he quit the profession, concluding that it was suborned by the corporations. He ended up as a ticket agent in one of the Newtons, and had a room on West Newton Street where E.A. often stayed with him when he was in Boston. In the spring of '23, when E.A. was about to go to England, he had written Burnham, regretting that he could not get up to Boston before sailing, to see "the man who knows me best, and—or so I like to fancy—overlooks the worst of my shortcomings." One day at the Colony, where Burnham usually visited E.A. once each summer, he was stumping along one of the forest roads beside Carty Ranck, with E.A. and me following at a little distance. E.A. said to me, "There goes the greatest man God ever put on earth." On another occasion Burnham assured me with his always exuberant certainty that

"Robbie" was among the greatest poets of human history. At the same time he was usually in a state of disgusted irritation at him for failing to achieve a systematic theology or philosophy. He himself was a Hindu, and in accounting for E.A.'s mysticism, Burnham's Brahma must be accredited at least equally with Emerson's Oversoul.

Because he also lived in Boston, after 1913, Carty Ranck usually shared with Burnham E.A.'s company during his semiannual visits after 1911, when he started migrating between New York and the MacDowell Colony. Of the unique and contrasted characters I knew best among E.A.'s friends, Carty was the only one whose uniqueness reached bizarreness. In age about halfway between the three others and me, Carty was a short, stocky, crude, ejaculatory, slobbering, popeyed, pugnacious misfit from the mountains of Kentucky. He was forever boasting that he had never lost one of his many fights because, having only one punch, he always surprised the other guy by hitting him first. His wife had run off with a musician, and Elizabeth Sparhawk-Jones, painter, said she hated to go walking in the evening at the Colony for fear Mr. Ranck would come "snorting out of the bushes like a moose." Inside Carty's doomed exterior there was passionate loyalty, a certificate from George Pierce Baker's "47 Workshop" at Harvard, and a flair of perceptive distinction that saw Robinson's poetic caliber, I think, before any other professional critic except Stanley Braithwaite. He had been a staff writer on the *Brooklyn Eagle* until 1910 or '11 when he moved to Cambridge and took Baker's drama course. In 1912 he appeared at the Colony as a dramatist. In 1913 he was already of the inner circle, for E.A. wrote Burnham that October, "I don't suppose any man ever had a better friend that [sic] you have in him." [11] In the same year, having become an occasional feature writer for the *Boston Transcript*, he published one of the first articles on Robinson, and about the same time he began to Boswellize him with E.A.'s knowledge. Since he never got a play produced under higher auspices than those of the Harvard Dramatic Club, his love of "Robinson"—he never called him "E.A."—and the prospect of doing the biography became the whole meaning of his life. In 1913 or '14, Carty had to go to the hospital for a small operation, and E.A. gave him all the money he had, which was sixty dollars. Then he wrote *Scribner's Magazine,* asking for an advance on his next three poems. He expected a hundred dollars and got forty.

Carty used to tell me with snorting delight that E.A. was yellow, and he cited an instance that had happened at E.A.'s table at the Colony during the First World War, Charles Wharton Stork being there, complete with Viking moustaches. Carty hated Wharton for what supposed reason I don't recall, but I held him in great respect because his *Contemporary Verse* had been the first periodical to recognize me! On the occasion in question Wharton said something favorable to Germany, whereupon Carty stood up and invited him to step outside. Instantly, according to Carty, both Wharton and E.A. turned chalk pale. Nancy Byrd Turner boasts that she once prevented a fight between Carty and Maxwell Bodenheim, and her interference might have been fortunate for Carty's swagger because Maxwell was as truculent as he and had done time as a professional fighter.

Carty's pugnacious slur on "Robinson's" courage was not supported by what little there is of record. There had been the case when he threw a bully down at Harvard and sat on him, and there had been the case before the fire one evening at Colony Hall when some pompous new arrival was haranguing the company, and E.A. stood up, told him he was a bore, and asked him to stop talking. Especially there was the dangerous incident of Joseph Lewis French, the journalist who early in the century in New York had done E.A. supposed favors in publicity and from that time had become an increasingly neurotic leech, calling on Robinson occasionally for the purpose of at once excoriating him and extracting any money that might be available. One summer, probably in the twenties when E.A. might have been in funds, French gave off round New York that he was going up to Peterborough to shoot him. He also wrote the proposed victim, apprising him of his purpose. E.A. told his friend Parker Fillmore, who told Mrs. MacDowell, and she urged E.A. to go to nearby Hancock and put up with his friends the Perrys until the maniac had come and gone. On the morning of the expected assault, E.A. at breakfast told Esther Bates, who was typing for him, not to bring him any typescript that day. Later that morning

Parker, who was in the Adams Studio perhaps ten rods from E.A.'s Veltin, heard angry voices there, then a report which he thought was a pistol. Parker hurried over, found that it was a screen door that had slammed, and there stood French and E.A. on the terrace of the Veltin, both red in the face. Parker said, "E.A., there's a long distance call for you." After the usual pause E.A. said, "It can wait." French went back to the village and back to New York, and that evening Parker told Esther the story. When she was alone with E.A. she asked, "Mr. Robinson, weren't you afraid?" E.A. wrinkled his forehead, looked up and down, and said, "No—it made me unhappy." Pause. "He got what he wanted." This meant a little money.

Throughout the period of my acquaintance with E.A., I was on the side of the unfortunates, the Rancks, the Burnhams, and the Frenches, and against the rich per se. I was in passionate, callow revolt against the respectability of my own background, and in consequence, while I knew E.A. had wealthy acquaintances, I managed to disbelieve that they were his friends as the "children of the night" were. Part of my passion in the premises was due to the weight on my conscience of the small competence I enjoyed. Most of my friends were in some phase of the dilemma that the poet X had been in when I gave him the party at the Colony, the dilemma which E.A. had been in most of his life. His comment, that he never advised anybody to write poetry unless they were willing to starve for it, was never far from my consciousness, and some time in those middle twenties, when I was in my early thirties, I decided that if ever I was to speak of and to humanity I must start where most of humanity started. I determined to give away my nest egg and do a little manly starving, a little walking of the streets penniless. I spent consecrated days making out a list of institutions and individuals worthy of my microscopic help. When at last I couldn't think of any shift for wasting more time on the calculation, I conceived that before putting the brokers to work I might just run up and show the list to E.A.—simply to get him to check over the objects of my largesse. When I came in, bright-eyed and brisk, he greeted me with his dubious expression, and continued to watch me, catlike. I recited my high purpose with gallant lightheartedness, and passed him the fateful document. For a long time he seemed to study it, wearing his little scowl, looking terriby grave. He didn't rock a single inch. Finally, he laid the list on the table, glanced up at my heroic eagerness, and tried to speak in his solemn vein, slowly, meticulously. "No. Don't do it. You want to do your starving before you're thirty."

E.A. was responsive and explicit where a particular person was concerned, or a particular experience or particular expression in literature. But he had little time for generalizations of a cosmic or social order. As he frequently proclaimed without shame, he had no rational philosophy or sense of "society" as a living reality. You soon learned in his friendship that his attention was sure to wander whenever you launched into any kind of theory, above all social theory. He was suspicious of people with causes, and the few causes he espoused involved matters which, like Prohibition, or Daylight Saving—"I don't like eating in the middle of the afternoon" [12]—touched him or his friends directly, in their daily lives. Between '21 and '27 he sat quietly rocking through the Sacco and Vanzetti fracas, and he refused to sign a petition that Edna Millay carried around the Colony. He did not know either of them personally, but from the news he suspected that they were guilty. Even worse, he suspected that they had a panacea, that they thought they knew the "whole truth!" As for injustice in the trial and the procedural flaws in the criminal law of Massachusetts, he knew only that the world was everywhere speckled with injustice. He trusted fate far more than he did law or reform. Things were too absurd, too unreal to be final. Neither he nor any other human could straighten them out, but some day everything would come right in accordance with the now incomprehensible but certainly benign plan of the "Scheme." Ever since I began to know E.A. I have looked dubiously on poets with causes. I have presumed that in joining parties and picketing government buildings they have been exhibiting some kind of social virtue, but not the virtue of poets.

As a part of his indifference to theoretical groupings of people and their joint doings, he had no interest in history as a drama between conflicting social, which is to say general, forces. He had little sense of historical evolution. On the whole the world didn't change much. As an addict of the twenties of the "wild young people," the Lost Generation, and their self-expression, I used to plead with him to understand that most of the misery of our then world was due to the peculiarly unhealthy repressions and hypocrisies of that late Victorian culture which was his. But he would only rock a little, blow out cannon blasts of Sweet Caporal smoke, and not hear me. The only historical generalization I ever badgered out of him was the appalling statement, "I suppose that the period between 1870 and 1914 was on the whole the happiest that mankind has known." On the cosmic side, he had recourse, when necessary, to a statement so sweeping that it was sure to stop conversation in a field that nettled him: "The world is a hell of a place, but the universe is a fine thing."

IV

E.A.'s declaration of the contrast between the world as a "hell of a place" and the universe as a "fine thing" was fundamental, not only cosmically but also as a revelation of one of his basic mental qualities. We may call it contrapositivism, intending for later purposes the philosophical pun involved, but meaning for the present no more than the necessity of looking on both sides of every question. Like all pure Yankees, E.A. saw everything cautiously and therefore double. Basically, the "Scheme" had its contrasting "world" and "universe," and as part of it every smallest phenomenon had its two aspects, its front and back, its top and bottom, its outside and inside. If you announced the affirmative of any proposition, you must immediately look behind you and acknowledge the negative. If you made a denial, you must watch out for the possible affirmation. Every thesis must have its antithesis. This dualism, this contrapositivism, deep in the instinct of every humblest Yankee, was one of the evidences that in their culture the search for truth was primary.

E.A.'s contrapositivism everywhere enriched his letters and conversation. Two or three examples from the early period will suffice here. After leaving Harvard in '93, he wrote his friend Arthur Gledhill that it was there that "I discovered and cultivated what is best and strongest in my nature—which I fancy is not much." [13] Also, to his friend Harry De Forest Smith, "I suspect . . . that I am pretty much of a damned fool in many ways; but I further suspect that I am not altogether an ass." [14] And four years later: "Solitude is the best means of getting acquainted with one's self, but if one gets too well acquainted there is likely to be trouble." [15] He was still at it in the late period when I knew him. There was still the world versus the universe. And there was the recommendation of starvation as a qualification for writing poetry, but with the reservation that you should do your starving before you were thirty. In '28 he wrote to Alice Tilton Gardin, "I used to worry for fear of not living long enough, but now I worry, when I think of it, for fear of living too long." [16]

All of these contrapositives are of course on the border line of that creatively selected incongruity which is humor, and which, in its whole gamut from the silly to the tragic, represented E.A.'s lifelong attitude towards both himself and the world. Again, we shall find his correspondence full of it, early and late, and a few pointers will be sufficient here. In 1915 he sent Daniel Gregory Mason a piece of high musical criticism: "The old-fashioned hand-organ isn't bad . . . , but its proper setting is a small town in the early spring just before sunset, and then it makes a fellow think of shooting himself out of sheer homesickness for a previous existence that he wouldn't like if he got back to it." [17] And in the same letter: "I carried a bundle of new poetry into the Macmillans the other day, and I expect in the course of time to see it come out in the form of another unprofitable slender volume. Who in hell invented that word slender?" [18] On June 2, 1924—being my first day at the MacDowell Colony when I did him out of his seat at dinner—he wrote Mrs. Richards: "I have . . . been reading the Old Testament, a most bloodthirsty and perilous book for the young. Jehovah is beyond doubt the worst character in fiction." [19] One afternoon in New York in 1925 I was telling E.A. solemnly about experiments I was making with a new kind of systematically alliterated sprung meter. He listened with equivalent solemnity, and in a pause interposed: "Moody worked for years trying to invent a new kind of blank verse. One afternoon he came thundering up to my room and shouted, 'Robbie, I've got it!' I thought he meant he'd got the syphilis."

E.A.'s humor was generally less engaging orally than in his letters, except in enabling you to share his own delight in it, partly the triumph of being able to say something that would "make people laugh," partly the sensuous pleasure he took in sounding the key words, savoring every shading of them. He told me that at one phase in his bad period he "used to enjoy sitting in Battery Park, with the rest of the bums, watching the ships. There was a sign hanging on the old Battery which I recognized as Italian and, though I didn't know the language, it was so beautiful that I thought it must be a quotation from Dante Alighieri. It said, 'Non sputari sui pavimento.'" It had been his pleasure from infancy to pronounce bizarre or resounding words, especially the harsh consonants, combining verbal voluptuousness with infantile silliness. With apologies to the lady, a good poet, I must report that he used to take great joy in referring to his correspondence with Clinch Calkins, always clucking out the gutturals and hissing the dentals with relish. And each time the performance would throw him into a spasm of snorting chuckles, as if he were just hearing these excellent sounds for the first time.

Once at dinner at the Colony, he told of an adventure he had had in the afternoon with two female tourists. He had been outside his studio indulging in a favorite, bloodthirsty enterprise, that of knocking down wasps' nests from under the eaves with a long pole. From some way up the path he heard voices approaching, fled into the studio, stretched out on the couch, and pretended to be asleep. The pair of ladies came up to his big back window and peered in. One of them said, "Isn't it wonderful!" The other said, "That man's asleep." And the first said, "I know it, but isn't it won-der-ful!"

The anecdotes E.A. liked best to recount tended to be for gentlemen only, and usually they were engaging, not for themselves but for his naughty boyish delight in recounting them. One night when there was no audience at the pool table, but a few ladies were sitting over by the fireplace, he told of having just visited his home town, incidentally to being "doctored" by Bowdoin. On the street he met an ancient lady, a friend of his mother's. "Well, Edwin," she said, "I suppose you've got so you can do it pretty fast now." This threw him into his half-suffocated laugh, but, glancing at the ladies who had looked round and might have heard, he added, "That was all she knew about poetry."

Later that night he told us of a very old man known as Uncle Ezra whom he met on the street during the same visit to Gardiner, a man who had been already old when E.A. left town in '99. He stopped to reminisce with him and finally asked, "Uncle Ezra, do you find there's any particular change in the way you feel about things with the passage of the years?" "Why, no, Edwin, nothing that would be worth telling about." "For instance, Uncle Ezra, do you find any particular difference in the way you feel about women?" At this the old man thought a long while and finally said, "Yes, Edwin, I believe there is a difference. I believe that now I don't think about it *all the time.*"

E.A.'s full-length stories were a little on the juvenile, and each was signalized by an incisive sentence or phrase, usually the last one. He loved to tell about the unmarried couple who drove out into the country for what E.A. called a "sporting weekend." When they were well out of town they stopped at a farmhouse and asked the farmer if they could have a room. He allowed they might, then squinted at them and asked, "You two married, be you?" "Of course," said the man. "Would you mind showing me your marriage license?" "Not at all," said the man, and he took out and handed him a dog license. The couple went upstairs and were opening their suitcases when the farmer hurried up and knocked at the door. "Come in," called the man. Through the door the farmer called, "*If you ain't done it, don't do it. This ain't fer it*"—E.A. shaking his head and biting off the dental stops.

He also liked to render on request a Wild West story whose appeal to him was its explosive title, the "Brush Broom Cock Tail." It appeared that a friend of E.A.'s, being on the frontier, entered a saloon, and while he was sipping his whiskey a cowboy came in and ordered a brushbroom cocktail. The bartender put a little of everything in the bar in a pitcher, stirred it, poured out the drink, reached under the bar, and stood up a brushbroom beside it. The cowboy tossed off the potion at a gulp, fell down, writhed briefly on the sawdust floor, got up, brushed himself off and departed.

Nancy Byrd Turner told me of E.A.'s recounting at dinner the misadventure of the sonnet *Reuben Bright*. Reuben was a worthy butcher who greatly loved his wife, so when she died

> He packed a lot of things that she had made
> Most mournfully away in an old chest
> Of hers, and put some chopped-up cedar boughs
> In with them, and tore down the slaughter house.

E.A. said that an "inspired printer" set it that when Reuben had put her things in the chest he

> . . . put some chopped up cedar boughs
> In with them and tore down to the slaughter house.

"It got by the under proofreaders," said E.A., opening his eyes very wide and considering the saltcellar with detachment, "and it got by the head proofreader, and it got by me, and the book came out with it." Silence. Then, "That kind of thing has happened to me more than once. . . . I shouldn't be surprised if some of my things are improved by these changes." (The *Reuben Bright* mistake was, I think, in the collected sonnets, and Macmillan got most of the copies back before they reached the public. A few of the original form are said to be in existence.)

The only oral expression of E.A.'s humor that approximated the incisiveness of that in his letters was in the pithy retorts that would come out of him quickly, before there was time for his social self-consciousness to summon up his shyness. During his period of starvation, Daniel Gregory Mason once asked him if he didn't think that his sense of humor had lengthened his life. To which he replied, "I think my life has lengthened my sense of humor." [20] There was the young smart aleck at the Colony who said to him at table, "The trouble with you, Mr. Robinson, is that all your work is in blacks and browns and grays." "Good, fast colors," said E.A. And there was the young poet who, distracted by the horror of life, frequently remarked that he was going to shoot himself. One evening, having remained silent through dinner, he left the dining room early and presently was discovered in front of Colony Hall, face down in the grass in the center of the circular drive. One after another, the writers went out to him, offered solacing wisdom, elicited no stir from the prostrate one, and ended standing around him in a circle of concern. Presently E.A. joined it, and for a long time he considered the unhappy form. At last he spoke—"The ants will get him."

It was a different young writer, a bouncing lady novelist, who made a daily practice of joining E.A.'s table at dinner, beaming at him, and announcing her achievement of the day—never less than five thousand words. Finally, following one of the silences her proclamations always caused, E.A. creased his brow in his scowl of excruciating precision, pursed his lips and said: "This morning I deleted the hyphen from 'hell-hound' and made it one word; this afternoon I redivided it and restored the hyphen." [21]

On another occasion at dinner a young man was telling how Edna Millay and some man had crossed the Alps. At the height of the pass the narrator got stuck and kept repeating, "They crossed the Alps on a donkey—on a donkey—they crossed the Alps—" When he paused for breath, E.A. asked, "One donkey?" [22]

One morning Nancy Byrd Turner was early to breakfast, she and a new colonist, female, being the first at E.A.'s table. Presently he came downstairs, looked dubious, and advanced. Nancy introduced him—"This is Mr. Robinson." The stranger exploded: "Robinson!—not E.A. Robinson!—not *the* Mr. Robinson?" Long, bleak silence. E.A. spoke—"A Mr. Robinson."

A snatch of Robinsonian eloquence occurred one quiet evening in Colony Hall when, as usual, a pool game was in progress, and over by the fireplace a game of anagrams. E.A. had a secret scorn for anagrams, but on this evening he suddenly left the pool table, went over to the other game, rested the butt of his cue as usual on the toe of his shoe, and gravely surveyed the array. It happened that a dignified lady he was fond of, and who notoriously had a sense of humor almost as perpetual as his, had, in the fury of battle, just taken the word "wore" from a neighbor by inserting an *h* between the *w* and the *o*. E.A. stood gazing at it, rapt. So did the lady. So did everyone else at the table. For once, the laconic comment was beyond words; it was in the realm of universal silence. For a long minute he stared, in a trance. Then his partner in the pool game came to tell him it was his turn. He looked up with surprise, gave his little jump of decision after indecision, and returned to the uninspired, everyday world.

The most famous Robinson anecdote occurred at breakfast on a balmy August morning during the open season for Freud in the twenties when everyone was familiar with his common symbols. I was at E.A.'s table with three of his usual retinue, all so-called old maids of a moderate to high degree of sophistication. As on all of the tables for six, there was in the center a little brass bell for the purpose of calling the waitress. Our sixth member sailed in on the wings of ecstasy and paused in transport behind the empty chair. She was a Victorian old maid, somewhat atavistic in her innocent sentimentalism, tall and addicted to trailing gowns and subjective beauty in all forms. "I must tell you all of the beautiful dream I have had," she sighed, and as she sat down she began to recount her exquisite experiences of fire and water in her recent midsummer night's dream. When she had finished her account, there was a silence of amused embarrassment. E.A. broke it by extending his long arm and tinkling the little bell in the middle of the table. The waitress came running—"Did you want something, Mr. Robinson?" "No," said E.A., pausing after each word in his most contemplative style. "No, I didn't want anything. I just wanted to ring the bell."

V

It was common talk among the bright young geniuses of the twenties that Robinson was a celibate old pickle and always had been. And reluctantly, during the first year or so of my acquaintance with him, I came of the common view. Apparently here, in violation of the reputation of poets and of the sacred canon of Sex in the twenties, was a lifelong ascetic who, nevertheless, had written some good poetry—and, in my opinion since I had begun to read him seriously, some of the great poetry of the world. So dedicated was I, on the one hand to the current cult of Truth,

Beauty, Poetry, and Freud, and on the other to E.A.'s own interest, that some time in the second winter of our acquaintance I tendered him a piece of solemn advice which could hardly be approached for impudence. In just what weighty tone and language I can't recall, I hinted that, being then fifty-five or fifty-six, he might enhance both his personal composure and the realism of his verse through the therapeutic device of an affair! E.A. froze in his chair, looking straight in front of him, and I felt the shadow of the guillotine. The fact that he did not cut me out of his acquaintance forthwith was a guarantee of his infrangible loyalty.

One ground for E.A.'s reputation for ancient virginity was his excruciating shyness with women. Even with the old friends who provided his court at the Colony, four or five of them always assisting at breakfast and dinner, he was rarely at ease. At least once when he was dining with one of them in Boston, he had George Burnham, with whom he was staying, telephone that a telegram had arrived for him. Elizabeth Sparhawk-Jones once said to me, "E.A. locked the door on the inside, threw the key out the window, and thereafter couldn't reach it to let himself out." Two of his old friends told me that he always blushed crimson if a woman inadventently touched him, and that he blushed likewise when you reported at his studio in compliance with an invitation for lunch. These reports lose a little of their edge in view of the fact that E.A. colored on any slight provocation, such as a pleasant thought, an arresting remark, or a little physical exercise.

Early in his acquaintance with Esther Bates, in the first few years of the Colony, they walked to the village together after dinner. Hagedorn's account follows: " 'I'm afraid I'm not going to be able to say anything,' he remarked uneasily. She made some reply and they walked on. After ten minutes—'I'm not saying anything,' he stammered, in evident distress. At last, on their silent return, they approached the [Colony]. 'Well,' he murmured, 'I don't seem to have said anything.' " [23] In the same period, beautiful Jean (wife of Herbert) Gorman boasted to the ladies that she could get some action out of E.A., and one evening when he was settled in an upholstered chair she went to him and sat down on his knee. He did not stir. Time passed. Jean peeked around at him. He gave no sign. She slid off his knee and walked away, looking back at him, as Esther Bates put it, "like a disgruntled cat."

Perhaps the chief significance of E.A.'s committee of faithful priestesses was to keep him consistently a little uneasy and lonely at dinner. When he would seem to be far gone in poetic contemplation of a remnant of butter, was he perhaps quashing the ungallant wish that more men would crash his table and give him a little relaxation and fun after the tension of the day's work? Was it perhaps this wish that made him such an abandoned addict of the masculine game of pool, evening after evening following female dinner after female dinner?

The counterpart to his shyness with women was, as I said earlier, his seemingly compulsive chivalry, and at the beginning of our acquaintance I used to wonder whether in its extremity it was not a psychological compensation for his actual helplessness with them. Only recently, in preparing this book, I have realized that his early experience taught him that women, all the way from his mother down to the prostitutes of Boston, were, of all the people who are tortured in this world, the greatest and the least deserving sufferers. Wherefore, his chivalry was only an extreme case of his general, compassionate humanity.

The legends of E.A.'s gallantry are numerous, and some of them are probably true. There is the story of his trying to teach one of the older ladies at the Colony to smoke, in order to discourage the mosquitoes, the lady, being clumsy, tending to blow through the cigarette instead of sucking at it. There was the case of the female neophyte at the Colony who was afflicted with swollen hands from arthritis. One evening she sat at E.A.'s table at dinner, and thereafter he stalked her for forty-eight hours before he could catch her alone. Then, as Esther Bates told me, he tacked up to her and gave her some scented bath salts some woman had given him, suggesting that she put it in warm water and soak her hands in it.

What was probably the acme of E.A.'s chivalry was reached in an adventure at the Colony which Nancy Byrd Turner recounted to me. I give it in her words: "E.A. and I had been picked up at separate points on the grounds and persuaded to take a drive with two other colonists (how he hated that word in that connection!), a man and wife, very insistent, for neither of us wanted to go, I because the weather was cold and I had on no wraps, E.A. because he never wanted to go anywhere unless he had picked the going. Well, captive on the back seat we sat . . . silent while our hosts tossed over their shoulders various incentives to conversation. Finally, asked whether we were comfortable, I had to confess chilliness. . . . To my astonishment, Robinson seemed to feel something must be done (very possibly turn the car around and go back). He fumed slightly, in his austere, gentlemanly way—suggested closing this window and that—or whether turning up my collar might help. . . . Presently he gave a kind of grunt of satisfaction, made a dive at something on the floor and came up with what he considered a good solution of the difficulty, a big, greasy cloth that had done good work, apparently, on the car's innards. 'Here, this will do,' said he, and he cast it around my neck. There was nothing to do but wear it. E.A. rode on in silence, looking fierce." Nancy Byrd was one of two women in E.A.'s dining room entourage whose dominant attitude toward him was a kind of tender delight in his mannerisms and unpredictable sayings. She was the only person except Ridgely Torrence who I admitted could imitate him with more disrespectful accuracy than I could.

E.A.'s shyness, or sensitiveness, with women was simply an aspect of his touchiness about himself as a supposed awkward ass in the world generally. To his men friends it was annoying and absurd, but to women it was pathetic and appealing; and it was natural that to be made a fool of by a woman would disturb him more than an equivalent, supposed affront by a man. In The Eaves the women used to puzzle and confer about any little favors or presents they might foist on him without touching him on the raw. Esther Bates told me that she knew he suffered from fallen arches, and sometimes at breakfast heard him doing exercises for them overhead; yet she never dared let him know that she knew, though she had helpful suggestions to make. One evening when people were assembled in the Regina Watson studio for music, E.A. came in, and one of the younger women hopped up to give him her chair. He gave a sniff of rage and sat somewhere else, causing the girl to go out on the porch in tears.

Besides his temperamental shyness, chivalry, and touchiness with women, he had a few settled reservations against them. One was his lifelong insistence on their cruelty to each other. I have seen women pleading desperately with him that it isn't always so, while he sat smiling as smugly as any of the businessmen in his narratives. One evening at dinner a new arrival at the Colony explained at E.A.'s table that sometimes she had seizures at night, but that if someone would wake her when she screamed, all would be well. Esther Bates and Nancy Byrd Turner were at the table, but that night when she screamed neither responded and the screams subsided. At breakfast, the afflicted one being absent, they confessed to E.A. with amusement, and he was outraged. Esther gave him a piece of her mind for his gullibility. There were no more screams, but neither was there any assurance that E.A. accepted Esther's account.

Illogical also was the failure of his usual compassion in the case of a woman in the respectable world who committed adultery and suffered some kind of retribution. As a matter of course, most of his greatest fictitious women—Vivian, Guinevere, Isolt, Gabrielle, Laramie—were guilty and retained their author's sympathy. But in real life, his feelings conformed to the Victorian stereotype. He could pity the "fallen," the poor, and the outcast. But if a respectably placed woman took her fate in her hands, she must take her own chances. Likewise in conformance to the Victorian double standard, the men involved did not suffer his disapproval as did the women. On the other hand, the nearest to intolerance of which he was capable fell on men who in any other respect were guilty of the smallest failure of consideration for their women.

Besides indulging these general prejudices, E.A. was accurately observant of individual women, especially the predatory ones, and his spotting of one in particular led to my prize case of his telepathy. The villainess was a young poetess at the Colony who had all the men there, and a considerable company elsewhere, in a state of blazing folly. Her panoply was beauty, high seriousness, talent that needed reassurance, devotion to her art above all things, and distressful confusion in the practical, literary world. It was an irresistible array. She had three or four of the most distinguished men of the country at leash, and I joined the pack. I followed her to New York and through the ensuing winter had my moments of false dawn. But my conquest was always deferred, and at long last I decided on the ultimately humiliating concession for young genius in the twenties. I decided to offer her the bourgeois honor of my hand in marriage. But, as in my previous apocalyptic decision to give away my inheritance, I thought I'd just run up and tell E.A. of the happy prospect. I had reached this decision at a time when I hadn't seen him for two or three weeks, so, although he knew *ad nauseam* of my toils, he had had no hint of my recent high resolution. Incidentally, I went up to Frasers' to see him without phoning, which was against orders and not likely to invite his sympathy. The maid announced me on the house phone and E.A. had her send me up.

When I stepped into his room he was in his suspenders, sitting in his usual rocker with his back to the open door. He was rocking a little inordinately and seemed unaware of me as I entered and stood. A long time passed, perhaps a minute. I conceived that he was annoyed at me for coming without phoning, and I was going to slip out, when abruptly he set his breadboard desk off on the table and stood up. He advanced on me slowly, scowling, not his scowl of anger or uncertainty but his scowl of concentrated concern and search for accurate expression. When he was almost upon me he stopped and looked down at me with his eyes blazing black fire. "For God's sake," he said, "do anything you want to that girl, but don't marry her!"

Some years later the same girl made a pass at him, and he told me about it with great unchivalry. "I got a note from Miss Z inviting me to call on her at a certain time, so I did. When I rang the bell of her apartment she called, 'Come in.' So I did. When I came into the sitting room she was lying on the couch with almost nothing on. So I went home."

There was never any question as to the universal appeal to women of E.A.'s helplessness, his chivalry, his perception, his integrity, and his mystery. At the Colony it was assumed that at least the seven steadiest members of his breakfast and dinner harem—five of them figured as old maids—were far gone in love with him, and that each nursed the delusion that she was the unique devotion of his life.[24] I dare assert of six of the seven that the assumption was in varying degrees nonsense. Only Elizabeth Sparhawk-Jones, at once romantic, candid, and humorous, confessed freely to her friends that E.A. was the center of her life. Sometimes she read a declaration in those big, infinitely understanding eyes, and once he bowled her over by breaking a silence with "The less I say the more I feel." Yet she had no delusions, unless in the not implausible conviction that she was "Isolt of the white hands" in *Tristram*. At the Colony, she left a basket of fruit at the door of his studio every morning before he came. He invited her to lunch with him once every week, and I believe she was the only person so honored. Long after his death she told me that if his spirit should walk into the room she would apologize to it for having disturbed him with her love. Her strong, impressionistic sequence, portraying a dozen or so phases of his life, is perhaps his most distinguished pictorial monument.

High on E.A.'s list of mutuality, both at the Colony and especially as a hostess in New York, was the poet Leonora Speyer, she happily married to the former Sir Edgar, but withal harboring for E.A. sentiments more tender than were implied by her frequent, robust assertion that she "doted on" him. He frequented their house on Washington Square, and Leonora, who was a big, handsome woman, powerful of body and spirit, used to boast in E.A.'s presence that she was the only woman in New York who knew how to manage him without frightening him. In confirmation of her claim he several times said to me in his tone of considered commitment, "I like Mrs. Speyer." She was possibly the last woman to get his attention when he was dying.

One of E.A.'s admirers from afar, a plain little old maid from Chicago, not an official camp follower—indeed a colonist for only one year—received a unique accolade from Fate. Looking out of her window in The Eaves one hot summer night, she saw two tall figures audibly counting the insects swarming on and falling from the big carriage lamp in front of nearby Colony Hall where E.A. slept. One of them was himself. And he was in his nightshirt! Shelley plain! The next day the little lady humbly described to her sisters in The Eaves the glory that had descended on her. Apparently she was permanently exalted.

E.A.'s reputedly closest miss of serious involvement at the Colony must remain nameless. She was qualified by youth, comeliness, appreciation of E.A.'s distinction and humanity, affectionate delight in his foibles—along with Nancy Byrd Turner—, generally a sense of humor of the first order, sometimes edged with malice and pointed with a sharp tongue. More than once E.A. was observed, when he held her coat, letting his hands linger on her shoulders. In the early years of the Colony she was considered dangerous enough by her sister geniuses to have advices reach Mrs. MacDowell that E.A. wanted to marry her, wherefore, for his protection, she ought to be excluded from the Colony. This, of course, was not done. Once she fished for his sympathy by telling him fictitiously at breakfast that the women were treating her badly. About eleven that morning he appeared at her studio and inaugurated his call by saying "Don't ask me to stay." He had brought her some candy and a copy of the *London Times Literary Supplement* to solace her feelings. Also he gave her a Sweet Caporal, smoked one himself, and so rose to go, having done his good deed. At the door he said, "You may ask me again if you wish." On another day he gave her a bag of many-colored mints which she took to her studio. At dinner she thanked him again for them, emphasizing how delicious they all were. "Have you eaten them all?" he demanded. She said, "Yes," and he gave her a disapproving sniff and scowl. Again, he favored her with a bag of mushrooms which he had gathered in the woods. As he presented them he said, "For every one of these I have a mosquito bite." Undoubtedly, one of E.A.'s charms for women was that when he did say anything it was never what was expected. After they had eaten the mushrooms he confessed gravely that he was not always certain of the difference between the benign ones and the deadly ones, and he offered comfort in the intelligence that they usually did not kill you for twenty-four hours. And the next day he congratulated her on being alive.

Sometimes he showed jealousy of the lady who was rumored to be threatening his bachelorhood. Coming into the dark dining room one night, he switched on the light, found her there with a notoriously dangerous musician, and stamped out. Another time he asked her about the same man, "What does Y talk to you about?" Once, about 1917, he courted disaster by telling her that a woman with brains and good looks could do anything she wanted. Shortly after that they were in a war discussion in front of the fire in Colony Hall, when she said playfully, "If I don't like the Germans, what do you think I think of you?" E.A. left the room and avoided her for three days. On the fourth she went to his studio and apologized. He said in his slowest, most solemn manner, "I am glad you came, because I had decided to withdraw my friendship from you and leave the Colony." This threw her into tears, and at that moment they heard Emil Tonieri approaching with the truck on his rounds with the lunch baskets. They were both in a panic lest he should see that she had been crying, so she hid. She hoped E.A. would take her basket from Emil and invite her to stay. But he didn't, and instead fell into agonies of embarrassment trying to confess to her that he had a lunch date with someone else.

But all these domestic scenes within the family of the Colony, with the accumulating tales of them, tended to confirm rather than to allay the horrid suspicion of E.A.'s celibacy which I suffered for nearly the first two years of my friendship with him, namely until April or May of '26. I did not then know his work well enough to realize that his enormous and subtle gallery of women could not possibly have been the creation of a monk. Nor had I yet observed in his work his casual acceptance of adultery. Carty Ranck assured me that he had had "two or three affairs," but Carty himself was such an innocent by necessity that I could not be sure that by "affairs" he meant more than flirtations. The pass that Isadora Duncan had made at E.A. in New York was notorious, but that involved his retreat from involvement and tended to confirm the rumor of chastity. To be sure, there were persistent whispers of the one great love, with two common attempts at particularity. One involved adultery with a friend's wife, which was unthinkable for E.A. The other and more plausible candidate was Olivia Dunbar, petite, dark, beautiful and intellectual short story writer, as of some time before 1914 when she married Ridgely Torrence. Ridgely and Olivia both used to tell how in those days in New York E.A. disappeared every weekend and no one ever doubted that he spent them with some lady. The later evidence that he spent some of those periods with his old friend Seth Ellis Pope, then a librarian in Brooklyn, still did not account for the rest of the weekends. Olivia Torrence, taciturn, Yankee, and indeed Robinsonian in her tense reticence, but forthright and honest when she did speak—Olivia was more convincing in her negation of E.A.'s involvement with her. While he lived, and indeed as long as she survived him, she used to deny passionately to her best friends that E.A. ever asked her to marry him or showed her more than normal friendly and chivalrous attention.[25] Olivia's grim self-sufficiency in general was evinced one morning at the Colony when Ridgely inadvertently left her locked in their room and went off to his studio for the day. Though a call out the window would have been heard immediately, Olivia sat in silence for several hours, till the maid came to make the room and released her.

For me the trail that led later to the complicated truth of E.A.'s great love opened in the spring of '26 when he had already been working for almost a year on *Tristram*, with another year to go. Before I learned that he had started the poem in '25, I used to plume myself in the suspicion that I had been in on the original combination of circumstances that set it off. Instead, I merely saw a late resurgence of one of the contributory impulses.

Coming up to his room late on that spring afternoon, I entered as usual, received no greeting, and stood. He was fully dressed and, what was unusual, was sitting in the visitors' rocker between the guest bed and the window. He was rocking almost violently, and had a fierce scowl that was in contrast to the puffy one that expressed his annoyance when his privacy was invaded. Every now and then he whacked his knee with one of the weeklies which I sensed carried a review of him.

I had stood there only a moment when he fixed his glare on me as if I were the culprit. Snapping each word and emphasizing the stops, he said, "They call me a dry New England psychologist! How in God's name do they think I wrote Guinevere?!"

With that, fury overwhelmed him and he sprang up and

started pacing the room, slapping his thigh with the wicked weekly. It was the only fighting rage I ever saw him in, and it was magnificent. I ducked by him, stood by the chair he had vacated, and seized this, the first confidence of the kind he had given me. In a tone as fierce as his I demanded, "Did you do your great love in Guinevere?"

He stopped pacing. "Yes." We glared at each other for a few seconds, then he relaxed a little, stepped over to the window, leaned against the sash and stared out at the twilight. I threw my coat on the bed, sat down, thought of things I wanted to ask him, but lacked the nerve to, or felt that I had got the one essential. Presently he looked around at me, wrinkled up his forehead in his normal expression of concern and sat down in his usual chair.[26]

So I came into the certainty that the great love had indeed occurred, and I saw the caliber it must have had. Already Robinson's Guinevere was, in my opinion, one of the great women in literature, the equivalent of Héloïse in her climactic gesture. Having long kept Lancelot from the Grail, finally, Arthur being dead, when Lancelot came to carry her off to France and make her his queen, still loving him she said she had stood in his way long enough. And she sent him off on his lonely quest:

> "I have not what you have
> To make me see, though I shall have, sometime,
> A new light of my own.
>
> .   .   .   .
>   . . . I shall not be alone.
> And I shall tell myself that you are seeing
> All that I cannot see."

Nine or ten years later, soon after E.A. died, I was talking with Ridgely, trying to persuade him to do the official biography. In what connection I don't know, I suddenly asked him, "Was E.A. celibate all his life?" "Hell, no," said Ridgely. "Was there one great love?" "Yes," he said. "It started back in Gardiner, and he fought it out in the *Octaves*. It ended along about '08 or '09, and after that E.A. took the veil."

I never asked Ridgely any more, for after E.A.'s death we

stopped exchanging irreverent pleasantries about him. Also, I thought Ridgely's testimony was dubious because of the apparent association of the *Octaves*, mostly composed in '97, with events in 1908 or '09. Twenty years passed before I was able to reconcile the apparent inconsistency and fill in the particulars of the story.

Part II

A WRECKED EMPIRE

> The time-infuriating flame
> Of a wrecked empire, lighted by the torch
> Of woman, who, together with the light
> That Galahad found, is yet to light the world.
> —*Merlin*

Prologue

PERHAPS the fundamental comment on Robinson is that through most and probably all of his life his favorite poem was the *Ode* on *Intimations of Immortality from Recollections of Early Childhood.* More purely than in most poets his Inner Self remained the active self, its function of uninterrupted perception—or Love—his real method of self-fulfillment, and its Inner World of simple, timeless Being his consciously real world. In *The Night Before,* the most pretentious of his juvenile poems, he identified truth with "something that followed me down from childhood . . . and kept me . . . just out of hell." In his thirtieth year, right after making his saddest sally into the outer world of successive appearances, he wrote to his friend Harry DeForest Smith: "I do not expect anything from my friends but impatience and perhaps disgust, but there are a few things that my friends do not know—things that I have known ever since I was four years old or whenever it was that I began to think rationally—and these things act as a kind of sorry prop for my shortcomings. . . ."[1] And sixteen years later, when he was getting the first flickers of recognition, he wrote to Amy Lowell, recording at once his early independence and his final choice of the throne upon which to exercise it: "When I was a small child . . . I used to rock myself in a chair many sizes too large for me and wonder why the deuce I should ever have been born. I was indignant about it for several years, but I've got over all that now. . . ."[2]

But in spite of this indignation at the outer world for impinging upon his privacy, his poet's necessity to perceive or love whatever was the essence of it began from infancy to send out beams of curiosity to explore its alien features and procedures. His personal life was a drama of the clash between these probings of the environment, both inquisitive and practical, and the forces he encountered there. And his verse was the running report of the play. It was an O'Neill drama of the ideo-neurotic tensions in a strong Yankee family in a typical Yankee community. From the point of view of the hero and baby of the family, we can identify four minor and four major themes of the play. One of the minor themes, that of his effort to fit himself into society, was never resolved, for to the end of his life he was self-conscious about poetry not being a respectable calling. In terms of the other three minor themes, his victory was in the outer world of time and place, and the play was therefore a comedy. Two of these were his gestures toward food and shelter and toward male friendship; and the third, flavoring the other three, was his humor, his perception of everything in the outer world, or simply "the world" as distinguished from "the universe," including "long Robinson" himself, as dual and dichotomous, ideally perfect and materially imperfect, and therefore absurd. In terms of the four major themes, namely his composition and publication of poetry, his love of mankind, his love of his family, and his love of a woman, his victory was universal, it was in the inner world and independent of the accidents of time and place, and with respect to them, therefore, the play was a tragedy. These eight themes in Robinson's life are all touched upon in the books about him, but at least the last two are dealt with sometimes sentimentally, and always inadequately. Since an understanding of these major loves, especially in their relation to his inner life, is fundamental to an understanding of the personality of the poet, they, rather than the other more familiar themes, will be emphasized here.

With respect to the material of Robinson's verse, he was forever protesting too much that all of his work was "objective"—though he admitted that it was sometimes touched by "personal coloring." In 1897, writing to his friend Harry Smith about his first book, he denied that there was much of "me" in it.[3] In 1917 he informed Lewis Nathaniel Chase that "I do not recall anything of mine that is a direct transcription of experience."[4] And about the same time he told Esther Bates that he "precipitated his own characters."[5] Minutely scrutinized, each of these statements may be found to be literally true, but their combined implication of godlike creation of something out of nothing is no more true than the common denials in novels that any character in this book is drawn from an actual individual living or dead. While full-length literary portraiture is rare, yet in any kind of fictitious writing there never was a character not drawn in part from some individual or synthesis of individuals, the whole duly distorted to fit the context for purposes of aesthetic unity and disguised for purposes of discretion. Likewise, even in works "precipitated" by the fancy, there never was a story not derived from a synthesis of the author's experiences. At the farthest remove, his observation and experience may be in reading, but this is rare in Robinson, as in most creative writers, and I doubt that a case of it can be found among the essential personalities or actions in any of his important works.

In looking for identifications in Robinson's work, it is desirable to distinguish between his objective poetry, which comprises the majority of his titles, and his autobiographical, including his subjective, poetry, which, characterizing most of the long poems, comprises the greater number of lines. The identifications in the objective poetry are of little value for biographical purposes. John Evereldown, Charles Carville, the clerks, Aaron Stark, Fleming Helphenstine, Reuben Bright, Uncle Ananias, Isaac and Archibald, Levi in *The Field of Glory*, Oakes and Oliver, the friends in *Captain Craig* and at Calverly's, the veteran sirens, the metaphysician in *The Burning Book*, Eben Flood, the hero in *Karma*, and many others, are apparently partial portraits, and their respective dramas partially authentic, but the spotting of these and other identities would have little value here, beyond the spotting of Robinson as a partial liar in his claim to have "precipitated" them in his fancy.

Far more significant was his partial lying with respect to the autobiographical poetry, which includes the bulk, though not all, of his great work. Here, it seems to me, the violation of the poetry by the dissection of it for the identification of people and experiences is justified when it helps to offer the world something perhaps as valuable as the poetry, namely the unique, elusive and saintly man behind it, not the prophecy but the prophet, not the imaginative perceptions alone but also the personal events and adventures perceived. In the autobiographical poetry, there is rarely even partial portraiture in the superficial sense of features and mannerisms, and only occasionally at the middle depth where prejudices, opinions, and even moral attitudes lie; and there is not, I believe, a single story that is a "direct transcription of experience," reproducing its original in consistently authentic detail of action. Yet within the disguises there are essential aspects or facets of the actual selves, inner or outer, of the two or three, at most the five, people nearest to Robinson. And in the fictitious settings there arise the actual tensions and situations between them, or between them and Robinson, that motivated the lifelong drama of his experience. Among his female characters, the widely miscellaneous Woman and Wife, Damaris Annandale, the wife in *Eros Turannos* and in *London Bridge*, Jane Wayland, Guinevere, Gabrielle Bartholow, the dark Isolt, Laramie Cavender, Natalie Matthias, Althea Talifer, the heroine of *The March of the Cameron Men*—each of these, together with many others less outstanding in Robinson's population, represents some quality of the same woman. Similarly, the villain in *The Night Before*, Argan, Flammonde, the husband in *Eros Turannos* and in *London Bridge*, Nimmo, Bokardo, Bewick Finzer, Avon, Arthur, Gawaine, Bartholow, both Tristram and Mark, Cavender, Nightingale, and Matthias, no two of them recognizably alike, are all drawn from some essential of one man. And, involving combinations of this man and woman with Robinson himself, or of any two in the triangle without the third, the poems in which they appear are all scenes in the same play.

Here we have in quintessence the quality of Robinson that all critics emphasize, namely his indifference to outward, physical paraphernalia, his almost exclusive concern with the psychological and spiritual problems of people in that inward world where each of them represents universal man or woman. The neglect of outward description has several significances. For one thing, it immediately directs the reader's attention away from irrelevant surfaces into the essential drama and the larger poetry. Also, it conceals in most cases the concrete experience of the poet in the interest of the universal situation. Certainly the paucity of sensuous symbols often contributes to his famous obscurity. Finally, on the score of discretion this outward obscurity was necessary, in the autobiographical poetry, to disguise the main characters, usually the same two or three characters, for they were his much loved, closest kin. For the purposes of disguise he used no cryptology, no code that can be broken by some verbal key so as to reveal who is who and just what happened when.

The only key is foreknowledge of the main situations in the actual drama. When they are understood, then each poem contributes to the understanding of the characters, especially the dramatist-actor himself, and to the development, climax, resolution, and implied preachment of his play.

Robinson was both less concerned and less secretive about his stage settings than he was about his dramatis personae. Most of his ocean scenes can be observed from and around Capitol Island in Boothbay Harbor, Maine, where his family went in the summer—the "stairway to the sea" in *Eros Turannos*, the little wharf in *The Return of Morgan and Fingal*, the beach in *Late Summer*, the gulls of Brittany, the cliffs of Cornwall, and the sound of Cornwall water. Informed opinion has it that the vanishing wake in the last *Octave* was that of the steamboat *Islander* which used to take the inhabitants of the Kennebec River towns down to Boothbay Harbor and its islands. Among these towns the most important one south of Augusta was Robinson's native Gardiner. He implicitly denied that it was the "Tilbury Town" of the poems by insisting that the latter was "any small New England . . . town." [6] In the universal sense, it was indeed any small *industrial* town in New England, but in recognizable fact, on the score of its aristocratic "hill" and squalid "downtown," and most of the characters in the objective poetry, it was Gardiner and none other. It was Gardiner, its vicinity and its 4,500 inhabitants that provided Robinson's subconscious album with its generic portraits and experiences, to which the later recruits from the bars and drawing rooms of Boston and New York rarely contributed more than refinements and disguises. It could hardly be otherwise, for Gardiner, with the surrounding farms and the cliffs and the seascape of Capitol Island thirty miles to the south, was the only world Robinson knew before he went to Harvard in '91 when he was coming twenty-two, and it was the only unacademic world he knew before he went to New York in '97 when, almost twenty-eight, he had already been tried and almost matured in the fires of the first three acts of his play.

In the eighteen seventies, eighties, and nineties, Gardiner on the wide and commercially busy Kennebec was a world in the agony of metamorphosis under the Industrial Revolution, the change from a shipping and farm economy to a manufacturing economy, to which was added the disquieting lure of the opening West. It was therefore a fruitful world for a dramatic poet. Its social pattern was still the paradox of the ancient New England agrarian-mercantile culture, the leadership of an intellectual aristocracy upon an otherwise one-class society. Gardiner enjoyed one exceptional ornament in the original Gardiner family with its stone-and-ivy early Victorian manor house just outside of town, its quasi-feudal acres and responsibilities, comprising with its connections—chiefly the Richards family—a small, Boston-type, hereditary aristocracy such as was rare in up-country Yankee communities. In three or four other families, Gardiner still had the intellectual gentry that had characterized most New England towns for two centuries and a half, a gentry still prejudiced by the soil and only latterly moved into the little city to fill the professions and administer the complicating finances of industry and the river trade, a fluid gentry open to all educated comers and exceeding the common citizenry in wealth by perhaps a hundred acres of farmland or its equivalent, or by a slightly bigger house having two chimneys instead of one. Under this responsible and respected ruling class, the bulk of the people were Yankees of the not-yet-old school, rooted in the agrarian economy and virtues, courtly in manner, humorous, intellectually and transcendentally disposed, semieducated, and from time to time casting up talented sons to go on from the local academy to college and qualification for the gentry.

Such were the still prevailing social and economic structures of Gardiner in Robinson's childhood. But already by the seventies the Industrial and Transportational Revolution had raised among them many ominous concentrations of power: numerous large plants exporting ice; many sawmills on the tributary Cobbossee River running through "downtown" to empty into the Kennebec; three paper mills; a crate-and-box factory; two machine shops.[7] The eighties and nineties added another paper mill and two large shoe factories. In the purlieus of these the aim of life was shifting from intellectual and moral to financial ascendance, and there was appearing a new social stratification between the increasingly ignorant, increasingly rich and the almost as ignorant, increasingly poor. In a few cases, scions of the respected families stepped on the industrial bandwagon, effecting a salutary combination of wealth and aristocracy; but in general the new rulers rose immediately from ignorance to power, were therefore impressed by their possession of the latter and little troubled by its traditional concomitants of education and responsibility.

Young Robinson, living among both the gentry and the new rich "on the hill," went steeply "downtown" to the dirty flat along the Kennebec where, on or near Water Street, crowded the three-story brick business blocks, the banks, the larger factories, and the small but not yet squalid houses of the poor. He saw the rich exploiting the poor and each other, with the physical distortion of the former and the mental and nervous distortion of the latter, including his closest kin. On the streets of Gardiner he saw most of the characters whom he set down in his objective verse. He identified the financial battle royal with the common experience of mankind, saw its casualties with the compassion that was his chief social trait, and chose for himself the increasingly uncommon and unpopular life of the inner self in the inner world. He concluded early that the outer world was "a hell of a place," so absurd that to explain it, even as "God's joke," the universe must be a "fine thing."

Gardiner was the backdrop and the macrocosmic projection of Robinson's drama. And within it the microcosmic drama, in terms of which he saw the macrocosm, was that of his family, the setting for the critical scenes being the big, white, clapboarded mid-Victorian house into which his father, Edward, retiring with $80,000 savings, moved them in 1870, a few months after Edwin, or "Win," was born. It stood under big maples on a two-acre corner lot at the edge of the city, and the side street, which it faced, ran a block to the main entrance of the cemetery—a circumstance which gave the boy an early awareness of mortality and, for the purpose of the family drama, proved both symbolic and expeditious. In architecture the house, built about 1850, remembered the Greek Revival style, its entrance of walnut double doors, duly glazed above, being off center on the end or short dimension. But the piazza which the Robinsons added around two sides was Victorian and up-to-date, as were the high ceilings within. On the left of the wide entrance hall was the stairway with its handsome walnut balustrade, on the right the large parlor with square piano, and behind it the equally large sitting room with a bookcase. At the end of the hall was a small square room with bay window which served as Edward Robinson's study. Upstairs the pattern was repeated, with two large bedrooms, a small, square bay-windowed room at the rear, and over the downstairs entrance an equally small hall bedroom at the front. The house was in the rural tradition of northern New England, with a long wing or L running parallel to the sidestreet, and at the end of it the barn attached. On the ground floor this L contained the dining room, kitchen, pantry, woodshed, and storerooms, and upstairs it had small bedrooms for guests, hired man, hired girl, and further storage space. In front of the barn on the side street was part of the orchard and the garden where "Win"—he never liked this family nickname—would one day practice his "farming." In the rear on low ground was the bulk of the hundred-and-forty-tree orchard, the hen yard, and a kind of glen with a little stream, a good place for an imaginative child to retire and wonder why the deuce he had been born into the strange world around him.

The stage and setting were the Robinson house, and the actors, including himself, were the five—presently six—people, all but one of them of major distinction, to whom "Win" referred later when he said, "There was a devil in all my family." By "devil"—in his verse he usually said "demon," sometimes distinguishing between them—by "devil" he meant humorously a streak of independence that would keep you from walking the self-righteous, "Sainte-Nitouche" chalk line of Victorian respectability. But seriously he meant much more than that. He meant the generic devil of the insatible lust for complete realization or Perfection, the compulsion upon the outer, self-concerned self, powered by unusual vitality, either "to plunge into the crater of the scheme," there to accomplish the absolute perfection of annihilation, or to shape the materials of the outer world into perfect form, whether symbolically in art or actually in the realization of some idea of service or of ambition. He meant that there was in the Robinson "blood the fire of time to warm eternity," or failing in that, to immolate the victim in secondary external excesses. In the members of the cast in whom the inner self and its imagination were strong, so that the diabolic demand from the outer world was only for the perception of its contents and the use of its images for symbols, in these the attainment or near approximation of perfection was foreseeable. But in the members of the cast who were relatively unequipped with imagination and who, therefore, looked to the manipulation of the actual outer world into conformity with the self's demand, in these the quest was more difficult, its consummation unlikely, its defeat almost certain. For all Robinsons, whether taking the inward and imaginative or the outward and rational-active road, divers secondary demons, notably alcohol or narcotics, or simply undrugged neurosis, lay in wait at the roadblocks and tunnels with their offers of pseudo-perfection to assuage frustration. But on the clearer highway of imagination these were less persuasive than on the twisted and rocky roadbed of the outer world—"Liquor was not the devil that would get me; poetry was the devil that would get me." With one possible exception, some devil, whether primary or secondary, was certain to "get" each of the five original Robinsons with their common, generic devil of perfection. Each of them, except possibly one, was Fernando Nash in *The Man Who Died Twice*: they "had it once."

The exception in the distinguished cast was not the mother, Mary Palmer Robinson, who was descended through two centuries of Yankee rural gentry from the Dudleys and the Woodbridges of Massachusetts Bay. Looking at us with hyperdelicate concern, her crayon portrait hangs today beside her husband's in their first house at Head Tide, both made from photographs and disfigured by hideously tinted, huge, late Victorian frames. Her demon is obviously that of high breeding run thin, of delicacy spun down into frailty, quality frittered into worry, of selflessness so utter that one wonders if she had anything more substantial than tremulous abstraction to give her sons. It is obvious that the high and sensitive perfectionism that qualified each of them was her all but fatal gift. Both her faults and her virtues were those of aristocracy: on the one hand, lack of physical stamina and the tendency to fret about her sons' devils rather than to cope with them; on the other hand, the sure perceptiveness of distinction, obliviousness to the snobberies, absolute loyalty, devotion, and service to and beyond her physical strength, and above all the continuous state of unqualified love. Whatever her superficial uncongenialities with her husband may have been, she was "completely wrapped up" in him. Life for her was only in the inner world of perception and love, unadulterated by the sensualities, vanities, and intellections of the outer. Win Robinson's quietly staring dignity, and his almost absolute purity of spirit, with its direct, unrationalized perceptions, in so far as these qualities did not descend out of thin air, surely came to him from his mother. One other trait of importance she may have given him indirectly. The fact that she wanted her third baby to be a girl may have contributed to that loneliness which was his earliest and one of his deepest wells of creation.

On the physical side, all contemporary witnesses agreed that her third son resembled her. She was tall but delicate, "very shy, but she had such a pretty, gentle dignity," a bearing at once stately and gentle. "She was beautiful" with the "satiny" or china-like complexion and "lovely clear pink color" which Win inherited and which was in distinction from the swarthy redness of his father, his older brother Herman, and probably his oldest brother Dean. Also, Win had from his mother "the soft hair growing close" down on the forehead, giving the impression that it was low.[8] Actually, Robinson's forehead was high, as appears in the later pictures when the "soft hair" had duly receded, but in his young manhood this apparent lowness of brow with the black hair growing down "close" is a striking feature in his pictures. Sartorially, Mary Robinson was fussy in all details, the fold of a lace handkerchief, the hang of a curl. One remembers that in his threadbare days Robinson was always fastidious about the cleanliness of his clothes. And one may recall also his minute exactness in every comma of his art.

On the intellectual side, specifically on the literary side, Robinson got little contribution from Mary Palmer. The fact that she penned a little verse is of small relevance, for all well brought up Yankee girls of her generation did that. In spite of eventual mutuality of sympathy and labor during the ordeals of the other members of the family, the mutuality never went as far as mental congeniality. Mary was thoroughbred and loving, but she was only narrowly educated, and the tenseness of her face in the portrait is not relieved by humor. She was aware of the high sensitivity of two of her three boys, but chiefly it worried her as a threat to their ability to support themselves in the real world. There is no evidence that she had any intellectual appreciation of them, and it was the less endowed and more practical one who became "the gift of God." For Robinson's important secondary capacity for intellectual generalization that could collate his perceptions, and above all for the special case of this capacity called humor, we must look to some other source.

The one possible, though far from certain, exception to the uniform distinction of the cast of the Robinson drama was Edward, the father. As Mary's delicate features in her portrait bespeak the inheritance of many generations of quality, so the heavy, neatly bearded, shrewd, wide-eyed, and jolly face in the companion crayon is that of the semieducated second level of the mid-century Yankee agrarian culture, the level that didn't go to college but figured that it knew a thing or two which perhaps the professors down at Bowdoin never found in their books. Edward Robinson, Jr., accomplished a rise in the world from the latterly unpainted, one-chimney colonial house in the town of Alna in which he was born and where he first took his bride. Having taught in the district school for a number of years, he married Mary Palmer of the local gentry and went in for speculation in standing timber. For $650 he bought a small mansion in the pretty hamlet of Head Tide and became a substantial citizen there. While serving as storekeeper, money-lender, postmaster, selectman and Member of the Legislature, he amassed a fortune of $80,000 as a timber dealer and laid it away in mortgages at 10 to 14 per cent. His naïve probity of the preindustrial world appeared in an early episode which his youngest son liked to relate. Soon after settling in Head Tide, having his first appreciable savings to invest, he drove up to Gardiner and got a banker's advice as to where to place it. A few years later the same banker, meeting him on the street, advised him to liquidate the stock he had recommended because it was now about to collapse. "But," said Edward, "if I sell it, somebody will buy it?" "Of course." "And they will lose when it goes down?" "Yes." "Then I figure I'd best keep it."

After his retirement to the "city" of Gardiner in 1870, where he paid the large sum of $4,000 for the big house on the corner of Lincoln Avenue and Danforth Streets, he arose into civic prominence there also. He became a director of the Gardiner Savings Institution and member of the school board—in spite of his persistence in pronouncing corps "corpse" and indulging in other rusticities. He was a big man with fine, easy bearing, full of gaiety and wit, and a great one to cut fancy figures in the square and contra dances that were held in the houses on the Hill. The Robinson house was a cheerful one, at least until the late eighties when the shadows of all five of its resident devils began to loom, a house that the neighboring boys ran in and out of freely, instead of waiting outside for their friends to appear. In the evening there was much singing round the square piano in the parlor, Mary at the keys, Edward leading the boys with his big baritone voice. One of his favorite songs was "The March of the Cameron Men," which many years later became an important autobiographical vehicle for Win. This domestic exercise no doubt accounted for Robinson's early enjoyment of church if, and only if, there was "lots of singing." Edward insisted on a sumptuous table, and all the boys, including Win, inherited from him a kind of Yankee *gourmandise*, a liking for rich and heavy food.

An element of Edward Robinson's hearty nature was the cosmic humor which had descended on the Puritans in compensation for the failure of their Heavenly Commonwealth, and had turned them into Yankees. Hagedorn happily calls him "droll." In Head Tide they called him "Duke of Puddlecock." When a customer in his store asked him why he sometimes talked to himself, he said, "Because now and then I like to talk to somebody that's got some sense." [9] Perhaps in an inchoate way he had his boy Win's perception of the world as "somebody's joke" which "may or may not be a good one." It seems likely that his mind, while lacking the discipline to order its contents into abstract thought, had native size. His interests were those of a naïve intellectual. Besides roaring the airs of mostly banal songs at home, he used to read to the family nightly from Bryant's *Library of Poetry and Song*, thereby giving Win his first direction away from Edward's own world of sound common sense. At the end of his life, whether through fear, or weakening reason, or because at last his Yankee conscience let him loaf and think, the devil of truth, though not fully decked out in its active aspect of perfectionism, was plainly at work in him. He drank too much, neglected his business, and went solemnly in for spiritualism. If Robinson's mother gave him his primary quality of hypersensitive perfectionism, his father probably gave him a natively large mind in which to exercise it, a mind able to encompass the outer world, measure it by its own inner standard, and find it tragic and absurd. And it may be also that the tremendous rhythms of the best *Octaves* and sonnets, of *Merlin, Lancelot,* and *The Man Who Died Twice,* remember a heavy baritone voice booming, always in perfect pitch and rhythm, "The March of the Cameron Men."

In the Robinson play, the function of the parents was to introduce the qualities—in Mary the perfectionism, in Edward the humor and bigness of mind—which in different ways defined the conflicts of the principal actors, their sons, all handsome and tall. In the oldest and youngest, the combination became imagination and the necessity of pursuing truth inwardly, in resistance to the practical lets and hindrances of the outer world. Horace Dean, the eldest, born in Alna in 1857, was throughout his life little Win's hero, and Win celebrated him *inter alia* in *The Pilot, The Dark House,* and *Calvary,* used him as principal contributor to the characters and minds of Captain Craig and Tasker Norcross, and finally delivered his philosophy of life through Garth in *Matthias at the Door.* They were alike in being sensitive and selfless, and both were bookworms from childhood, predetermined either for perfect realization or perfect failure in the inner world. In Dean's case we may attribute tragedy to a possibly less than complete inward self-assurance, so that his protection against his father's dictation of a false career was less than "impenetrable"; or we may attribute it to the fact that his own choice of a career, that of medical research, would have required further investment in him, thus making him peculiarly dependent on his father's sound judgment. We may remember, as between Dean and Win, that when the time came for Win's final choice their father was not involved, for as Win wrote in the *Colophon* in 1930, he "died . . . without suspecting "the grisly secret." [10] Win did not have to overcome the "mighty stranger." Of Dean one of his teachers wrote that "he had . . . a high-minded fine look, and he had very good features. He had the dignity that they all had, perhaps he had it most. He had a high-minded purpose and earnestness, and he was gentle. He planned to give himself to what [word not clear] that was best and highest in life, to give his life for other people." [11] Here was that encounter of love with the world that provided, in both Dean and Win, one of the main themes of the Robinson play.

The second boy, Herman Edward, born in Head Tide in 1865, was fated to defeat even more certainly than Dean was. In him the combination of the parental traits became a more than usual facility in the outer world without recourse in the inner, and it was driven by a compulsion to some absolute achievement so pretentious as to make failure certain. All three boys had extraordinary beauty of face, but where Dean's and Win's was delicate, favoring their mother, Herman's was strong, masculine, and intelligent like his father's, a face to inspire trust. He was a polished chip off the old block—no college nonsense for him—and his father doted on him and encouraged his rise towards ruin. The same teacher who described Dean wrote of Herman that he was "as handsome a young fellow as could possibly be. And oh, so merry! So sweet! And delightful! And he was friends with everybody. . . . Of all the boys I was teaching, Herman was *my* boy; but"—and here comes the tragic note—"I never thought he would amount to much. He was the kind that everybody would love, and that would never grow up." [12] What that teacher saw was what Win saw later. For here was Richard Cory and the young Flammonde, Gawaine, Roman Bartholow, and Tristram; and on the other hand, here also was "the gift of God," the villains in *The Night Before, Eros Turannos,* and *London Bridge,* the brother in *The Miracle,* and Bewick Finzer and Bokardo, Avon and Cavender, Nightingale and Matthias. Here was a split, a "small satanic sort of kink," which Robinson, for all the scores of times he produced facets of the character, could never explain. Perhaps there was a rudimentary spirituality that misdoubted his worldly ambition and impelled him to reach all the higher for escape from its whisper, so that defeat and humiliation were all the more sure. Here, almost, was external, to match Win's internal, greatness. But finally, when the test came, there was its mysterious flaw, the "broken link" that withheld him from the destinies that came so near to being his.

Act I

The play opens with little Win Robinson at four years of age— "or whatever it was that I began to think rationally" [1]—in Lord Fauntleroy costume, and with long curls framing his deep brown eyes, sitting in a grown-up rocking chair with his feet and button shoes sticking straight out, rocking vigorously and wondering why he was born. The scene of this opening is probably the sitting room, for its furniture at this time included the curlycued rocker which subsequently Robinson will appropriate for his den where it will become the seat of much meditation and prophecy.

Watching the gigantic and mysterious elders parade back and forth before him, little Win wonders about them continuously, but since he does not understand why either he or they are here, he has nothing to say and begins life as he mostly continued it, in puzzled, inquisitive silence. But already in that four-year-old's silence he was beginning to enjoy the ridiculous incongruity between that outside world and the one inside him. One day his mother took him into a shop in downtown Gardiner and left him on a high stool while she went off and did her shopping. Some "women came up and tried to make him talk. He remained . . . silent," staring back in enormous brown-eyed wonder. Finally one said, "I know why this little boy doesn't talk. He hasn't any tongue." Win stuck it out and showed her.[2]

It was probably at about this time, in the early seventies, that the Robinson boys got their permanent assignments to bedrooms in the house. Dean, the eldest, got the small front hall bedroom.

Herman, the favorite of his father, got the prize room, the one behind their parents' room and its equal in size. Win the baby did not get the rear hall bedroom with the bay window, but, adjoining it in the story-and-a-half L, the first room there, low-ceilinged, lighted by one dormer, normally a hired man's or a hired girl's room. Presently, and perhaps from the start, his furniture was as good as anybody's. Part of Edward Robinson's lumber business was the importation of mahogany, and he had much of the furniture of his house made of it, solid. Win's share was a big bed and bureau, both in American Empire style. Either at the outset, or soon thereafter, a picture of Poe hung on the wall at the foot of the bed.

At five Robinson went to private school in a neighbor's house, and his lifelong problem of "society" was posed. During the next six years—probably more toward the end than the beginning of the period—his one great quasi-worldly talent emerged, that for masculine friendship. He evolved from the age of solitary fancy into that of the group, and ran, swam, coasted, and stole apples with the gang. There is an anecdote of young Win and a companion in crime watching from the Congregational Sunday School window till they saw Mr. and Mrs. Robinson come to church, then slipping out and running home to the Robinsons' to play. In the early years one or two girls, the sisters of his cronies, were acceptable members of the gang because in normal situations— that is, outside of parties—their carriage at this age was not markedly different from that of boys.

But in general, girls were identified with gatherings where conversation consisted of giggling at nothing and pleasure was associated with meaningless games. From this time the artificial idiom of assemblies was and remained a mystery to him. "I realized, at the age of five," he once wrote Mrs. Ledoux, "that I was never going to be able to elbow my way to the Trough of Life." [3] So early he resigned himself to that lifelong social help-lessness which he later attributed to having only "half a brain," that is the imaginative, the metaphysical, and aesthetic half. Actually, his phrase for this public paralysis has always seemed to me rather literally accurate than figurative, for I recall the same absolutely tongue-tied helplessness as a child, the same mental void in the face of social necessity. A later, poetic friend of Robinson's remembers how the conscientious great-aunt who brought him up adorned him for a party at the great age of eleven with a tuxedo with short pants and a ruffled shirt, a costume somewhat advanced beyond the sartorial attainment of his peers. Up in the boys' coat room he crawled under the bed and remained there paralyzed throughout the festivities, listening to the racket below, the loud music and the make-believe fun. Many years later this friend gave up writing poetry, grew the other half of his brain, and made the normal compromises. But young Robinson's dilemma was fiercer than his friend's. From infancy he knew that the half brain he had was more important than the half he lacked. He kept on writing poetry, and stayed under the bed.

During this private-school period Robinson started a practice he never outgrew, his confederates in this case including the son and daughter of a neighboring sea captain, Gus and Alice Jordan, who ought to be remembered for their early perception of this youngster's literary bent. Almost as soon as he could read he would pounce on resounding words, run over to the Jordans' with them, and pronounce them to the family with slow solemnity —"Melchizedek" . . . "Nebuchadnezzar." This combined silliness and verbal voluptuousness got into the little exercise *Two Men* which he included in *The Children of the Night* and finally in the *Collected Works*. As already noticed, the auditory sensuousness remained a source of chuckling pleasure to him and his friends throughout his life.

Protoliterary also seems to have been his interest, not only in the names of ancient venerable worthies, but also in contemporary old men for their own sakes and for the wonderful stories they sometimes spun for him. He liked to be taken to his grandfather Palmer's farm, and there to hear the talk of the granduncles and twice-removed cousins who with very little distortion became Isaac and Archibald, the gardeners in Linndale, and others.[4] Conformable with this interest in rural characters, young Robinson seems to have been normal in the worldly matter of household and outdoor chores, what he later called his "farming." Apparently, long before he was ten he was feeding the chickens, weeding the garden, gathering—and guzzling—apples, currying the horse. Perhaps he found in these solitary activities some justification for himself in a world he didn't want and that he believed didn't want him, an honorable means of escaping from social exercises in the house or elsewhere.

Actually he did in these early years acquire a limited repertoire in the Victorian ballet of manners which became and remained a part of his rudimentary outer self. In high maturity he would—with fortunate rarity—come out with astonishing condemnations of people for small breaches of such decorum as he had mastered. More seriously, and also as an expression of his social maladjustment, the dwarf outer self became identified early with the generic "pride" or touchiness, the bantam pomposity which until late in his life would puff up—again with fortunate rarity—whenever it fancied itself detracted. Objectified, this hypersensitiveness both produced his valid individualism and remained a lifelong blemish on it. Already the two are combined in that late youthful statement, *The Night Before*, where the turn of the tragedy comes when "they were laughing at me and my fate. My God, I could feel it—That laughter!" Throughout his life Robinson remained ready to stick out his tongue at anyone who remotely implied that he didn't have one— as indeed he didn't.

In a year which looks like 1878 but which probably was '77, there occurred in the Robinson drama a crisis that we can best explain as relating to Dean and involving Win's devotion to him. In October of '93, writing to his friend Harry Smith and apologizing for having missed a week in their correspondence, he explained this grave failure, cryptically as always, by saying, "I had considerable to contend with, and hardly found time to do anything.—The fates have stirred me up considerably during the past fifteen years, and sometimes I fall to wondering how much I am to blame for my failure thus far in life." [5] We shall not find it hard to guess what he was having "to contend with" in '93, but what was it "fifteen years" before? By what means did the fates "stir [him] up considerably"—always "the fates," not any free individual, such as his father, who could be held responsible— at a time when he was in his ninth year and in the third or fourth grade in private school, enjoying a small gang of friends but already considering himself a misfit in the world generally?

Herman was then coming thirteen, probably in the eighth grade in public school, glitteringly popular there, cheerfully arrogant around the house, always first at *The Youth's Companion* though Win already had a better literary claim to it, permitted by his father to take the girls buggy riding behind the horse that Win curried for him. Also, being a powerful athlete, he was rowing in a four-oar boys' crew which Henry Richards, scion of the Gardiner clan, had organized, a distinction which made Herman the only member of the Robinson family then known to that high association of "friends not easy to be won." At this time and for years to come Win stood in admiration and awe of Herman and his success in the outer world; although it had baffled him since birth, he had not yet come to question its standards, but thought himself at fault for his failure to meet them. It is highly unlikely that as early as '78 or '77 there could have occurred any incident between him and Herman such as would color the next fifteen, and indeed all the rest, of Robinson's years.

Toward Dean, on the other hand, his feelings at eight were already deep and integrated. He was emotionally identified with him, and what happened to Dean happened to Win also. Besides, the external circumstances around Dean in '78 or '77 were appropriate to family explosions, which Win would have heard. In May, '77, Dean was twenty, and in the fall he was going to enter Bowdoin. There is a standing rumor that Dean the bookworm wanted to take the liberal arts course, but that his father required him to take the medical course, which did not then require the B.A. as prerequisite. In spite of old Edward's protointellectual interests in music, poetry, and eventually spiritualism, when it came down to brass tacks he was a country Yankee of his era, and he knew that such matters were the trimmings of existence, not the reality; the basis of life was economic, and the only excuse for a college education was a recognized profession, with the prestige and income it would fetch in. Also, it is probable that the Panic of '77 was puncturing some of his investments and starting them on their long decline. It was no time for his eldest son to go off vaporing in daydreams. It would seem quite likely that through the spring and summer of '77 there were debates at the supper table and in the sitting room afterwards. Little Win, listening big-eyed, heard his beloved, handlebar-moustached hero declaring gently what the boy knew for sure were the ultimate truths of life and love. And then he heard the harsh words of his father destroying these truths, not by other truths, but simply by power, the brainless power of "gold." In his full maturity Robinson said, "Dean knew more at twenty than I will ever know." [6] Dean was twenty in '77 and until May 31 in '78. The close coincidence of date with the later reference to a crisis fifteen years before '93 that had "stirred [him] up considerably" implies that at this particular moment in his life he began to sense, not only the alien but the sinister nature of the outer world, its organization for the purpose of nullifying the inner reality of such as Dean.

And at the same time, from things Dean said, comprising "more than I will ever know," he caught glimpses of that "wisdom" which nineteen or twenty years later he began setting down in the *Octaves*. Dean in disguised form appears less often in the poetry than do the other two leading characters in the drama, probably because, by the time Win was a practicing poet, Dean's antagonist was no individual but the world, and his story, therefore, was not good dramatic material. He was himself too pure, too free of inner conflict, or of outer personal conflict, to provide the necessary suspenses and climaxes. His accumulating torture was no more than brutal melodrama. But his wisdom at twenty became his brother's later wisdom, and the general fact of his crucifixion by the material world, with the necessity of his spiritual resurrection, became for Robinson the fact and the destiny of mankind. In the events of '77 and '78 we can see the seeds of his worldly pessimism, his cosmic optimism, and his "idealism."

Three years after young Robinson was "stirred up considerably," and no doubt in conscious formulation of the stir, he was writing his first poetry. Perhaps it was to this period between his ninth and twelfth years that he later referred when he wrote to a friend, "Writing has been my dream ever since I was old enough to lay a plan for an air castle." [7] In that fall of '81, possibly with the purpose of knocking this nonsense out of his head, his father sent him to the public school a little way down the street. There the teacher did her best to further the salutary purpose. Catching Win dreaming, she gave him a clip behind the ear and stirred up a slumbering mastoid infection which thenceforth impaired his hearing and was a continuing menace to his brain and life. The necessity of living with this threat deepened the gloom of his gathering interpretation of the world.

In '81 also, Dean had graduated from Bowdoin *cum laude*, and his father denied his wish to go into medical research instead of practice. For three years he practiced in Gardiner, meanwhile becoming engaged to Ardell Toby and building a small house across the street where they would live when he could afford to marry. In '84 he moved to Camden, presumably to gain a wider practice and prestige. As was customary, the burdensome job of City Physician was at once foisted on the newest and youngest doctor in town. Jingling or rowing to his emergency duties in the deep cold of the winter nights, he acquired violent neuralgia and began treating it as he or any doctor in the eighties would have treated it in a patient. At that time the destructive qualities of morphine were not appreciated. Whether the anodyne was also welcome against a way of life that starved his imagination, and again whether his fiancée's death while he was in Camden accelerated the habit, we can only guess. Also, we can only guess at the possible significance of Win's having gone up to visit him at least once during the three years he was there. Under whatever cause or causes, Dean came home in '87 addicted. By his father's requirement, he practiced two years in the old man's native town of Alna, after which he came home and stayed.

In those same years of the last half of the eighties while Dean's star was falling, Herman's was enjoying its spectacular rise. Though lacking in academic distinction or interest, he had been, like Avon, the most popular boy in high school and had delivered the Class Oration. In '84 he was assistant cashier in the Savings Institution and deep in the councils of its officers in the matter of investments, especially real estate. On the personal

side, he was at nineteen a heavy but svelte figure in correct frock
coat, silk hat, gloves, and fashionable longhorn moustache. Like
Talifer forty-nine years later,

> A power to bend
> Or break was in his face, and in his eyes
> The conquering gleam—which is a gleam sometimes
> Of more fire than is there; and in his voice
> There was a ripe repose—which might, without
> Its honest warmth, have been complacency.

It was none other than Herman that everyone stared at when he
came "down town" and who "glittered when he walked," who was
gentle spoken and yet "fluttered pulses when he said 'Good morning.'" In '86, when he was twenty-one, the bank appointed him
its Western representative, accredited to plunge into the scramble for millions of acres of lands then opening up, and to advise
the bank, its clients, and all and sundry local tycoons where to put
their chips on that great green table. This Herman proceeded to
do, instigating the investment of considerable funds from Maine,
including the reinvestment of most of his father's fortune, for the
old man, still in his sixties, was beginning mysteriously to weaken
and to trust in all things this one son who showed no signs of
being a mollycoddle.

Two years and a half after Herman went west, and specu-
lating from Minnesota to Kansas, had settled in St. Louis, the
impressive weekly *Real Estate Bulletin* of that city, in its issue of
August 25, 1888, gave him one of the lead stories on its front
page. The occasion was his speculative purchase of the McCune
or "Audubon Place" for $30,000—His father's? Or the bank
actually investing?—and the reporter gave him his best rhetoric:
"The buyer Mr. H. E. Robinson is a young man of twenty-four
years of age, and has from early boyhood been connected with
the financial interests of the country. At the . . . age of fifteen
years he entered the Gardiner (Me.) Savings Institution. . . .
He was soon recognized by the bank as an expert operator" in
real estate, especially western real estate, and so the bank sent
him out as its representative. It appeared that "his attention was
directed to St. Louis by Mr. A. G. Bradstreet, the prominent New

York Broker, with whom he was associated in several business enterprises." Also Herman had been in a certain famous "McRee deal" with Mr. Bradstreet and other celebrities, and his most recent venture was this of the "Audubon" or McCune property.

When the article appeared on August 25 Herman had recently left St. Louis in order to solicit eastern capital for investment there, and before he departed he had granted the reporter an interview in which he gave as good rhetoric as he received. He affirmed out of his expert knowledge that "St. Louis . . . is fast assuming a position among the first cities of the world," having at this moment the greatest commercial and manufacturing activity of "any other large city upon the continent." He declared that all that was needed to make the city a perfect utopia was a little publicity to raise money for the construction of an elevated rail-road. He said he was going first to New York—whose only point of superiority to St. Louis apparently was that it had such a rail-road—then to Gardiner for a rest, and then to Montreal. He hoped to coax to St. Louis some of the $40,000,000 hiding in Maine savings banks—which indeed he proceeded to do. There is no reason to doubt Herman's candor in this sumptuous vision, or to blame him if at less than twenty-four his expert opinion might have been blown up by flattery from childhood to a pre-tense somewhat too large for the facts. Incidentally, we may notice in this magnificent mirage the first outlines of little brother Win's future Camelot. Indeed, even while Herman was building his abstract utopia in the sky, events of equivalent moment in concrete terms were building toward crisis back in Gardiner. And on that very August 25, 1888, when the article appeared in St. Louis, Herman enjoyed a victory on the home front that gathered all that nonsense into serious reality with a local habita-tion and a name.

In '84, the same year that Dean went to Camden, Win, com-ing fifteen, had gone to high school. There, in spite of his father's forcing him to take the "scientific" course, thus disqualifying him for college, his interest in literature, especially the classics, began to bloom. According to a surviving schoolmate, he was considered lazy and "no-good" in school, sitting in the back of the room, his legs so long that he had to trail them out in the aisle—it was in

this period that he began to refer to himself as "long Robinson."
It is perhaps relevant to his lack of physical coordination, although he was muscularly strong, that he never took much interest in out-of-doors. Whatever he learned of nature he got from
reading, as distinguished from his perpetual, active curiosity
about people. One of his early friends, pointing to this difference,
says that as boys they never could get him to go camping, even
with his close cronies. "Win had a sort of dignity that it was hard
for him to overcome. I think he really didn't like the idea of
dish-washing and all the sort of scramble of a camp." [8] Perhaps
the point was not that he was toplofty about dish-washing, but
simply that he had never learned how to do it and, as in most
worldly maneuvers, his inability to perform aroused his stubborn
"pride." On the other hand, the same friend insists that even in
physical things "there was no laziness in him. Any task he set
himself or that had been set for him, he would dig in until it
was done."

Long Robinson's "no-good" literary instinct took several forms
during the high-school years. He indulged his extracurricular
reading not only by himself but in the company of three boys
with similar tendencies, including two who became the first of
his great friendships. They smoked pipes, not only as the pre-
rogative of profound wisdom and the delight of junior naughti-
ness, but in Robinson's case the indulgence of voluptuousness, for
from this time he rarely wrote to a friend without a reference to
the luxury of a "good pipe," either just past or in prospect.

His introduction to creative literary life was through a bizarre
neighbor, one Dr. Schuman, who lived on the other side of the
Robinsons' glen, a short block down Lincoln Avenue. He had
been spoiled by money, didn't practice his profession, was a
roughneck in conversation, more or less of an alcoholic, and always getting into and out of "engagements." He was not much
of a poet, but was an excellent prosodist and taught Robinson his
basic technique. It is obvious from the record that most ladies
disliked Dr. Schuman, but Robinson always delighted in him,
partly no doubt because he was a perfect Robinsonian failure,
having seen his poetic "gleam." In later years, when he would
show up in Boston or New York, Robinson would be careful in

his selection of those whom he should expose to the poetic doctor's foul tongue!

But, tongue or no tongue, in Robinson's high-school days
Schuman was a member of the Gardiner Poetry Society which
customarily met for mutual self-expression at the house of Miss
Caroline Swan, a former teacher who had lived in France and
understood French prosody, a composer of insuperably sentimental verse and the possessor of insuperable self-confidence in
her own omniscience in matters poetic. Early in Robinson's high-
school career, Dr. Schuman began to take him to the Poetry
Society meetings. Miss Swan reported that he was "very good
looking, . . . had a very bright color." [9] At fourteen or fifteen he
was far the youngest in the group and "sat very quiet, listening.
He did not talk, but his eyes were very bright, and I noticed he
listened intently the whole evening. . . . Sometimes Dr. Schuman brought some of Win's verse, or persuaded him to bring it
himself, and I went over it with him. . . . He was learning every
day. Our little club was of great use to him. But he *was very determined*. He had his own notions, he was one of those persons
whom you cannot influence *ever*, he went his own way." [10]

It is easy to guess but not easy to be certain as to what verse
may survive from the experiments of those days. Mrs. Richards
says that one afternoon Robinson read some of his verse to a
group in the high-school cellar and that when they laughed he
threw it all in the furnace—and so "we have no Juvenilia." [11] This
would seem an overstatement. In 1930 in the article in the
Colophon already mentioned in connection with his choice of a
career, he said that some of the poems in *The Children of the
Night* "were written more than forty-five years ago." That would
mean before the autumn of '85 and would point to his sophomore
year in high school. It would suggest the exercises in standard
French forms, the ballades and villanelles of the first two volumes.
A year later, being his third year in high school, when he was
seventeen, he "became excited about the structure of English
blank verse." [12] He translated Cicero's *First Oration* against Cati-
line. And so he was off.

Robinson's high-school class had been originally that of '87,
but because the instruction was found to have been inferior, a

new principal required another year for the diploma. Of Robinson's friends, Harry DeForest Smith left, but Arthur Gledhill, Ed Moore, and Robinson himself stayed on. They organized as the "League of Three" and wore a triangular insignia—the first of those masculine clubs within which, for the ensuing eleven years, Win fortified his social timidity. They persuaded the principal of the high school to put a Franklin stove in the laboratory, and there after school they smoked an improvised Turkish water pipe, sipped hot toddy—the first record of Win's tippling—and read Virgil. One night they burned up a school bench for fuel and grazed expulsion. Two years later, when the then collegiate Gledhill wrote him condescendingly of their last two years in the League of Three, Win took fire: ". . . don't for God's sake labor under the delusion that those days were wasted. This world is at best a diabolically practical place and if you are able to draw a little poetry somewhere out of the past, do it." [13] This reference to the past is, I think, his first recorded hint that reality is to be found not in the material world, but in the mind—the first glint of "thought's impenetrable mail."

High school and his male friendships there gave Robinson his first comfort in the outer world, including retreat from the shadows gathering over his father, and latterly Dean, at home. There also began the long and usually oversimplified story of his relations with women, which presently started to open into the future the widening vista of his subjective verse. Shy he certainly was, and both selfless and humble in the sense of finding it difficult to believe that any girl could care for *him*, the awkward and no-good "long Robinson." Also, conduct with girls was part of that external activity that he could never perform spontaneously or learn readily. Outside of the common code of good manners, there was no authoritative book to tell him exactly what it was you said and did to and with these nervous, giggling creatures. He pretended to dismiss them in mid-high-school career by writing a satirical poem on a classmate's unhappy involvement, and again at graduation he read an ode on the trivial sex entitled "Mulieria." But at the same time he was blessed with the exceptional beauty seen in the high-school graduation picture, deeply rather than superficially self-confident, and utterly sensitive, the large eyes very far apart, as in the face of Christ on the Chalice of Antioch. It was a beauty which no intelligent girl could fail to aspire to nurture, even while it frightened her with its clear, universal perspicacity.

Young Robinson was sympathetic with girls even while he was baffled by them and laughed at them, as he laughed at himself and all and sundry humanity. He was passionately curious about all human beings, and in the case of girls the passion was normally heightened by nature. From infancy his imagination enveloped his passion, along with all other outer phenomena, and took it into his inner life, what he later called his "idealism." But the process was not the common one of "escape." He always accepted and addressed the material world, even while he transformed it. It was as if matter were part of idea in one single reality whose central activity was mental, or as if idea were the one reality and matter an aspect of it or the surface of it. Thus, idealizing lust into love from the beginning, he did not thereby deny it. He kept it in its place as the outward function of an inward reality, but it never was reality itself. His feelings towards girls were normal, but his interpretation of the feelings, and consequently his demands upon the girls, were abnormal. Any love in which a girl would be able to follow him was sure to be a great love, inclusive beyond common experience and memorable as an example in the human record.

The earliest reported courtship consisted of calls on the favored member of a triple sisterhood during which the young suitor beguiled the difficult hours playing whist with the parents in the kitchen while the girls in the other room whispered and giggled. The first candidate of known significance was Mabel Moore, sister of Ed Moore, distinguished along with Arthur Gledhill by membership in the League of Three. In a later phase Miss Moore earned the high status of one of the two runners-up to the unique and incomparable lifelong queen. But, beyond the general and shadowy fact that she seems to have been the leading consort during much of high school, we know nothing specific of her agency, at this early time, for either Eros or Αγαπη.

In contrast, there seems to have been no doubt of the absolute finality of the main theme when it sounded. It was during that extra senior year of '87–'88, and the dramatic setting was an exercise which was of itself repugnant to Long Robinson, but which has been incorrectly denied the honor of any participation by him. During at least the latter part of his repeated senior year, fate sent him to dancing school, and there she was, a blazing stranger. The "torch of woman." Guinevere on the way to Camelot. Instantly they were no longer strangers. Her name was Emma Loehen Shepherd.

Emma's parents were of Pennsylvania Dutch extraction, and her father had been sent from Philadelphia by the Knickerbocker Ice Company to harvest ice on the Kennebec. He was a man of moderate substance and had bought a Greek Revival mansion looking down its terraces through trees to the great river. It was an older, larger and finer house than the Robinsons', and then, or soon after, it was painted buff with darker brown trim on the pilasters, the eaves, the door and window frames. It was in Farmingdale, then a separate village adjoining Gardiner on the north and having its own schools. For this reason, and doubtless because of their newness, Mr. and Mrs. Shepherd and their three daughters seem to have been socially unknown in Gardiner. From the Farmingdale District School Emma, the eldest, had graduated to the Hallowell Classical Academy, and had ended her formal education with two years at tony St. Catherine's Hall in nearby Augusta.

Why at the great age of twenty-two, coming twenty-three, Emma Shepherd first invaded Gardiner through the device of dancing school is not explained. Though we have no likeness of her for that year of '88, the pictorial evidence is conclusive that at seventeen, and again at twenty-five and thereafter, she was of a spectacular beauty to match Win's or any other young god's. She was short and sprightly, in contrast to his long slow lankiness. Her chin was too square, as befitted her determined nature, but its strength was softened by an irresistibly appealing, slightly snubbed nose. Her eyes were very large and very dark blue, disturbingly direct, intent, and earnest, her hair black, and she had the complexion of a May wind. Among all of Robinson's delineations of her qualities for forty-five years, his dark Isolt is apparently the least disguised physical portrait of her. Elsewhere

he recorded at least two mannerisms of hers in his work. Being
lightsome and nimble in all her gestures, she used her fingers
when talking, and sometimes paused suddenly and looked at
them. Similarly, Guinevere, generally well disguised, often stops
in the dialogue and gazes at her fingers "as to be sure again how
many of them she had." Another gesture of Emma's was that of
Avenel Gray in *Mortmain,* to look suddenly at someone as if to
speak—and then not speak.

Soon after their meeting in the winter of '88, Win was walking
the mile and a half over to her house to show her his verse, and
it is certain that no extremity of late adolescent passion would
have made him for long compromise his aesthetic integrity by
continuing to expose his poetry to criticism that was merely flattering. Through at least the next nine years of the family drama—
that is, through the third act—her belief in him as a poet was one
of the stones in the foundation of his career. In this, as in other
respects, it was significant that she was more than four years his
senior, she turning twenty-three on April 19, '88, he not to be
nineteen until December. She showed what would seem a little
more than perfunctory interest in her puppy lover by sending
him a bunch of roses for graduation!

The common summer resort for the well-to-do of the Kennebec towns was Boothbay Harbor, reached by the steamer *Islander*
plying up and down the river and out to the larger islands in the
Bay, in order from the shore Capitol, Squirrel, and Monhegan.
Residence around the Harbor was in either cottages or house-
boats, the latter towed down the river from their home ports and
anchored. Capitol Island, three-quarters of a mile long north
and south, was the retreat of an association of Gardiner people,
and time out of mind the Robinsons had rented the white Collins
cottage there, on the southeastern, seaward cliff, one of a line of
a dozen front porches along which the vacationists visited and
gathered and sang. The Shepherds of Farmingdale had a house-
boat, but presumably they had never tied up at Capitol, for in
the summer of '88 their eldest daughter had not yet been seen
there.

Beyond the southern end of the line of cottages, five or six
south of the Robinsons, near the seaward point of the island, its

highest point was a bare granite pinnacle commanding a more expansive view than the occupied sites to the north. Here, sixty feet down the gnarled but unscalable cliff, was the eternal, lonely lap and thump of what one day was going to be Cornish water, and out in the widening prospect past Squirrel and Monhegan to the open Atlantic were the white birds "flying, and always flying, and still flying, / And the white sunlight flashing on the sea." The bare summit had never been inhabited by anything but gulls and such dwarf junipers and spruce as could find nourishment in pocks and crevices. It was a fine place for a castle that might be called Tintagel, or even Joyous Gard, or Nightingale's "unnecessary house," but not Camelot, for that would be inland. In somber vein, the waves below the cliff were Nightingale's "imbittered sea," and from the top, positivists would one day be invited in *The Man Against the Sky* to "look sheer down / To the dark tideless floods of Nothingness" where they might do well to drown. From the high site there ran down the cliff a steep stairway to the beachless sea wheredown one day the blind of *Eros Turannos* would be "driven." Part way down the stairs there was a shelf where one could step off and sit, a belvedere where a nightbound lover might wait for his beloved to descend from the castle in order that they might be "in the world alone."

Before the summer of '88 the beautiful Emma Shepherd is not known to have visited Capitol Island. But now she made a startling move. She made that summer fateful for literature by bamboozling her parents into letting her go there alone. And further, as if by chance, it happened that the friend in whose cottage she found room and board lived three doors north of the Collins cottage, where from early June all but one of the Robinsons were normally in residence.

Already, when Win welcomed his Emma to the sea and sky of Capitol, he was completely possessed, and it would appear that she was at least impressed, by the remarkable love, at this time exclusively spiritual or ideal, which channeled the subjective stream of his poetry from then on. So far as may be conjectured, he first began celebrating it in verse a year and a half later in a lost first draft of *The Night Before*, not finished until four years after that, in '94, and even then juvenile and the worst long poem he ever published. On the evidence of this poem and *The Mira-*

cle, both in the contents of his first book, published in '96, it would seem that through that year, whenever he wrote more or less directly of Emma, he wrote passionate, versified prose, clichés of derivative rhetoric, the emotion conveyed being that of vicarious experience not transmuted into imaginative perception. But by the same token this immature writing embodies some of his least disguised confessions. The central experience of that summer of '88 comprised the first major crisis of his life, crystallizing two of his qualities, one transitory, one permanent. First there emerged his dualistic notion of female love, interpreting it as sometimes carnal, sometimes spiritual, as in imaginative young men; a dozen or more years passed before he outgrew this strange imperceptiveness. Also there appeared at this time or soon thereafter, perhaps as a by-product of his love of Emma, that universal compassion which was his greatest human endowment. Within a year or two after the crisis of the summer of '88, these qualities began to affect his attitudes and actions—though it took him almost six years to rationalize them to the point where he could record them to his satisfaction.

What we find in *The Night Before,* as finished in '94, is the situation of '88 clarified by much thought and some experience. In the poem the young man kept the girl he had married

> Here in my heart with as pure a devotion
> As Christ ever felt for his brothers . . .
> .   .   .   .   I loved that woman!—
> Not for her face, but for something fairer—
> Something diviner—I thought—than beauty:
> I loved the spirit—the human something
> That seemed to chime with my own condition,
> And make soul music . . .
> . . . .   My pulses
> Leapt with an aching speed; and the measure
> Of this great world grew small and smaller,
> Till it seemed the sky and the land and the ocean
> Closed at last in a mist all golden
> Around us two . . .
> .   .   .   .   .   The passion

Of that great love was a nameless passion—
Bright as the blaze of the sun at noonday,
Wild as the flames of hell; but, mark you,
Never a whit less pure for its fervor.
The baseness in me (for I was human)
Burned like a worm, and perished; and nothing
Was left me then but a soul that mingled
Itself with hers and swayed and shuddered
In fearful triumph . . .

This shuddering distinction between "the baseness in me" and married passion that was "never a whit less pure for its fervor" looks like the escapism of any sensitive, frustrated, and frightened adolescent of eighteen, especially one of Robinson's generation, which under the double standard practiced prostitution on the one hand and on the other taught the young that even married coition was something not quite nice, involving feelings which ladies did not have. This might have been true of the Robinson of '88, though even then, in a powerful and passionate imagination such as his we would expect a subtler, a stronger, and a more realistic attitude. In '94 when he wrote the draft of the poem that is preserved he was an experienced young man of the world and was beyond indulging the luxury of chaste escape. Yet his understanding of love was still almost as rarified as that of the boy of eighteen.

Robinson's lifelong understanding of love was as a relationship in which the reality was imaginative, and the carnal expression, like other bodily functions, was to be taken for granted as animal, undramatic, and uninteresting. It was both assumed and ignored. The entire emphasis is on the spiritual rapport. What he condemns as "baseness" is not the external act but the external concern, not the practice of lust but the preoccupation with it, the putting of second things first, the elevation of the material above the ideal. With Robinson from the beginning and throughout his life, it was the inner point of view that mattered. Love as a motive, the entire identification with the other person, was true and right. Lust, the use of another person for the indulgence of the self, was false and evil.

But if Robinson's understanding of love was spiritually mature at eighteen, his capacity for the application of it, like his understanding of women, was still juvenile. Though he may have recognized carnal consummation as ultimately an aspect of love, he had no notion of any gesture short of it, physical, verbal, or telepathic, that might be essential in courtship. About twelve years later, when he was creating the character of Damaris in *The Book of Annandale*, probably in 1900, he seemed for the first time to grasp a woman's need for some kind of external demonstration on the part of her suitor, some confirmation, primarily by words, of his need of her, that would give her the right to cherish him; but in the case of Damaris, the expression of love was still in the unearthly "golden" "mist" of poetry. We shall see that as late as 1913 Robinson was still assuming, in his own life, that the mutual sense of congeniality, of inarticulate "soul music," with a woman was tantamount to a declaration, an acceptance, and an engagement to marry! It was not until Jane Wayland's cry to *John Gorham*, written soon after that—"Somewhere in me there's a woman, if you know the way to find her"—that he shows that at last he has learned that there is something special a man must *do*, perhaps something he must *feel*, to awaken a woman fully. And, by that time also, he had matured into the knowledge that a woman's love is single and unconditioned, integrating soul music and desire in one fact that contains them both.

It is to the glory of Emma Shepherd that from the beginning she saw the distinction and the possibilities of this golden boy through both his inarticulateness and his ignorance. Though it is unlikely that she ever emerged into the fullness of love out of the tender condescension of four years' seniority in youth, yet it is undoubtedly true that throughout the sweet and bitter diversions of forty-seven years she never failed him in a deep sympathy which lent some justification to his early dualistic interpretation of her. Throughout that lifetime she remained, with few and brief hiatuses, his central human preoccupation. The greater part of his autobiographical verse is the running record of his changing perceptions of the nature of her feelings towards him and towards the third member who completed their triangle. During more than half of that forty-seven years, specifically during the first thirty years of it, he stayed of the persuasion that, whatever might be her passing frailties, her affection for him remained what in youth he called "soul music" and later believed to be integrated love. It took him thirty years to discover Emma. And it took him at least ten years after that to discover himself, with her help, and to find out just what it was, from the beginning to the end, that he should have done or felt, but was unable to do or feel, that would have fetched her.

At this remove it is probably impossible to draw with assurance a psychological portrait of Emma Shepherd. Surely Robinson nowhere sketched her all-round, for his concern was as much to conceal her identity as it was to isolate and use particular qualities of hers in particular, mostly fictitious, stories. Presumably the best physical portrait is that in *Tristram*, the best account of her self-sacrificing nobility in *Lancelot*, of her supposed conflict between love and loyalty in *Cavender's House*, her sense of intellectual inadequacy in *Roman Bartholow*, her lifelong love of Win, or his sometimes presumption of it, in *Talifer* and *Matthias at the Door*. And there are scores of glimpses of her in the shorter things. Perhaps the most complete statement of the quality inside her outward dark beauty is that of Althea in *Talifer*, who, like most of the other heroines, wears a blonde disguise:

> A beauty that is made of more than faces,
> A mobile and a multiple confusion
> Of humor, truth, and passion, and of love
> That outwears time.

The few surviving personal recollections of Emma are all reflections of prejudice, some for her, some against her, from which we may infer that it was impossible to feel indifferent toward her. One surviving friend makes her a mighty blur of all the virtues, without any faults and crags on which to hang a personality. Another report has her of a literary bent and an omnivorous reader, and she did have at least as much education as two years in the best finishing school of the region could give her. Yet she never became a part of the small intellectual group in Gardiner, and we shall see that late in life she felt unqualified for the great literary world. The obvious guess is that neither her home environment nor St. Catherine's in Augusta quite fitted her for intellectual society, and that from this inadequate start, sensitiveness, independence, and pride kept her solitary and prevented her native intellectual capacity from developing to its potential.

Among the reports of negative prejudice, one has her a "tigress mother," which I take to mean passion in cub defense rather than in cub eating—in either case a woman of strong passion slumbering behind that strong beauty. Another report calls her a "stupid woman," which may be no more than a charge of undereducation, or it may suggest a point of congeniality with Robinson. Settling in Gardiner as a stranger, and inevitably sharing the local disapproval that was then beginning to fall on her new connections there, she probably withdrew into a reticence that became a habit of social taciturnity. I have heard people of conversational facility call Robinson's silence "stupid," and similarly qualified people, especially if already prejudiced on other grounds, might have applied the same epithet to Emma's differently originated reticence. Whether or not they had a bond in silence, they seem to have had one in the kind of rapport that characterized Robinson's silence with his friends. Of their later years, the family report is that it was a joy to be with them together because they gave off such a warm aura of mutual understanding, and were both so perceptive of each other's wishes and meanings. Also, they had a secret code, involving glances and a few cryptic phrases that would stir them into smiles and chuckles but which no one else could translate. Elsewhere, there are evidences of Emma's playfulness and gaiety, but here, I think, is the only hint of a sense of humor to match Win's major one.

In the summer of '88, pursuant to Emma's sally against Capitol Island, Win Robinson did not long remain alone in the field. She blossomed into major popularity with the young crowd, was courted by several, and seems to have come to the verge, though not the fact, of commitment to one. Yet all the time, as it were in a separate compartment, there glowed her interest in her young poet, so adoring, so sensitive, so needful of understanding, so different from anyone she had ever seen, and withal so safe in his four-year juniority that put marriage beyond present consideration. He was like a sweet dream, a retreat from the not quite overwhelming, realistic rage of her contemporaries who wanted to carry her off to church here and now. And yet he also was a man. If he now provided only sanctuary from the assaults of the outer world, yet he too might one day be aroused. In some not incredibly distant future, he too might speak. And when he did, might not his declaration be the most beautiful ever heard before on land or sea? So, when she walked out with him on the rocks in the sound of the ocean in the evening, she might only be resting from the cry of the pack, she might only be mothering him, or big-sistering him; but also, consciously or subconsciously, she was challenging him to win her if he could. In the depths she waited for something, some overt sign of a tangible reality in this man that her tangible reality with its senses could rely on; some declaration, "one true word of yours," as he would have Isolt say almost forty years later; if not that, then some special, tender gesture; and if not even that, then as better than nothing a violent gesture that she could know she alone was the cause of. Any of these might have awakened her, might have assured her that she was more than a symbol for the reality that was in his mind, that she also was a reality to him even if a secondary reality. It was a juncture, not only in their lives but also in literary history. For if the word had been spoken and Emma had fully responded, we would in all probability have had only the objective poetry, without the lifelong, subjective love song.

But under the direction of what he would call "the unseen powers," determining his future and that of literature, beautiful young Win failed to measure up. He remained the puppy in love and indeed probably settled himself, from the woman's point of view, in that status for the rest of their lives. Completely possessed himself, he could not conceive that this glory could be solitary, that they were not united and mutually contained within "nameless passion," that anything remained for him to do but to "sway and shudder" in "fearful triumph." To do more would be "base." And Emma, understanding and honoring that, yet remained restive in suspended readiness. Through those summer evenings, sitting on the beach of the inner cove of the Island, or on the outer cliff above the lap and crash of the surf, indulging in delicate caresses and the long, golden silences of his love, she

waited for the word, like Isolt waiting for "your step behind
me . . ."

June slipped away. And July. There was no question of the
eternity, of the inner perfection, of his love. But she waited for it
also to enter time and the hours and the days. August began tick-
ing away. Still she waited, and the longer she waited the more
desperate became the need. Mid-August passed under the golden
moon. Perhaps she began to despair of Win, began seeing less of
him and more of that other young man with his more ordinary
quality but greater realism withal. And then suddenly, out of
the earthy and adventurous West came one whom Legend identifies as

> The man Flammonde, from God knows where,
> With firm address and foreign air,
> With news of nations in his talk
> And something royal in his walk,
> With glint of iron in his eyes,
> But never doubt, nor yet surprise,
> Appeared, and stayed, and held his head
> As one by kings accredited.[14]

As Lancelot, committed to Guinevere, brought her to King
Arthur, as Tristram, committed to Isolt, brought her to King
Mark, so Win introduced Emma to King Herman, who was sover-
eign of all the towers of Camelot beyond the sunset. But where
neither Arthur nor Mark had the emotional credentials to possess
their queens, Herman, being Emma's age instead of four years
younger, brought exactly the tangible, worldly assurance that the
woman required, and brought it with a dash and a distinction
that her other older suitor lacked. Like a storm with high flying
spray, he went into action, and a few evenings after his arrival
pinned Emma into engagement on the dramatic bare pinnacle
near the seaward end of the island. On that same evening of personal triumph, on that same August 25, 1888, the glorious article
on Herman was appearing in St. Louis, that fabulous metropolis
that was "fast assuming a position among the first cities of the
world." Back on the porch of the Collins cottage, Win sat alone,
rocking, wondering why he was born. And American literature
turned a corner.

Thus all the great triangles of Robinson's dramas were cast, and his relation to his brother became as unique as was his relation to Emma. Characteristic of him throughout his life was a kind of generous envy, the wish that he also possessed some quality which he admired in another. But jealousy, the twisted desire for something to be wrested from someone else, was outside his experience except in trivial ways. Professionally, he was entirely free of it. And with respect to women, its rare and momentary flare-ups were only sparks from his touchiness about his person. It may be doubted that even in that extreme trial of late August, '88, his reaction to Herman was jealousy for more than an alembic moment. His desire for Emma was not possessive. It was a highly emotionalized sense of an inner unity already existing, an emotion in which there was no separate identity, no outer self capable of being acquisitive. What Herman had done was irresponsibly to violate that inner, imaginative state which, as Win saw it, could not be destroyed. Not being capable of it himself, Herman had, in Win's view, substituted for it the external or "base" condition of carnal desire. As Win's desire for Emma had expanded into an almost impersonal state of union, so now any jealous impulse he may have felt toward Herman expanded into a concept of all worldly men who live without imagination in the outer world. His emotion toward them became an almost impersonal, generalized contempt. Having previously admired and envied Herman his worldly charm and facility, he now saw all this for the emptiness which in the final draft of *The Night Before* became a "genial craft that cloaked its purpose,/ Nigh to itself," of "sounding . . . the depth of a woman /Fooled by his brainless art . . ." Now for the first time he understood "this fellow" as

> one of the popular sort who flourish
> Unruffled where gods would fall. For a conscience
> He carried a snug deceit that made him
> The man of the time and place . . .
> The cad was there, and his ease forever
> Shone with the smooth and slippery polish
> That tells the snake.

This cad became a part of Robinson's world, ready in future to put on the costumes of the several villains and truncated heroes who have already been named.

Of all these Hermans, the original and central one was the "fellow" who in '88 had lured Emma out of the world of imagination with his "brainless art," who had "weakened / A woman's love to his own desire." Twenty-seven years later Robinson still carried this substitution of carnal desire for love as high among the expressions of that self-centeredness which is the central sin of humanity. And so he presented it as the fatal flaw in Camelot whose towers Arthur had raised to be a perfect model for mankind. Robinson's Merlin divided the fatal flaw into two, "two pits of living sin." One was Arthur's casual and loveless sensuality in begetting Modred, who eventually killed him. The other, be it observed, was not Lancelot's adultery with Guinevere, for that was a ritual of love; the deadly sin was Arthur's, who, making of love "More than he made of life and death together," yet insisted on marrying the golden Guinevere,

> albeit he knew
> That her unsworn allegiance to the knight
> That he had loved the best of all his order
> Must one day bring along the coming end
> Of love and honor and of everything.

This, in Win's conviction, was what Herman had done, putting sensuality above the love that he knew or should have known was mutual between his brother and Emma. Their triangle became mankind, and the Robinson house in Gardiner became Camelot. Win—again be it observed—did not charge Herman with physically seducing Emma on that romantic rock overlooking what was to become the Cornish sea. Physical seduction was not the point. Herman had done something far worse than that. With his morally irresponsible "craft" he had corrupted Emma's "innocence," he had caused her to exchange spiritual for carnal love, inner for outer desire. In the dualism that Win then attributed to her, he believed that the congeniality that continued between them was her true love, her soul music, as it was his. Wherefore, in inner truth they remained one.

Besides this dualistic notion of love, the other and deeper crystallization that occurred in Win's nature from the crisis of '88 was universal compassion. Indeed it would seem that his love of Emma, first enlarging into a spiritual union between two persons, expanded further into a general and impersonal love for mankind. And certainly his loss of her to Herman strengthened this sublimation. Six years later he proclaimed it in *The Night Before:*

> The woes I suffered
> After that hard betrayal made me
> Pity, at first, all breathing creatures
> .   .   .   .   Like brothers
> And sisters they seemed to me then . . .

Of at least equal importance with Emma, young Robinson's problem in '88, after the graduation, the ode, and the roses of June, was the disposition of his own separate life. There was now no question of what he wanted, but of almost equal exigence in him were the inherited Yankee economic virtues and the current Victorian respectability, both of which revolted from the prospect of his being a parasite on the present family establishment and the prospective inheritance. In late '88 and through '89 conditions at home gave him increasing pretexts for procrastination. Herman, having bagged his girl, returned in the late fall to his imperial affairs in St. Louis, taking with him, informally if not formally, the management of his father's investments and along with it Edward's reason for living and most of his vitality. He gave up active life at the savings bank and on the school board, and sank into a kind of mild, domestic alcoholism. Being in his seventy-first year, he began to fail in some obscure fashion that showed itself in weakening muscular control and general lassitude. In the Lincoln Avenue house he would lie hour after hour on the couch with his head in his Mary's lap. Or he would sit on the front porch stroking his beard. He walked with difficulty, and his muscularly strong youngest son lifted the massive old man in and out of bed. Sometimes he and Mary would go buggy riding; and if they happened to take the pretty drive up the Kennebec through Farmingdale, the old horse, having been at

Herman's disposal during the fall, never failed to turn out of
Main Avenue up Sheldon Street toward the Shepherd house on
the corner.

Sometimes old Edward's vitality revived sufficiently to demand diversion, and Win played checkers and seven-up with him,
again hour after hour. He gave up song and Bryant's treasury
and went in for spiritualism, which was then fashionable and had
its appeal for a curious but declining and ill-equipped mind. Although he had trouble navigating himself, he became adroit at
making tables galumph around the sitting room. Win later wrote
Harry Smith that his father lost his reason, though he himself
also fell into a brief flirtation with Edward's spooks. One night
when he was driving through the cemetery he was impressed
when the stolid horse shied at a ghost which Win happened not
to see.

During part of the winter of '88–'89 he salved his conscience
by getting up at five every morning to go down and keep time
for one of the ice companies on the Kennebec. But he also found
time to go back to high school and do further work on Horace
and *Paradise Lost*. He plugged along at the French forms and
sonnets and translated a good deal of Virgil. So far as appears,
the only work from this time to make the permanent record was
Horace to Leuconoë in an early version. Undoubtedly he had a
furtive eye on college, but after Dean's debacle he knew it would
be useless to broach the matter to the "mighty stranger." At some
time in '89 Dean came home from practice in Alna, hopelessly
possessed by morphine and alcohol. But for occasional hallucina-
tions, in which he was never violent, his mind remained clear
while his physical steadiness declined. For a while he served as
city physician. He compounded his pathos by joining his brothers
in the love of Emma, giving her a perfect score for the family.

Through '89 she was frequently in the Robinson house, and
she seems to have relieved her future mother-in-law at the piano,
playing for the boys to sing the old favorites they had sung with
their father. Meanwhile, Win did not yet throw in the sponge
in the battle of earthly love. His contempt for Herman was so
great that it justified to his generally meticulous sense of honor
the most egregious disloyalty. Scornfully he told Emma that she

and Herman had nothing in common but their pretty faces—
one wonders whether, on the affirmative side, he ever said anything to her as decisive as these negatives! And so even was the
tug in her between the two attractions—or perhaps the three,
counting the former, favored suitor at Capitol—that during '89
she twice broke the engagement. In November Win wrote Arthur
Gledhill, now teaching in Massachusetts and engaged to be
married: "My girl is still designated by the character (x) unknown quantity doncherknow. I am afraid, Art, that I shall have
to advertise in the Police Gazette when I yearn toward matrimony. How would this do: 'A young man of good character and
unquestionable ability, having wearied of his hitherto celibate
life. . . .'" 15

Herman's aplomb seems not to have been shaken by Win's
idealistic machinations and Emma's vacillation, for during '89
he bought a small and possibly non-speculative house in St.
Louis to receive his bride. About the first of the year '90 he was
back in Gardiner, and early in February Win wrote Gledhill of
having "just returned from Herman's hymeneal symposium," 16
that is, his bachelor dinner. On February 12, the prettiest girl and
the most promising boy in two towns were married at the home
of the bride's family. Herman was described in the *Kennebec
Reporter* as "of St. Louis, Missouri, formerly of this city, and at
present one of the rising young railroad men of the West." The
wedding was a splendid, evening affair, involving Farmingdale,
Augusta, and Gardiner. Emma was "attired in a handsome gown
of white faille française, en train, with a petticoat of silver and
gold brocaded silk, square corsage and short sleeves filled in
with trimming of ostrich feathers and a pendant of diamonds,
the gift of the groom." 17 Emma's little sister Josephine was to
have strewn the aisle before her with Jacqueminot roses, but
elected instead to spend the evening in tears. Neither Robinson
brother attended the wedding. According to the family legend,
Win stayed home and then and there started the first draft of
The Night Before. Late that winter night Dean was found unconscious beside the Kennebec.

As was then fashionable for the rich and great, Herman and
Emma honeymooned at Old Point Comfort, but they were called

back early by a supposed stroke of Mr. Shepherd, which did not
turn out to be serious. One afternoon a few weeks later they took
the four o'clock train for the fifteen-hundred-mile journey [18] to
their waiting home in St. Louis. Although Win did not publish
Cortège until twelve years later, he must have written near the
event a draft including the first stanza with its fresh emotion both
in the substance and in the onomatopoeia of the trucks of the
train that was Emma's funeral procession:

> Four o'clock this afternoon,
> Fifteen hundred miles away:
> So it goes, the crazy tune,
> So it pounds and hums all day.
>
> .   .   .   .   .
>
> Best for them the grave today.

Dean survived the loss of Emma and got engaged to Della
Collins, daughter of the dean of river pilots. Herman and Emma
stayed in St. Louis until August, when they were back in the
Collins Cottage on Capitol Island, bringing guests from the
metropolis. Probably at this time, Herman entered into a lease
with either a contract or an option to buy the seaward pinnacle
where he and Emma had got engaged; and either then or the
following spring he had work started on the cottage which still
stands there. They returned to St. Louis, but in November Emma,
probably with Herman, was back in Farmingdale where their
first child, Ruth, was born on the thirteenth. On January 12, '91,
Herman wrote to a friend in Minneapolis a letter whose retained
copy is in the then legible hand of *Win!* Having turned twenty-
one three weeks before, he was perhaps being initiated into the
financial mysteries of the family. In the letter Herman asks his
friend "Ben" to take over some of his interests in Minnesota. He
explains:

. . . You know my position—I've been bled right and left in
Minnesota and not only lost more than I ever made there but
have lost a good deal of my credit and standing here. These
people went into the thing on my say so. . . . The most of the
loans are secured by double lots at the rate of $200 per half

acre, and as Hayward and [?] have sold adjoining property @ $600 to $1,000 per quarter acre lot, I doubt that there is any chance for loss. Let me hear from you at once. . . .

Not fatal surely. Still the large language of the great financier of twenty-five. But also, perhaps, the first far footfall of doom.

For Win the year '90 had been one of important though obscure developments. From the point of view of his calling, the marriage of Emma to Herman was beneficial, for it put her squarely where she belonged, in the world of idea and poetry, while settling her in enough propinquity to keep him at productive pressure. When she and Herman were back East they stayed either at Capitol or with her family in Farmingdale, so Win was rarely subjected to the extreme stimulation of her presence in the house.

On the personal side, subconsciously if not consciously, Emma's marriage was not an unmixed misfortune for Win. At least it excused him from the ominous possible necessity of action in the outer world. Hagedorn's sketch of his haphazard life at this time shows him in a debonnaire mood: "He gave up chewing tobacco; raised a moustache and cut it off again; studied stenography and gave it up as a waste of time; . . . took to the clarinet and learned to play 'The Flying Trapeze' and 'Abide With Me.' The family tomcat fled whenever he drew his clarinet from the drawer. . . . When the animal began to tolerate the 'Miserere,' he felt encouraged, and he suffered a shock when he discovered that the creature had built up his own defence and gone deaf." [19]

Meanwhile, three weeks after Emma's marriage, whatever relief that may have given him had been hardened into positive confidence by a cosmic event, soundless on earth like the birth of stars. On March 3, 1890, the Gardiner *Reporter Monthly*, organ of the gods, issued his first publication, the sonnet *Thalia*. It is juvenile but clearly Robinson. Much of it is banal, but not with the stereotyped banality of Victorian sentimentality. There is not a hint of a "poetic subject," not a breath of "poetic diction." It is all honest feeling and honest expression. In the whole listening empyrean, there was in March, 1890, not one person except

Robinson himself, twiddling his clarinet, who knew that "modern American poetry" had begun.

The safe enthronement of Emma as the queen of Ideal Heaven, and the accolade of history in the guise of the *Reporter Monthly*, doubtless contributed between them to a third major development in 1890. Forty years later Robinson wrote of the great decision which, from the reference to his father, seems to have been made in that year:

> . . . I realized finally . . . that I was doomed, or elected, or sentenced for life, to the writing of poetry. . . . I kept the grisly secret to myself. . . . My father died—two years later —without suspecting it . . . Something told me . . . that they whose lives are to be chronically hazardous and uncertain should take only short views ahead. Before the family fortune . . . went to smash, I could see it going and could see myself setting out alone on what was inevitably to be a long and foggy voyage. . . .[20]

One reason Win had leisure for these indulgences and impractical considerations was that in '90 he had by necessity, as well as by inclination, to forego his impulse to earn an honest living. Not only did his father take increasing time, but, for economic reasons that can be guessed, it fell to Win to plant, cultivate, and harvest a considerable vegetable garden, besides tending to the orchard.

It was inevitable that once Robinson had settled on the high and perilous career of poetry, his contrapositivism should require him to look at himself and see how unworthy he was of such pretension. The gay clarinetting became a whistle in the dark upon the only phase of near self-pity in his record. In July he wrote Gledhill:

Dear Friend Art;
    . . . . Dean is weighing ice down at Smithtown, . . . and consequently I am left here alone with mother to take care of the "farm" and look after father. . . . Taking things all around my life is rather a dull one, though of course I can not complain. . . . Keep on with your pedagogic work and go through

college if you can, and sometime when you are strolling around the campus after twilight, alone (with a big chew in, I hope), you may think of the fellow down east who never seemed to amount to much in school (or anywhere else) but who was prone to believe that he was not altogether a nincompoop. He never had a great many friends, this fellow, but those he did have he has never forgotten and never will. . . .[21]

Two months later, again to Gledhill, now a divinity student at St. Lawrence University:

. . . No, Art, I have entirely given up all ideas of going to college; my school education was completed when I left the friendly doors of G.H.S. [Gardiner High School] . . . Father always talked down colleges and claimed they did more harm than good. . . .[22]

At about this time Dean, old Edward's prize exhibit in the harm colleges did, got a job as teller in the savings bank, and did well enough to inherit presently Herman's old position of assistant cashier.

It happened that under the same date as the latter letter, September 27, 1890, Robinson's second great correspondence began. Harry DeForest Smith was then entering his senior year at Bowdoin, and while at this time Robinson seems emotionally closer to Gledhill, he is from the start more congenial intellectually with Smith. The bulk of the correspondence over forty-two years consists of criticism. In the first letter his literary judgment is based in the contemporary prudish or "moral" standard which was at once so consistent and so inconsistent with his large idea of love, and which comprised the current form of that diminutive specter of respectability that walked beside him always. In this letter of September 27, 1890, he informs Smith profoundly that he has

come to the conclusion that Wannamaker did about right in suppressing the *Kreutzer Sonata*. . . . There is altogether too much low-necked truth in it to be circulated among the young idea; it would teach them how to shoot without taking a fair aim. . . . We are not all rakes, and there is such a thing in

the world as a good woman, excluding those angular spinsters
who preach about woman suffrage. . . .[23]

Six months later we have the last of this:

If a man must have something essentially filthy, why can not
he satisfy himself with the work of the ancient and venerable
Moses? . . . Here is the book—or Book—which we are all
told to peruse, and in it lies enough offal to choke the throats
of millions . . .[24]

Perhaps we can accredit Smith with fetching Robinson out
of this childish, inverted prurience, for it seems likely that his influence bore upon another healthy development which explodes
like a bright bombshell in the early phase of the correspondence.
In November Robinson visited Smith in Brunswick, and then on
December 5, without any recorded transition from the hopelessness of July, August, and September, he wrote him casually, "I
have about come to the conclusion that I shall take a year at
Harvard next fall." [25] And, for good measure, he wrote Gledhill
two days later: "For the past two or three months I have been
harboring an idea that I may take a year's course at Harvard.
. . . Of course this may never come to pass, but I see nothing
now to hinder it." [26] In other words, his recollection, forty years
later, that he saw the family fortune going "to smash" in '90 probably claimed a little longer prescience than he actually enjoyed.
Or perhaps he later identified this mature foresight with his
twenty-first birthday, on December twenty-second of that year.
For about three weeks after that event, namely on January 12,
'91, it fell to him to copy Herman's financially ominous letter that
has been cited.

From that time Win's hopes for Harvard wax and wane
monthly and weekly, and we must presume that the oscillation
was due both to inconsistent expressions by old Edward and to
varying reports from the western front by Herman. Two weeks
after the letter of January 12 Win reveals to Smith doubt of the
Harvard project. But now the dark mood of the pre-Smith period
has vanished in basic self-confidence, and he faces cheerfully the
prospect of making "another garden." He even tells Smith a little

airily, "Someone must be at home to run the place." [27] And his humor is in excellent order: "Sometimes I think I shall go into the missionary business and teach the chattering Hindoos how to read the *Police Gazette* and *Town Topics.* They never would take the trouble to barbecue me, my bones are too large." [28] On March 11, a letter to Gledhill shows that he has turned down offers of interim appointments as principal of the high schools of Bennington, Vermont, and China, Maine. Throughout his life, although he was grudgingly willing to do manual labor, when it came to intellectual work he would have nothing but the best. A little later he wrote Smith: "If I am ever fortunate enough to secure employment in some publishing house or in the office of some one of the higher grade of newspapers, I shall be perfectly satisfied." [29] Even this turned out to be a larger claim than he could make good.

Meanwhile, in a letter to Smith on March 10, '91, he showed new hope that the Harvard plan might work. But by the end of April he was deep in his "cucumbers, cauliflowers, onions," and was leaving the major project to fate. ". . . I shall stick to the dirt this season, at least, and trust in Providence." [30] Incidentally, Emma brought her baby to visit her in-laws that spring, and Herman also was there. Win wrote Gledhill something which the latter interpreted as "indicative of a sort of mental depression or perhaps the expression of someone in love." To this Win replied with jovial disingenuousness:

> To tell the truth, I wrote that mess more to see what you would say in reply than for any other reason. As to its sincerity, of course the idea is ridiculous. I have these spells of moralizing occasionally, and considering the sentiment expressed from the standpoint of psychological affinity, there may be some chance for an argument in its favor. But I can assure you that I entertain no such notions.[31]

"Psychological affinity" is of course prose for "soul music" and represents Robinson's notion of love. It is too bad "that mess" has apparently vanished. It might have been in effect a major confession.

In May he writes Smith that he "plans to go to Cambridge the first of July," but it does not appear whether the motive is academic or therapeutic, for his chronic ear has been giving him much pain, and whether he really means "Cambridge" or whether that is a wishful euphemism for Boston.

In June he is externally pessimistic but inwardly still self-confident. To Smith on the tenth:

> I am well aware that memories and ruminations occupy altogether too much of my time, but when I behold one of those excruciatingly active and practical individuals [Herman?] the same awakens no feeling of awe or admiration within me. . . . I have a presentiment that my life is not to be altogether a fiasco.[32]

And on the twenty-first:

> I cannot feel that I have altogether wasted the past three years [that is, since Harry went to Bowdoin]. . . . Knowing as I do that I should never have been satisfied had I taken up with some work with the sole incentive of "doing something" and given up the idea of a further literary knowledge, my hopes for the future are not as dark as they might be.[33]

He adds a disillusionized word about friendship, but not in the pathetic tone he had used to Gledhill the year before:

> I have about come to the conclusion that friends are scarce; I can easily count mine upon the fingers of one of my hands and still have fingers to spare. You will understand that I am speaking of friends in the higher sense. . . . I never thought much of having a host of acquaintances. . . .[34] [Herman?]

Some time early in the summer of '91 there occurred an event which is not reflected in Win's correspondence, and he may not have known of it. Either the previous summer of '90 or in the spring of '91 when Herman was in Gardiner, he had started the construction of the cottage on the pinnacle of Capitol Island looking out over the Cornish sea with its white birds flying and flying. But now his local credit had shrunk to a point where he could not see the work to completion. It was a clear clap of thunder on his horizon. Mr. Shepherd, his father-in-law, took over the construction and had it finished that summer. The work was carried on under some kind of contract with the owner, R. Harrison Potter of Haverhill, Massachusetts, presumably an option to buy. The scale of these operations which Herman could not finance appears in the fact that in March of the next year, '92, Mr. Shepherd bought the rock, then capped by the cottage, for $131.[35]

It does not appear when Herman and Emma came east that summer of '91, or whether the Robinsons took the Collins cottage as usual. On July 28 Win was in Boston having his ear treated. The drum was destroyed and the bone diseased, and the advice was that he should have regular treatments in the hospital there. It looks like a smile of fate to settle him in residence in Cambridge. But there is no evidence that old Edward was impressed, or of any comment by Herman. On August 10 Win's tone in a letter to Gledhill is negative. For the first time it appears that Mary is following Edward into decline: ". . . Father is very low (but not suffering) and Mother very weak." [36] It also seems for the first time that they have been without a domestic—vacation, or financial pinch?—though she is coming back.

Meanwhile the saws, hammers, and paint brushes were finishing their work on the romantic site near the end of Capitol, and probably in the middle of August,[37] little Tintagel stood there complete on the highest point of the island, high peaked, the steep cornices frilled beneath with appropriate jigsaw lace, the siding of smooth, matched boards painted yellow, the shutters green, the wide front porch, windows, and doors white. From the top of the cliff near the southern end of the porch the "stairway to the sea" ran down to the water, passing on its left, halfway down, the shelf with its natural seat. Below was the endless, impersonal murmur of the water, the senseless seaweed heaving and falling. And always the gulls.

One evening soon after the cottage was finished and Herman and Emma moved in, they gave a housewarming party. It was both a dance and a sing, involving "gay music." As at the wedding two and a half years before, Win declined to participate. As soon as it was dark he slipped down the stairs and sulked on the shelf, with the lights and the racket up there behind him.

Thirty-four years later it became a "fanfare of malicious horns,"
and what he gazed at "down through the gloom" became

> a moving blur
> Where foamed eternally on Cornish rocks
> The moan of Cornish water . . .

He thought of the "shuddering unreal miracle" of Emma up there
at the focus of all that artificial rumpus, and then heard again

> the changeless moan below
> Of an insensate ocean on those rocks
> Whereon he had a mind to throw himself.

His departure had been remarked at least by Emma, and suddenly he knew that someone was there

> above him on the stairs.
> Coming down slowly and without a sound
> She moved, and like a shadow saying nothing
> Said nothing while she came.
>
> .   .   .   .
>
> Came nearer still to him and still said nothing,
> Till terror born of passion became passion
> Reborn of terror . . .

So far the story follows the biographical facts as reported. But
in the embrace that follows, factual memory perhaps gives way
to wishful memory and certainly to the requirements of the
Tristram theme as conceived in 1925. The opening scene is full
of flashes from the first act of the Robinson drama that ended
in '91:

> "What have I done to you, Tristram!" she said
>
> .   .   .   .
>
> "But God! for seizing you,
> And having you here tonight, and all his life
> Having you here, by the blind means of me . . . !"
> "O God, if only one of us had spoken—
> When there was all that time!"
>
> .   .   .   .

"You mean, if only I had been awake
In paradise, instead of asleep there
. . . ."

"Had you been someone else,
You might have been . . . like Mark.
God—you like Mark!"

All these are sparks struck by imagination from Robinson's memories of this early phase of his great love. Also, as will appear later, *Tristram* has important autobiographical significance as of the period of its composition, 1925–27. But, except for snatches like the above, and for the setting and the physical description of Emma with her "blue black" hair and her dark blue—sometimes "violet"—eyes, there is probably no personal revelation of Robinson in the actual story. As I said earlier, he was already writing *Tristram* in '26 when he told me that Guinevere (in *Lancelot*) was his real love, Guinevere who more than Isolt was, therefore, essentially Emma, though physically she resembled her hardly at all.

For this opening scene of *Tristram*, the family legend provides only the facts of the jolly party, of Win's absenting himself to go down and sit on the shelf in the cliff, of Emma's following him down the stairs and trying to persuade him to come back. The legend says nothing of whether Herman, like Mark, followed her down to heighten the tension and banish him from the premises—to be distinguished from Arthur's banishment of Lancelot which has a later and greater significance. If Herman did not banish Win at the party, he nevertheless did it at about this time, and more subtly. For in late August or early September he threw his weight, always definitive with Edward, on the side of Win's taking a year at Harvard. Parenthetically, it looks like an odd piece of inconsistency that he should recommend this extravagance only a few months after he had been unable to finance the completion of the cottage! But the cottage had been in all probability his private venture, and his own assets never amounted to much more than a flourish of credit from his reputation as a prodigious financier. The financing of Win's academic dreams, on the other hand, would be for Edward's resources, which, though already precarious in their investments, were not yet seriously depleted.

On the affirmative side of this sudden swing of fortune to Win, we may doubtless recognize Flammonde's generous wisdom about the boy who had in him "the rare seed of learning." But we may wonder also how responsible Emma may have been, both directly through intercession with Herman and indirectly through Herman's suspicion of her soul music with Win. He might well have looked with contemptuous relief at the prospect of the mooning young whippersnapper being banished to a safer distance—a possible first hint of Avon's much later contempt and fear of the young intellectual leech.

Whatever these speculations may amount to, on September 13, '91, Win wrote Smith, ". . . my application to Harvard has been accepted. . . ." [38] And he comfortably associated the opportunity with "the unseen powers." On the nineteenth, he wrote Gledhill that he heard the old Gardiner High School bell ringing, and that it made him homesick. On the twenty-seventh he wrote Smith that he was leaving for Harvard the next morning, and that on the way he would probably smoke too many cigars because he was nervous and had "an affinity for the smoker." [39] Here were the only two aspects of the external environment with which, at almost twenty-two, Win Robinson was maturely comfortable: tobacco smoke, and masculine society.

Act II

The Harvard period, consisting of the academic years 1891–92 and '92–'93, was a typical Second Act in that it presented elaboration in the introduction of corollary themes rather than much development of the central ones, the clarification and mainte- nance in suspense, rather than the advancement in action, of the principal drama. For Robinson, besides providing the luxury of systematic learning, it was a time of the polishing of surfaces, the smoothing down of the outer personality before the filling out of the inner. In the consistently intellectual routine, the continuous association with "the friends of my life," the relative financial ease, the freedom from domestic tension and from immediate erotic entanglement, it was probably the happiest period of his existence. His room the first year cost only $180.00—the maximum was $400.00—but he ran through the impressive sum of $1,000, much of it for books, and duly bewailed his extravagance at the end of the year.[1]

Like that of all creative people, his primary interest from first consciousness had been in himself, not in his case in a self-centered or egoistic way, but simply because the outer self that stood between him and the outer world was the nearest and clearest external thing that the inner or real self could see. No question of its virtues or importance or ascendance was involved, merely the two queries, What is it? and, What is its relation to the rest of that strange, outer environment? If he couldn't solve those questions he couldn't solve anything. In most artists the outer self, even while being censored and censured by the inner, develops into a mighty and self-celebrating titan in the world, complete with armories of vanity and aggressiveness. In fact it is the compressive frustrations of these superficial impulses that account in most artists for the so-called "creative" drive, even while the actually selfless or objective inner self, the watching eye, is the real perceiver or lover and creator. In Robinson, unlike most artists, the process of maturing was the gradual withering away of much of the outer self, leaving as its final repertoire the orderly performances of art, including the formulation of ideas and notions, a minimal drill of conventional manners, and occasional petty explosions of touchy "pride." In the two years at Harvard, he made major advances towards this simplification. The near resolution of his social uncertainties was of much greater importance than his scholarly performance as a special student, moderately distinguished in languages, especially under Norton—"by all odds the greatest man in America" [2]—and undistinguished in philosophy, mostly under Royce—logic was "too much for me. . . . Worse than hell itself." [3] The friendships "of my life" that developed there, being of the inner world, made the outer adjustment easier.

The first thing Harvard did for Robinson was to clear out his Victorian prudishness of the double standard, as a prerequisite to learning to think. In one of his first letters from Cambridge, he blushes apology for inditing a swear word, and in another he refers self-righteously to the "fast set." But in the latter letter he also celebrates a thoroughly "satisfactory" "Bohemian" party of "beer, oysters, pipes, cigars and literary conversation." [4] (He bought a "bull-dog" pipe soon after settling in Cambridge.) And two and a half months later, in early February, '92, he records a heavy beer brawl at the Old Elm in Boston and calls himself a "bloody fool" for doing it before an exam—in spite of the hangover, he passed the exam.[5]

On the seventh of Februray he reported to Smith [6] the beginning of a passing concession to then current custom that led quickly to the crystallization both of his finest particular social trait and of that general renunciation of the double standard which made him a leader in the humanitarian as well as the poetic aspect of the subsequent revolt against Victorian hypocrisy. Between midnight and four in the morning, he and four of his friends went on a round of inspection of eight of Boston's palaces of sin. This departure on the part of a young man of extraordinary sensitivity represented in fact a confluence of two of his characteristic qualities. Certainly it was his strong social trait of male friendship that made him go along cheerfully with his gang on an enterprise which he would hardly have undertaken by himself or in the company of strangers. On the less engaging side, this adventure, and others of the kind through the month that followed, exemplify his lifelong, wistful conventionality, his desire to be like other people—in this case a high percentage of Harvard students—whenever he found that he could actually do the things they did. Of the same sort, during the same period, was the normally sophomoric, prurient vocabulary which pops up in his letters to Smith during the ensuing four months. In his account of February seventh he commented familiarly, like an experienced roué, on the smartness of one of the madams and her little flock, and he enclosed a souvenir for Smith's edification. Three months later, when he was cutting down on his drinking, he deplored as effeminate the crème de menthe he was reduced

to, said he felt like a "charley" [fairy] sucking at it.[7] Just one
of the little boys strutting among the other little boys. (And a
little old for it at twenty-two.)

But two months before this last epistolary swagger, and only a
month after his first tour of the underworld, he had made a gesture that in two respects brought him to maturity. It is a pity that
censorship on the part of the head of a great library postpones
quotation from the eloquent letter to Smith of March 6, '92.[8] In it
Robinson declared for the first time that extreme chivalry which
characterized him henceforth; and at the same time he put himself in the forefront of that upsurge of intellectual and emotional
honesty which two decades later had become a social revolution.

In this letter he recalled having visited, during the past month,
thirty or forty of Boston's "houses of seclusion," as he calls them
elsewhere. He said that the experience had given him—presumably for the first time—a real understanding of women, and in
consequence full realization of the horror of prostitution. He
declared his contempt for men who thus debased women for
pleasure only; and from the depths of his characteristic humility
he even dared value himself above such men(!)

From this letter it is quite possible to draw an inference that
Robinson himself had not thus debased a woman, and thereby to
find early support for his absurd reputation for celibacy. But it
is equally possible to interpret his impassioned denunciation,
combined with his profession of a newly acquired understanding
of women, as an implicit assertion that he spoke from experience.
As always, Robinson's condemnation is not of carnality categorically, but of carnality for its own sake, carnality without love. If
ever in one of the dives Robinson did leave the general company
with a "damsel," it is certain that part of his impulse was concern
for her. A week after the letter of March 6 he reported to
Smith that one of the pathetic creatures had sent him word that
she hoped he would come again, and he acknowledged pleasure
in her having remembered him.[9] Whether or not they had progressed beyond drinking and talking, it is certain that he had
treated her as a human being. One wonders why in *The Growth
of "Lorraine,"* written nine years later, the name of the tragic little
harlot is enclosed in quotation marks.

In the letter of March 13, in which Robinson mentions the girl who inquired for him, he also expressed loathing of the carnal spectacles he had seen in the dives. His final report in this field was on June 5, and he reveals that since the denunciation of three months before he had in fact visited one of the houses at least once more.[10] In all probability that was his last venture of this kind; but if ever, during the Cambridge period or later, he did go along with a crowd that was visiting one of the "holes," it may be taken that his part was that of an uncomfortable spectator only. What is memorable out of this brief passage, besides what has been mentioned, is that Robinson's condemnation of prostitution was the result of experience. It was based, not on smug and timid propriety, but on the immediate human grounds of suffering on the one hand and selfishness on the other. He never had any patience with the inverted prurience that looks away from the unpleasant prospect and suppresses the record of it. He always walked all the way up to supposed evil, looked at it directly, addressed it kindly, and hoped it might turn into good. Self-righteousness and the callousness that goes with it were the only sins he did not forgive.

Besides maturing his chivalry and exemplifying his flair for male companionship and his penchant for conventional conduct, a further significance of Robinson's little passage in and out of the underworld was that it brought out, probably for the first time, his remarkably easy control of secondary devils. He was already hopelessly pinioned by the generic fiend of truth in her costume of the art of poetry. But once his imagination enjoyed a perception that condemned one of the lesser, outer demons, his outer self, in this case his body, submitted almost without a fight. Because of the great power of his desire in its sublimated form, whether aesthetic or "idealistic," the point with him was not weakness of lust but strength of imagination. His method of overcoming devils was not to escape from them but to face them. Having denied for himself some lure of the outer world, he did not thereby condemn those who still pursued it and withdraw with monastic loftiness into his inner self. Instead, he remained with them in the outer world, looked with steady love at their inner selves, and forgave them their outer failures.

Besides meeting and overcoming the devil of loveless sex, during that first year at Harvard, Robinson also inaugurated his astonishing, lifelong control of the demon of alcohol, astonishing because he liked liquor "for the effect"—although its immediate effect on him was slight—, liked intellectual conviviality, and in this case there was no appreciable social taboo to bolster his self-control. By December of his first year at Harvard, when we find him reporting his first beer parties, we find also the instinct for moderation and the counterdevil that strengthened it. Excess interfered with his sleep, and he seems to have been prone to hangovers. In the letter of May fifteenth, cited above, in which he described himself sucking a crème de menthe, he told Smith positively, "There is no fear of my ever becoming a drunkard." He also reported that four bottles of "Dublin Street" had made him sick, but that he overcame it in the morning by eating beans! Here, at the end of his first year, he declared that he had drunk everything—except the standard hard stuff—from pousse-café to bottled cider, and that he didn't give a tinker's dam for any of it except Guinness's stout. In February of his second year, 1893, he says the last word on his academic drinking when he reports that his friend Saben "got drunk, as I expected," and read a lot of poetry. "The audience seemed well amused, but there is something rather degrading in it after all. Perhaps I would have enjoyed it more if I had drunk something, but I have practically given it up, if ever I drank enough to say that. The pipe does me very well." [11]

A year before reaching this grown-up status, that is, in the winter of '92, he had reported after a beer party in his room on Cambridge Street that "the smell of the 'innumerable pipes' has not yet left the room. . . . There is a sociability about pipes that I cannot explain. They seem to bring us nearer to each other and I think upon the whole that the world should be thankful for the weed—so called." [12] Here was his mystique of friendship, with the pipe for ritual, something that he had felt from his first initiation to tobacco in high school. At the end of the first year at Harvard, in June, '92, he was experimenting with a variation which had less mystical value. "I have contracted a habit of smoking [Turkish cigarettes] which I must stop. They make a man dull and sleepy, but there is a fascination about them that is hard to describe. I suppose they are loaded. Peters hit it about right when he said each puff from them feels as if it were killing you." [13] Tobacco was one devil he seems never to have renounced or even moderated for long. So far as appears, he had no cause to.

Before Robinson settled solidly into the company of "the friends of my life" with their "innumerable pipes," he experimented in two other social directions. Throughout his life he had a kind of wistful admiration—not exactly a social inferiority complex, but bordering on it—for the cultivated gentry with their courteous manners and especially their ability to talk easily and well, if for no reason but to make their listener comfortable. If they were to interest Robinson personally, they must also have for him some community of intellectual interest, and at Harvard of course there was a formidable pool of wellbred young highbrows for him to draw on. They were running, among other things, the university's literary world, and after Robert Morss Lovett called on Robinson, as a courtesy in rejecting "Thomas Hood" for the *Harvard Monthly,* he wanted to be of their fellowship. It was flattering for a "special" to be called on by a prominent upper classman. He even laid a plot. "If I am a little foxy," he wrote Smith that first December, "I may get in with the whole gang, which will be rather more pleasant than my present situation. Of course I have found some good fellows—but you will understand precisely what I mean." [14] The "whole gang" of undergraduate literati then included Hutchins and Norman Hapgood, Charles Flandrau and R. M. Lovett; William Lyon Phelps and George Santayana were graduate students. After Robinson had three times cracked the *Advocate* before the first Christmas, he made good. He was invited around to meet the editors. This was his chance.

And as he doubtless had foreseen, he failed. "I sat there among them," he told one of his new real friends, "unable to speak a word." [15] Apparently he was not invited again. Outwardly, the experience depressed him. But inwardly, it had a different significance, one he could never explain to anyone, probably did not even formulate himself. The truth was that all those bright young men had failed to meet a condition more profound than that of courtesy or even of intellectual congeniality. They had failed to understand Robinson on the one level in which he was adept at communication. Silence. They had failed to meet his chief requirement of friendship, that its essential expression be in that language of the inner self and the inner world. The language of reality. Doubtless if he had continued to be "foxy," if he had called on some of those bright young men singly, as Lovett invited him to do and had done to him, he would have found reality not too far under the surface. His challenge to them to make the first articulate move out of the common pool of Being would have been met. But Robinson's quasi-snobbery didn't go that far. It was difficult for him to make one slight gesture, to accept an invitation. After that they must go all the way. And when they failed, one of the effects was to strengthen his inner assurance, his self-sufficiency in loneliness.

His other early, experimental, and definitive gesture toward people in groups was "social" in the common sense. And this offered no compensation for its embarrassments, as did his adventure with the intellectual bosses. When in the fall of '91 he was invited to one of his professors' at-homes he wrote Smith, "A 'society man' is something I can never be, and never wish to be"; and he proceeded to prove his point. His report was that he "fed an Annex girl on chocolate and bilious cocoanut cakes. I did not eat any myself, though she urged me to most earnestly. . . . We talked for an hour on French novels. She thinks they are shocking in their immorality and hopes I will not read them. They will injure me. . . . Her simplicity and innocence, or mine, was startling. I do not think she was trying to seduce me, however; her eyes were too large and earnest. I do not remember her name, but she was apparently growing quite fond of me when I left her. She seemed to have a sisterly regard for me that gave me a 'temporary feeling of safety for the time being.' Her nose was a trifle one-sided and she carried a whole arboretum on her bosom." [16] Three and a half months later he wrote: "I have been to two or three receptions at Mrs. [Professor] Sumichrast's but will not attend any more. . . . It [is] fairly a mystery to me how a fellow can mix himself with a roomful of strangers and enjoy himself. . . . passing through one of these 'at-homes' here

in Cambridge . . . is like passing through Hell. . . . When I
watch these 'polished young gentlemen' floating around from one
girl to another, keeping their tongues wagging all the time and
saying things that no man or woman that God ever put on earth
could remember five minutes, I begin to realize the difference in
humanity. . . . No, the truth is that I never enjoy myself so
much as when I am with one or two congenial souls talking on
some congenial subject, and smoking the pipe." [17] This letter was
less than two weeks later than the one in which he had condemned and renounced prostitution. Thus in two fell swoops he
eliminated both low society and high society from his vital activities. The one stirred up his imagination in the form of compassion, only to violate it. The other stirred nothing.

Long before these two cleansing renunciations, Robinson had
settled into the aura of the innumerable pipes of "the friends of
my life" [18] who accepted him at his own valuation, not a "society
star," nor yet "one of the boys" (Herman?) but something "about
midway between." They called him "Robbie," constituted themselves The Corncob Club and met in each other's rooms. Actually, only three of them remained his active, lifelong friends.
Preeminent was two-wooden-legged George Burnham, now at
twenty-four an impoverished law student, a Hindu, and a man
of passion; once at a baseball game he disagreed with a decision
of the umpire and ran out on the field on his stump legs, proposing to beat him. The second lifelong friend was Mowbry Saben,
rich, a superannuated freshman and a universal rebel. In March
of '92 he was fired because he had low marks and one of the
club's meetings in his room got too drunkenly noisy, two Cambridge policemen being among the guests; Saben stayed in residence, leading rebellion on the alcoholic and other fronts.
"Robbie's" third permanent friend from that era was William
Edward Butler whose father owned a department store on Tre-
mont Street. Among its other members the Club included an
Oxford Movement Christian and a Swedenborgian. William
Vaughn Moody, who was Harvard's great poet at the time and
high in the official intellectual set which "Robbie" failed to make,
was drawn to him and so was in and out of the Corncob crowd.
Then and always Robbie was satirically and indulgently de-

lighted with Moody's enormous vitality and enormous rhetoric.

From the beginning, Robinson's sense of humor was liberated by Cambridge, in the same proportion that his perceptions were freed from their swaddling of Victorian prudery. Here he is writing to Smith the December after his arrival:

> Harvard University is a great place to set a man's thoughts going. Yesterday I watched two able-bodied men spreading fragrant New England dung on the campus. . . . There is a kind of poetry in scattering dung—if the dung is good—that must needs awaken a fine sentiment in the mind of a man of any imagination. The excrement gives the increment to the emerald grass, etc., and when the spring zephyrs begin to blow the transformation becomes apparent . . . The faculty are obviously poets. They use no prepared fertilizer whatever, but cling to the mushy manure of our, and their, ancestors. . . . The odor made me homesick. . . . In the play *Alabama* just closed at the Tremont Theatre there is an artificial odor of magnolia raised by burning something or other. It affects the southern students wonderfully. So you see that it is only . . . natural . . . that the frank sincerity of the odor I have mentioned should turn my thoughts towards Maine.[19]

His attitude towards himself when in the company of his friends was usually humorous. When he was working on *Supremacy*, apparently the first of his great sonnets to be written and surely the first to be published (*Harvard Advocate*, June 16, '92), he sent Smith the first quatrain, opening, "There is a drear and lonely tract of Hell," and commented: "I don't know how long this Hell business will last, but I may sigh out two or three more. It is a damned cheerful subject and my muse is merry whenever she gets into it. . . ." [20]

A month later he reported solemnly that a friend recently came to his room and "after a silence of some minutes he made a statement that startled me a little. . . . 'Robinson,' he said, 'I can't see what this life of ours amounts to anyway. What is the object of it? What are we here for?' I could not give him a definite answer, so I blew a stream of Bull Durham smoke into the air and shook my head." [21] This was a lifelong gesture of amusement with him. At the same time he would have opened his eyes very wide in apparent astonishment and wonder.

Six months after this he seemed to be trying to give himself a more "definite answer," and his humor sank to its sardonic genre. But it is still humor, not cynicism; it is his sense of the absurd incongruity between the world and the universe. ". . . life is a curious mess. . . . Sometimes I sit here by my fire and wonder how it is all coming out. I look back upon the millions who lived and died a thousand years ago and wonder if it makes much difference how it comes out, after all. I do not look pessimistically upon the matter. I am inclined to regard it more in the light of a big joke—whose joke it is, or whether it is a good one, I cannot tell. Maarten Maartens has written a novel called *God's Fool*. Think I shall read it." [22]

Although Robinson's sense of humor deepened at Harvard, it never completely effaced the banal wish for respectability and the banal vocabulary appropriate to it. In the same letter in which he first reported a beer brawl in Boston, Gardiner still spoke its paragraph:

> Every day that I live I realize more and more the existence of several elements or characteristics in my make-up that, unless they are put down, will be of decided disadvantage to me in the future. In the first place, I am and always was too much of a dreamer; I have no sympathy with the cold, matter-of-fact contriving nature [Herman?] that has made the fortunes enjoyed by multitudes all around us . . . and this is a dangerous state to be in. . . . The sight of success awakens a feeling painfully approaching envy, and I am inclined too much to look upon its achievement as a kind of destiny. . . . [23]

And a year and a half later, in June of '93 when he was about to leave Harvard, respectability was still nibbling at him. At the advanced age of twenty-three he writes Gledhill with typical ambiguity:

> The idea of leaving seems a little strange, but I doubt if I should care to come another year under the circumstances. I am getting to be an old man and must do something to bring

in the ducats instead of throwing them out all the time. . . .
This "job" question is beginning to interest me to an extent that
it never did before. Most of the people who have them seem to
be better off than those who do not, but most of the people are
not so hopelessly fettered by their individual tastes as I am. I
do not wish to teach school or work with tools or anything
else that brings money to a man. And yet I do not consider myself altogether lazy.[24]

As an offset to this maundering, it is refreshing to find him
confessing a little healthy improvidence at a time when he probably already knew the family fortune was disintegrating. He
stays out of Boston on a Saturday night in order to save money,
and so goes down to McNamee's bookstore and "blows" four
dollars and a half. Again he celebrates the purchase of "elegant"
bindings that will "make your heart glad and improve your
appetite." [25] Finally, in his last letter to Smith from Cambridge,
he confesses that during the past three weeks "I have spent over
twenty-five dollars for foreign books and have about come to the
conclusion that it is time to stop." [26]

In the matter of "ducats," Robinson undertook while at Harvard what was probably the only venture of his life in that field of
private enterprise in which he had observed that a "cold, matter-
of-fact contriving nature" might get rich. In the fall of '91 he
wrote Smith: "I think some of taking a private class in penman-
ship to pay for my tobacco." [27] At that time his writing was clear
and still a little boyish. Whether the proposal got beyond the
conceptual phase does not appear, but the practical impulse
ended, as might have been expected, in anticlimax and confusion.
Six months later he was writing Smith again, "I wish you would
tell me honestly whether you can read my writing or not." [28] In
the middle of the next academic year despair looms: "I would
give a hundred dollars (if I had them) to get over my nasty
habit of microscopic writing. I cannot seem to cure it, try as hard
as I may. Four or five years ago I wrote well enough, but I seem
to have gone steadily down hill in that way (and perhaps in every
other) during the later years of my life." [29]

This late and declining year was his twenty-fourth. At this

time his calligraphy was already maturing into its small, distinguished, quasi-seventeenth-century quasi-legibility—a hand which curiously suggests that of Thomas Hooker, that first great Yankee. Often, as he gives off these epistolary wails of helplessness, he tries deliberately and carefully to make a few letters according to the book; it is a curious thing that while it is possible with great patience to decipher his casual, fluent writing, these self-conscious curlycues are entirely meaningless and unrelated to any orthodox sign. Later, in '94, he had given up the attempt: "So much has been said to me of late on this subject that I have become somewhat alarmed, and am beginning to wonder if it would not be better for me to give up writing with a pen altogether. . . . The more I try to improve, the worse success I seem to have; for the criticisms often come after what I consider a praiseworthy effort. I suppose the real fact . . . is that I don't care enough about the matter." [30] In short, he had become a professional writer.

Besides his dull mood of only partly hypocritical worry about "ducats," Robinson's other external imp, that of touchiness about his physical person, approached full petty stature during the Harvard years. At some time when they were home together in Gardiner, Smith duly photographed him and in course sent him a print. The young man who replied had already written one or two of the great poems of the world: "I have received your letter and the picture. The latter seems to me a jot idealized. If you have kept a copy for yourself, destroy it for God's sake and mine. Do not think that I am finding fault with you—nothing of the sort. Besides the underdevelopment of the negative I remember that I was looking into the sun. The natural consequence was that I squinted. Hence that diseased droop about the under eye-lids. . . . If I had that look naturally upon the day the thing was taken, you ought to [be] shot for not saying so. There is an appearance of a painful attempt to look very tough, also, which I never anticipated. I showed it to Johnson and he said, 'Good God, Rob, you must have had a hell of a good time in Maine.'" [31]

Actually, on the physical side, Robinson cut in the outer world a figure of a kind of lankily awkward gracefulness that he had no need to be touchy about. Although he was sedentary by

inclination and practice, it should be remembered that early in
Harvard when he was baited by a bully he instantly accepted the
challenge, put the other man down, and sat on him. About the
same time he wrote Smith: "There are eight bowling courts in
the gym, and I am quite a fiend for that antiquated sport. As to
the other appliances, I have not touched them. I fear I am not an
enthusiast on the subject of physical culture, though I am an excellent subject to [be] experimented with. My stooping shoulders
are disfiguring, but I cannot bring myself to a regular course of
training. . . ." [32]

Not at all absurd, and in fact gallant, were his reactions to
real physical trouble—his eyes, and always the highly dangerous
business of the ear. In October of '92, when he was starting his
second year at Harvard, he wrote Smith: "That ear operation has
got to come and I have made arrangements to submit myself to
the carver's hands on Saturday next at 3:00 P.M. You can think
of me then stretched out for all the world like a corpse, filled with
ether and letting Dr. Green and two assistants (probably Harvard
Medics) do whatever they think will give them the highest satisfaction. . . . I have had an idea all along that the necrosis has
got in beyond the small bones. If it has I may hear a trumpet
blow a little sooner than I would ordinarily—that's all." [33]

A few days later he wrote a letter whose objectivity is premonitory of an expression of his to Ridgely Torrence over forty-
two years later in a similar situation: "Well, I have had my ear
bored out, and cannot say that I feel much the worse for it. . . .
This hospital life has few attractions for me . . . but I suppose
I ought not to complain when I think of those in the house who
are so much worse off than I am. . . . About all I can do is to
pity them, and ache to get away myself." [34] That was the great
Robinson speaking, the near saint.

Throughout the Harvard years, even while the outer self was
sniveling and equivocating about its appearance in the world, the
ideas and world perceptions of the combined inner imagination
and outer reason were moving toward maturity. The notion that
remained always the cornerstone of his social "philosophy,"
namely the perception of the inviolable individuality of every

queer and unfortunate duck, appeared early. In December of
'91 he congratulates Smith for his "breadth of human sympathy"
in understanding that "all men are in a way themselves." [35] And
the following spring: "We all live in a world of our own and
wonder what it is to others. They wonder what it is to us." [36]
Meanwhile, in his verse he was carrying his cult of individual
idiosyncrasy to the point of the celebration of failure. In *Villanelle of Change*, the poem he placed with the *Harvard Advocate*
immediately on arriving, we have a phrase which no one but
Robinson could have uttered, "the glory of Greek shame." If we
delete the proper adjective and assimilate "shame" to "failure,"
we have a theme, "the glory of the unfulfilled," drawn from the
tragedy of Dean, that runs through a large section of his verse
throughout his life. *Thomas Hood* is another expression of it from
his first year at Harvard.

Balancing this earthly pessimism, his lifelong cosmic optimism
also appears in that early period in *Supremacy*—"I heard the
dead man singing in the sun"— and the following year in *Luke
Havergal*—"The dark will end the dark, . . . and if you trust
her she will call." The latter poem—the only surely great one of
the Harvard period—is not simplified by Robinson's characteristically misleading later references to it, first as a piece of deliberate "degeneration" and later as "my uncomfortable abstraction."
It will be his indomitable optimism that will keep him through
the dreadful years ahead, his mystical perception, his faith. "The
world as a whole is surely growing better and better." [37] In this
merely uneasy period he was already saying it in his letters. "I
feel that things are coming out all right sometime but the action
is slow." [38]

And perhaps fundamental to the individualism, the pessimism,
and the faith, his "idealism," the belief in the primary reality of
the life of the mind, was also taking shape at Harvard. In March
of '92 he reports to Smith that it is a fine day and he wishes they
were back in their "bower" in Gardiner. But then he considers
that "there may be more pleasure in the thought than in the reality." So-called reality, material reality, is often "humbug." We
may feel uncomfortable in a situation, but "after the whole thing

is over we begin to realize that we were having a good time without knowing it." [39] That is, the memory may be more real than the current experience was. Four months before, during his first autumn at Harvard, he had begun experimenting with a "long meter triolet . . . dealing with passion and death (that is the stuff we need)." [40] If, as is likely, this is a second start of what became *The Night Before*, it expresses the principal specific form of his idealism, that of idealized love.

But even more important than these early formulations of his lifelong notions was the awareness of roots that Harvard gave him, the sense of belonging to something actual, strong—and incidentally respectable. He learned for sure that it was not a disgrace, as his father had taught him, to be an intellectual. He never entirely outgrew his impulse to apologize for his inability to do anything but write poetry, but after Harvard, the apology was neither so frequent nor so desperate, and it carried no hint that he might still try his hand at gathering "ducats." Just before leaving Cambridge, he wrote Smith: "I suppose this is the last letter I shall ever write you from Harvard. The thought seems a little queer, but it cannot be otherwise. [A reference to the state of the family fortune.] Sometimes I try to imagine the state my mind would be in had I never come here, but I cannot. I feel that I have got comparatively little from my two years, but still, more than I could get in Gardiner if I lived a century." [41]

In appearance he had matured considerably during the two years. The omniscient young god whose picture was taken at the time of graduation from Gardiner High School is still there in the elegantly moustached and high-collared young man who left Harvard in '93. But now the god has come to earth and is looking directly at its spectacle. By June of '93, the stage was already bleakly set for the third act of the play. A year before, Edward Robinson had died peacefully, probably without realizing the "grisly truth" about either his second or his third son. By the spring of '93, in the auctions of St. Louis real estate at panic prices, the family fortune under Herman's management was crumbling. The precarious future of the poet, which Robinson had long ago foreseen, was now the present.

Act III

The Robinson who returned to Gardiner, presumably for good, in June of 1893, differed chiefly in self-assurance from the boy who had gone to Harvard in '91. The traits that he took away with him were less altered or augmented than they were solidified in what, in his twenty-fourth year, was a kind of tentative maturity. He knew now that his compulsion into the life of the mind did not make him a wastrel; on the contrary, it qualified him for admission to the small company of the finest human beings. The realization of this at once fortified his inner assurance and increased his inner humility before the responsibility fate had laid on him: he must now prove himself, not before Gardiner but before enlightened humanity. He knew now that he must be a poet and nothing else. As always, his contrapositivism figured in his thinking. When he was praised, or was alone with his introspection, his humility made him doubt his ability to fulfill his calling. But when he was challenged by his neighbors his certitude bristled. A letter to Smith on the first of October revealed that he had already written and shown him at least a draft of the most famous of his early sonnets: "I am half afraid that my 'dear friends' here in Gardiner will be disappointed in me if I do not do something before long, but somehow I don't care half as much about the matter as I ought." [1]

> The shame I win for singing is all mine,
> The gold I miss for dreaming is all yours.

The Win Robinson who came home in '93 was not essentially different from the Win who had gone away in '91; but in the big white house on the corner of Lincoln Avenue and Danforth Street, the big white house with its comfortable trees, wide veranda, orchard, and garden, the family drama was in a twilight of transition, the older generation surrendering the leading parts and the young having not yet replaced them. Edward Robinson, who, both for better and for worse, had been the center of the domestic cast, was in the cemetery to which Danforth Street was the entrance a block away. Mary Robinson, always frail, was steadily failing and, now finally deprived by poverty of hired help, must get it from one or more of the boys. Dean was increasingly delirious and sometimes bedridden,[2] and since there is no further mention of the engagement to Della Collins, that, it may be presumed, evaporated about this time. Most of the time his mind was clear, and on days when the bank examiners were expected, even when he had been unable to come to work and was unsteady on the street, the officers would send for him to come down to check the accounts. A picture taken of him in this phase shows the once jolly-faced, immaculately bearded physician now shorn to a moustache, emaciated and sheet-pale, his expression heartbreakingly wistful—suggestive, not of his old self but rather of a sickly Win, who was always lean-faced and close to him in spirit. According to legend, Dean's "insufficient eyes, forever sad," in this failing state were the model for Charles Carville's.

In '93 Herman was still fighting against defeat. The western lands, in which he had sunk most of the estate, were selling at ruinous prices, and even more humiliating than the impoverishment of the family were the large amounts he had persuaded banks and other Maine investors to pour down the same drain. The vision and gamble had been large, and the debacle was major. "One of the rising young railroad men of the West" had turned out to be merely another overenthusiastic youngster. Until now he had never known anything but success and popularity; so, since he had almost no intellectual resources, the fall was bottomless for him. The elegant and generous "man Flammonde" began to succumb to his "satanic sort of kink," the "broken link," that "Withheld him from the destinies / That came so near to being his." The kink was a necessary self-defeatism or self-destructiveness, commonly the dark side of imagination but occurring in this case with only a rudimentary affirmative side to offset it. One wonders whether a strong streak of this compulsive negation may not have been in Dean also, gradually corroding in defeat his intellectual strength, and whether the relative weakness of it in Win, its relegation to a merely external pessimism pitted against his tremendous internal, affirmative power, one wonders whether this different balance of positive and negative in Win may not have been his essential distinction from his brothers.

In Herman, always convivial, long accustomed to sending "the midnight home with songs and bottles," it was inevitable that the first turn of the negative necessity would be against himself in alcoholic excess. And the next turn would be in the form of suspicion of others, and here he had ready material in his belief, perhaps justified, that some of his western associates had cheated him. A picture of him in silk hat and frock coat at one of the auctions in St. Louis in '93 shows him worried, dubious, with the suggestion of a suspicious leer. Liquor and bitterness were his anodynes from now on, and perhaps he was already beginning to ejaculate that "unhallowed laugh" which Win, according to the legend, later identified with him as the *Doctor of Billiards*. Yet in '93 he was still fighting, and some of the statements of his western real estate companies still showed solvency. Also, he was rarely present to contribute confusion in the Lincoln Avenue house. Through '93, and probably for four or five years more, he was not much in Gardiner, spending most of his winters and some of his summers in the West or otherwise in parts unknown. And when he was in town he and Emma stayed with the Shepherds in Farmingdale. Writing to Smith in November of '93, Win took occasion to mention, in another connection, the burden that a steadily drunken husband is to a wife, and in his correspondence he began to speak a little contemptuously of "business men."

When Herman was out of town by himself, Emma likewise stayed with her family in their mansion looking down over the Kennebec, where Marie, her second daughter, was born in April of '93. During the summers she was frequently alone with the children on Capitol Island in what was now the Shepherd cottage, and her solitude there began to raise the doubts in her mind and in the minds of "the harbor side" which eventually produced *Eros Turannos*. Through '93 and most of '94 she seems not to have been in the Lincoln Avenue house more than was necessary to bring the children over to see their grandmother. The situation was ideal for Win's production. On the one hand, there was still enough coming in from the estate to defer the need of his contributing more than some "horny-handed" work in the garden and at chores. On the other hand, Emma was visible just enough and not too much to perform her function as a stimulating Beatrice. Also, she performed the important secondary role of fending him against his always devoted and always worried mother. "God will take care of him," Emma assured her.[3]

And so, Dean being usually *compos mentis* and congenial, there was an Indian summer peace in the house which permitted Win to buckle down to his calling. He fixed up for den the only room where mid-Victorian Mary would let him smoke, namely the small square room adjoining his bedroom at the rear end of the upstairs hall, the room above what had been his father's study on the ground floor. It was a pleasant, varnish-brown little room, and now or soon thereafter the lower half of the walls were covered with bookshelves. The east side was a bay window looking down behind the house into the orchard and glen which had been his childhood retreat, and over it to the backs of the houses on Fremont Street. The chief and perhaps the only furniture were an eighteenth-century desk that had been his grandfather Robinson's and the curlycued wicker rocking chair brought up from the sitting room to become the first of a great creative triumvirate, the second to be a wooden "mission" rocker in New York, the third a wood-and-cane one in his studio at the MacDowell Colony. Before long he got a typewriter for letters, but never for verse. In November, the unheated hideout being "too cold for free thought," a radiator was installed. Here in four years he hammered out on "the anvil of God's forge" the bulk of the contents of *The Torrent and the Night Before* and *The Children of the Night,* together with how much other material for later publication we can hardly infer. Sitting in the rocking chair with pad and pencil, occasionally rocking a little to release a stubborn word, he sometimes found his moderating control in a quid of tobacco, sometimes in deep, bronchial drafts from his pipe. When he smoked too much it made his hand tremble, which, as he confessed to Smith, made his chirography all the more difficult.

Meanwhile, in spite of his ear being semiacute through most of '93, he pitched into his "farming" and the chores: "I have done great work in forestry this fall and have now arrived at the last stage—'blowing up' the butts. When they are sawed and split

I shall consider myself free from a long but upon the whole rather pleasant piece of work." [4] And in the spring of '94: "My farm work takes almost all my time, and I am . . . getting to be a horny-handed son of toil. My face and neck are burned to the color of leather, and I think I feel a little proud of the fact." [5] A dash of rural respectability.

But he was losing hope of making an adjustment to the town. In October of '93 he wrote Gledhill: "About all I find here in Gardiner to interest me is what I conjure up from my own fancy and memory." Earlier in the same letter: "If I had a little of your general intellect and faculty of making yourself popular wherever you go, life would be a different thing for me. I have lived nearly twenty-four years and am thankful chiefly that I haven't them to live over again. . . . My life hasn't been such a pleasant affair as some men's seem to be. Perhaps it is partly my own fault, but I hardly understand how it can be to any great extent." [6] About the same time his optimism broke out to Harry Smith: "I am thankful that I cannot *see* a life of failure before me. When I picture it to myself there is a dim vision of something else that renders it impossible for me to wholly give up the fight. I half feel that I have a Palladium somewhere that sends a 'ruling effluence' upon my life, and though the waves of fight seem just now to be rolling against me I have not yet fallen . . ." [7]

If he couldn't adjust to Gardiner generally, he did attract whatever equally isolated distinction was languishing in the community. The Jordans and Herbert Longfellow had been kid neighbors and now presently became his mature friends. So did the cultivated Barstow boys, two of whom were his contemporaries. The three of them used to read Shakespeare in the Barstows' little new-fangled telephone room, Win slapping his knee after a good passage and exclaiming, "Isn't that great!" He and Smith, now teaching in Spencer, Massachusetts, started their translation of the *Antigone*, Smith to provide the letter of it and Robinson to whip it into meter.

In mid-February he made to Smith an interesting comment on his taste for music, in view of his later addiction to opera: "My fondness for music is wholly of an emotional kind." [8] On the twenty-fifth he sent Smith a copy of *The House on the Hill*, typically deprecating his current penchant for the old French forms and saying that he tossed off this villanelle in "twenty minutes"! (Twenty-seven years later he changed two stanzas for the *Collected Poems*.) Early in March he gave Smith as good an explanation of his fundamental humor, his owl-like delight in the world, as we are likely to find:

> Most of my . . . happiness is of a negative quality—a kind of sublimed selfishness [that is, emotional self-indulgence]. . . . As you know, I seldom laugh. The smoothest part of my face is around my mouth, where the only wrinkles of youth rightfully belong. [He had been doing a little mirror research for a reason that will appear!] My wrinkles are in my forehead. . . . That, I fancy, is because I think more than some people, and do my laughing in my gray matter instead of upon my face. Real solid laughter is almost a physical impossibility with me. When it occurs it almost frightens me. I grin upon the slightest provocation. . . . At a theatre . . . I may be highly amused, but I cannot give way to my feelings in the ordinary manner. . . . One might find a comparison to this intense mental receptiveness in the bursting of a barrel of beer.[9]

Many years later, Nancy Byrd Turner spoke of his *"inner laughter,* which was entirely lacking in tone and facial expression."

By the time of this letter to Smith, Robinson was embarked on an enterprise that turned out to be no laughing matter. At what must have been an age not far below his own, his old high school girl, Mabel Moore, adopted an unladylike plan to get educated. In January her family hired Win to tutor her in French and otherwise to devote '94 until September to qualifying her for admission to Wellesley. In his letters to Smith, Robinson rejoices that at last he is going to be of some use in the world. Remembering the teaching and other jobs he had turned down before, we cannot fail to detect here the first recorded deviation from Emma, whether through normal fickleness or as a conscious practical effort to translate an impossible passion into a possible one. Without noticeable comment in the correspondence with Smith, the tutoring proceeded through February, March, and April. Then on May first, at the end of a normal letter of literary criticism, the beer barrel of simmering, Robinsonian silence burst quite unhumorously:

This is a gray sticky day that makes me think of everything but the sun. I am not wholly in a grouch, but I think it is just as well for you that I am not with you. I fear that my company would not be much better than my handwriting. Perhaps you will understand my feelings a [little] better, and perhaps not, when I tell you that my French lessons are over. You may interpret this as you like, but I fancy you will not get far out of the way in your conclusions. Anticipation and realization are two different things [clearly a step, probably conscious, in his developing idealism]. Take this for the text of this letter, and remember it. It may do you good someday, and lead you to be more careful in your actions than I have been. . . . Kindly tear this into seventy pieces after reading it, and when you write next Sunday tell me what you think of *Views and Reviews*.[10]

In another letter three weeks later, Robinson confirmed the implication that there had been an engagement, but many years later Miss Moore denied that there had ever been any such thing. This split in authority we may resolve by either of two guesses. The obvious guess is that Win by uncareful "actions" had indeed brought on an agreement of engagement (in high circles at that time a kiss was tantamount to a proposal); whereupon the transfer of the scene of love from the inner opera house of "soul music" to the stage of external action would have brought serious misgiving. Subjectively, Win would have found the immediate pseudosensuality of a few chaste hugs and kisses a "base" emotion after the imaginative richness of "love's elemental overglow." In objective terms, the inexperienced young lady's joyfully sordid concern for their practical future, including her lover's gastronomic and sartorial well-being, would likewise have been stultifying. Both the subjective and the objective experiences would have repelled Win into silences empty of everything but terror before the responsibility he had let himself in for. Without anything so unchivalrous as a verbal recantation on his part, Mabel would have detected that in dumb reality she was being jilted, and would thereafter have persuaded herself and all in her confidence that in fact there had been no engagement.

This might have been one way of it. Or, the more peculiarly Robinsonian account, conformable with what had probably happened with Emma five years before, and what certainly happened in the case of another close shave some twenty years later —the pure Robinsonian account would have it that Mabel told the whole truth in denying that there had been any overt engagement, while Win, luxuriating in "nameless passion" and assuming that it was mutual, would have believed there was one in fact. Just as fatally as if he had uttered an ill-considered word, the inward light of love would have faded into the illusory and frightening light of outer day. Just as fatally as if he had spoken, he would have lapsed into desolate silence, feeling incidentally guilty of an ungallantry for which he had not qualified. And presently Mabel, detecting an incomprehensible rat where there was yet no food for one, would have suggested, and Win by silence would have acquiesced in, his release from the tutorial contract.[11]

And so, after three months of treasonous experiment abroad, Win returned, and Emma, still strong in unavailability, again reigned alone on the throne of Love. Once more the still undefined idealistic tendency, here identified with "anticipation," reigned unruffled over materialism, here identified with "realization." After her hour in the center of the stage, Miss Moore lurked in the wings of his dreams a little longer. There is a reference to the supposed engagement in a letter written three weeks later. And her last appearance is in another sad letter early in June: "My failure thus far to accomplish anything or to be anybody in the world, rather than my separation from the one who is and always will be part of my daily life, is the cause of all this. . . . My pride is almost unnatural and sometimes I wonder if it is not killing me by inches." [12] (Does this mean that after all Mabel had done the jilting?) Then a week later he makes a different reference which finally overshadows her, for either it is in the line of causation of Emma's *Cortège*, if it was not yet written, or it is a report of a poetic coincidence involving that poem and his continuing interpretation of her marriage: "In reading Tennyson the other day, I came across a little poem in blank verse dedicated to the Princess Beatrice, in which she speaks of her marriage as 'that white funeral of the single life.' A Poet Laureate is worth while when he says things like that." [13] Thus we return from an evanescent love to the permanent one.

Meanwhile, Robinson's emotions, having burst out in the confession of the broken engagement, had continued through May of '94 to overflow on the confidential floor of his letters to Smith. He has a "horrible dose of the blues." He is "afraid I have made a giant blunder in this literary business." [14] (He had sold nothing in '93, and he sold nothing in '94 until September.) But he admits that he has a few real friends who don't mind his shortcomings. And so he comes up to the great letter to Smith of May 20, which reveals so much of the inner Robinson in his outward relations that I shall quote most of it:

. . . I hate to disappoint you, but I was not in the least startled by the fact that you are engaged to be married. I knew well enough that you were in love with somebody and have known it for a long time. . . . I don't suppose you will believe me when I tell you that you have been slowly putting me away from you for the past six months but such is the truth. . . . Do not misunderstand me in this; do not think that I mean to hint that you really think less of my friendship than you did two years ago, for I know that is not the truth. It is merely a case of "not that I loved long Robinson less, but—oh, yes, Adela —more." In short, I have lost you, and, for your sake, I am heartily glad of it. . . . Of course we shall sit and read and smoke together next summer, but there will be another person there besides myself. . . .

Ever since the great change for higher things came over you—it began three or four years ago—I have felt your worth and have had a corresponding admiration for you. I have felt the countless weaknesses of my own flickering nature and wondered that a man of your strength should find so much in me to like. All this was well grounded before I went to Harvard. Then I found that there were other people besides yourself who could find something in me worthy of their friendly attention.

The only thing that saves me from total discouragement is the knowledge, or at least, the belief, that such men as you, Tryon, Saben, Butler, and Ford, look upon me as a person worth knowing. This leads me to think that I am not wholly an ass. These I have named, with one or two others, are my friends; and where are they? You alone are where I can still feel that you are near me. . . . So you see I am pretty much alone, and perhaps you will not think it so strange after all that I am not so jolly as some fellows you know. More than this, all my life at home has been a kind of hell from which there seemed to be no release until I broke from my harness and went to college. I have queer feelings of cowardice as I write this, but I depend upon you to take it in the right spirit.

You are engaged to be married, you are happy, and the world and the future look bright in your eyes; I am not (*now*) [italics added to emphasize the implication referred to earlier] engaged to be married, I am not happy, and the world and the future look so dark and gloomy that I look mostly into the past. Here is the difference.—But the Fates have been kind to me in one respect—they have given me the ability to rejoice in the happiness and good-fortune of others. So I am happy on your account and am glad for what seems to be in store for you. Did I ever tell you of a kind of intuitive sense of prophecy I sometimes feel in the presence of my friends? . . . You may be glad to know that I have never once had the trace of a doubt as to your ultimate welfare. I do not think that you will ever be rich, or publicly great (in the bow-wow sense of the word) but you will, if you live, fill an eminently respectable place as an intellectual American citizen; as a married man you will be happy and make your partner the same; and whenever long Robinson comes to see you for a day or so, you will treat him like a brother. So speaks my prophetic spirit. [In fulfillment of this prophecy, Harry DeForest Smith became and remained a distinguished professor of Classics.]

Yes, I am glad you are going to be married. I have always looked upon a bachelor as only half a man. . . . I have always believed in love, and always shall believe in it. The fact that so many thousands go astray sometimes shakes my faith a little,

but it always rights itself after a time. There are natures that
positively cannot be faithful to a single companion, and sometimes the people who have them seem to be the happiest in the
world; but I think if we knew them as well as they know themselves . . . we should find there is something in their souls that
is never satisfied—their lives are not complete, they live without a mission. Their life is a fevered irregularity, and, when
they are past their forties—and oftentimes long before that—
the original nature stamps itself in the face, and those lines of
hardness . . . tell us that something is wrong. . . .

"L'Amour" is pitifully abused in spoken and written literature. . . . Love and lust have become so mixed by our poets
and novelists that we poor puritans are half inclined to wonder,
as we read, whether there is such a thing after all, as a better
nature in man or woman. . . . When you get to read Shakespeare (you are bound to do so someday) you will find in all
his later plays an undertone of manly melancholy, which you
will naturally trace to a love of a higher kind, which, for some
unknown reason, was never satisfied. [A little anticipatory,
comparative conceit?]

. . . Do you fully understand that I am glad that this
change has come to you? . . . When the time comes to put
away childish things, the individual stands in a new light. The
lost days of boyhood and youth begin to put on the appearance
of broken toys in a dusty garret. The man has come and has
taken the boy away. . . . This is something the way it is with
most people, I fancy, but somehow I, with my crotchets and my
childish sensibilities, cannot put away the old things [i.e., the
permanent inner reality of the first "Intimations."] . . . When
I look far into the future, I see myself—sometimes in the light
of a partial success—living alone in some city—Boston, most
likely—with a friend or two to drop in upon me once in a while,
and a few faithful correspondents. [An exact understatement
of what did eventually happen.]

When you are married you must not ask me to come to your
wedding. I can fancy now the effect it would have upon me,
and the sorry figure I should cut. When I began this letter I
intended it to be good-natured rather than melancholy, but

I fear I have only half succeeded in my purpose. Do not read too much vinegar into it, however, and consider, as one of its lessons, the inevitable truth that a man cannot be a good husband and still be one of the boys [surely Herman]. There comes the time when Memory [like anticipation, to a form of protoidealism] must take the place of Reality [that is material reality], when the new life must draw its curtain over the old. All I ask or hope is that there may have been some one little act or word on my part that you will feel and remember as a part, however small, of your life. You have my heartiest congratulations and best wishes. In the meantime, I await a long pipe under the pines, and remain,

Always sincerely,

E. A. R.[15]

But, significant as was Robinson's report of the breaking of his engagement on May first, and more significant as was his reaction to Smith's engagement in the letter of May 20, that month of passion was to contain still another definitive expression. Soon after the letter to Smith he made what was probably the third start on the first and one of the most autobiographical of the triangular narratives. As was noticed, he is said to have started a now lost draft of it the night of Emma's wedding in February of '90. Then, during his first autumn at Harvard, in November, '91, he had written Smith of having "a long meter triolet in my mind, dealing with passion and death." There had followed silence on the subject for two and a half years. Then on May 27, '94, a week after the great letter of friendship: "I have been too much occupied of late to do any writing except two sonnets [already the great *Two Sonnets*?] and some ninety lines of a queer poem called 'The Night Before'. . . . It is a tragic monologue written in unrhymed tetrameters. . . ." This could be a development of the "long meter," with the triolet form abandoned, and it certainly fulfills the earlier announcement of "passion and death." A week later, in the same letter in which he refers pathetically to the one who "always will be part of my daily life," he reports progress on the poem and begins his lifelong process of more or less mendacious transmutation of subjectivity into alleged ob-

jectivity: "I have written 225 lines of 'The Night Before,' and
am getting rather enthusiastic over the thing. . . . The story is
unpleasant, founded upon my system of 'opposites' that is, creating a fictitious life in direct opposition to a real life which I
know"[16]—meaning of course an artistic distortion of a real life
which he knows very well! In '96, two months before its appearance in his first book, he wrote to Gledhill of the poem that it was
"an attempt to be absolutely impersonal which, of course, is an
impossibility."[17] Two months after its appearance, in February,
'97, he assured Smith that it was "purely objective";[18] but late
in the same year confessed that it involved something more than
"mere objectivity" which is "at the best unsatisfactory."[19]

And yet as always the poem transcends Robinson's experience
while it records it. Reproducing the emotional crisis of the summer of '88, it goes far beyond it in human content. Founded in
Robinson's universal compassion, which was noticed earlier, it
opens with an assertion of the "glimmer of good" in all people,
and proceeds into his doctrine of the inviolable separateness of
every individual.

> When I was a boy the world was heaven.
> I never knew that the men and women
> Who petted and called me a brave big fellow
> Were ever less happy than I . . .
>
> .   .   .   .
>   Then slowly—
> And yet so swiftly!—there came the knowledge
> That the marvellous life I had lived was my life;
> That the glorious world I had loved was my world;—
> And that every man and every woman
> And every child was a different being,
> Wrought with a different heat and fired
> With passions born of a single spirit;—
> That the pleasure I felt was not their pleasure,

(Then that tremendous outcry of compassion, quite unnecessary
to the dramatic development:)

> Nor my sorrow—a kind of nameless pity
> For something, I knew not what—their sorrow.

(And that gloomy rationalization to which, for the defense of his own hypersensitivity, he had occasional, deliberate recourse throughout his life:)

> And thus was I taught my first hard lesson,—
> The lesson we suffer the most in learning:
> That a happy man is a man forgetful
> Of all the torturing ills around him.

Then comes the love passage, quoted earlier, to which Mabel Moore doubtless made a vanishing contribution but whose main reference, with the "sky" and the "ocean," and the plot of the invasion by the "cad" with his "genial craft," seems to refer to Capitol Island and Herman in '88, and so to Emma.

These are within the first ninety lines of the poem which he told Smith he had written by May 27. A week later, in the letter in which he refers sadly and finally to his loss of the unnamed Mabel, he reports the completion of two hundred and twenty-five lines which include the account of the perversion of Emma by Herman that was quoted before, and then a more detailed record—dramatically superfluous as was the original cry of pity— of the expansion of his concern from himself to mankind. Now he associates his compassion for all people with that compelling curiosity about the life and story of each which made himself a dramatic poet:

>   The woes I suffered
> After that hard betrayal made me
> Pity, at first, all breathing creatures
> On this bewildered earth. I studied
> Their faces and made for myself the story
> Of all their scattered lives. Like brothers
> And sisters they seemed to me then; and I nourished
> A stronger friendship wrought in my fancy
> Between these people and me.—

And then, as human if not dramatic anticlimax, comes the Robinsonian flaw, the shallow aspect of his social touchiness. Even as Win could *feel* the people of Gardiner laughing at his inadaptability, so the cuckolded hero in the poem "could feel [the neighbors] laughing / At me, and my fate." And so Robinson's superficial "pride" takes over the story and leads up to the melodramatic "passion and death."

In that same spring and summer of '94, while Robinson's somber side was expressing itself in the sad letter to Smith and in *The Night Before,* his affirmative side was declaring itself more positively in *The Altar, Credo, Two Sonnets, Three Quatrains* and *The Torrent,* as it had already done in *Supremacy* and *Luke Havergal.* The worst poem of the period, probably the worst poem Robinson ever published, including *The Night Before,* was *The Miracle,* so autobiographical that the names might as well have been used for the "brother" and "sister" and "friend." It is perhaps his most literal statement, here in terms of Victorian clichés about roses, of that dualism which he then assigned to Emma:

> "Dear brother, dearest friend, when I am dead,
>   And you shall see no more this face of mine,
>   Let nothing but red roses be the sign
> Of the white life I lost for him," she said.
> "No, do not curse him, pity him instead;
>   Forgive him—forgive me; God's anodyne
>   For human hate is Pity; and the wine
> That makes men wise, Forgiveness; I have read
> Love's message in love's murder—and I die."
> And so they laid her just as she would lie,
> Under red roses. Red they bloomed and fell;
>   But when flushed Autumn and the snows went by
> And spring came, lo! from every bud's green shell
> Burst a white blossom. Can Faith reason why? [20]

Through most of '94, Robinson's steady literary occupation was the versification of the installments of the translation of the *Antigone* which Smith was sending him. In October his mother had apparently chased him out of his den down cellar even for chewing purposes, for he is planning to write the *Tavern Songs* "down by the furnace with a chew . . . 'in.'" [21] In November Emma is obviously much in the house. "Since the middle of last week I have been hopelessly 'out of sorts' on account of the kids, who keep running by my door and shake the house generally. Sometimes I get desperate and go down street or anywhere I can cool off." [22] (This galloping cavalcade consisted of Ruth, his future executor, just turned four, and Marie, a year and a half, both of whom were already on the way to preempting his permanent devotion.) At this time he was experimenting with short stories, all now lost. In late November he wrote *Ballade of Dead Friends,* and reported that he was "morbid." His entire magazine sale for '94 consisted of *The House on the Hill, The Miracle,* and the more promising *Sonnet,* "Oh for a poet . . ."

In '95 the barometer rises with such enthusiasm that one tends to wonder how much domestic gloom he is whistling down. In March he declares, "I am . . . rather radiant over something— though I haven't the slightest idea of what that thing is. I think it is the knowledge (or at least the belief) that I can do anything, in my own way, that I undertake." [23] At about the same time he quits both smoking and chewing with appalling ease, his reason being, "I think I do a little better work without it and sleep better—though it may be all fancy." [24] In April: "I have got pretty well through the 'creative' part of the book [his first book that eventually he would call *The Torrent and the Night Before*]. I shall try to publish in the fall . . . the rest will be revising and rewriting—a long and hard summer's work and all, perhaps, for nothing. But there is one grand consolation: if it is for nothing, another may be for something else. I have made up my mind that I am going to do this thing, and that is all there is to it. Some day you will see a printed edition of *Scattered Lines* even though it be printed on toilet paper with a one-hand printing press." [25]

In May his humor is high: "In *The Story of an African Farm* the chickens were wiser than the human beings; and I wonder now if my six hens are wiser than I am. They are saying something down there behind the barn that I cannot understand, and for some reason they are making me think of the whole scheme of life and of its final outcome. . . ." [26] Also his musical sentimentality: "I shall hear no more of Reece's Band, which . . . has been with us all the week. At the end of the closing concert last night they all stood up and played 'Auld Lang Syne' in a way that sent seven distinct kinds of crinkles up my spine and through my hair. . . . I felt as if an epoch in my life had ended." [27]

In June there is a relapse into the whimper on practical grounds: "A man who is earning his living, to say nothing of holding a position of responsibility and respect, has a peculiarly depressing effect upon me just now. . . ." [28] Possibly related to this general depression was the fact that on June 25 Harry Smith got married far away, and Robinson wrote a draft of what became *On the Night of a Friend's Wedding,* attributing its motivation to the nuptials of some strangers which he happened to observe. In terms of literary achievement also, the year was another depressing one, for he sold only *Kosmos* and *For a Book by Thomas Hardy.* In November his humor revives: "I am making all sorts of poems nowadays, and do not dare stop for fear I might realize what a damned fool I am." [29] He ends the year with the cheerful hope that the book of verse will be "pretty well shaken out" and sent off by the first of February. In discussing the likelihood of rejection, he first begins to show professional literary stoicism in the matter of rejection slips, which presently he was amassing in the hope of papering his den with them.

In '96 he is approaching a permanent ground of compromise between hopelessness and hope. In February, still working on the book, he says: "The past three months have been a grind for me, and . . . have probably been all for nothing. . . . I have partly succeeded in looking at such things as steps to what I am going to do later. . . . Anticipation is more than half of life anyway, and this is particularly true of a life like mine, which is, in reality, almost wholly selfish. . . ." [30] What he means by his "selfish" life is, of course, either the quiet of the inner self or the external self-indulgence of symbolizing the inner truth in outer words. At his most depressed, I don't think he ever accused himself of being selfish in the ordinary, externally predatory sense. Later in February he wrote: "I am cheered sometimes by the conviction that I am not a total damned fool. This is something for a man to say in the first person. . . ." [31] Three weeks later, in March, the book, which he then called *The Tavern and the Night Before,* has gone off on its first cycle of the merry-go-round of the publishers, and the poet has reverted to his hobby of collecting stamps and reading stamp catalogues. In April, anticipating the return of the manuscript, he determines that ". . . I shall keep on having the same faith in myself. That faith has become chronic. . . ." [32]

A month later the manuscript has indeed come back, and as always when a major blow fell, it struck through his self-concern and laid bare his objective inner self: "I was so thoroughly satisfied that the stuff would be rejected, that the information hardly touched me. . . . I don't seem to have any capacity for discouragement, no matter how much I may be running over at the heel. I have done a few things which I know are worth while and that is a great deal to be sure of. If printed lines are good for anything, they are bound to be picked up some time; and then, *if some poor devil of a man or woman feels any better or any stronger for anything that I have said, I shall have no fault to find with the scheme or anything in it* [italics added]. I am inclined to be a trifle solemn in my verses, but I intend that there shall always be at least a suspicion of something wiser than hatred and something better than despair." [33]

Earlier in the same letter: "I am trying as hard as I can to get over my almost helpless dependence upon my friends, but I find it sorry work. I say to myself that I was not made to live in solitude (and my present life amounts to little more than that). . . ." [34] But the next week, near the end of May: "I suppose I can stand more letting alone than any man who ever breathed. Two or three good friends . . . and some oatmeal porridge are the things that keep me going.

". . . I have been a wallowing degenerate ever since I painted the dining-room floor last week. . . . There are seven shades of yellow in it and I have a symbol for every devilish one of them." [35]

On the worldly side, '96 was his best year yet for magazine sales: *The Children of the Night, Thomas Hood,* the sonnet "I make no measure . . . ," *The Clerks, Verlaine, God's Garden, Boston, The Pity of the Leaves,* and *Shooting Stars.* The book of verse sashayed out to a few more publishers and back, and in September, now entitled *The Torrent and the Night Before,* it

went off for respectable private printing at the Riverside Press,
at a cost to the author of $52—"which," he reported thirty-four
years later, "I am told is appreciably less than one pays today for
a single copy." [36]

Immediately Win's humor associated the prospective book
with the current campaign of McKinley and Hobart. He wrote
Smith in Germany: "The American air is full of politics now just
as the German air is full of patriotism. I think I like the American
article a little better, because it appeals directly instead of indirectly, to my sense of humor—which is about the only sense I
have. My book of poems . . . is one of the funniest things ever
written by a mortal man. I do not know of anything funnier unless it be *Werther* or a *Life of McKinley and Hobart*." [37] A month
later his humor is still going nicely: "Whenever I feel out of sorts
I take a look at that new school house on Plummer Street. I have
a good view of about half of it from my window upstairs, and I
tell you the sight of it gives me a feeling of spiritual encouragement. At times I am troubled to think of what the effect of so
much hideousness may have [*sic*] on the children who will in-
habit it, but I have lately come to the conclusion that they will
all be poets." [38] After the election the theme of politics becomes
even funnier than his book: ". . . it is rumored that the blood
went to McKinley's head a little when he read the telegram. I
fancy his old mother is the most thoroughly tickled person in the
United States, and I feel glad for her. I fear my own mother will
never be tickled in any such way, though I may get to be a Common Councilman sometime if I am foxy. After that the White
House is a matter of destiny." [39] Alas, there is no evidence that
his always shy, stately, exquisite, tense, tired, and probably
humorless mother was ever tickled by anything her dreamy and
improvident youngest did or proposed to do.

Actually, Win's cheerful determination and industry, both at
writing and farming, were, second only to her integrating love,
the healthiest elements in the home through '95 and '96, when the
heavy undertone was of crumbling foundations. As early as
September of '94, Win had written Smith of the disintegration:
". . . if things are bound to go to the devil anyway the best thing
for me to do is to let them go with a feeling that I have done as

well as I can." [40] During '95 Dean declined rapidly, until a great part of the time he was delirious, either in bed or moaning and pacing backward and forward, backward and forward, in "the dark house" which was at once his little hall bedroom, his original devil of truth now perverted into the demon of drugs, and finally the devil of self introverted and shut in.[41] Writing of him twenty years later in this great poem of defeat, Win still affirmed that his beloved Dean had finally heard "murmurs" of ultimate love and wisdom, "a music yet unheard / By the creature of the word," whereby the door of his prison had opened wide so that he was "living, having died." Through '96 he sank farther toward earthly oblivion, and the resources of the family had to undergo a further drain in hiring for him an attendant named Wakefield.

Through '96 the decline of Herman became irreversible. He gave up compounding losses with new losses, and so was more in Farmingdale and Gardiner, adding his cruder alcoholism to Dean's tragic addictions. The generosity of Flammonde began to succumb finally to his negative "kink." Richard Cory ceased to "glitter," though he may still have "fluttered pulses." Among the features of Herman in defeat, three are recorded in Win's poetry and reported in the family legend. First, as portrayed with apparent accuracy in *Bewick Finzer*, and superficially in the smugness in his photographs in this period, he kept up the swagger of worldly greatness, "the fond imponderable dreams of affluence," pathetic in Finzer, merely coarse in the pictures and, a few years later, in the gestures of the husband in *London Bridge*. Secondly, the business man's patronizing contempt which he had doubtless always felt for bookish, namby-pamby, unrealistic little Win began to harden, in one who lacked introspective power, into more serious attitudes. Out of probable exaggeration of Win's little successes in magazine publication, and his final dispatch of *The Torrent and the Night Before* to the printer in September, '96, came envy and jealousy. Out of unadmitted guilt, while watching Win composedly going about his "farming" and helping their mother in her last, tired effort to hold the home together, out of guilt and gathering sense of inferiority, there began to develop the hatred that is recorded presently in *London Bridge*

and which much later became Avon's pathological terror of his
young intellectual leech. And finally, there was already gathering
in '96 the serious but never consistently explained chill between
Herman and Emma.

In two respects, common jealousy probably contributed to
Herman's cooling and his gathering aversion to Win. There was
Emma's sympathy for his poetry and her defense of him in the
family circle. More serious, there was the growing attachment
between Win and Herman's children. Children annoyed Herman,
but no matter how much Win grumbled about the "kids" stam-
peding all over the house when he was working, he still took to
them naturally and they took to him. Through '96, because
Mary's capacity was weakening, Emma and her brood of coming-
six-, -four-, and -one-year-olds, were much of the time in
the Lincoln Avenue house, and a tradition was established involving Uncle Win. At five o'clock every afternoon he would
emerge from work into the upstairs hall and would tramp downstairs to the playroom, formerly his father's office under his den.
There he would stare solemnly at the squealing girls, then would
kneel down on all fours, and so for a children's hour would plod
or cavort as any kind of vehicle or beast of burden their fancies
might require. Then at six o'clock the fun was over and he went
downstreet to get the mail. Uncle Win fitted in with the family,
and from this time Ruth, Marie, and Barbara thought of him *in
loco parentis* rather than their more dourly grinning and resourceless sire. On or about November 13, Ruth's sixth birthday, Uncle
Win wrote her a sonnet:

> You Eyes, you large and all-inquiring Eyes,
> That look so dubiously into me,
> And are not satisfied with what they see
>
> . . . .

One of the poems in the contents of *The Torrent and the Night
Before* was entitled *Her Eyes*, in celebration of Emma's with their
"gleam of heaven to make them pure" and their "glimmer of hell
to make them human." Originally, Uncle Win committed self-
plagiarism by borrowing her mother's title for Ruth's sonnet. It

was and remained for life a high triumph for Ruth, even after, ten years later, the sonnet was published anticlimactically in another's honor and with a different title.

The frequent presence of the children and Win's domestic efforts were integrating elements in that disintegrating home, but the factor that was indispensable was the mother as focus, loving everyone, beloved by everyone, worried about everyone but judging no one, absolutely to be relied on. Win had kept secret from her the fact that *The Torrent and the Night Before* was in manufacture in the Riverside Press in Cambridge, because he wanted to surprise her with it at Christmas. A day or two after Ruth's birthday in November, Mary went to visit friends in Boston and returned ill. Emma, with the girls, moved into the L and took charge of the family. In a few days the trouble was diagnosed as "black diphtheria," one of the most dreaded plagues in those preantitoxin days. The doctor refused to treat her further. Ironically, Dean's special interest had been diphtheria, and he pulled himself together and did what he could.

On November 22 Mary Robinson died. No one would enter the house. The undertaker left the coffin on the porch, and the boys put their mother in it. Likewise, the minister read the service on the porch. The boys borrowed a delivery wagon, loaded the casket, drove it the block to the cemetery, and lowered it into the grave. Returning from the interment, Win, according to the Legend, disappeared upstairs and started what became *The Book of Annandale*.[42] The deceased wife Miriam, whom George Annandale was amazed to find he missed so calmly, was the poet's mother. The skirts that Annandale heard "scudding on the stairs" outside the closed door were Emma's.

In a few days little Ruth, who had run to her grandmother when they first came to take care of her and whom Mary had kissed impulsively, came down with diphtheria. But the strength of youth prevailed. Outside of the family, no one came into the house for five months, late November till late May. Semiquarantined in that former temple from which the altar had been removed were the three "wise brothers" and their several devils, Emma, the three little girls, and Dean's attendant, Wakefield, who fetched from downtown the requisite whiskey and morphine. From now on Herman's family lived permanently in the house.

A day or two after Mary's funeral, the bundle containing *The Torrent and the Night Before* arrived, and two weeks later, on December 7, Robinson wrote Smith: "Things have been going so like the devil with me for the past two months that nothing short of idealism would have kept me together; and a fortnight ago, to put a finishing touch to the whole business, my mother died of diphtheria. . . . She has gone ahead and I am glad for her. You see I have come to look on death as a deliverance and an advancement." This, I think, is Robinson's earliest surviving affirmation in prose of immortality, also of "idealism" as a systematic recourse (*cf. Kosmos, Two Sonnets,* etc.). He continued: "Speaking of the book, I received the whole thing (312 copies) the other morning, but did not take enough interest in them to open the package until evening. In fact, I feel as if I should like to kick them from here to Augusta and never see them again. They looked so small and so devilish blue to me that they made me sick; but now I am feeling better and am beginning to foster my same old ridiculous notion that they may amount to something some day." [43]

As a matter of sentiment, the corner is identifiable in Robinson's den where the unwanted package of devilish blue little books languished. Presently he distributed thirty or forty of them among his friends, and to at least one of them, Will Gay, he said, "Keep that, Will, it will be worth money some day." [44] The rest he sent out into the cold, critical dark. The reception was excellent, and he sent batches of the mail to Smith, with the typical caution: "Don't mistake my motives, for I assure you I haven't the smallest symptom of a 'swelled head.' . . ." And at the end of the letter: "Tear this business up when you have read it." [45] He refused the request of a Bangor editor for a picture and autobiographical note, writing Smith, "I appreciate his kindness, but I do not sympathize with his notions of human sanity." [46]

Characteristically, Robinson soon reacted to the impossible situation in the house with a declaration of optimism and a surge of humor. In mid-January: "We mortals are all fools and most of us are damned fools; but the time is coming when we are going to be something else. My philosophy says so and you say 'to hell with my philosophy'; but that's all right—we'll wait, and someone else will see. There's where the altruism of it comes in. There's a good deal in altruism—particularly when the pipe is drawing well." He announces the receipt of a letter from "an unknown female who seems to be in a very bad way about my verses." [47] And thus begins his third great correspondence, that with Edith Brower.

In February he seems to be settled into a less forced and more profound optimism: "I . . . make free to say that many of my verses [were] written with a conscious hope that they might make some despairing devil a little stronger and a little better satisfied with things—not as they are but as they are to be. This is the point the critics will not see. [In thirty-eight years they never did see it!] Because I don't dance on an illuminated hilltop and sing about the bobolinks and the bumblebees, they tell me that my world is a 'prison house, etc.'" In the same letter he makes, I think, his first important statement about organized religion: "I have been interested to find out that Christianity is in reality nothing more than Buddhism humanized; and that Nirvana and Heaven are from the idealist's point of view . . . pretty much the same thing." [48] And he goes on into Emerson and the Oversoul. On February 11, in reaction from a particularly flattering fan letter from a bank president in Vancouver, Washington, he draws and sends Smith a fierce caricature of himself as a long-haired genius smoking a corncob. There ensued a month's blank in the normally weekly or biweekly correspondence.

This strange hiatus in the ritual of what was at this time his most intimate association doubtless had several causes, but the astonishing one was his active involvement in the administration of his mother's estate. Edward, dying in '92, had left to the boys a dollar each, and the rest of his property, with the executorship, to Mary his wife. When she died intestate in November, '96, the estate must have been worth in the vicinity of $15,000 in personalty, mostly in securities, besides the house which a few years later was appraised at $2,500. This was no great fortune for a family of four adults and three children, but with parsimony, "farming," controlled wastage, and sound reinvestment at the then conservative 6 per cent, it could have done them for ten years.

At the outset, namely in December of '96, Dean as the eldest was appointed administrator, and the next summer Herman succeeded him. But, at least through '97, it seems to have been the feckless poet who directed the successful policy of the estate. Among surviving acquaintances of the family it is still remembered that Win stepped into the breach left open by the more or less incapacitated brothers. Nathaniel Barstow, then vice-president of the Maine Banking and Trust Company, and oldest brother of Win's friends Joe, George, and Jim, when asked later if he didn't find it remarkable that it was the poet who saved the situation, said emphatically, "Why no. . . . Everyone who knew him knew that it was Win who would carry them through, and he did." [49] It was a case where the artist's perception, though he had only contempt for the financial motive in life, yet when confronted with a specific situation, penetrated to the essence of it. It would seem that Win, had he wanted to, could have been a better doctor than Dean or a better gambler than Herman. (He did like to play poker!)

The course adopted by the estate has the mark of Win. No high and fancy finance with the hope of vast unearned increments from vague and distant prairies. Rather an understanding of an immediate need right there in Gardiner that could be exploited by industry and—what was more important than the economics of it—a project that at once could utilize Dean's professional knowledge, thus contributing toward his recovery of self-respect, and would facilitate his supply of morphine which was his only alternative to torture. Herman with his spacious memories would hardly have considered a petty, small-town mercantile enterprise. Certainly, in the tradition of association with the most pretentious and hypocritical Victorian respectability, he must have looked with horror on a proposal which, far from concealing Dean's "weakness," indulged it and even flaunted it. But Dean was on Win's side. Two to one, and Dean was then the administrator. On February 13, '97, two days after Win had sent Smith the caricature of himself as a long-haired and rolling-eyed genius, the estate bought for $2,700 from F. M. Noyes, not the drugstore at 207 Water Street, as is biographically reported, but simply the stock of the store.[50] The bill of sale ran to Horace Dean Robinson, and it was not until the following July, on the day when Dean withdrew as administrator, that, by the sale of some mortgages, the price was paid. But the new project, in the name and style of "H. D. Robinson & Co.," went into immediate operation, under what must have been a lease from the owner of the block, Henry Johnson, though no evidence of the lease has been found. A competent pharmacist, Edwin Emery, was employed and was soon taken into the company.

A Gardiner history says that Edwin Arlington Robinson for a time "found employment" in a local drugstore.[51] In an undated letter to Smith some time in '97 he says that he is downtown every day until six o'clock.[52] Presently we shall see that H. D. Robinson & Co. was not the only place downtown where he might have spent his days. Also, although it was not yet the time of high pressure salesmanship, the vision of this tall, silent, grave, hesitantly spoken poet dealing as clerk with the customers is not suggestive of what the drugstore seems to have become, namely the most popular of the three in town. Probably Ed Emery was clerk enough, and Win's business there was chiefly to check the accounts and perhaps to keep an eye on Dean whenever he might make his way downtown to preside over the "company" that carried his name. In any case, the store provided Dean with his needs, and it flourished outwardly, though there may be doubt whether it flourished financially as well.

One reason for the hiatus in Robinson's correspondence with Smith between February 11 and March 15, '97, was doubtless this unwonted busyness, leaving him too little time even for his own work. But probably more throttling of the impulse to communicate was the "nightmare" in that supposed pest house where more than usual passion for truth suffered more than usual perversion, and more than usual love was bound within more than usual frustration. Twenty-five years later Robinson published a record of the undrugged part of the tension in the double sonnet *Not Always*. First, there was Win himself in his almost hopelessness, his self-accusings, and then the compensating and composing escape of his imagination into the light:

In surety and obscurity twice mailed,
And first achieving with initial rout
A riddance of weak fear and weaker doubt,
He strove alone. But when too long assailed
By nothing, even a stronger might have quailed
As he did, and so might have gazed about
Where he could see the last light going out,
Almost as if the fire of God had failed.

And so it was till out of silence crept
Invisible avengers of a name
Unknown, like jungle-hidden jaguars.
But there were others coming who had kept
Their watch and word; and out of silence came
A song somewhat as of the morning stars.

And there were Emma and Herman, where love was being
twisted into disgust in the one and surly suspicion in the other:

There were long days when there was nothing said,
And there were longer nights where there was nought
But silence and recriminating thought
Between them like a field unharvested.
Antipathy was now their daily bread,
And pride the bitter drink they daily fought
To throw away. Release was all they sought
Of hope, colder than moonlight on the dead.

Wishing the other might at once be sure
And strong enough to shake the prison down,
Neither believed, although they strove together,
How long the stolid fabric would endure
That was a wall for them, and was to frown
And shine for them through many sorts of weather.

Then there was Dean, beloved by everybody, usually pacing
and moaning behind the closed door of his little room. And there
was Herman, leaving the house to no purpose except to come
home drunk and have to be put to bed. The guilt, envy, hatred,
and jealousy that comprised Avon's devil within him were com-

pounded by the fine press of Win's devilish little blue book which
Emma would tell Herman about if Win didn't. And worst of all,
the effeminate little book was full of insinuations and insults
against Herman and his friends that not the dullest and drunkest
ex-financier could miss. In things like *Dear Friends* and *Three
Quatrians* all solid citizens were belittled. And just who is the
girl and the "brother" in *The Miracle,* and just who is it that he
is supposed to "pity"? And what about *The Night Before* and this
fellow with the "brainless art" who is a "cad" and who shines
"with the smooth and slippery polish" of a snake? As Herman
had been cheated by his big financial colleagues in Wall Street
and the West, now he saw that his lightweight little brother was
trying to undermine him, and with his wife's sympathy and
encouragement.

In spite of Win's score of supposedly disguised, bitter satires
of Herman, he continued to include him in his love of the family,
the love that years later said to Carty Ranck, "People may say
or write anything they like about me, but leave my brothers
alone," [53] the love that treated Herman with entire compassion
in *Flammonde, The Wise Brothers, Old King Cole*—who is
Robinson himself—and all the later poems with one dubious
exception. It seems likely that through '97 it was Win's inclusive
love, as much as Emma's, that replaced Mary's and provided the
cohesiveness the family continued to enjoy. Increasingly Uncle
Win was at home romping with the nieces, now six, four, and two,
and increasingly they expected and depended on his ministra-
tion. Every night after they were in bed he would come and
lean over them to be sure they were all right. And he would
reassure them when they could hear Uncle Dean acting so
strangely, pacing back and forth in his room and moaning. After
his death in 1935, Ruth said that she always associated with
Uncle Win himself the line in *For a Dead Lady* about his mother
leaning over children: [54]

> The beauty, shattered by the laws
> That have creation in their keeping,
> No longer trembles at applause,
> Or over children that are sleeping;

And we who delve in beauty's lore
Know all that we have known before
Of what inexorable cause
Makes Time so vicious in his reaping.

And always, within Win's general love of the family, both the
strongest and the most disruptive individual force was his love
for Emma, at once intensified and more firmly disciplined in consequence of their functional intimacy as the two responsible
people in the house, she doing the housekeeping, he helping with
the chores, the farming, and the errands, both concerned about
the children, and she encouraging and to some extent criticizing
his poetry. Certainly there was close congeniality between them,
which to Win was still soul music and true love, as distinguished
from what he still considered her secondary ensnarement by
Herman.

And so Camelot was crumbling into a "wrecked empire,
lighted by the torch of woman" that, "together with the light /
That Galahad found," was "yet to light the world." And even then
Win's inner voice was whispering as it did to Lancelot twenty
years later, ". . . A world has died / For you, that a world may
live." Even in that month of silence in his correspondence, Robinson, against all the diversions, was beginning to raise with his
verse "another Camelot," beginning to chart with the *Octaves*
the course of his new quest for the light that Galahad found.
As *The Night Before* is the record of the first crisis of his life,
the *Octaves* are the record of the second. But now the juvenile
moralist and rhetorician of *The Night Before* has in three years
vanished in the mature thinker and the great rhetorician, sometimes rising into the great poet.[55]

Of the twenty-three *Octaves* preserved in the *Collected
Poems*, the bulk are mostly of impassioned rhetoric setting down
with precise, steel-like "clean wisdom, and strong skill" what we
might call Robinson's secondary notions, now finally formulated:
"the splendid shame / of uncreated failure"; the fact that "God's
accomplishment / Is always and unfailingly at hand"; the notion
of the world as "some crazy regiment at arms, . . . led resource-
lessly along / To brainless carnage by drunk trumpeters"; the

"record of All-Soul whereon God writes / In everlasting runes the truth of him"; Emma, "the purest thing God ever made," ensnared by the flesh until it seems "An angel has come back restigmatized"; the affirmation of his mother's immortality, ". . . the free life that would no longer feed / On fagots of outburned and shattered flesh / Wakes to a thrilled invisible advance, / Unchained (or fettered else) of memory"; and many other observations that are part of his mature store. But beyond these, in five or six of the *Octaves*, the same irresistibly questing power lifts him to both final truth and consummate expression, and it is in these five or six that, in the early part of his twenty-eighth year, he makes his first bid for the anthology of the greatest poetry in the world.

In mid-April he reported to Edith Brower that he had written forty "Octaves," [56] and he probably continued writing them through May. Of these, twenty-five are printed and preserved, twenty-three in series. With the exception of the penultimate one, originally the Twenty-fourth and finally the Twenty-second, written in early April, we have no external evidence of the order of composition. But in general, with a few parenthetic deviations, there is a steady progress, recalling the *Symposium*, from the immediate and prosaically stated observation expansively upward to the united absolute idea and absolute love that can be expressed only in poetry. With the exception of the Fifth *Octave*—

> There is one battle-field whereon we fall
> Triumphant and unconquered; but, alas!
> We are too fleshly fearful of ourselves
> To fight there till our days are whirled and blurred
> By sorrow, and the ministering wheels
> Of anguish take us eastward, where the clouds
> Of human gloom are lost against the gleam
> That shines on Thought's impenetrable mail.

—with the exception of this Fifth, which is among the five or six great ones, they are all found after the Thirteenth. In the absence of evidence to the contrary, and in view of the April date of the Twenty-second, it seems plausible to presume that about the first half of the *Octaves*, the exploratory half, were

written before the fifteenth of March, for on that day Robinson
seems to pause and make a comment on his quest for truth which
sums up the burthen of the *Octaves* he has written thus far and
announces the theme of idealism and love which characterizes the
rest. This comment is in the form of a letter to Smith, breaking
the silence since February 11. It is Robinsonian that out of his
blazing mind he starts with an attempt at humorous antisenti-
mentality which in this case turns into no more than a piece of
pathetic vulgarity. From that brief false start he strides off into
a country of clearly defined certitude from which he never
returned:

Dear Smith:

How long do you think a man can live in hell? I think he
can live there a good many years—a hundred, perhaps, if his
bowels keep in decent order—but he isn't going to have a very
good time. No man can have a very good time—of the right
sort, at any rate—until he understands things; and how the
devil is a man to understand things in an age like this, when
the whole trend of popular thought is in the wrong direction—
not only that but proud of the way it is taking? The age is all
right, material progress is all right, Herbert Spencer is all
right, hell is all right. These things are temporal necessities, but
they are damned uninteresting to one who can get a glimpse of
the real light through the clouds of time. It is that glimpse that
makes me want to live and see it out. If it were not for that
glimpse, I should be tempted, as Tennyson used to be, to stick
my nose into a rag soaked with chloroform and be done with
it—that is, if I could screw up the courage. But now, thank
God, that is not the kind of courage I am praying for; what I
am after is the courage to see and to believe that my present
life is the best thing for me, and that every man has it in his
power to overcome whatever obstacles may be in his way—
even the seeming obstacle we call by the name of Death. I
have not said much about my life for the past three years—I
mean the past ten [that is, since '87 when Dean came home
addicted]—because with all its lack of anything like material
hope and pleasure—it was tolerable. For all my long lean face,

I never gave up; and I shall never give up. I can't do it; but I can suffer like damnation, which shows there is something wrong with me somewhere. The past three months of my life, however, are quite another thing. If they had come two years ago, or even one, I think they would have finished me. The book has helped me out a little—in fact, I was rather bewildered by its reception—but that counts (the praise, I mean) for very little. There are things here at home that are pulling me back, and I've got to look out for them. I can't get away, just now—I don't see how I can for a year—and the result is that all my best strength is required in keeping my thoughts in some kind of rational order. The one great pleasure of my life is the knowledge that my poor dear mother is out of it. I can't quite understand—yet—the laws of compensation that make a woman suffer what she did and from so many causes. We say she died of diphtheria. What does that mean? It means just this: she had endured all [she] could and was ready to die. I had been watching it for a year. If she had not had diphtheria, or membranous croup, or whatever it was that took her off so hellishly, she would have gone crazy. *I am not going crazy, for I see some things she did not see—some things she could not see; but I am going to lose all those pleasures which are said to make up the happiness of this life and I'm glad of it. I'm glad to say that I am strong enough to do without them. There is a pleasure—a joy—that is greater than all these little selfish notions and I have found the way to it through idealism* [italics added].[57]

And so back to the *Octaves*. This is from the Eighteenth:

> Like a white wall whereon forever breaks
> Unsatisfied the tumult of green seas,
> Man's unconjectured godliness rebukes
> With its imperial silence the lost waves
> Of insufficient grief.

And here is the Nineteenth:

> Nor jewelled phrase nor mere mellifluous rhyme
> Reverberates aright, or ever shall,

One cadence of that infinite plain-song
Which is itself all music. Stronger notes
Than any that have ever touched the world
Must ring to tell it—ring like hammer-blows,
Right-echoed of a chime primordial,
On anvils, in the gleaming of God's forge.

And the Twenty-second, in process on April fourth:

Forebodings are the fiends of Recreance;
The master of the moment, the clean seer
Of ages, too securely scans what is,
Ever to be appalled at what is not;
He sees beyond the groaning borough lines
Of Hell, God's highways gleaming, and he knows
That Love's complete communion is the end
Of anguish to the liberated man.

And the final, Twenty-third:

Here by the windy docks I stand alone,
But yet companioned. There the vessel goes,
And there my friend goes with it; but the wake
That melts and ebbs between that friend and me
Love's earnest is of Life's all-purposeful
And all-triumphant sailing, when the ships
Of Wisdom loose their fretful chains and swing
Forever from the crumbled wharves of Time.

This last *Octave* might record a bright, windy day in April or
May when Emma and Herman took the old *Islander* down the
great River to Boothbay Harbor and their cottage on Capitol
Island. Perhaps Win went down with them to the pier and saw
them off. Then he walked the mile up to the house to take care
of Dean, passing on the way the northeast corner of the Common
where forty years later his memorial stele would stand.

In the *Octaves*, together with the letter of March 15, '97,
which is their prose equivalent, we have the record of the second
crisis and the second great step in Robinson's life. The first step,
beginning with his crisis of '88, ended in '94 with his declaration

in *The Night Before* of the differentiation between love and lust, comprising an emotional dualism in women as well as men, of his own awakening to universal compassion, and, derivative from this, his doctrine of individualism. The second step began with the crisis precipitated by the death of his mother in November of '96 and was completed with the definitive expressions of the following March, April, and May.[58] Its achievement was the integration and articulation of that "idealism" that had always been potential in him, meaning in his case the recognition of the seat of reality as in the mind, and the recognition of love as its expression.

Also, we find in the emotional style of the *Octaves* and in the key statement of the letter Robinson's remaining sin, his early blind spot to the eventual "light" which will require another crisis to become clear to him. "There is a pleasure—a joy—that is greater than all these little selfish notions and I have found the way to it through idealism." By this "joy" Robinson means two things which he does not yet distinguish. He does mean the "imperial silence," the "unclamoring peace," of the selfless inner self, the seat of the ultimate Idea combining Truth, Beauty and Love. But he means also and especially the quasi-orgastic ecstasy of "creating" or consciously formulating particular perceptions and "ideas" in the colloquial sense, and especially embodying them in words. As distinguished from inner peace, this is outer gratification, sublimated out of carnal into mental experience but still external in its delight, its emotional self-indulgence. Generally, it is the mood of romantic poetry. Specifically it is the mood of Robinson's subjective poetry which characterizes much of his work for his first forty years, including some of his great work, notably those few *Octaves*, a few sonnets, and a few passages in the longer poems. This ecstasy, this "joy," is a hindrance to Robinson's growth to his full poetic stature, and it is the villain in the drama of his personal development toward saintliness. He acknowledges the emotional self-indulgence of it when he calls himself "selfish." We shall see that eventually, in his mid-forties, he will outgrow the orgastic-ecstatic mode of creation and will distinguish it from the calm "Light" of the inner self in universal perception and love. Yet in this process of maturing he will never repudiate that aspect of the outer self that is the artist. In his humility he will always ignore the possibility of his own sanctification, for which he was congenitally qualified, and will continue through life to practice a merely less ecstatic, creative selfishness as the necessary condition of his fated performance as a poet.

Robinson's catharsis of March 15 left a composed state of assurance behind it. On April fourth he wrote Smith "I have had a golden opportunity this winter to study the possibilities of mental resistance" [59]—apparently the defensive aspect of "idealism," "thought's impenetrable mail"—"and it is the triumph of my life to know that I am good for something." The correspondence with Edith Brower in Wilkes-Barre was getting up to cruising speed: "My female correspondent has done wonders for me and has proved to me that I possess the power of helping others, which, after all, is about the greatest thing a man, or a book, can do." Miss Brower, unavailable by distance, looks like a possible new rival for Emma, and probably has also the special virtue of more literary understanding than Emma possessed. "She is infernally bright and not at all ugly and has something of a literary reputation." But one element of her unavailability, while especially comforting to Robinson and ensuring her permanence, yet disqualifies her for rivalry with Emma in love's highest "elemental overglow." "The best of [Miss Brower] is," said Robinson, "she is too old to give me a chance to bother myself with any sentimental business."

The letter of April 4 is full of other developments: "I have been to Cambridge and Boston where I tried, without success, to find a publisher. . . .

"I was treated magnificently and ought to have enjoyed myself; but somehow I felt out of place, and could not quite bring myself to believe that I cut quite the figure in men's eyes that they would have had me think. I was much lunched at the Colonial Club and A. S. Hill gave me a cigarette. I drank rum punch at the St. Botolph and talked with men who can stand on their feet and not feel as I do (no reference to the punch)." [60]

In the same letter he reports the first of the two social escapes he enjoyed from the hell of home and Gardiner: "At last I have a downtown den to crawl into." [61] Four friends, respectively "the

Banker" (Arthur Blair), "the Pedagogue" (Seth Ellis Pope), "the
Scientist" (Linville Robbins), and "the Poet," organized themselves as "the Quadruped" and rented for two dollars a month a
room over Brown's store, complete with Franklin stove. It was
at the top rear of one of the three-story business blocks on Water
Street, the windows looking out over the final millpond of the
Cobbossee before it emptied into the Kennebec. Typically, Robinson excoriated village clubs as "just a little the foulest things I
know of in a way of social gatherings. Four shall be the limit.
Three, ordinarily, would be much better and there is a great
deal to be said in favor of two." [62] Thus he propounded his defi-
nition of tolerable society from which he never deviated. The
almost nightly assemblies of the Quadruped, with pipes, beer,
clarinet, and fiddle, were one of the things that kept him from
"going crazy." Also, possibly from the start and certainly a little
later, he used the room sometimes to work in during the day.

The other salvation, beginning in early April of this same
packed spring, was the contact with the Richards-Gardiner clan
which, next to his family and a few of the male "friends of my
life," became his most important lifelong association, certainly
his most satisfactory association with a sizable mixed company.
Laura Richards, children's story writer, was the daughter of Julia
Ward and Samuel Gridley Howe and kin to half of Brahmin
Boston, including the Emersons. Henry Richards' mother was
a Gardiner of the manor house "Oaklands" on the edge of the
village the family had originally owned. In '76 Henry moved
to Gardiner and bought the finest colonial house in town, in order
to help his brothers with the paper mills which had been their
father's. Until the spring of '97 the Richardses had met of the
Robinsons only old Edward in his capacity of a director of the
savings bank until his death in '92, and young Herman in his
capacity of a boy oarsman in the four-oar crew Henry Richards
organized. When Win came into their ken they knew that his
mother was dead, but they did not learn until later, and never
from Win himself, that she had died only the previous fall. Laura
Richards heard of him and his verse from the poetess Caroline
Swan. She considered Miss Swan a bore, but invited the poet
round to one of her literary and musical evenings in the "Yellow

House," looking down Vine Street and over the Kennebec. In
her note, Mrs. Richards, who was a good deal sounder woman
than was implied by her occasional Victorian poeticisms, wrote,
"Prithee, good Hermit Thrush, come out of thy thicket." This gave
Robinson great pause, but his prosody coach Dr. Schuman persuaded him. He replied, "I shall be glad to come to see you on
Monday. I am not a Hermit Thrush." [63]

Very soon the engaging new connection gets into Robinson's
correspondence with Smith: "Went down to Mrs. Richards' again
last evening and had a pretty good time. I was invited, with a
villanelle, to tea; but I couldn't stand that, so I told her I'd be
down about half-past seven or eight. . . . I had a good time, as
I said, and the three [dogs] again to help me out. They put their
heads up on my knees and give my hands something to do. . . .
There was some small literary talk (I can do that well enough)
and then there was some good music. Hays Gardiner said all the
pleasant things . . . between selections and I had a good time.
I repeat this, because it has been such a devil of a while since I
had the last one." [64] John Hays Gardiner, Henry Richards'
nephew, a popular associate professor of English at Harvard,
was six years older than Robinson and was like him in the essentials of inward humility, outward dignity and reticence, cheer-
fulness in adversity, and devotion to literature. Gardiner had a
chronic heart, and on account of it sometimes spent winters at
Oaklands in semiretirement. This seems to have been the situation that spring of '97, and after meeting Robinson that April
evening he had him out frequently to Oaklands, besides meeting
him often at the Richardses'. Mrs. Richards and Hays Gardiner
were Robinson's most valuable early friends, immediately by
appreciation on the level of the only real literary distinction in
town, and ultimately in the practical literary world. [65]

A month after that second soiree at the "Yellow House," Robinson wrote Smith: "I got lonesome the other evening and went
down to Mrs. Richards', where I found two daughters and a dog.
I tried to make myself pleasant and entertaining to the daughters
and I think the dog understood my position. At any rate he came
up and let me scratch his ears again, and looked at me in a way
that implied, 'Go ahead, you're getting along first rate.' After

that there was some more music, but I didn't quite have the nerve to ask for 'Mandalay' again, as the *pater* had a visitor in the next room. The only trouble with that family is they are too abnormally happy and unconscious of the damnation that makes up nine tenths of life." [66] Thus Robinson embarked upon his innocent social hypocrisy, his very special kind of double standard. With the Richardses and, following them, a series of comfortable, cultivated Victorian families elsewhere, he found the only domestic happiness he ever knew after he had begun to be "stirred up considerably" at home at the age of eight or nine. Yet the real world that he acknowledged in his poetry and closest friendships was the world of hardship and defeat, the world of his mother and Dean and George Burnham, of Luke Havergal, Eben Flood, and The Town Down the River.

Mrs. Richards saw Robinson's quality at once, both as person and poet. She always had an unsophisticated preference for what he called his "jingling" things, his *Klondikes* and *Wildernesses* and *Twilight Songs*, and in their later intimacy he used to kid her about it. But in the large she saw his fineness and promptly set out on the hopeless enterprise of making him socially easy. "We knew nothing at all that he had been through . . . but his loneliness, his need, were patent. Our chief idea was to accustom him to a cheerful household. . . . I tried, among other things, to teach him to shake hands warmly and cordially, not to give a limp flap of a cold paw. . . . I only partly succeeded. To the end, I think, he still pinched with his fingers [He did, "to the end"!]. . . . I am not sure whether I told him . . . that he must look people in the eye when speaking . . ." [67] (This he did learn to do, sometimes.)

Mrs. Richards' valiant failure is most apparent in the record and pictures of Robinson's visits to the numerous family and their numerous guests at their camp on Belgrade Lake in the woods. "I really think he enjoyed his two visits to our camp. Hays Gardiner was there both times. . . . There was much merriment. We sang over the dish-washing; sang in the canoes when the moon shone; played games by the fire . . .[68]

"In everything E.A. took his part quietly, cheerfully. [Mrs.

Richards gave him that nickname, which he instantly preferred
to both 'Win' and 'Robbie.']

"E.A. always, I think, in black, but wearing for the most part
the white hat I gave him . . . an Italian fisherman's hat. . . . It
was extremely becoming to his sombre beauty. Did he know this?
Anyhow, he liked the hat, and wore it, I think, through several
years and in various places." (This big, floppy white hat was
undoubtedly the spiritual grandfather of the golf hats that years
later he always wore at the MacDowell Colony and elsewhere in
the summer.)

Alas, most of these excerpts from Mrs. Richards' record comprise *in toto* a desperately generous lie. Compare his earlier, high-
school friend's account of the boys' efforts to get him camping.
Undoubtedly he was cheerful and quiet, but it is incredible that
he "took his part" in dish-washing or other than quietly chuckling
merriment. There is a photograph of him in one of the Richards'
canoes, sitting in his sombre black suit and "sombre beauty" as a
sombre passenger while two healthy girls paddle him. I doubt if
even Mrs. Richards ever dared assert that he sang "when the
moon shone." Elsewhere, she describes him beautifully: "I don't
believe E.A. was ever happy. Merry, yes . . . the effervescence
of childhood (except when he found a new word) was not for
him, nor that of boyhood. Quiet: his book in his hand; yet seeing
everything . . ." [69]

Perhaps the best capsule of Robinson's whole life in the external world is a group picture of one of those house parties. In
the center is blondly beautiful Mrs. Richards with, I think, three
daughters and three sons around her, together with miscellaneous young cousins and guests on the ground in front; in the
background, Henry Richards and all but one of the men standing,
including Hays Gardiner. They are in rough clothes, no hats or
coats, mostly soft collars without ties. The women likewise are all
in the long sports skirts and shirtwaists of the era, the girls in
pigtails. And there sits E.A., the only man not standing, at the end
of the back row of women, alone, staring intent and black-eyed
at the camera out of his indeed sombre beauty, on his head the
ridiculous big white hat, on his person a complete, black city suit

that looks like a frock coat and in any case would become an
undertaker, round his neck the highest possible wing collar and
the enormous four-in-hand tie that in '97 was already out of
fashion. It was not that E.A. didn't have plenty of decent, old
"farming" clothes that he could have worn, but he simply *could
not* have put them on to go out in company, any more than he
could take his jacket off. He didn't know how you did these external things. He had learned one way of dressing, and that he
could and must do. In time he could have learned another. But
two house parties, indeed the whole summer, would not have
been enough for that.

The contrast between Robinson alone and that family assembled is a section of his biography. Not that he isn't a match for
them all, both in strength and in gentility, for in outline he is his
mother and she had their high quality, only in its rural instead
of its cosmopolitan aspect. His strength is entirely of the inner
world looking out through those black eyes. Theirs includes the
outer world at its best, the easy intercourse of cultivated minds,
the courtesy towards all, the active generosity towards the misfits
with whom E.A. instinctively identified himself. His limitation is
social, it makes him feel inferior, and it is a complex. And yet it
is not a social inferiority complex in the ordinary, snobbish sense:
he does not feel inferior to these people as individuals or as a
class. He simply doesn't know what you *do* with them, any more
than he would know what to do with a company of angels if he
encountered them on the highway and they asked him to come
along. There is an anecdote by way of comic relief that occurred
one evening round the campfire when E.A. was sitting obscurely
behind one of the sisters, Julia, then ten years old. For a long
time he considered her long red-gold braid while the fire glinted
on his black eyes. Presently he reached forward, tweaked the
braid. The girl looked around and smiled. He smiled, "with his
gray matter." That was all.[70]

With the support of the Quadruped and the Richards-Gardiner family, Robinson's correspondence with Smith takes on a
subdued but sure optimism: "It is only when I forget what an
ass I am that I find life tolerable; but I am putting the ass away
more and more—to my own mind at least—and recognizing my

place in the scheme of things. It is quite a place; so is yours; . . .
There's a good deal to live for, but a man has to go through hell
really to find it out. . . . The process is hard, but the result
pays." [71] His humor is aglow. "I want to go to New Zealand. Ever
since I lied so like the devil about 'my northern pines' [in the
truncated sonnet *Boston*—"My northern pines are good enough
for me"] I have had visions of Auckland. I think if I buried myself there for five or six years I could write a sonnet." [72]

Three months before this, in the letter of March fifteenth,
Robinson had said that he wanted to get away, but he didn't see
how he could for a year or more. Perhaps he wanted to stay until
Dean died, in order to watch over him and keep the drugstore
going. Perhaps he felt he must stay to help Emma with the house,
and especially with the children. Dean, although he never did
anything violent, was getting more and more frightening, pacing
up and down in his "dark room" for hours without stopping, and
groaning loudly and continuously. One night when Win was
downtown, Emma herself got panicky, took the children out on
the front porch and tucked them together in the hammock. Win
came home at about eleven, "felt dreadfully," quieted Dean
quickly, and got everybody safely to bed. Rosalind, one of the
Richards daughters, wrote a charming sketch of Ruth the eldest
niece, then in her seventh year, she the one who always resembled
her Uncle Win in looks and the air of sensitive perception. When
they were walking down the street together, "It wasn't just that
her hand was in his . . . she looked up at him, laughing and
talking and frolicking along; it was the way in which he held
her hand, the utter confidence with which she seemed to own
him." [73]

All this does not imply that Herman was getting any closer
to his family or to Win. He presumably was around that summer,
for on July 10 Dean resigned as administrator of their mother's
estate, and on July 12 Herman succeeded him, Dean and Win
going on his bond.

Meanwhile, a vanity publisher, Badger, in Boston had flat-
tered Win into letting them issue a new volume for him, and his
Harvard friend William Butler offered to pay the bill. He sub-
tracted five titles and added seventeen to the contents of *The*

Torrent and the Night Before, made *The Children of the Night* the title poem of the new book, and sent it off that summer. There isn't much of the new material that can be attributed to Emma. Very dubiously, the Legend holds that *The Story of the Ashes and the Flame* records her cooling toward Herman at this time, together with her wiles for holding him—compare the unmistakable and mature treatment of the same theme later, in *Eros Turannos.* Of the *Octaves* only two or three can be directly associated with Emma, though she probably knew that the personal aspect of the passion behind them was for her. But, of more significance than particular instances in the contents of *The Children of the Night, The Book of Annandale,* presumably started in late '96 but not finished till 1901, associates a woman either with *The Torrent* as a whole, with *The Children* as a whole, or, more likely, with both. Also *Partnership,* whose date of composition between '97 and 1901 can only be guessed, seems to associate Emma with the later volume.

Both *Annandale* and *Partnership* portray a woman's commitment to a man's artistic accomplishment. In the first great passage in a long poem of Robinson's, *Annandale* celebrates poetry itself and records the effect on a woman of poetry which she knows was "made for her, / For her alone." Originally *Partnership* was entitled *The Wife of Palissy,* but a curious thing about it is that it has nothing to do with Palissy, the great sixteenth-century potter, or his wife, except in so far as he was an artist who underwent years of agonizing experiment before achieving the glaze he wanted. Robinson got his idea from Longfellow's *Kéramos,* which he admired as early as '93. But neither in *Kéramos* nor in any other secondary source is there any statement about Palissy's wife dying; and neither in *Kéramos* nor in any other source, primary or secondary, is there any evidence that Palissy's wife was ever anything but a termagant and a frigid woman who compounded her husband's torture through his years of struggle.[74] In *Partnership,* on the other hand, the beloved shares joyfully in the lover's triumph. And in her monologue she spells out with great poignancy exactly Win's belief about his and Emma's relationship at the time of a new climix which overtook them some time that summer of '97, presumably after Herman's appointment as administrator in mid-July, and not later than the early fall.[75]

On a warm evening in this period, Herman came home dignified and drunk as usual. It does not appear where Dean was,
but Win was downstreet, probably at the Quadruped rooms
where he went almost every night. Emma put Herman to bed,
and while there is no record of what occurred between them it
does appear that by this time she was habitually berating him
for drinking. After she had tucked him in, she went downstairs
and out on the porch, where she sat in the hammock in the dark.
As was usual in the days of gaslight, the central hall light was
left on, turned low, and it was visible from the hammock through
one of the parlor windows. Presently Win came out Lincoln
Avenue, stepped up on the porch, and sat down beside Emma in
the hammock. Little or nothing needed to be said by her to tell
him of the situation, and it can be assumed that he said nothing.
He put his arm around her, she cried a little on his shoulder, and
presently fell asleep.

Above, in the master bedroom, Herman got up and came
downstairs in his nightshirt. He turned up the gas in the hall,
went into the parlor, looked out the window, and the light
showed him the scene of domestic tranquillity in the hammock.
There was no pugilistic gesture, but in that moment biography
accelerated and much literature germinated. Chiefly this mild
incident became in due course Arthur making his surprise return
from the hunting at Carlisle, catching Lancelot in Guinevere's
bower, and sending their love off on a road of great poetry to
the light that Galahad found. Also, this became Roman Bartholow
catching his friend Penn-Raven kissing his wife, with the opposite result of great pity, futility, and death, in poetry that is
less than great. What happened materially as the shadowy prototype of all this ideational reality was that Herman and Win went
upstairs to Win's den and shut the door, and thereafter Emma
heard much loud and angry talk which she did not understand.
Since Win was never known to shout, the loud words must have
been Herman's, and because of the dilemma of Damaris in forthcoming *Annandale*, it is possible that a part of Herman's oratory
informed Win that he would make Emma promise him never to
marry Win if he died. There was quiet talk too, and it surely

comprised verbal financial arrangements between the administrator of the estate and one of the other two heirs. Since it appears that in November Win had $600 in hand, the plan may have been to provide him with a fixed allowance from the estate, perhaps in the vicinity of $750 a year. It could scarcely have been less than this, for during the next four years Win, while often pinched, was never *in* financial *extremis*.[76]

The next day Herman went downstreet to his devices, and Win spent the morning packing his clothes and effects, including his clarinet but not his manuscripts. About noon he finished, and irrespective of how much or little of the external action it records, it is hard to explain *Partnership* otherwise than as the true inward account of that epic parting. Not a great poem, it is a great personal record, and like *Cortège* it is too passionately subjective to have been written, at least in first draft, very long after the event. In spite of the early title of "The Wife of Palissy," there is nothing of that disagreeable lady in it, and there is nothing of Palissy the potter except the fact that the artist holds something in his hand that he has at long last achieved. The manuscript of *The Children of the Night,* Win's first commercial publication, and he himself went off into the great world at about the same time. And since Emma was involved in both dramatic departures he combined them in the poem. Instead of Palissy's cup, Win is showing her the manuscript, and she is responding:

> Yes, you have it; I can see.
> Beautiful? . . . Dear, look at me!
> Look and let my shame confess
> Triumph after weariness.
> Beautiful? Ah, yes.
>
> Lift it where the beams are bright;
> Hold it where the western light,
> Shining in above my bed,
> Throws a glory on your head.
> Now it is all said.

(It doesn't matter whether the imagery here recalls Mary Robinson's deathbed and Win's wish that she might have seen and

appreciated some achievement of his, or whether in literalness
Emma was napping in the master's bedroom, which was the
western large one, when Win came in to say good-bye.)

The third and fourth stanzas are more clearly Emma and Win,
and no one else, asserting Win's belief in the identity of the idealism of love and that of imaginative or poetic perception:

> All there was for me to say
> From the first until today.
> Long denied and long deferred,
> Now I say it in one word—
> Now; and you have heard.
>
> Life would have its way with us,
> And I've called it glorious:
> For I know the glory now
> And I read it on your brow.
> You have shown me how.

The fifth stanza involves the embrace which may have referred
to either his mother or Emma, and it closes with the one shadow
in the poem, the suggestion that Win was not unequivocally
satisfied with the relationship of soul music alone:

> I can feel your cheeks all wet,
> But your eyes will not forget:
> In the frown you cannot hide
> I can read where faith and pride
> Are not satisfied.

Then the sixth stanza, which is the central declaration of the
poem, recording more passionately and perhaps more clearly
than elsewhere Win's belief in Emma's dualism, spiritually his
in her true love, physically Herman's in superficial infatuation:

> But the word was, two should live:
> Two should suffer—and forgive:
> By the steep and weary way,
> For the glory of the clay,
> Two should have their day.

Here are the two "two's," Emma and Win in the great love that suffers and forgives, Emma and Herman in what is for her the "steep and weary way" for the indulgence of the "clay." Robinson was too good an artist not to have intended the pun touching Palissy and Herman.

The seventh and eighth stanzas confess the triviality of all the "clashing" there has been with Herman, all transcended now in Win's achievement, and ending with Emma's tender question, one of the occasional, early intimations of Robinson's potential understanding of women and their love as of a different emotional texture from his own:

> Did I doubt you now and then?
> Well, we are not men.

And the last stanza, while it probably recalls his mother's death, combines it with the equally ultimate realities of the lovers' parting and their assurance that Win is going on to great achievement in their separated life ahead. It is not great poetry, but it is a great romantic moment and a critical moment in the history of literature.

> Never mind; we know the way,—
> And I do not need to stay.
> Let us have it well confessed:
> You to triumph, I to rest.
> That will be the best.

And so, a little after noon Robinson left the big house near the cemetery, where he had lived since before his memories. At supper Herman regaled Emma with the information, suggestive of Roman Bartholow's later sentiments in similar circumstances, that a man who took another man's wife was a "scoundrel." And so the war moved out of the towers of Camelot into the open world.

Act IV

Robinson's departure from home in the late summer or early fall of '97 was final, but for two years he postponed establishment elsewhere, probably in order to keep an eye on Dean. His location for the first month or two after he walked down Lincoln Avenue carrying his bag is conjectural. Since he already had a habit of retreating downtown to the Quadruped room in order to find peace to work, he doubtless went there first, and it is possible that he put up there briefly. But, since three or four months later he is found bunking in with his fellow Quadruped Arthur Blair, in Winthrop across the Kennebec where Blair had a job in a bank, it is more likely that he went to him straightway. After he settled there, he walked across the long footbridge every morning and spent the day working in the club room, with its quiet and its outlook over the millpond of the Cobbossee.

Generally this transitional period was marked by incidents that are uncertain in fact, in date, or in both. Not long after leaving home he returned there for an essential errand, and his niece Ruth remembers watching him hammering in the nails to box up some of his manuscript, notably the almost finished poetization of Harry Smith's translation of the *Antigone* on which they had spent more than two years. As things turned out, this was the last view either of them ever had of this effort. In spite of the fact that Robinson had already written *Luke Havergal,* the *Octaves,* and two or three other major pieces, this boxing of the *Antigone* can be taken as the winding up of his youthful phase.

Robinson's preliminary sally into the great world occurred late that fall of '97, at the suggestion of one Titus M. Coan, son of a minister, poet, member of the Century Club, and collector of pornographic pictures, to whom he had sent a copy of *The Torrent and the Night Before.* Robinson went to New York and put up with George Burnham in a boarding house on West 64th Street, that "greatest man ever born" then practicing law on Wall Street, with a number of years to pass yet before he walked out of the profession on his two wooden legs. Coan inducted Robinson into an intellectual group with whose assistance he seems to have first learned of his abnormal capacity for whiskey and of its magic power to loosen his tongue. The new association included his permanent friend Graven Longstreth Betts and his transitory friend Alfred H. Louis, an ancient, learned, prophetically bearded, and once distinguished Anglo-Jewish derelict, a former protégé of Gladstone's and now his abominator. The forth-coming "Captain Craig" stank, starved, shivered, pontificated, and wore a shiny Prince Albert turned up at the collar to conceal the absence of shirt.

On December 6, *The Children of the Night* appeared and got a flutter of attention. Robinson was entertained at the Century Club and at the Authors Club, and his reaction was as in Boston earlier: "Meeting this man or that is nothing to me. I must have a chance to know him, and that chance . . . must come about of its own accord." [1] Later in the month he went back to Gardiner to meet some brief emergency involving Dean. This time he surely stayed with Arthur Blair in Winthrop during the few days before he was away again.[2] On January 5, '98, he was in Cam-bridge, and on the thirteenth he was back with Burnham in New York, settled down and making a probable second start on what he then called "George Annandale." During the ensuing winter he visited his "great aunt" Edith Brower in Wilkes-Barre and was de-lighted with her. In the spring he went to Cambridge where he started *Captain Craig*, first called "The Pauper." The composition and recomposition of this, his first memorable long poem, became his regular occupation, relieved by excursions into other works, during the next two years.

Modeled externally on Alfred Louis, and internally on Louis and Dean, *Captain Craig* represents both a transition and a kind of sophomoric island in the body of Robinson's work. Alone among all of the long poems and all of the significant short ones, it is, but for a few passages, not an imaginative transcription of imaginatively perceived emotional experience, but a conscious versification of much derivative or deliberately concocted wis-dom. Most of it, therefore, is not poetry at all but rationalistic pseudopoetry. The generalized observations and didactic apho-risms are Robinsonian in manner only; they are Robinson with the passion drained off and only the mind speaking. It was as if in '98 and '99, when his emotional life had been frustrated and diverted into the life of the mind, he was negating emotional motivation entirely and giving himself, not to the heat that in the *Octaves* shimmers off "thought's impenetrable mail," but to a cool, objective intellection that wanted to be civilized and sophisticated. Life, including his own, was not to be lived but observed as the half-humorous material of drama and poetry. It was as if Robinson during these two years, having found no peace on the plane of his always impassioned and essentially unphilosophical "idealism," was experimenting on a more truly philosophical level, one that has been called his "stoicism."

Dean is supposed to have shared with Alfred Louis the provision of the enormous array of wisdom set out in *Captain Craig*, and it would be possible perhaps to divide it into two parts, an aggressive, self-assertive, essentially pagan part which might be attributed to Louis, and a humble, essentially Christian part which might be attributed to Dean. The pagan wisdom is hot and affirmative, usually associated with the image of the sun— "good courage of the sun." It recommends enjoyment of living, self-understanding, and artistic creation as subjective achievement rather than as objective perception. Nothing achieved is wasted, "the songs all count." Altogether, the pagan side of the Captain's mind, represented by Phaethon and all "high-flyers," is Robinson's literal and conclusive celebration of the romantic, sublimated orgastic "joy" which, up to the time of beginning the poem in the spring of '98, he had identified with his "idealism" in its aspects both of love and of poetic composition. Finally, the wisdom attributable to old Louis includes the interpretation of the whole "Scheme" as God's joke, to be taken lightly and climaxed with the gay and absurd flourish of "trombones" in the Captain's funeral march. This image was supplied by the "Dead March" from *Saul* which Robinson had heard many times in the processions of Knights Templars rounding the corner of Lincoln Avenue and Danforth Street on the way to the cemetery. Years later he repudiated the notion that the universe was "God's joke," holding the view to be Hardy's pessimistic "blunder, both philosophical and artistic." [3]

As distinguished from Alfred Louis's aggressive individualism, the wisdom of Captain Craig attributable to Dean is of the humbler sort that was congenital with Robinson, and that eventually led Captain Craig's hot "sun" to fade into the selfless "Light." It is embodied in the best poetry in the piece. Passionately it celebrates the glory of "the unfulfilled,"

           the rhythm of god
That beats unheard through souls of shattered men,

and akin to it, the compassion for every

        cursedest mean thing that crawls;

  .   .   .   .   .   .

You may not ever crush him but you lose,
You may not ever shield him but you gain—

And again, the Christian injunction "to learn your trade in Nazareth."

    In the early summer of '98 Robinson was in Gardiner again, living in Winthrop and working in the Quadruped room which he now called his "eyrie." There, through the summer and fall, he debased his personal musical expression from the clarinet to the saxophone, finished a draft of "The Pauper," and started *Aunt Imogen*, then and for some time thereafter known as "The Old Maid." Aunt Imogen, with her niece and two nephews, represents with near literalness Uncle Win and his three nieces, who always gave him a "tempestuous welcome" [4] on the occasions—presumably rare—when he appeared at the old house. As portraying a selfless love, indifferent to the quasi-carnal luxuries of "soul music," the poem is of biographical interest as showing that he was already outgrowing the pagan self-expressionism which he had just been celebrating with such gusto in the pronouncements of Captain Craig.

    Whether or not there was any connection between this change and his personal experiences of that summer, it does look as if Robinson made at this time a deliberate effort to backslide from his hopeless "nameless passion" for Emma, to replace her "soul music" with a more realistic strain. Opening his susceptibilities to the acceptable currents in his acquaintance, he relaxed into involvement with the most highly qualified woman he ever walked out with, the most formidable runner-up Emma ever encountered, the one who probably represented Robinson's nearest miss of that married love he had so eloquently celebrated in his letter to Smith in May, '96, and which he had forsworn in the letter of March, '97.

The young lady, whom Hagedorn calls "the girl of the woodland walks," was a birthright member of Boston Brahmin society
at its most intellectual, and she sometimes visited the Gardiners
in Oaklands, notably in that summer of '98. Robinson was often
in the house to see his friend Hays Gardiner, and presently he
and the girl were walking out together on the paths in the spacious woods, largely beech, maple, and oak, around the mansion.
She was of a golden blondness and frequently, perhaps habitually, wore white. Her features were small and of patrician
fineness, her eyes blue-gray and large, her expression tense, concerned, and consecrated, her bearing highbred in delicacy and
grace. At every point she was cast for a queenly role, and as
Emma provided Robinson's Guinevere's passionate soul, and
some of her gestures, the Woodland Girl has no known rival as
the model of her bearing and "white and gold" exterior. She was
highly educated, wrote both poetry and fiction herself, was genuinely and intelligently appreciative of Robinson's work and remained addicted to it throughout her life.

Of the women who are known to have tempted Robinson
towards "those pleasures that are said to make up the happiness
of this life," the Woodland Girl was the one least likely to blemish
the glory of "anticipation" and soul music with the crudity of
"realization," such as concern for her lover's physical state or for
the nature and degree of his passion for herself. But, in the absence of epistolary evidence or of poetic evidence seeming to
point both strongly and exclusively to her, it must be doubted
that they did indeed achieve any fullness of spiritual rapport.
Also, though the thought of marriage to this highly eligible and
attractive girl must surely have entered Robinson's mind, at the
same time there would have weighed against it, not only his
aversion to complicated activity in the outer world, but also his
pride of poverty, the intolerable fact that it would be impossible
for them to maintain a ménage without help from her family.
The intellectual aspect of the Woodland Girl's Brahmin tradition
was strongly in her favor. But the possibility that her family
might have been of that Boston fellowship that lived easily on
the income of its income, this weighed gravely against her.

Robinson's fundamental relationship with a lady of his desire, as we have inferred in the cases of Mabel Moore and Emma and shall see in at least one other case, was that of the ineffable fact of mutuality, whose appropriate ritual was the interchange of silent surges of "fearful triumph." In this relationship, which he assumed to be settled without need of further confirmation, any articulate word was not only unnecessary, it was a violation, a sacrilege. But short of absolute and silent mutuality, there were relationships where articulate expression was not only permissible but desirable. As was noticed with respect to some of Robinson's female friendships at the MacDowell Colony, he commonly deplored his conversational helplessness with ladies. Most of his worried attention during encounters with them would concentrate upon his unhappy silence and upon ways of breaking it. If and when some expression were finally formulated and delivered, its reference was not likely to be anything in the superficial scene. Rather it would be to Robinson's inner perception and dramatization of his present situation with relation to this lady here present, not with any purpose of instigating outer action, but merely as a creative gesture of the imagination, a poetic naming of a perceived truth. The epitome of such pronouncements was Robinson's sudden comment, already noticed, to Elizabeth Sparhawk-Jones at the MacDowell Colony after they had been lunching some minutes in silence: "The less I say, the more I feel." To an expectant lady with imagination, such a remark, combined perhaps with a straight glance of those huge dark-brown eyes, would strike with more overwhelming power than any literal declaration. In effect this guileless and appealingly helpless poet, this chivalrous champion of women and condemner of men who in any way humiliated them, became, where his ideal of love was less than wholly engaged, a dangerous flirt and philanderer, one who incited love in woman without any purpose beyond pleasantly beguiling the time!

By combined inference from observations from four disconnected sources—of varying degrees of credibility—it seems likely that something of the kind occurred between Robinson and his companion of the woodland walks. One credible comment has it that he made her a declaration of love, less than a proposal of

marriage, to which she was unable to respond in kind. Another
report that is no better than gossip has it that she was in love
with him. A better source, speaking long after the event, says
that when Robinson was charged with this he replied that she
was "very fanciful," meaning that she tended to romanticize her
feelings beyond actuality. An interesting general comment on
Robinson, made by one who knew both parties but without
specific reference to their experience together, is that he "wanted
to do all the loving," that the moment he felt any current returning he retreated. The same source said that "anything like personal contact was repugnant to him."

From these scattered bits we are left to our guesses. The one
high probability is that where there were so many wisps of
smoke there must have been fire, on one or both sides. In any
case the woodland walks ended. In at least five poems there may
be references to them or the companion of them. There is the
doubtful allusion in *Aunt Imogen,* which was in composition late
that summer of '98 but had plenty of "grief" in its own model
story at home:

> Some grief, like some delight,
> Stings hard but once: to custom after that
> The rapture or the pain submits itself
> . . . .

Suggestive in its piquancy is the sonnet *Another Dark Lady,*
which Robinson at a later time dashed off in twenty minutes in
a contest, and whose title would be a typical Robinsonian disguise for this blonde girl. The sestet sounds right:

> I cannot hate you, for I loved you then.
> The woods were golden then. There was a road
> Through beeches; and I said their smooth feet showed
> Like yours. Truth must have heard me from afar,
> For I shall never have to learn again
> That yours are cloven as no beech's are.

The family legend identifies with the Woodland Girl *The Tree
in Pamela's Garden,* with its humorous identification of Robinson

with Apollo; but equally respectable opinion attributes it to a friend of his, a supposed old maid, who had a happy affair with someone else:

> Pamela was too gentle to deceive
> Her roses. "Let the men stay where they are,"
> She said, "and if Apollo's avatar
> Be one of them, I shall not have to grieve."
> And so she made all Tilbury Town believe
> She sighed a little more for the North Star
> Than over men, and only in so far
> As she was in a garden was like Eve.
>
> Her neighbors—doing all that neighbors can
> To make romance of reticence meanwhile—
> Seeing that she had never loved a man,
> Wished Pamela had a cat, or a small bird,
> And only would have wondered at her smile
> Could they have seen that she had overheard.

Beyond these slight records, there is the possibly weightier one in the second part of *Annandale*, which will be noticed presently. And finally, there is the likelihood that twenty years later the Woodland Girl still survived to lay her "white and gold," for the duration of literature, over the figure of Emma on the throne of Guinevere.

Whatever the circumstance of the suspension of the woodland walks, probably in September, Robinson was not happy in his narrow escape. On October 12 he wrote Smith, "Everything has stopped for the time being and I am chiefly occupied in trying to figure out how long I can hold myself up on a foundation of abstractions." [5] But later in the letter he is easing back into composure in a state of exclusively idealistic love: "Today I am remarkably good natured, but tomorrow I may be reading *The Ring and the Book*. . . . Do you know I have a theory that Browning's life-long happiness with his wife is all humbug? The man's life was in his art, but he was big enough to make the world think otherwise." [6] A month later, in a letter to Hays Gardiner, Robinson is restored to his normal high contempt for the carnal aspect of human experience. "Donne doesn't seem to me to interpret much more than a sort of half-mystical sexual uneasiness and a rather uninteresting religious enthusiasm which seems to have been quite the thing in those days for a fellow who had raised the devil for thirty-five or forty years and so worked up an appetite for symbols."

The period now beginning, from the early fall of '98, in Robinson's twenty-ninth year, to July of 1905, was probably the one of which he later said, "For seven years I had ab-so-lute-ly nothing but the bottle." Besides getting along most or all of the time without any active love, he enjoyed almost none of the gratification of publication. Only two things of his appeared in magazines, both in the subworldly and non-paying *Harvard Monthly;* and Houghton Mifflin's subsidized edition of *Captain Craig* in 1902 came after so debased an "odyssey" of the Captain, and the response fell so far short of the recognition Robinson expected it would bring him, that it was a little worse than "ab-so-lute-ly nothing." On the practical side, the period became, after the first two years, one of gradual descent into want approaching squalor, a testing by hunger and outer failure of his determination to write poetry without benefit of either "ducats" or the "pleasures which are said to make up the happiness of life." In the October letter to Smith previously noticed he delivered one of his great understatements: "To be born with just one thing to live for, and that thing a relative impossibility, is to be born with certain disadvantages. . . ."[7] His one compensating benefit, the one glow in the lugubrious twilight, was friendship. During those seven years of lovelessness, literary neglect, and increasing poverty, his old friends watched him and gave him what little he would accept, and of the new friends who gathered round him several proved to be of the permanent fellowship.

Through '98 and '99 Robinson was getting enough from the estate to provide a meager subsistence. Nevertheless, the margin above want was thin. He wrote Betts that if he came to New York, "I expect to work most of my meals out of the ash cans that spot the landscape o' mornings between Fourth and Eighth Streets. I am told that those on Eighth are the more nourishing. . . ." [8] His friends had an eye out for "ducats." In December of '98 Willie Butler, who had financed *The Children of the Night,* offered him a job as nightwatchman in his father's store in Boston, and he was about to accept it when a seemingly more desirable opening appeared. Hays Gardiner had been trying to find him something at Harvard, and finally got him hired as a sort of long-legged office boy in "University 5," one of the rooms of the administration building, his duties to begin early in January. Robinson thought that the consequent slowing up of "The Pauper" would be a good thing. He wrote Betts: "I am a great believer in Parnassian pickle. . . . My ideal method of writing books of verse is to spend a year in getting together the first draft; let it soak six months; work on it another six months; soak it again—ditto; and then fix it up. This would mean one book every three years, which God knows is often enough." [9]

At Harvard, Robinson took an immediate dislike to President Eliot, who told him on first meeting that young men ought to marry. He always looked back on the job as the most degrading of anything he ever tried. The only comfort of that winter of '99 was as usual in terms of friendship. He made the acquaintance of Josephine Preston Peabody, poet and friend of Mrs. Richards, and of Daniel Gregory Mason. More dubiously, he struck up an acquaintance with Joseph Louis French, a ne'er-do-well currently functioning as a salesman for Badger, publisher of *The Children of the Night.* Without explanation, Robinson turned down the kind of respectable newspaper job he had once said he would accept. Through the influence of his friend Jimmy Barstow's sister, who lived in Kansas City, he was offered the literary editorship of the *Star,* and when he refused it Barstow took it himself.[10] The office boy position ended with the academic year, and Robinson wrote Smith, "Three months more of the life I have lived for the past half year would make an imbecile of me if not a corpse." [11] Later he wrote apologetically to Gardiner: "My performance was pretty bad, but you see I have only half a brain. You fellows who suffer from the disadvantage of having whole ones can hardly understand how it was possible for me to cut the figure I did."

After the college year ended, he stayed on in beloved Cambridge through the summer of '99. He tried for a civil service job and failed to get it.[12] In July he wrote Mason: "The octopus of superficial self-respect . . . refuses for some reason to take hold of me . . .

"I am in ridiculous good spirits just now, sending the Pauper [that is, *Captain Craig*] along at a rate that makes him red in the face, eating anything that comes along [that is, not eating much], drinking nothing unpermitted by the laws of Cambridge, and feeling every morning the joy of a liberated idiot for the thought that I am no longer a 'necessity' in University 5." [13] In August, again to Mason, he is so gay as to show signs of maturing out of his petty "pride" in matters involving his person: "I enclose a copy of Butler's photograph which may interest you as a harmless freak. I have a look that might lead one to think that I had just eaten the lining out of my own coffin, but that is the fault of an uncomfortable feel somewhere in my spinal column." [14] A little later, in September, he is still in a merry vein: "My spirit, like my feet, moves slowly but generates a good deal of momentum. When it gets fairly started something is bound to happen. . . .

"September is everything to me that June was to Lowell, though I don't ask nature to lay her warm, or rather cool, ears down on the earth. Or was it Heaven that had ears?" [15] About the same time he writes Smith that he is playing golf—"I can tear up the turf and occasionally send the ball whizzing for as many as fifty or sixty yards." [16]

A few days after he wrote this letter Dean died, probably in suicide from an overdose of morphine which he been accumulating from the allowances sent up to him from the drugstore.[17] Just as Robinson had been glad when his mother was released by death from the hell of the world, so it may be presumed that he was relieved when Dean escaped. It is interesting that in the later sonnet *How Annandale Went Out* and the much later poems *Annandale Again* and *The March of the Cameron Men*, he seems to justify euthanasia. Professor Nivison associates the sonnet specifically with Dean's death; which raises the question whether Robinson had not been wishing that Dean would die, for his own sake, perhaps by the method he used, for Win would have been privy to his getting the allotments from the store. Thus Robinson might have suffered a sort of sense of guilt in the matter, which could account for his lifelong preoccupation with the subject.

With Dean and both parents dead, with the estrangement from Herman keeping him from any usefulness to Emma and the children, and with the woodland walks apparently at an end, Robinson's emotional ties with Gardiner were finally broken. And with Dean's physical need of the drugstore gone, its value as the source of "ducats" was of little weight against Win's necessity to escape from the province into open civilization. He went up for the funeral, and heard Captain Craig's wish for "trombones" fulfilled in Dean's funeral procession behind the Knights Templers' band. He stayed in Winthrop two days, which offered the last known possibility of the encounter with Emma later reported in *London Bridge*, and which she is supposed to have said occurred in "about 1901." On the third day, in a drizzling rain, he left Gardiner, virtually forever. He returned to Cambridge, and thence, in that mid-October of '99, to New York, also virtually forever. From that time his only active connection with his home town was his fourth great correspondence, that with Laura Richards, which had begun in '97 [18] and lasted, weekly by her and biweekly by him, for over thirty-five years.

He first took a room on Washington Square, from which he was driven by "the competent bed-bug," and so joined Burnham in a clean boarding house at 71 Irving Place, where he found congenial company and had a fifty-cent picture of Beethoven in his tiny hall bedroom, "for the sake of having the presence of a fellow who did things without ears." [19] He met Clarence Stedman who had taken *Luke Havergal* and two or three other things to be "soused in anthological pickle," [20] and Stedman introduced him and Ridgely Torrence as "Torrence—and the Night After." [21] Early in April, 1900, he wrote Smith: ". . . I am a veritable volcano of assurance . . ." [22] And ten days later to Mason: ". . . I feel impelled to give you the dregs of my creative intelligence and to say that I am, as usual, a howling optimist. . . . I have been twice this spring to hear *Tristan und Isolde*, which I maintain to be the only opera, as such, ever written. All the rest of

them are abortions and monstrosities. . . ." [23] In May he finished
Captain Craig and sent him off on his first voyage.

In that summer of 1900 Robinson's new friend Craven Longstreth Betts took him into his apartment in Harlem, and he wrote
Mason: "I have Betts's word for it that when he sees me snoozing
in the morning, on my hospital cot, I look like the dog in Durer's
'Melancholy.' " [24] In August, Mason and William Vaughn Moody
were at Chocorua in New Hampshire. Robinson wrote Mason:
". . . I am glad to know that you and the man of odes [Moody]
are enjoying yourselves. . . .

"My chief recreation is riding to Bronxville on Sundays and
consuming Mr. Stedman's tobacco. . . . Sometimes we go to the
back lot behind the house, where we sit on ant hills and talk
about farming and what is Art. . . .

"I have just received a letter from Miss Peabody in which she
tells me that Moody has written a 'rousing' poem on Gloucester
Moors. If you think Moody has a stray copy of it in his jeans . . .
I wish you would tell him that I should like very much to be
honored." [25] Robinson never felt as close to Moody as he did to
the rest of his friends. He found his rhetorical pretentiousness
endlessly amusing—"There is a possibility of his growing up
someday and writing like Shakespeare." [26] At the same time he
thought he had talent and, as Hagedorn says, "he could not . . .
evade the thought that Moody was his one dangerous rival for
poetic supremacy in America." [27] He told Torrence about a walk
he had with Moody. "We had walked a long time saying nothing.
Suddenly I turned and looked at him, and found that he was looking at me. We found that we were watching each other. He
wanted to know what I was up to, and I wanted to know what
he was up to." [28] At some time in the summer of 1900, Robinson
received news of "the last smash in my western real estate"
which, as he wrote to Mason in September, "has left me guessing
a little, and I am amusing myself by trying to transform a draggle-
tailed poet into something practical." [29] He had not, however,
yet exhausted whatever was the last installment Herman had sent
him, for he was able in December to buy in the remaining copies
of *The Children of the Night* in Badger's bankruptcy proceed-

ings.[30] He was not destitute, but retrenchment did seem to be indicated, and instead of returning to Irving Place he and Burnham moved out to cheaper quarters in Yonkers.

Meanwhile Robinson had produced what he first thought would be two crops of poetry. In May he had sent off *Captain Craig* to Scribner's, who duly rejected it. It went off to Small, Maynard in Boston, who temporized for six months, and in December, being gently bullied by Mrs. Richards, they accepted it. During the previous summer as Betts's guest Robinson had finished *Aunt Imogen*—to Mason, "I did it in the rough two years ago when . . . I had a good mill-pond to look out on . . . Maybe I thought she ought to have drowned herself." [31] Besides, he had worked in his objective vein on *Isaac and Archibald,* in his musical vein on his "long-legged lyric" *Twilight Song,* and on short pieces to fill out what he intended to be his fourth volume, following *Captain Craig.* Through the winter in Yonkers he got this volume in penultimate shape, with *The Book of Annandale,* on which he had been working sporadically for four years, for title poem. This volume never materialized, but most of its contents were presently incorporated in the *Captain Craig* volume. These included eight subjective poems, namely *The Return of Morgan and Fingal, Cortège, The Woman and the Wife, Partnership, Sainte-Nitouche, The Book of Annandale, Aunt Imogen,* and *As a World Would Have It.*

Of these poems, the first is biographically unimportant as the account of a melodramatic incident in a storm that long before had involved the three Robinson brothers on Capitol Island. *Cortège* has been noticed as a declaration of the funereal error of the marriage of Emma to Herman. *The Woman and the Wife,* the first of the series of poems which Robinson successively believed to be "the best I have ever done or am likely to do," [32] is the dramatic portrayal of that error after it has been proven. The first of the two sonnets recalls Emma's premarital efforts to break the engagement between August, '88 and February, '90; and the second is Win's analysis of the situation between her and Herman in the years between '97 and 1900:

I—THE EXPLANATION

"You thought we knew," she said, "but we were wrong.
This we can say, the rest we do not say;
Nor do I let you throw yourself away
Because you love me. Let us both be strong,
And we shall find in sorrow, before long,
Only the price Love ruled that we should pay:
The dark is at the end of every day,
And silence is the end of every song.

"You ask me for one proof that I speak right,
But I can answer only what I know;
You look for just one lie to make black white,
But I can tell you only what is true—
God never made me for the wife of you.
This we can say, — believe me! . . . Tell me so!"

II—THE ANNIVERSARY

"Give me the truth, whatever it may be.
You thought we knew, now tell me what you miss:
You are the one to tell me what it is—
You are a man, and you have married me.
What is it worth tonight that you can see
More marriage in the dream of one dead kiss
Than in a thousand years of life like this?
Passion has turned the lock, Pride keeps the key.

"Whatever I have said or left unsaid,
Whatever I have done or left undone, —
Tell me. Tell me the truth. . . . Are you afraid?
Do you think that Love was ever fed with lies
But hunger lived thereafter in his eyes?
Do you ask me to take moonlight for the sun?"

This double sonnet is one of Robinson's clearest statements
of the dichotomy between passion and love which he still attributed to Emma. *Partnership,* as already noticed, makes the

same distinction, more poetically but less literally. So does *Sainte-Nitouche*, but with a difference. There the minister Vanderberg has practiced hypocrisy by having a mistress, equivalent to Robinson's hypocrisy in his secret love for his sister-in-law. Through the death of the mistress Vandenberg escapes the immediate, practical hypocrisy, as Robinson had done by leaving Gardiner. But in both cases the life without the beloved becomes simply another kind of hypocrisy, for now she is identified with ideal reality, opening the mystic way, "The dark and starry way that leads / Right upward and eternally." *Sainte-Nitouche* is an obscure poem, and bits of it are great poetry. Its biographical importance is in the question it raises as to whether the ecstasy of idealized love, the soul music that opens the "starry way," is not, after all, merely a function of passion, a "half truth" of which the other half is physical, while love is something of a different order. Here Robinson seems to be disassociating love not only from carnal expression but also from the "joy" of sublimated Eros, and identifying it with Αγαπη:

.   .   .   .   .   .

> The fight goes on, the triumph clings,
> And there is yet the unseen crown.
>
> But was it his? Did Vanderberg
> Find half truth to be passion's thrall,
> Or as we met him day by day,
> Was love triumphant, after all?

The distinction is carried farther in *The Book of Annandale*,[33] which is Robinson's first narrative containing whole passages of greatness, two or three passages that are the first since the best of the *Octaves* to belong in his final major list. In *Annandale* there is no passion at all. There is merely the quiet transport of Αγαπη in personal terms, very far removed from the violent, sublimated desire of *The Night Before* and even the *Octaves*. The same change is sometimes apparent in the style. While the highly emotional, subjective ring is still strong in some passages, in others it is already quieting into the detachment from which

Robinson in his maturity will present his autobiographical as
well as his objective material.

The story opens with Annandale's return to his empty bedroom after the funeral of his wife Miriam—supposedly representing Robinson's mother Mary—and he is troubled by his
failure to grieve for the pretty girl with whom he had lived
happily for five years. Occasionally during their matrimony he
had been aware of the abstraction of ideal love that was not
Miriam, but it had not disturbed him—

> the other face—
> The searching face, the eloquent, strange face—
> That with a sightless beauty looked at him
> And with a speechless promise uttered words
> That were not the world's words. . . .

Similarly, it had not been any conscious frustration that had made
him gradually accumulate a "book," presumably of poetry, his
private statement of truth, which he had eventually bound up in
red leather. It was not written with Miriam or anyone in mind
except that abstract face whose "searching . . . eloquent" quality
may suggest Emma's. Not Miriam or anyone had ever seen or
heard of the book.

The ideal quality of the love is emphasized by the fact that
before the death of Miriam, Annandale, so far as appears, had
never heard of one Damaris, now a five-year's widow. There is
no explanation and no account of his dropping in on her and
leaving her his private record. The conflict in the poem is provided by a promise Damaris had given to her dying husband,
Argan, that she would never love another man, a seemingly
anachronistic feature in a poem of Robinson's begun in '96 and
finished in 1900. Herman did elicit from Emma a specific promise
that she would not marry Win after his death, but according to
the Legend, and in all reasonable probability, this was several
years after 1900. Whether or not Herman had at some time baited
Win with the boast that he would get such a promise out of
Emma, Win by 1900 was enough aware of Herman's animosity
and jealousy to anticipate it.

With or without biographical basis, Damaris in the poem had made the promise to Argan. And so, the stranger Annandale dropped in on her, left her "the book" and departed, thereby causing her to fall in love with his "prophetic voice" in the poetry—not his physical voice—and so with "the man within the music." It is pointless to speculate whether the book represents *The Night Before* or *The Children of the Night*, but it does recall the talisman in *Partnership* which represents concretely, as this does abstractly, a joint spiritual achievement of man and woman.

It is worth noting that Damaris's promise had been simply never to "love" again. Nothing is said about marriage in the poem. The subject is mutual, idealized love, disembarrassed of any external action or of passionate derivation—Robinson still sees no essential difference between men and women in their experience of this central reality. For an appreciation of the calm glory of this poem, it is important to remember that it is not, as conventional expectation interprets it, a mere delicate love story ending in a marriage and two people living happily ever after. Robinson is not dreaming of the time when Herman's alcohol may carry him off, as Dean's morphine had carried him, leaving him and Emma free to marry. He is possessed by their idealistic love for its own sake, as it is for him, and as he believes it is for her, at this moment. The development of the poem is the gradual emergence of this perfect love in the woman, against the weight of the promise she had made.

Damaris's description of the book which released her from

> The grave-deluded, flesh-bewildered fear
> Which men and women struggle to call faith,

is one of Robinson's most personal outcries. It is his profession of his own ideal of poetry and, at a time that was his lowest for neglect, it is his declaration of what he believes that his own work at long last is fated to become. In his humility he is oblivious to the fact that in this very passage, which indeed the world would not recognize for a long time, he has realized his hope. Phonetically, it is prophetic of his supreme achievements, in *Merlin* and *The Man Who Died Twice*, where major material rolls in waves of the back vowels *o, u, ah,* and *aw,* and the liquid consonants:

> They were eternal words, and they diffused
> A flame of meaning that men's lexicons
> Had never kindled; they were choral words
> That harmonized with love's enduring chords
> Like wisdom with release; triumphant words
> That rang like elemental orisons
> Through ages out of ages; words that fed
> Love's hunger in the spirit; words that smote;
> Thrilled words that echoed, and barbed words that clung
> . . . .

In *The Book of Annandale* Robinson still implicitly distinguishes between passion and love in female experience, but he separates love entirely from its passionate sources and assimilates it to the selflessness of Αγαπη. Also, he here begins to show, for the first time, an awareness of the difference in texture between male and female love. Subjectively, Damaris's vision is of herself as the fulfillment of the man's vision of truth and beauty:

> There were the words that he had made for her,
> For her alone. The more she thought of them
> The more she lived them, and the more she knew
> The life-grip and the pulse of warm strength in them.
> They were the first and last of words to her,
> . . .

the assurance that he had set down his idea of her perfection to *him* even before he had seen or heard of her. Objectively, her awakening is not to an abstract, masculine perception of ideal reality but to a concrete, feminine version of it, not to the music of the poetry but to "the man within the music," a specific person.

And yet in 1900 when Robinson wrote this, he still believed that the woman's perception of the whole person is ideal and not sensuous. It is of the reality of someone who is physicaly absent, a reality that the woman, like the man, experiences alone:

               The shield of love
Was clean, and she had paid enough to learn
How it had always been so. And the truth,
Like silence after some far victory,
Had come to her, and she had found it out
As if it were a vision, a thing born
So suddenly! — just as a flower is born,
Or as a world is born—so suddenly.

Here, in this final receipt of Grace, we have, I think, the first
intimation in Robinson's poetry of that quality of primeval silence
"where nothing had occurred," the *tabula rasa*, the emptiness
which later surrounds the descent of Grace upon mankind in the
person of Lancelot, also silent and alone.

Robinson's exclusive concern with the idealized love of the
principals individually and separately is evident in his indifference to the question of their possible subsequent marriage. Having dealt with Damaris in ideal terms, he paid no more attention
to her and her matrimonial prospects. Instead, in his next book,
The Town Down the River, he disposes of Annandale in *How
Annandale Went Out* by means of euthanasia, and if we think of
Damaris at all in connection with that poem, it is hardly in terms
of an "ever-after" happy marriage. Years later, in *Annandale
Again*, Robinson notifies us that there was indeed a short marriage, and that Annandale's final suffering was brought on by an
automobile accident. Whatever the motive of the late poem was,
it had no relation to the original poem and its action which was
laid in an ideal region where there is neither marriage nor giving
in marriage.

In this poem, the extreme maidenly delicacy and reticence
with which Damaris finally awakens provides a hint that here,
as elsewhere, Robinson was not portraying one person or one
experience in a particular character and situation, but was reaching out for whatever material would serve his dramatic need.
In general it is to be presumed that Emma and her experience
is at the foundation of his love stories, and she is obviously here
in the promise not to love again; also she is probably here in
that "searching . . . eloquent . . . face." Nevertheless, the im-

palpable daintiness of the budding of Damaris's love seems virginal. We recall that, whether "the book" was *The Torrent* or *The Children,* Robinson first showed it as a *fait accompli* to the young and sensitive Woodland Girl; and from that time she remained both emotionally and critically possessed by his verse.

In *The Book of Annandale* Robinson moves towards both an objective style for autobiographical material and the concept of calm and selfless love. In *Aunt Imogen* he associates the latter with his long settled doctrine of fate and carries it almost all the way to Αγαπη in its universal sense of the love of mankind. Facing the fact that, like her creator and avuncular prototype, she must dedicate herself to nieces and nephews instead of to children of her own, she awakens to the reality that

> she was born to be Aunt Imogen.
> Now she could see the truth and look at it;
> Now she could make stars out where once had palled
> A future's emptiness; now she could share
> With others—ah, the others! — to the end
> The largess of a woman who could smile
> . . . .

And on a parallel line of growth, Robinson in *As a World Would Have It,* where Alcestis speaks for his mother in her complete devotion to his father, comes in sight of the full glory of woman's love, absolute and unconditioned, integrating physical and imaginative union in one transcendent fact:

> "I would have given everything? — gone down
> To Tartarus — to silence? Was it that?
> I would have died? I would have let you live? —
> And was it very strange?"

In the four poems just noticed, out of the eight subjective ones to be part of the *Captain Craig* volume, Robinson seemed on the verge of the mature resolution of two of his lifelong themes. In particular he glimpsed the integrity of female love where passion and selflessness are combined, and in general he came in sight of the ultimately satisfying reality of Αγαπη where there is no passion and no self at all. There he stood in 1901. And yet for

successive reasons, some of which could be laid to fate and some
to his own backsliding from idealism towards respectability, he
hesitated here. Not until thirteen years later did he again pro-
claim the vision of selflessness that he had glimpsed in 1900 and
1901.

Two sordid blows of fate had been gathering through the
previous winter. Having accepted *Captain Craig* in December,
Small, Maynard welshed on their acceptance a couple of months
later, but couldn't find the manuscript. The fact was that one of
their editors had left it in what Robinson elsewhere called a "house
of seclusion" and had forgotten it. Come spring, he returned and
found that the madam, more responsible than he, had kept it for
him. So the *Captain* went home to his creator, and all was to do
again. It was during or just following this juncture that Robinson
did the most cruel thing of his life. Old Alfred Louis, the very
Captain in person, had become intolerably importunate, not only
of Robinson's small treasure, but even worse, of his time and
always helpless sympathy. Robinson turned him from his own
hall-bedroom door and forbade him to return. His confession was
in terms of a contrapositive: "I have kicked my real self out of
the way and done a thing that I shall always regret but shall
never be able to consider quite unjustifiable under the circumstances." [34]

Robinson's dismissal of Louis, uniquely cruel in his experience, might well have been related to descending impecuniousness and gathering despair. The news from Gardiner was all
bad. In February the stock of the drugstore was transferred from
Mary Robinson's to Dean's estate, and because of debts to be
paid, no distribution was yet forthcoming. The last of Herman's
western lands and stock in land companies had failed to sell and
fetch Win the installment whose expectation had caused him to
write Betts early in the winter, "I have good reason to suppose
that my affairs will be in better shape before long." [35] By March
they were in precisely no shape at all, and he moved to a dingy
cubicle in a crumbling brownstone at 450 West 23d Street because the owner of the house, in gratitude for a personal favor,
told Robinson to take the room and pay the rent whenever he
felt like it. At about the same time Robinson, parading spiritual

self-assurance to compensate for the lack of practical assurance in Gardiner, and feeling no doubt that he spoke with authority in the matter of triangles, wrote his friend Mason some composed, grandfatherly advice. Mason was involved in a triangle which also was based on a sister-in-law. Said Robinson:

If you go to Paris you will have at least the satisfaction of knowing that you have made a definite move in the matter . . . the very question of test and probation . . . comes to me now in the light of something like a duty. [Compare Robinson's departure from Gardiner.] You will say to yourself that I am thinking only of you, perhaps, and I assure you that I do not forget that there is the other. . . . The man always gets along somehow, and the woman knows it. . . . When two people are sure of each other, as you are, perhaps it is not so much a question of what one of you can bear as it is of how the other is going to suffer while he is bearing it, and . . . I suppose there is nothing better or less emotional to be said than that she must look on it as the price she has to pay for the right to believe in the possibility of a great happiness. . . ." [36]

Apparently, Robinson believed that he had left Gardiner with a clear understanding between "two people [who] are sure of each other."

In 1901 the situation in Gardiner was approaching its all-time low, in personal as well as in financial terms. The pattern of Herman's and Emma's life was semiannual migration between the Robinson house in Gardiner and the Shepherd cottage on Capitol Island. But Herman was still away a great deal on errands supposedly beneficial to the estate, and probably consuming much of its vanishing capital in legitimate if unprofitable "administration expenses." When he was at home there was increasingly bitter tension, and the little girls, ten, eight, and five in 1900, were old enough to carry into maturity the memory of bickering between their parents, sometimes loud enough to wake them at night. Understanding nothing of it at first, they learned with the passing years that the disagreements often involved a lady named "Madame Cliquot" who turned out to be a euphemism for alcohol.

A full understanding of the state of continuing crisis in Gardiner after 1900 would be useful as bearing on the understanding, if any, between Emma and Win after he went away. But the evidence is meager, inferential, and sometimes contradictory. There is said to have been a correspondence, now lost, running both ways between Emma and Win in New York, and it is possible that this might account for Robinson's knowledge of conditions and incidents between Emma and Herman which he recorded in verse probably written at this time though published later. One reason for attributing *London Bridge, Eros Turannos,* and *The Clinging Vine* to this period is that there is a passionate subjectivity in them which is comparable to the same quality in the *Octaves* and the earlier love poetry. Also there is in these three poems an unrelieved contempt for Herman which is softened in *The Unforgiven,* in *Bewick Finzer,* and *Bokardo* of the next period, and is qualified by compassion, objectivity, and recognition of Herman's virtues in *Flammonde, Nimmo,* and all of the later poems in which he figures.

Besides Herman's general state of defeat, with the necessary recourse of his perfectionist but resourceless soul to "Madame Cliquot" and bitterness, he was both harassed by Emma's upbraiding of him and gnawed by jealousy of her. In *The Whip* he attributes his final collapse to her having had a "lover." Years later, Cavender's murder of his wife was due to jealous suspicion. In the terrible *London Bridge* the wife feels compelled to confess to her husband, "Yes, I met him, and I talked with him—today." The "him" might have been the man she almost married before Herman appeared; but Herman's sneering reference to her friend as a "genius" fits Win and not the other. Also, Emma, years later, contributed to the Legend that the poem dealt with an actual meeting with Win, "about 1901." All the probabilities are against this recollection as to date. There is no grain of evidence that Robinson went to Gardiner in or about 1901, and in the impoverished years from 1900 through 1904 he would not have taken the expensive trip without strong cause. It would seem likely, either that Emma later fabricated the "meeting" with Win, consciously or unconsciously, out of a sympathetic letter, or—what is more probable—that the meeting occurred at an earlier date, almost any time in '98 or during the three days in the

fall of '99 when Win was in Gardiner for Dean's funeral. Also,
the earlier dates are more persuasive because of Herman's reference in the poem to an opulence which was almost gone by
1901. The actual incident and dialogue of the poem are presumably all of the poet's contrivance.

Whatever the facts, the importance of *London Bridge* is the
revelation of Win's attitude: his contempt for Herman's insensi-
tivity, and his belief about Emma's feelings. On the one hand he
assumes that she loves him, Win, at least in the old spiritual
fashion:

> For I have heard the stars of heaven, and they were nearer
>   still.
>
> .   .   .   .
>
> For their music on my heart, though you may freeze it, will
>   fall always,
> Like summer snow that never melts upon a mountain-top.

And, on the other hand, he believes that she hates Herman,
that she considers herself one of those

>   women who are giving
> All they have in holy loathing to a stranger all their lives
>
> .   .   .   .

Incidentally, Herman apparently did keep in his desk a pistol
such as the one the husband threatened the wife with in the
poem. This flourish might exemplify crudely Herman's destructive "satanic sort of kink." Besides *Flammonde*, it is alleged in
Nimmo, on the whole an affectionate poem about Herman, but
with the qualification:

> The painter put the devil in those eyes,
> Unless the devil did, and there he stayed;
> And then the lady fled from paradise,
> And there's your fact. The lady was afraid.

Avon's Harvest is exclusively a study of this perverse element in
Herman. And finally, in *Exit*, Herman's obituary, Win suggests,

> May we who are alive be slow
> To tell what we shall never know.

In the gathering estrangement between Emma and Herman,
he was alcoholic, bitter, jealous, and possibly a little fiendish.
The first hint of Emma's alienation is her attempt at adjustment
to Herman's absences in the summer, leaving her alone in the
cottage on Capitol Island. *Eros Turannos*, with its "stairway"
down the cliff in the great last stanza, is the only poem of large
caliber, before the later, book-length poems, that came out of
the tension at this time:

> She fears him, and will always ask
> What fated her to choose him;
> She meets in his engaging mask
> All reasons to refuse him;
> But what she meets and what she fears
> Are less than are the downward years,
> Drawn slowly to the foamless weirs
> Of age, were she to lose him.
>
> Between a blurred sagacity
> That once had power to sound him,
> And Love, that will not let him be
> The Judas that she found him,
> Her pride assuages her almost,
> As if it were alone the cost.—
> He sees that he will not be lost,
> And waits and looks around him.
>
> . . . .
>
> The falling leaf inaugurates
> The reign of her confusion;
> The pounding wave reverberates
> The dirge of her illusion;
> And home, where passion lived and died,
> Becomes a place where she can hide,
> While all the town and harbor side
> Vibrate with her seclusion.
>
> . . . .
>
> Meanwhile we do no harm; for they
> That with a god have striven,

Not hearing much of what we say,
Take what the god has given;
Though like waves breaking it may be,
Or like a changed familiar tree,
Or like a stairway to the sea
Where down the blind are driven.

Then, in *London Bridge*, there is the basic trouble, the sensitive woman's desperation with the coarse-minded businessman:

"Do you conceive, with all your smooth contempt of every feeling,
Of hiding what you know and what you must have known before?
Is it worth a woman's torture to stand here and have you smiling,
With only your poor fetish of possession on your side?
No thing but one is wholly sure, and that's not one to scare me;
When I meet it I may say to God at last that I have tried."

.   .   .   .

"Will you tell me what intrinsic and amazing sort of nonsense
You are crowding on the patience of a man who gives you—this?
Look around you and be sorry you're not living in an attic,
With a civet and a fish-net, and with you to pay the rent."

.   .   .   .

"For you have taught me more than hides in all the shelves of knowledge
Of how little you found that's in me and was in me all along.
I believed, if I intruded nothing on you that I cared for,
I'd be half as much as horses,—and it seems that I was wrong;
I believed there was enough of earth in me, with all my nonsense
Over things that made you sleepy, to keep something still awake;

.   .   .   .

Is there anything in all your pedigrees and inventories
With a value more elusive than a dollar's?"

Following the quarrel of *London Bridge*, there is the mutual, quiet desperation of *The Unforgiven*, probably written later.

And then, back on Capitol Island, there occurs, in Robinson's opinion, the separation and final descent of the cold in *The Clinging Vine*:

"Be calm? And was I frantic?
    You'll have me laughing soon.
I'm calm as this Atlantic,
    And quiet as the moon;
I may have spoken faster
    Than once, in other days;
For I've no more a master,
    And now—'Be calm,' he says.

"Fear not, fear no commotion,—
    I'll be as rocks and sand;
The moon and stars and ocean
    Will envy my command;
No creature could be stiller
    In any kind of place
Than I . . . No, I'll not kill her;
    Her death is in her face.

.   .   .   .   .

"If she were the whole story,
    If worse were not behind,
I'd creep with you to glory,
    Believing I was blind;

.   .   .   .   .

"But you—you came clear-sighted,
    And found truth in my eyes;
And all my wrongs you've righted
    With lies, and lies, and lies.

"You've killed the last assurance
    That once would have me strive
To rouse an old endurance
    That is no more alive.

.   .   .   .   .

"No more—I'll never bear it.
I'm going. I'm like ice.
My burden? You would share it?
Forbid the sacrifice!
Forget so quaint a notion,
And let no more be told;
For moon and stars and ocean
And you and I are cold."

The charge here is the only hint, I think, of Herman's having
been interested in another woman—except "Madame Cliquot."
It is probably fictitious, and, as Emma states in the poem, the
point is unimportant in comparison with the other incompati-
bilities. About fifteen years later, in *Nimmo*, a poem sympathetic
with Herman, Robinson implies the permanence of Emma's
coldness to him:

The calm of men forbidden to forget
The calm of women who have loved and changed.

From the point of view of Robinson's own relationship with
Emma, the first question about her coldness to Herman after
1900 is what it signified as to her feelings towards Win. And the
second and more important question, whose answer may or may
not be the same as the first, is what he believed it signified. As
to the fact of her feelings, she seems to have made contradictory
revelations to two confidants conformable to their different respective expectations. Agreeing in most things, these reports
together comprise the Legend of Emma that is in the main accredited here. But, diverging upon the love theme, they founded,
within the body of the Legend, what may be called an Orthodox
Account and a Dissenting Account. Somewhere between them
runs Robinson's own shifting interpretation of Emma's feelings,
providing the central personal theme of his own drama. And,
reflected variously in all of these accounts, there is the fourth
one which is the truth and which biography must try to decipher.

According to the Orthodox Account, Win was always Emma's
great and single love, beginning in the winter of '88. The mar-

riage to Herman in '90 represented at first a superficial infatuation. After five or six years, in which the cold descended, it
became a round of duty. And finally, after about 1900, it was an
exercise in pity. Meanwhile, from the time of the end of the
infatuation in the mid-nineties, Emma was "entirely faithful to
Win," by which is implied the virtual end of the marriage.

In contradiction of this, the Dissenting Account holds that
Herman was Emma's single, lifelong love, that the apparent
coldness of the later period represented her superficial resentment
of his drinking, but that there was no change in her basic attachment, that her affection for Win was never more than big-
sisterly—"They loved each other but they were never in love."
This view would seem to conform to normal expectation in such
cases, namely that a woman who has first known a man as her
much younger puppy lover can never quite see him in any other
role.

In spite of the apparent irreconcilability of these two interpretations of Emma's feelings, I shall in due course attempt to
draw the inference that the truth borrows something from each
of them. For the present, the important observation is that Robinson himself, perhaps beginning with Emma's change toward
Herman in the late nineties, and certainly by the time of the
climax ten years later, believed that her love had returned to
him, although—contrary to the Orthodox Account—it had left
him in the meantime. As indicated in *As a World Would Have It,*
he was beginning to outgrow his notion of a dichotomy in women
between spiritual "soul music" and physical desire. Perhaps the
first record of his maturing view with respect to Emma is the
title of *Eros Turannos* and the reference there to "Love that will
not let him be / The Judas that she found him." Then comes the
freezing and loathing of Herman in *The Clinging Vine* and *London Bridge,* which to Win now means the end of a former complete love. And finally, first intimated in the music of "the stars
in heaven" in *London Bridge,* and later confirmed for him by the
action of 1909, as recorded in *Lancelot,* comes his belief that her
complete love is now his.

Remembering Robinson's later statement that he set down his
great love in Guinevere, one may wonder whether he did not

find in the situation in the first decade of the twentieth century
a suggestion of the second phase in *Lancelot,* the sixth and
seventh sections, where Guinevere, besieged with Lancelot in
Joyous Gard, begs him to cut their way out and carry her off to
France, but Lancelot instead returns her to Arthur, whom she
hates, under the safe conduct of Rome. Not that Emma, whose
surest motive was always duty, would ever have proposed to
Win that they make a break, or would have acceded if he had
proposed it. But in this situation where he was at least partially
convinced that she loved him and loathed Herman with whom
she was forced by convention to live, Win must have suffered
occasional inchoate impulses involving the plume and the white
horse, always dissolving under his combined sense of propriety,
of his poverty with the three little girls to be taken care of, and
of the demands of his calling. He must sometimes have been
swept by violent waves of sadness and self-blame when he
thought of her valiancy up there in Gardiner, probably loving him
and yet performing as the dutiful wife of Herman, which is to say
King Arthur and the husband in *London Bridge.* Seventeen years
later, this sadness, with its pity and its touch of shame, may well
have confessed itself through Guinevere in that second act of
Lancelot:

> "Am I so old
> And dull, so lean and waning, or what not,
> That you must hurry away to grasp and hoard
> The small effect of time I might have stolen
> From you and from a Light that where it lives
> Must live forever? Where does history tell you
> The Lord himself would seem in so great haste
> As you for your perfection? . . .

> .   .   .   .

> "If I were God," she said,
> "I should say, 'Let them be as they have been.
> A few more years will heap no vast account
> Against eternity, and all their love
> Was what I gave them. They brought on the end
> Of Arthur's empire . . .

> .   .   .   .

but they knew not what they did—

.   .   .   .

For it was I who gave them to each other.'
If I were God, I should say that to you."

In 1909, Herman's alcoholism and the freezing tension between him and Emma were the harbingers of the still distant
climax of the play. But the financial crisis and debacle were then
and there. Perhaps on the insistence of the bank which held notes
against it, Mary Robinson's estate, formerly Edward's, was given
a final appraisal in January, 1901, and this was apparently part
of its winding up, for it does not appear again in the probate
records. The appraisal showed a value in the estate of $6,740 in
securities, besides the house. But no obligations are set out, and
the chances are that the bank held notes in approximately this
amount which Herman as administrator had put in from time to
time in order to raise money for distribution between himself
and Win. In any case, this sum vanishes from the record, and
subsequent evidence makes it doubtful that any penny of it ever
reached the poet in New York, who now for the first time faced
actual destitution.[37]

In February, a month after the appraisal of their mother's
estate, that of Dean, now dead over a year, was created on petition of Herman, also signed by Win in New York.[38] The stock
of the drugstore, which had appeared on Mary's appraisal at its
original cost of $2,700, was transferred to Dean's estate, pre-
sumably in the winding up of Mary's, and became its only appreciable asset. The administrator appointed was one Henry
Sewall Webster, a considerable personage in Gardiner, not only
a former judge of probate but also a poet, a former member of
Caroline Swan's poetry group where young Win Robinson must
have observed him well. As usual Win contributes the only light
touch in those dark days of final liquidation. He wrote Mrs.
Richards a little later that his "skirt-crazed reprobate John
Evereldown" was drawn from John Tarbox, a local reprobate
indeed, plus "a . . . projection of H. S. Webster, Esq." [39]

Having moved in March to his dismal cell on far West 23d
Street in New York, Robinson suffered there his second attack of

grippe that winter, and on April 2 he wrote *The Growth of "Lorraine,"* [40] perhaps recalling the pathetic "damsel" who had liked him ten years before in Boston, but no doubt revealing also his weariness with his own "worn-out, cast-out flesh." In July he is frying in his little oven, having through poverty declined Mason's invitation to join him on the Cape. In his letters he is still his old "imperturbable" self—"I am not quite so damned lazy as my friends think. I am simply incomplete and made up as far as I am made at all of what must have been left over after the manufacture of sixteen or seventeen other fellows. . . . By this description, if by no other, I am a man of parts. . . ." [41]

In the same letter there is hope of relief from the heat in the revelation that a "good fellow," certainly Betts, has invited him to occupy his empty apartment in Harlem "again." And on July 27 there stirred hope of more substantial relief in the fact that Administrator Webster of Dean's estate sold the stock of the drugstore in Gardiner for $2,400, representing only a $300 loss from the original investment. [42] On August 15 Win got a first bite of $100 from the distribution of these proceeds, and on the thirtieth he got $400 more. In September, back at West 23d Street, he wrote Mason out of opulence, recalling the time when "I spent two dollars of a final four for a couple of opera tickets—to the peanut gallery of course." Now he has just committed the "moral crime" of buying a writing table and it makes him feel "much better." [43] Earlier in September he had written Mason: "I look ahead either two hours, like the wise men of old, or at least five years." [44]

In the August letter he reported that *Captain Craig* had just come back for the fifth time, but he was still "on the march." At this point Hays Gardiner stepped into the picture and that fall sent Robinson's proposed fourth volume, still entitled *The Book of Annandale,* to Scribner's who rejected it with their usual alacrity. Gardiner and Mrs. Richards then went to work on Houghton Mifflin, and by the spring of 1902 had worn them down into the acceptance, under a financial guarantee, of a volume to be entitled *Captain Craig* but to contain also much of the material of the proposed *Book of Annandale* volume. The book came out in October, and was successful enough so that the publishers made a second run of two hundred fifty copies. But the notices were cool and patronizing. The *Captain* whom Robinson had expected to put him on the literary map did nothing of the sort, and the slow sordidness of his two years' adventures among publishers left his creator at what was his spiritual, as it presently became his financial, nadir.

The $500 he had got from Dean's estate in August, 1901, apparently had done him through that fall, and with further increments of $60 in January and $133.25 in March, through the following winter. But the rate and amounts of the payments were now decreasing. The March payment must have all gone to arrears. So must the early April payments in the diminishing amounts of $40 and $14.86. And then the checks from Gardiner stopped entirely for seven months. On November 5 he got $25, and on the same day another payment of $12.54. And, so far as appears, the latter summary amount represented the last benefit he ever enjoyed from the once considerable fortune of Edward Robinson.

Beginning in that fall of 1902, Robinson had no apparent means of support for about a year, and he entered the long valley of borrowing from which he never entirely emerged until after the success of *Tristram* twenty-five years later. He ate on fifty cents a day, and became expert in the use of the free lunch in saloons, thus partly killing two needs with one nickel. About this time he met James Fraser the sculptor, but the great promise in that event was not fulfilled until after this darkest time was over. Sometimes his dinner consisted of a roll. Once in the Old Homestead Restaurant on Eighth Avenue a waiter was so touched by his looks that he offered to lend him two dollars. He tried to save up money for a new pair of pants, but when he almost had it he happened to pass the Metropolitan and spent it all on *Tristan und Isolde.* He wrote Mrs. Richards, proposing to end their correspondence because they had nothing in common and he probably would never see her again—she of course permitted no such self-punishment. It was probably at some time during the ensuing winter of 1902/3 that he said to Ridgely Torrence, "I guess my trouble is that I was born with my skin inside out."

It is not easy to explain events in Gardiner during that year of 1903 on any ground except Herman's entire loss of responsibility. Even in 1901 and '02 it is hard to imagine where he got the money for his family's support, and for his own alcoholism, which was now complete, unless some of it was provided by David Clark Shepherd, his father-in-law. By 1903 he had finished the last of his mother's and brother's estates, and there remained only the house, which either was still in his mother's name or, if her estate had been closed, belonged jointly to him and Win. Early in the year he sold it for $2,200, being $300 less than its appraisal two years before, and $1,800 less than his father had paid for it in 1870. After the sale he instructed his twelve-year-old daughter Ruth to write her Uncle Win that it was sold, to tell him that he, Herman, was very tired and that he would write him later. Presumably he did, but there is no evidence that Win ever got any share of the proceeds. This was probably the basis of his direct charge against Herman in *Bokardo*, "Your last flight went rather low," and in *Old King Cole* he implied a general charge of misappropriation against his two brothers, including long-dead Dean.

After the sale, the family moved up Danforth Street nearer the cemetery and rented a house, where Herman was reported as down and out. In October Mr. Shepherd died, probably from a fall while pruning his apple trees, and Emma and Herman moved the family into the Farmingdale house. Some of the contents of the former Robinson house were moved there, and Win's box of manuscripts, including the *Antigone*, went into the attic and was set by one of the chimneys. An incident occurred which reminded Herman that he was not welcome to all of Emma's family, whereupon, being in his thirty-ninth year and his hair gray, he packed up and went down to Capitol Island in what turned out to be a permanent desertion of Emma.

Thereafter Herman lived sometimes in the Shepherd cottage on the promontory above the sound of Cornwall water, sometimes, especially in the winter, in a boathouse on the back cove, probably because it was easier to heat, possibly because he did not feel comfortable in the cottage now owned by the heirs of David Shepherd. With respect to his mother-in-law no such uneasiness was justified, for Mrs. Shepherd took the trip down to

Boothbay Harbor and return for the sole purpose of begging him to come back to the Farmingdale house. But he would not come. His only known sources of subsistence were the dwindling proceeds of the house, and his facility as a fisherman and clam-gatherer. In the years following 1903 he was sometimes seen peddling lobsters in the market in Gardiner, possibly Flam-monde's and Richard Cory's last appearance in their native town. Probably in 1904, when he was approaching forty, he faced his demon of alcohol and, mostly alone, began the one known inner fight of his life.

Meanwhile, Mr. Shepherd's estate, through confusion in the consolidation of his Knickerbocker Ice Company with another company, had turned out to be only $9,000 besides the house. On this amount and Emma's expert dressmaking, which she now undertook professionally, she and her mother and the three girls lived until 1909, with occasional small and unreliable contributions from Herman. Sometimes she took a loaf of bread or a cake or batch of doughnuts down to him in his solitude on Capitol. According to the Orthodox Account, this was the work of pity. According to the Dissenting Account, it was the work of love.

In New York, Win didn't have even the tag-end of the estate, or clams and lobsters, or visiting pastry cooks to live on. Later he wrote Betts: "Sometimes I think the funniest thing in my whole life, and pretty much all of it is funny, is my staying alive since 1903—I mean since 1902." [45] Through the summer of 1903 he stayed in his hall bedroom on West 23d Street. Frequently his friends took him out to dinner. From the street they could see his back in his top floor window, just sitting there. Late into every night his neighbor in the adjoining room heard the slow creak of his rocker. What he was doing, of course, was not troubling about himself, probably not even about Emma or Herman, except as material for poetry. What he was doing was composing on his little pad, pursuing his calling. "The great art of life," he wrote Mason, "is to suffer without worrying." [46] Between 1900 and 1905 he sold not a line to a periodical. One dis-tinguished magazine editor asked him not to trouble to send him any more. It was probably in this period that he wrote of Claver-

ing that he "clung to phantoms and to friends / And never came
to anything."

In the fall of 1903 Burnham's brother, an engineer, found
Robinson a job at two dollars a day as timekeeper in the subway
construction, and from then on he spent the working day underground, mostly in the dark but for a smoking lantern. His humor,
fortified by sustenance, made the somewhat pathetic best of the
situation. In January of 1904 he wrote Miss Peabody: "Think of
me only as a well-meaning and well-wishing friend with one little
wheel somewhere in back of his cranium that never got started.
It may start yet. And then there may be some fireworks. Fizz!
I don't know." [47] In the same month he wrote Hays Gardiner one
of his most gallant little notes: "After thanking you most sincerely for your last letter I can only say that I believe in the
subway—for the present at any rate. If my mind is not large
enough to include a few months of monotony and dirt, surely it
is not large enough for you to think about. As for money, let me
answer you that I am getting along very well. —If I were to
come out of my hole now I should feel that I was making the
mortal blunder of my life." [48] In May, Joseph French, formerly
of Badger, now one of Robinson's failure friends, and a sponge
when there was anything to soak up, got published in the *Sunday
World* an article with the heading, "A Poet in the Subway—
Hailed as a genuius by men of letters, Edwin Arlington Robinson
has to earn his living as a timekeeper." "In a circle in the center
was a reproduction of a photograph of Robinson; on the left,
a facsimile of the title page of *Captain Craig*; on the right . . .
a drawing of a man in an ulster and a black hat, carrying a
lantern." [49]

In August he was laid off and came out of his hole, and in
the light his humor soared. He wrote Miss Peabody that he had
just taken a ride over his old rails. "Dark and stuffy, but smooth
and otherwise satisfactory. . . . On the whole, I'm rather glad
that I built it." [50] And in response to an invitation of Gardiner's,
his eternal self-belief and his gallantry:

Thank you for your letter and for your very friendly invitation. Under other conditions I should surely take advantage of

it, but I am sorry to say that it will be out of the question this time—for reasons that I need not go into at greater length than to say that I am not travelling at present. I got out of the subway a month ago . . . and I am willing to say that I am rather better on the whole for the experience. . . . Sometimes I . . . look with envy at any fellow who has an enthusiasm for anything so practical . . . as running a peanut stand or swallowing swords. If I were to go into the peanut business I should burn more than I sold. If I were to swallow a sword the results might be more satisfactory to . . . my friends, though I might not enjoy the process any more than I did the subway. I write this in the greatest good humor. . . . For, among other things, I know that I can keep on waiting for some time longer in the dark. . . . The present day disregard of everything save dynamics and dollars does not worry me in the least. If I happen to be ground to pieces in the hopper, I still have faith in the pieces. One of the things that gives me faith is the knowledge that I have had a few friends like you.[51]

At the time Robinson wrote this letter, in September of 1904, his "Unseen Powers" were already astir, specifically in the person of Henry Richards, Jr., who was teaching English at Groton and imbuing his students with enthusiasm for *The Children of the Night;* Kermit Roosevelt, son of the President, was one of the students. But Robinson, having no hint or immediate hope of any miracle by his "palladium," lapsed into the old life with no means of visible support except a landlord who told him to pay the rent when he "got goddam good and ready" and his friends who dined him.

At an uncertain date, probably in December because of the subsequent reference to the "cold," [52] one of the latter festivals was toward. Robinson and Burnham were just emerging from his quarters at 450 West 23d bent on dinner when one of the Unseen Powers, this a malign one, appeared. On the sidewalk, the unannounced, big, gray-haired, pale and haggard man who stopped and stared at them was Herman. He was probably sober, being already in grim war with his demon, and he probably had a slight cough. He was probably silent and surly in what had

become his customary mien. Having come down from Capitol
Island, he must have been in some slight funds, and any guess
will do as to what he and Win and Burnham did then. But in
course, after dinner, Herman and Win were alone in the latter's
tiny bedroom on the top floor. *Bokardo,* one of the most literally
autobiographical of the poems, takes up the account.[53] Win leads
off with affectionate welcome, an invitation to share his diminutive quarters, and follows with the home truths:

> Well, Bokardo, here we are;
>   Make yourself at home.
> Look around—you haven't far
>   To look—and why be dumb?
> Not the place that used to be,
>   Not so many things to see;
> But there's room for you and me.
>   And you—you've come.
>
> Talk a little; or, if not,
>   Show me with a sign
> Why it was that you forgot
>   What was yours and mine.
> Friends, I gather, are small things
>   In an age when coins are kings;
> Even at that, one hardly flings
>   Friends before swine.
>
> Rather strong? I knew as much,
>   For it made you speak.
> No offense to swine, as such.
>   But why this hide-and-seek?
> You have something on your side,
>   And you wish you might have died,
> So you tell me. And you tried
>   One night last week?

Herman has thawed out of his disagreeable silence and has
said something about "honor," perhaps suggesting that it calls
for him to break the law by killing himself, perhaps justifying his
criminality in stealing from Win in order to carry out his honor-

able duty to provide for his family. Win reminds him that you can't break the laws with impunity, implicitly including the laws of nature against abusing your body:

It's a comfort, if you like,
    To keep honor warm,
But as often as you strike
    The laws you do no harm.
To the laws, I mean. To you—
    That's another point of view,
One you may as well indue
    With some alarm.

.   .   .   .   .

Learn a little to forget
    Life was once a feast;
You aren't fit for dying yet,
    So don't be a beast.

.   .   .   .   .

—an early hint of the major theme of *Matthias at the Door.*

Apparently Herman wants to provide for Emma and pay Win what he stole from him, but he can't find manual work at this season back home on Capitol Island, and it is assumed that no one will give him serious employment in Gardiner or anywhere.

There's a debt now on your mind
    More than any gold?
And there's nothing you can find
    Out there in the cold?
Only—what's his name—Remorse?
    And Death riding on his horse?
Well, be glad there's nothing worse
    Than you have told.

Leave Remorse to warm his hands
    Outside in the rain.
As for Death, he understands,
    And he will come again.
Therefore, till your wits are clear,
    Flourish and be quiet—here.

> But a devil at each ear
> Will be a strain?

Presumbably the devils of guilt and alcohol. Win says they'll attack them together, and Herman will be astonished when he finds how easy they are to overcome:

> There'll be falling into view
> Much to rearrange;
> And there'll be a time for you
> To marvel at the change.
> They that have the least to fear
> Question hardest what is here;
> When long-hidden skies are clear,
> The stars look strange.

However Robinson might criticize and condemn someone intellectually, whenever he was confronted with actual suffering that he could alleviate, the outer self that made judgments vanished, and he was only the inner and selfless self. This was especially true with respect to his family, even his father and Herman, who were his enemies. Whenever he could actually do something for them, he was happy and ignored all other interests. It doesn't matter whether gigantic Herman and long Win did actually squeeze together in Win's niche for a few days, or whether Herman dispensed some of the last drops of the estate putting up elsewhere. What matters is that Win, as previously after his mother's death, when faced with a financial crisis involving the family other than himself, went into practical action. As before, his Harvard friend Willie Butler appeared at the right moment to meet a crisis. He offered, and in January Robinson accepted, a job assembling advertising copy for his father's department store in Boston, the employment to be on a third-time basis, the wages $10 a week. There is no evidence that Herman had as yet any occasion to call at the City Hospital in Boston, and the chances are that he went back to winter-bound Capitol Island.

And now it seemed that Win's having taken even slight action was enough to prod the Unseen Powers to their larger devices.

On March 24 he sold *Uncle Ananias* to the *Century*, the first poem he had sold in five years and the first he had been paid for in ten years. A week later he found in the hall in his rooming house a letter from the White House. It was in the President's hand:

My dear Mr. Robinson:

I have enjoyed your poems, especially "The Children of the Night," so much that I must write to tell you so. Will you permit me to ask what you are doing and how you are getting along? I wish I could see you.

Sincerely yours,
Theodore Roosevelt.

A week or two after that came the offer of a job as immigrant inspector in either Montreal or Mexico City at a salary of $6 a day. Robinson turned it down, and the fierce Teddy became obsequious—"Will you let me know what kind of a place it is that you could accept?" It was pure Robinson that on April 15, at the height of these negotiations for a job that would enable him to support Herman and help Emma he wrote Betts: "Don't throw away the rest of your life, even if living it in your own way does make some disturbance in the lives of others. There is nothing in the law or the prophets that says a man must crucify himself to please his relations."

In May he accepted a position in the New York Custom House as "special agent of the Treasury," at $2,000. Instructions would be given his superiors that he was not to be supervised. The employment was to begin on July 5. Years later he characteristically accredited the powers: "I got the Custom House job just when Herman needed me . . ." [54]

Act V

The fifth and last act of the Robinson drama shifted between Boston, New York, Capitol Island, and Farmingdale, and the external action resulted from Herman's needs and vicissitudes. It is far from certain that Win ever went up to visit him on Capitol;[1] but if he did, a natural time for it would have been in the spring of 1905, after he had accepted the Custom House position but before he left Boston for New York to begin his duties. That would have been the time for them to agree upon the partition of the forthcoming bonanza of $2,000 a year, and it was an easy boat trip from Boston to Boothbay Harbor. Also, Win would have wanted to strengthen Herman in his fight to escape the dungeon of his demon into the objective light. If we wish to follow the analogy of *Lancelot*, we can find here the great knight's last visit to Gawaine dying, and their final reconciliation.

More convincing because somewhat documented, is the possible analogy to *Roman Bartholow* which, according to the Legend, Emma said was autobiographical. If she paid one of her visits to the cottage while Win was there, there was set up something like the situation of that poem, to be written eighteen years later. As Penn-Raven lifted his friend Bartholow out of a futile egocentricity into some kind of quasi-mystical assurance, so Win seems to have awakened Herman to a new grip on reality, which involved the conquest both of his alcoholic demon and of the devils of self that first had let that demon in:

> "Those devils
> Had coiled a snare for you so cunningly
> That long before your knowledge they had caught you
> .   .   .   .
> Penn-Raven,
> having found the soul
> In Bartholow that ailed him, had with ease
> Ineffable healed it. . . .

This is to say that in Herman the surly, frustrated spoiled boy became again the affectionate boy who loved everybody and whom everybody loved—though his affection for Win at its most extreme perhaps ran a little short of Bartholow's who loved Penn-Raven "almost as a novice loves God"! After 1905, Herman, looking in the "reassuring glass," began to see

> a face at least agreeable,
> And surely not the blank and haggard mask

That he had seen so long there in the dark
Of his devouring fear and hopelessness

.   .   .   .

And gradually, through the next year or two,

"it was done.
There were no mummeries, no miracles;
There was no degradation of the wits,
Or of the will; there was no name for it;
Yet something in me opened and the light
Came in. I could have given him all but life
For recompense."

And straightway the passage, without even a paragraph break,
runs into the other principal aspect of the situation in *Roman
Bartholow:*

"Also, I could have killed him,
Indifferently, while he was on the floor,
And I was at his throat."

Penn-Raven had been having an affair with Gabrielle, the wife
of the friend he had saved; Roman Bartholow caught him kissing
her, and the assault ensued. In the model Robinson triangle, there
was no adultery. But if, as Emma said thirty years later, *Roman
Bartholow* was autobiographical, then at this or some other time
there was something actual to account for this spatter of literary
violence, if no more than Emma's obvious delight to see Win
again after more than seven years. Something, however slight—
perhaps a big-sisterly kiss, or, if Win did not come up to Capitol,
something she said about him or about a letter from him—something occurred during 1905 or '06 to revive Herman's jealousy.
Only now, complicated by his sense of guilt, his gratitude to Win,
and his fundamental affection for him, it was a pathetic rather
than an ugly jealousy; it was weary and self-pitying rather than
aggressive.

Having committed himself to some kind of provision for
Herman, and perhaps Emma as well, Robinson went down to
his Custom House job in New York and a social life more congenial than any he had known since Harvard. He settled in the
Hotel Judson on Washington Square, and in place of the old

crowd of bohemian intellectuals assembled around Titus Coan and Alfred Louis, among whom the emphasis had been on the "bohemian," his new association was with the boarders and frequent visitors at the hotel among whom the emphasis was on the "intellectual," and on distinguished production. The group included Moody, Mason, Torrence, MacKaye, Ledoux, Lyman Beecher Stowe, Nazimova, May Sinclair, and Olivia Dunbar, the latter dark beauty destined to work no slight havoc on two of the assembled geniuses, including Robinson. Regularly the men took him out on nightly "shopping" expeditions,[2] by which was meant the rounds of the neighboring saloons. There was an Italian restaurant, which Robinson immortalized as "Calverly's," where they frequently dined and talked the night away. In this fellowship one group of his friends was permanently cemented, including at least Moody, Torrence, and MacKaye.[3]

Besides the stag association, the men and women alike dragged Robinson out of his unsocial shell into mixed company as good as their own. There is the hilarious incident of Isadora Duncan's attempt to seduce him, casually and hastily while leaving her Christmas champagne party roaring in the other room. There is the romantic scene of May Sinclair and Robinson leaning on the rail of Brooklyn Bridge at two o'clock in the morning. There was Mrs. Clara Davidge, the widowed daughter of Bishop Potter, who presently built him a studio in the garden back of her house on Washington Place, and she and her sister used to pray—presumably in his presence—that he might be empowered to overcome the demon rum. There was the dubious inference that was drawn from Robinson's unexplained disappearance each weekend from the Judson and the congenial company there.

Meanwhile the high office of Special Agent of the Treasury in the Custom House was providing Robinson with some of the gayest epistolary ammunition of his career. To Mrs. Richards: "In reply to your letter of the second instant I have to say that bananas and skeletons may be imported free of duty. I regret to inform you that there is a duty of ten (10) per centum on baked ant's eggs. . . ."[4] Again: "The soulless Secretary of the Treasury has taken away my steamboat. . . . His dinner disagreed with him sometime ago and since then he has been dreaming that he is going to be the next President. . . . I assume it to be true that there is in him something that is as human as a stomach." [5] And finally: "Sometime there is going to be something to do—otherwise there would be no Custom House. As it is I look out upon Wall Street and see men going to their ruin and to their luncheons. It is a sad life. If my next book turns out pessimistic you are to attribute the fact to T.R., not to me. By nature I am jovial and sunny but I can't continue so unless there is crime in the world to cheer me up and give me something to do. . . . If you are really a friend of mine you will go abroad at once and smuggle something. . . ." [6] (Robinson's daily round of duty in the service of his country consisted of opening his roll-top desk, reading the paper, closing the desk, leaving the paper in his chair to show he had been there, and going home.)

But inevitably the new situation brought moral doubts as well as freedom and lightheartedness. In so great a change Robinson detected a kind of dramatic finality, as if his main work of writing poetry had ended along with the hardships that had been its setting. Roosevelt had bullied Scribner's into getting out a new edition of *The Children of the Night* in the forthcoming fall of 1905, and in August Robinson wrote about it in his last published letter to Smith:

> . . . I shall feel secure and not have the distressful experience of looking longer on my own offspring as orphans of the night.—I don't know whether I deserve anything or not, but I have been through enough to feel that it is about time for something in the way of a change. . . . Unless I can contrive to get some time for myself . . . [the Custom House job] merely [means] that I shall remain here a little longer than I should otherwise. I often wonder if there's any reason why I should remain, after all. The best of me is on paper—and God knows how much or little it is worth.
>
> Yours sincerely,
E.A.R. [7]

During the next eight years it looked as if this lugubrious prognostication about his work being done might be justified. The new edition of *The Children* came out in October, and the

President personally reviewed it with extravagance. But the press generally was as indifferent and patronizing as it had been towards *Captain Craig*. More serious, Robinson seemed unable to release his larger perceptions under official patronage. The poetic output of the period up to 1910 contains one great poem, *For a Dead Lady*, immortalizing his mother. But the rest is all competent and minor comment on life, typified by *Miniver Cheevy*, in celebration of whose excellent facility Frost in the Introduction to posthumous *King Jasper*, and the New Critics generally, tried to kill Robinson with faint praise. It is a comment on his creative emptiness at this time that he dusted off the sonnet he had written for his niece Ruth twelve years before, dedicated it to Arvia, the five-year-old daughter of his friend Percy MacKaye, published it in *Scribner's* in 1908, and included it in the contents of his next volume. Nowhere in the work of these years is there a subjective, lyrical shout; and no more is there an objective comment that advances his familiar notions about fate, idealism, the brutality of the world, "the glory of the unfulfilled," the goodness of the cosmos. It is his most muted time. "I shall do better soon," he wrote Mrs. Richards. "At any rate I am not likely to do worse." [8] He experimented with drama, writing *Van Zorn* and *The Porcupine*, both of which Broadway declined.

A partial explanation of this poetic slump may be found in his eternal suspicion of government. He fretted under the obligations created by private patronage, yet if it was marked by a convincing show of friendship, it also stimulated him. But the "soulless Secretary of the Treasury," even the generous President of the United States, represented something powerful, material, incomprehensible, and remote that he couldn't identify with his ideal world or credit with concern whether or not he did well in it.

Another and more significant account of these subdued years was in the fact that between 1905 and 1910 Robinson himself, approaching forty, was in major transition. He was growing out of his subjectivity, his "joy," both in his "idealism" and in his poetry, but his objective poems were yet minor, like all of his previous work of the kind, except in a certain sense *Captain*

Craig. Some new turn of experience, some shock, was still necessary to awaken him to a maturity that would both enlarge his objective vision and, on the subjective side, be nearer to the selfless, inner light of Αγαπη, a maturity that would in fact deal objectively with his own feelings and personal perceptions. As he told Mrs. Richards, "I don't yet know where I am or where I am going. Chiefly I seem to be drawing semi-long breaths and looking around." [9]

Finally, the immediate cause of Robinson's uncertainty and resulting insignficant production in these years must have been his awareness of the gathering climax in the drama back home, of his personal involvement in it, and of the responsibility he must carry in its resolution. Without writing a word about Emma, he must have been thinking about her "all the time," the beautiful singleness of her love that had been Herman's and that he now believed was his, the little he had done to deserve that love, what further he must do, actively, to deserve it in the future.

Meanwhile, most of the time alone on Capitol Island, Herman fought his demon of alcohol for two years and defeated it, probably in 1907, thus raising himself to a moral, as distinguished from a spiritual, stature as high as either of his brothers, if not higher. Many years later, Robinson celebrated his victory, not only in *Roman Bartholow* but more specifically in *Battle after War:*

> Out of a darkness, into a slow light
> That was at first no light that had a name,
> Like one thrust up from Erebus he came,
> Groping alone, blind with remembered sight.
> But there were not those faces in the night,
> And all those eyes no longer were aflame
> That once he feared and hated, being the same
> As his that were the fuel of his fright.
>
> He shone, for one so long among the lost,
> Like a stout Roman after Pentacost:
> "Terror will yield as much as we dare face
> Ourselves in it, and it will yield no more,"
> He said. And we see two now in his place,
> Where there was room for only one before.

It may be that Herman emerged, at least partially, from the single, "only one," external, and self-indulgent self, into a second, or objective, inner self. It may be also that he overcame his guilt and so much "terror" as was associated with those "faces in the night" and "eyes," presumably of delirium tremens, which suggest so closely some of the non-alcoholic terrors of Avon whose "harvest" appeared only two years before this "battle." But one terror that Herman did not overcome in his recovery was his jealousy of Win. And for those disposed to accept the Orthodox Account of the triangle, this failure becomes important in the history of literature.

This relatively petty failure, or at least its chief demonstration in action, was attributable to the fact that as Herman was conquering alcohol morally, tuberculosis was weakening him physically. In 1907 [10] he went to Boston and began to take treatments at the City Hospital. There seems to be no evidence that Win came up from New York to confer with him, and, as earlier, the Legend denies that he was in Gardiner or Farmingdale. Herman got steadily worse until his larynx was partly destroyed and he could only whisper. He had collected letters of introduction to help him to a new start, but he had to give up the possibility. One day when Emma was bringing him supplies, the lurking jealousy broke through. He rasped to her that he loved her more than she loved him, for if she should die he would never remarry, but when he died she would marry Win. Whereupon, although her dying husband did not ask the promise, she did promise him never to marry the man who already believed that she loved him and whom, according to the Orthodox Account, she had always loved.

Not long after this promise, at the end of 1908, Herman went down to the Boston City Hospital, enrolled as an in-patient and stayed. Early in February, 1909, the once most popular and promising boy in Gardiner died alone in the ward, without a relative or friend present. Emma, tied down by her children and an ailing mother, wired Win to go to Boston and bring the body to Farmingdale, which he did. Two days after the funeral he returned to New York, postponing the resolution of the play to propriety and a quiet time.

For what we owe to other days,
Before we poisoned him with praise,
May we who shrank to find him weak
Remember that he cannot speak.

For envy that we may recall,
And for our faith before the fall,
May we who are alive be slow
To tell what we shall never know.

For penance he would not confess,
And for the fateful emptiness
Of early triumph undermined,
May we now venture to be kind.

Twenty-two years after 1910, Win's mood had hardened. Herman became again, as he had been earlier, a "devil," and his unattended death in Boston became the basis of the passive euthanasia in *The March of the Cameron Men* where the doctor-friend and the wife of the incurably suffering fiend "let him die."

From the funeral Robinson returned to his job at the Custom House where, as for the four years now past, he reported daily, opened his desk, considered its lack of contents, closed it, and went home. In March, a month after Herman's death, Taft succeeded Roosevelt in the White House, and William Loeb, the former "soulless Secretary of the Treasury," sank to Collector of the Port of New York. He told Robinson that he would have to keep regular hours, and that he intended to put him in uniform. Robinson must have wrinkled an amazed and amused forehead at the vision of himself in buttons. But, of course, he resigned. Later, when he was back in Gardiner, he completed to Emma the statement of which a part was quoted earlier: "I don't understand how it was. I got the Custom House job when Herman needed me, and, when he didn't need me any more, it was over." [11] Obviously, the Unseen Powers.

He rested in New York until July, when the pressure of the Powers for the resolution of the family drama became irresistible. He began writing people that he was planning to go to Gardiner. To Ledoux on July 22: "I expect to leave these parts for an *indefi-*

nite stay [italics added] before long and would hate to go without another sight of you." [12] He was still in New York in August,
when Emma's mother died. In September he finally went to Gardiner, and so to Farmingdale, and the last scene of the play
began.

Emma installed him in a comfortable bedroom with a Franklin stove, on the northeast corner of the second floor. The east
windows looked out through the trees over the wide, peaceful
Kennebec, and the north window looked across a hollow to a
neighbor's Victorian mansion and its stable, whose cupola had for
weathervane the running "little horse" of *The Long Race*. One
afternoon Win came back from town and found Emma entertaining a lot of people for whose society he felt no need. So he went
on and called on the neighbor whom he had known slightly fifteen
or so years ago. He experienced the mutual blankness recorded
in the sonnet, and so came home when the coast there was clear.
Looking out his window at the neighbor's stable with the
weathervane, he realized how far he had moved away from
Gardiner. He concluded that "the little horse [whose name was
Time] had won."

But if his feelings for Gardiner had faded, those for Emma
and her daughters had not changed. He spent each working day
in his room, polishing the contents of the forthcoming *The Town
Down the River*, and divided most or all of the rest of the time
between doing the chores for Emma and courting her in his
fashion. Scattered through the poems of the next twenty years,
we find flashes of settings and episodes, all fictitiously recon-
ceived, from the script of that climax and resolution of the
family drama. In *The March of the Cameron Men*, one of the
most autobiographical of the poems, we are told that he arrived
at the Farmingdale house one starlight evening that September of
1909, when Emma was carelessly "rippling" the old Cameron
march, as she used to do twenty years before at the Robinsons'
during her engagement. Now she was "calling" Win with it. He
entered the house and the parlor quietly, and then "you were in
my arms," this gesture perhaps comprising the "lapse" which he
afterwards "regretted"—and Emma punished him for the regret!
In the parallel final scene of *Lancelot* we have the golden, har-

vest weather which was no great hyperbole for any New England
landscape in late September and early October. In *Mortmain*
Emma and Win are in her garden, surely in Farmingdale, where
there is "languor" in the air. In the *Cameron Men* again they are
out rowing in the "autumn twilight" on the "lake," which is obviously the broad Kennebec, with the house almost hidden in the
trees. In *Late Summer* it is another evening and they are on an
ocean beach, probably on Capitol Island

> where the tide threw forward

> Its cold, unconquered lines, that unceasingly
> Foamed against hope, and fell.

A little later, probably in November, Hagedorn [13] has them sitting
"through the crisp autumn evenings" before the stove in Win's
room.

And all the time he was asking her to marry him, and she was
temporizing, as in *Rahel to Varnhagen*, or refusing, as in *Late
Summer* and *Mortmain*. All we know for certain is the result, but
through the three months we can detect three shifts in the
weather of mutuality. By the end of the first month the prospect
was hopeless: Win revised his intention for an "indefinite stay,"
and on the thirtieth of September wrote Ledoux, "I hope to see
you again some time before Commander Peary goes crazy . . .
The kids coming home from school make me feel blue and old.
I've been out of school for twenty-one years and am not yet of
age with the publishers." [14] Some years later he wrote Smith:
"I'm sorry to say that when I was in Gardiner, in 1909, I tried
in vain to find my 'Antigone.' I remember boxing it up with some
books of mine, but I found that the box had been opened . . .
and its contents more or less scattered." [15] Subsequently, Robinson told a friend he was glad that early work had vanished.

On October seventh some hopeful turn had reversed his plan
for immediate departure. He wrote Edith Brower, "I expect to
be in New York this winter." [16] He lingered on through November into December. The "kids" were out of the house all day.
This would have been the time, if there was any such time, for
the consummation of his lifelong love, as implied in his state-

ment to me about Guinevere, and about himself as a "dry New England psychologist," and as asserted to me positively by Ridgely Torrence.[17] Against this possibility was Robinson's idealism, which was none the less real now that it had accepted the flesh as part of ideal love. Without the mutuality that he used to call "soul music," he would have found carnal "pleasure" not only false but humiliating. And Emma, even if she had suffered at this time the generous impulses of a great woman toward a man who had loved her beautifully for twenty-two years, still understood him and would not humiliate him. Robinson's later implication that he had experienced a completed "great love" may have referred simply to his belief at this time that Emma now loved him wholly, thus perfecting a mutuality more mature than his juvenile "soul music," a mutuality that was of the order of marriage and in relation to which consummation, whether accomplished or not, was a secondary and irrelevant matter. When Emma, some time in December, finally and categorically refused marriage, all such concerns would be annulled. Yet for nine years more, he cherished the belief that she did love him, and that her rejection of him was in spite of her love and for the noblest of extraneous reasons.

Already we have noticed the bases of four possible accounts of the rise and fall of this romance. There is the Orthodox Account which holds that Emma always loved Win; that she was swept into an infatuated, unhappy and actually brief marriage, of which she kept up an outer show, partly through duty and partly through pity; that as incident to the pity she made a foolish promise not to marry Win; and that it was this promise alone that kept her from marrying him. The Dissenting Account, on the other hand, holds that she never loved Win except in a big-sisterly way, that Herman was the one, enduring love of her life, which fact accounted for her refusing, after his death, to marry any of the applicants, of whom Win was only one.

As between these two accounts, both oversimplified, the view taken here favors the second with qualification. It seems incredible that a deathbed promise, made by the noblest of women, could stand against a new, fully awakened love. Robinson himself denied the possibility in *The Book of Annandale* and, near the end of his life, in *The Cameron Men*, where he had Emma expressly flout certain analogous promises that "are best forgotten" and "would be treasured more if broken and lost." The obvious fact is that in spite of all the bickering Herman was Emma's one and permanent love who was never replaced. In a woman of her intensity, this inner fusion with a particular man could not be cooled by his most egregious omissions and misconduct, not by his entire lack of perception or consideration for her, not by his indifference even to the point of desertion and infidelity. Any of these failures on his part might lead to the hysterical freezing of her outward responsiveness in the manner of *London Bridge* and *The Clinging Vine*. And yet, according to the Dissenting Opinion and the view taken here, the very violence of the freezing would be the measure of the inner love that could not freeze. That essential love would remain Herman's, beyond death, unless and until there should arise the unlikely but possible event of its being superseded by another love of equal pervasiveness and power.

And here, as back in the beginning in '88, idealistic Win failed to meet the requirements. Though her feeling for him was not of the order of her love of Herman, yet it was a great deal more than the patronizing, sisterly affection of the Dissenting Account. She was a person of exceptional sensitivity and a creative instinct which never found expression beyond a little amateur painting, exquisite dressing, and expert sewing. She was an artist *manqué*. From the youthful start she saw Win's distinction of mind, appreciated his poetry, and sympathized with his loneliness, which was like her own. In a small town, where for some uncertain reason, perhaps a combination of pride and lack of intellectual background and education, its literary coterie never opened to her, Win was probably the only real companion she ever found. Certainly, as in the beginning, there was that in her that wanted to marry him. But the essential woman was stronger. He must say the magic word that would fetch her. She would cheer for him with her mind; but he alone must make the gesture that would gather her emotions and transfer them from Herman to himself.

So the final situation repeated the original one when little Win at eighteen had been unable to meet the female conditions. Now it is no longer the boy with his dualistic notion. Now he sees love truly, as all one wave. Furthermore, he is a man of the world who, while socially halting, is perceptive of women and not helpless with them in ordinary circumstances. He is not, and never was, a man of weak emotion such as might turn to homosexuality or get along with almost no sexual life. As a mind and body, Robinson was of the vitality of Wagner and Beethoven and Brahms, of Chaucer and Shakespeare and Browning. His art was not of the exquisite but of the resounding kind. As he said of his sense of humor, the pressure of emotion within was great, but it did not know how to break out of the barrel into outer action. The more it fermented and bubbled within, the tighter sat the bung. By long study, he learned how to get along with women as long as he was not deeply involved, to understand them and sympathize with them. But when his feeling for one of them became impassioned, all the outlets of action closed. Intercourse without love he understood and deplored. But the art, the "craft," of arousing a woman's full response he never learned. His only heroine who falls in love as a result of male courtship on stage is Damaris in *The Book of Annandale*—and Annandale's whole technique consisted of calling formally and leaving a book! When Robinson himself was impelled to make major advances, nature turned inward and closed its eyes while the darkness seethed. Later he described his life generally when he said to the unhappy young woman who did love him, "The more I feel the less I say." He also meant more than action in the masculine marketplace when he said, as he did several times in his life, "I never could have done *anything* but write poetry." Out of embarrassment he could ask Emma to marry him, and could make other prepared speeches. Perhaps he could even kiss her according to plan. But it must all be learned. He could not relax into the role of the spontaneous male and win her.

Because of their congeniality and her intellectual need of him, Emma probably considered marrying him without loving him. But here, the enterprise being in the field of the mind, the reasonable objections raised their heads. One such might have been the promise to Herman, the thought of which, incidentally, would reawaken him and his power over her. But to give that as the whole reason to Win would provide him no comfort. More considerate and real was the objection of poverty. They were all penniless, and if Win married her, with the three girls, he would be bound to take some absurd job like the subway. Probably he would find one right there in Gardiner where it would not only steal his time but would starve him for the company and resources of New York. His career would be ended just as he was getting a foot in the door. Perhaps Win even assured her that he would become a breadwinner! Certainly this was the reason she gave him for turning him down, for this was what he believed, then and for some years to come. The view taken here accepts the main premise of the Dissenting Account, that Emma never loved him; but it adds the qualification that she still might have married him but for extraneous reasons, of which the one she gave him was the future of his career.

The fourth account of the failure of the romance was Robinson's own, and it combines elements from the Orthodox view and the view taken here in an explanation that transcends them both. In 1909, and probably through 1917, he believed that Emma loved him but gave up her own happiness in order to help his calling. It was in this role of supreme womanhood that he cast her as Guinevere.

Lancelot, planned with *Merlin* in '15 and written in '17, is autobiographical in almost no physical detail. The great knight himself, being the world's leading bruiser and only a second- to third-rate intellectual, is hardly suggestive of Robinson. And "white and gold" Guinevere recalls Emma superficially in only a few minor, although telltale, gestures. The autobiography is internal: the great decision of Emma, and in consequence the great awakening of Robinson. Guinevere in the first part of the epic, the first five sections—what we might call the first Guinevere— was no more than Robinson's generalized Woman. She loved Lancelot completely; there was no dichotomy in her that left anything on any level for Arthur, whom she simply despised. The second Guinevere also, the one of Joyous Gard and the pathos of her return to Arthur on Rome's command, the Guinevere of the sixth and seventh sections of the epic, is no more than Woman crying out against the masculine world of law that makes light of her love. But the third Guinevere, the Guinevere of the last section of the poem, has enjoyed through loneliness and mental torture a change which is Grace. Through the long nights when she was Modred's prisoner in the Tower she emerged from Eros into Αγαπη, from her self-indulgent love into the selfless love that understood what it was Lancelot had always wanted and she had withheld from him. Like Emma in Robinson's understanding of her, Guinevere not only bowed before the masculine idea of perfection, the Grail, which is every woman's rival, but she espoused it and supported it. She rose from the general woman into the ideal, the transcendent woman. To the function of Beatrice she added that of Héloïse when she sent Abélard back to Paris to continue his career.

When the war was over, Arthur and Modred both dead and Lancelot still in France, Guinevere entered a convent at Almesbury. If we wish we may assimilate her novitiate vows to Emma's promise to Herman, and their unimportance when Lancelot came, to the equivalent little that Emma's promise meant to her when Win came for her. More important than the vows was now Guinevere's new understanding of the man she had always loved; and in her vision of him and the prospect of his fulfillment, she experienced the same simple and inclusive mystical assurance that she knew he would attain in coming to the Grail. As his Grail would be the Light of ultimate Truth, hers would be the vision of him seeing that Truth. Thus, between 1910 and 1917, Robinson interpreted Emma's attitude toward him and his poetry. As he had come up to Farmingdale from New York to marry her and jeopardize his calling, his prospect of seeing the light of his life's accomplishment, so Lancelot came from France to the convent in Almesbury to carry off Guinevere. Their interview is one of Robinson's greatest dramatic dialogues:

> He found the queen,
> But she was not the Queen of white and gold
> That he had seen before him for so long.
> There was no gold; there was no gold anywhere.

The black hood, and the white face under it,
And the blue, frightened eyes, were all he saw—

.   .   .   .

Their eyes met, and she smiled: "No, Lancelot;
We are going by two roads to the same end;
Or let us hope, at least, what knowledge hides,
And so believe it. We are going somewhere.
Why the new world is not for you and me,
I cannot say; but only one was ours.

.   .   .   .

                              You are good to me,
Coming to find me here for the last time:
For I should have been lonely many a night,
Not knowing if you cared. I do know now;
And there is not much else for me to know
That earth may tell me. . . .

.   .   .   .

                              There is nothing now
That I can see between you and the Light
That I have dimmed so long. If you forgive me,
And I believe you do—though I know all
That I have cost when I was worth so little—
There is no hazard that I see between you
And all you sought so long. . . .

.   .   .   .

See me all white and gold, as I was once.
I shall not harm you then; I shall not come
Between you and the Gleam that you must follow,
Whether you will or not. There is no place
For me but where I am; there is no place
For you save where it is that you are going.

.   .   .   .

                              I have not what you have
To make me see, though I shall have, sometime,
A new light of my own. . . .

.   .   .   .

                    I shall not be alone.

> And I shall tell myself that you are seeing
> All that I cannot see."

So Lancelot, following Guinevere's will more than his own, turned from her and set out on his final quest. And Robinson, following Emma's will, turned from her and set out into a new world, under a new sky cleared of everything but the stars.

> A word stronger than his willed him away
> From Almesbury. All alone he rode that night,
> Under the stars, led by the living Voice
> That would not give him peace. . . .
>
> .   .   .   .
>
>   Under the stars,
> Alone, all night he rode, out of a world
> That was not his, or the King's; and in the night
> He felt a burden lifted . . .
>
> .   .   .   .
>
> . . . the Voice within him said: "You are not free.
> You have come to the world's end, and it is best
> You are not free. Where the Light falls, death falls;
> And in the darkness comes the Light." . . .
> And he rode on, under the stars,
> Out of the world, into he knew not what,
> Until a vision chilled him and he saw,
> Now as in Camelot, long ago in the garden,
> The face of Galahad who had seen and died,
> And was alive, now in a mist of gold.
> He rode on into the dark, under the stars,
> And there were no more faces. There was nothing.
> But always in the darkness he rode on,
> Alone; and in the darkness came the Light.

Robinson's quest was to require three or four years instead of one night before he would see his "Light" and qualify to record the experience of Lancelot and Guinevere. It started in December, 1909, when we may imagine him at the rail of the Boston nightboat, watching the cold phosphorus of the bow wave, and on the New York train, listening to the rhythm of the trucks. Seething with the capped emotions that were going to do his greatest work over the next fifteen years, there was also in the center of the turmoil a still shrine of peace, a barely conscious gratitude to the powers that Emma in her role of Beatrice was not to be handicapped by the exactions of marriage to a pauper, and beyond that a larger gratitude, wholly unconscious, that his love was to continue in its long-tried terms of idealism rather than risk the precarious ones of material and social embodiment. Here at the start of his quest for the Light, or very soon thereafter, realizing that love's full consummation of marriage was not to be for him, he rejected thenceforward the possibility of its "counterfeit." On a day that must have been very near his fortieth birthday, he showed once and for all the ease with which an idea could overcome an outer devil. He "took the veil," and remained celibate for the rest of his life. The final curtain fell on the play.

Epilogue

The end of the personal drama in late 1909, when Robinson was forty, was the end of the preparative phase of his life, as the publication of *The Town Down the River* in 1910 marked the end of the subjective phase of his verse. As in the case of his Lancelot, there remained a quest before he should come to "the Light," less a continuing drama than a kind of epilogue, an extended application and revision of the truths already learned. As with Lancelot also, the course of the quest would be marked by a sequence, less of dramatic climaxes than of more or less ignominious anticlimaxes. For Lancelot these were moral, as when, being about to set out for the Grail the second time, he returned to Guinevere for one last tryst and got caught in her bower; or again when, Camelot being destroyed, he was again about to set out, but again must deviate to say good-bye to Guinevere; and finally it was her will not his that sent him off to find his Light. With Robinson, the anticlimaxes will be rather in his mind, the pursuit and abandonment of successive false lights, and finally,

The poet's parents, Mary Palmer Robinson (1833–1896), Edward Robinson (1818–1892)

The Robinson House in Gardiner
The poet's "den" in the bay window, second floor

1888: High School Graduation

The poet's brothers, Horace Dean (left) and Herman Edward (below)

Emma Shepherd Robinson, Herman's wife

1896–1901: *Octaves, The Book of Anandale, Captain Craig*

1913–1923: *The Man Against the Sky, Merlin, Lancelot, The Three Taverns, Rembrandt to Rembrandt, The Man Who Died Twice*

1928–1934: *Cavendar's House, Matthias at the Door, Amaranth*

after he sees the true one, the abandonment of that also for what might seem to be a less noble aim.

Actually there will be for Robinson two successive quests. First, he will struggle intellectually merely to see or understand the distant "Light," the vision of life's meaning, that will become more than ever exigent after the empty return to New York at the end of 1909. This quest will involve three years of vacillation, two of preparation, and two of execution. It will reach its consummation in the composition of *Lancelot* in 1917, the statement of his doctrine of self loss, which as theory he maintained through his great productive period and qualified only a little near the end of his life. The second and final quest will be Robinson's own in terms, not of imagination but of living. Neglecting for himself the Light he has seen, he will declare in *Merlin,* even before he writes *Lancelot,* for a different goal. Yet the true perception of Robinson's imagination will remain Lancelot's. He will write *Merlin* first because it presents a contrasting and preparative theme, because dramatically it serves well as a curtain raiser for the main play of *Lancelot.*

The quest for Lancelot's Light was the first and true one, and as Robinson's imagination pursued it through the early teens, so his poetry in the same period moved into its maturity. During the previous decade he had outgrown the pagan, self-indulgent, quasi-orgastic "joy" that had characterized the composition of *The Altar, Credo, Two Sonnets,* the *Octaves, Sainte-Nitouche,* most of *The Book of Annandale,* and had provided the argument of *Captain Craig.* In the verse collected in *The Town Down the River,* 1910, objective art had generally superseded subjective self-expression. But the personal verse in that contents, though mature in style, was, with the exception of *For a Dead Lady,* minor in content. It represented a transition into the next period when much of the personal poetry in *The Man Against the Sky,* 1916, would combine the old sweep of greatness with the new objectivity. It would show that he had indeed outgrown adolescent ecstasy, that his personal poetry was no longer subjective but simply autobiographical, that he could now treat his own involvements with the same detachment he had always shown in his proprio objective work. As in the preparative period, the verse of objective drama after 1910 would continue to provide about twice as many titles as the intellectual verse and the autobiographical verse combined. But, whereas before 1910 the objective dramatic poems, notably the character sonnets, used to comprise also the preponderance of the lines, after 1910 the many long autobiographical poems, whether intellectual statements or dramatizations of the triangle, would gradually preempt the bulk of the lineage also. It seemed that as Robinson's art matured, the prodigal inspiration for all kinds of short poems failed. Once in his later years, having been asked why he didn't do any more short things, he said, "They don't come any more." And he repeated it sadly, "They don't come any more." [1]

The first fiasco or anticlimax in Robinson's quest for the Light consisted of his turning his back both on it and on his calling for three years! Possibly through numbness after defeat, but more probably in order to convince both Emma and himself that he was capable of financial respectability, he began to experiment with novels, in addition to plays. The decelerating poetic output of the preceding five years came to a full stop. Four poems, probably written in 1909, appeared in magazines in early 1910, and there was no more publication through the rest of that year, or in '11 or '12. For three years and a half, until the late spring of 1913, he devoted himself to unsalable and forgotten prose.

Meanwhile, his economy, instead of fulfilling its pretense of self-support, merely shifted back from public to private patronage. From collateral indications it appears that Hays Gardiner was helping him. For residence he returned to the cottage in Mrs. Davidge's garden on Washington Place, and in 1912 followed her to a brick castle with a ghost on Staten Island where she moved with an artist, Henry Taylor, whom she had reformed and married. In New York there was Ledoux, among other valuable friends. In the summer and fall of 1910 an old acquaintance entertained him at Chocorua, in New Hampshire, and there he met Hagedorn. In October, *The Town Down the River* appeared, and while it was generally treated like another slim volume of verse, it did get a review by William Stanley Braithwaite in the *Boston Transcript* and so started a friendship and further association in Boston.

The next year, 1911, Robinson went, very suspiciously, to the MacDowell Colony in Peterborough, and met Isaacs. His life began to assume its permanent routine: four or five free months each year at Peterborough; a few migratory weeks in Boston, spring and fall, with the Perrys, or with George Burnham in his room on West Newton Street; longer visits with the Ledoux' at Cornwall-on-the-Hudson, the Hagedorns in Westport, the Isaacses in Pelham; two or three months of free bed and breakfast with the Taylors and their ghost on Staten Island. There was very little provision left to be made up by the ravens, and this little was minimized through his friends inducing him to do one of his more sustained stretches on the wagon. The deprivation was unusually sharp because of the current folly of devoting his life to trying to make money, and because of some unspecified tension in the Taylor household. Robinson was always examining himself with suspicion as to whether his affection for all these kind friends was sufficient to justify his accepting their largess; and he always concluded that it was. In 1912 he wrote George Burnham from the Colony that someone not accredited had sent him a check for $200, "which I thought was rubbing it in just a little. I returned it to the sender." [2] And two weeks later: "Few damned fools have ever invited disaster so cordially as I have and received (to date at least) so little of it."

In the spring of '13 Robinson awoke with apparent suddenness out of his three-and-a-half-years' delusion that he might be an honest breadwinner. His usually perceptive friend Hays Gardiner had encouraged him to try novels, and on March 9 he wrote him:"When I come out of myself and try to write for the crowd, I perpetrate the damnedest rubbish you ever heard of. . . . At last I can see the light again, and I am going to write a book of poems. . . . I don't believe the human brain was ever constructed that could stand much more of the wear and tear of conflicting activities that mine has undergone during the past three years. . . . I feel that I have given the thing a fair trial and it would be unfair to you as well as to myself to waste any more of my life in doing something for which I have come to see that I am not fitted." [3] And two weeks later to Burnham: "The powers that pull the strings are not going to let me write popular plays. I'm sorry, for I wanted to make some money; but instead of doing that I've got to make some more poetry. This will be distressing news to you, but there doesn't seem to be anything I can do about [it] . . . Sometimes I almost hope that I have had my last dream of independence and respectability, for the waking up hurts more and more as I get to be an old man." [4] On his way to the Colony in June he wrote Harry Smith in his old vein of full commitment: "I hope to leave enough behind me to leave a small dent. Perhaps I have done as well as I could under the circumstances, and perhaps I have made my own circumstances. I'm damned if I know." [5] He had to borrow money from Fraser, Ledoux, and Gardiner to get to Peterborough, but in Boston on the way he had the satisfaction of enjoying his first flurry of journalistic attention, because the young Alfred Noyes was there and had announced that Robinson was the leading poet in America.

And so, back at the Colony, with no prospect of support but the generosity of his friends, he cut his last reputable cables and embarked upon ten years of work that, both for quality and quantity, were the most productive of his life. Passing through Boston, apparently on the way back to New York, he met his old friend Herbert Longfellow, who asked him why he didn't run up to Gardiner when he was so near. "I don't expect to go back," Robinson said, "unless something definite should call me. You know there is a good deal there." [6] By that time he must have learned that the Powers, being duly defied, were beginning to hedge in his favor. Hays Gardiner had died in May and left him a legacy of $4,000. Though he didn't get it till the following spring, the prospect of so great a sum changed the color of the sky. Later he said to Rollo Brown: "Somehow I was always able to keep going after that. It almost makes a man feel that maybe there is somebody somewhere who makes it [sic] a business of looking out for people." [7]

Back in New York in the fall of '13, Robinson ran into complications in what had been, so far as appears, his first attempt since the Woodland Girl to obliterate the chief part of the "good deal" that had been in Gardiner for twenty-five years. Gossip has it that he had had an affair with Olivia Dunbar, who was still living in the "tower room" of the old Judson on Washington Square. However that may be, it was another case where Robinson, because he felt emotional rapport in the air, seems to have thought the relationship was settled and sealed, even to the point of engagement—just as he had done twenty years before with Mabel Moore, and twenty-five years before in his soul music with Emma, just as he had done in reverse with the Woodland Girl when he may have made what sounded like a proposal but which was not one because the spiritual union was not clear in his perception. Returning from the Colony in the fall of '13, he hurried up to Olivia's room and found Ridgely Torrence there and engaged to her. Robinson bolted downstairs and out. It took Torrence several blocks to catch him, and then a very long time to persuade him to come back to Olivia's room, where they duly talked all night.[8] Early in February, 1914, Olivia and Ridgely were married, and on the ninth Robinson wrote them a slightly stiff note of congratulation:

I have no means of knowing how much or how little my best wishes are worth to either of you, but you may be sure that you have them, and that they are entirely genuine. I was not very much surprised by the news, for the occurrence seemed in the order of things likely to happen.

I hope most sincerely that all will go well with you, and that you will forgive me for not saying so in more brilliant language. But I can't be brilliant when my teeth are chattering with cold.[9]

There followed between Robinson and Torrence, not an open break, but a lapse in their former intimacy which lasted about ten years. Olivia Torrence always insisted to her intimates that "E.A." never came within a mile of proposing to her, and since she was a desperately honest and forthright woman, she may be believed. The truth seems to be that Robinson's friendship with Olivia had always been chiefly intellectual, and on a level somewhat above Torrence's capacity; wherefore, Robinson could not conceive that she could have discarded him in favor of his lighter and gayer friend. Faintly the situation recalled the scene of the triangular drama twenty-five years before when it had been incomprehensible to young Win that Emma should have succumbed to Herman's trivial realism. So now, it was beyond his understanding that Olivia, after eight years of waiting for him to act, should succumb to another who had nothing to recommend him but personal charm and the banal fact that he asked her to marry him.

During Robinson's great period, 1913 through '23, it is not possible to date precisely most of the shorter pieces. Since, as he told Hays Gardiner in March of '13, he was setting out deliberately to write a "book of poems," we may presume that the first thing he did was to look in his box of unbooked things and pick out what might be worth working over. Also, since Herman was now four years dead, this would be the time to dust off a number of items reporting on the tense days of the triangle, which he had suppressed out of consideration for Emma and for Herman in his agonizing years. It is hard to conceive that in his new state of realized independence, and on the threshold of major production, he could have lapsed into the several angry moods that had produced *The Clinging Vine, Eros Turannos, Lisette and Eileen, Bewick Finzer,* and *Bokardo,* all to be included in the new book of poems. Incidentally, all of these except *Eros Turannos* are minor sketches of hardly more than biographical and technical interest to recommend them to the immortality of the *Collected Poems. Eros Turannos* is usually assigned as written in the summer of 1913, and its publication in *Poetry* in March, '14, supports the view. Yet it is incredible that, at least fifteen years after the very special circumstances involved, Robinson should have reboiled into the mood of resentment against Herman that motivated that poem. Rather, it must have been at least sketched in the mid to late '90's, set aside for years, as was frequent with Robinson, and then revamped in the summer of '13. Of the other poems of triangular reference in the forthcoming contents, *Flammonde* treats Herman gently, as Robinson tended to do after his death, and *The Unforgiven* portrays the old tragic impasse between Emma and Herman in the same way. The two wicked brothers in *Old King Cole* are playfully dealt with, while the spacious resignation of Old King Cole himself looks more like the Robinson of 1913 than the Robinson of the earlier, more irascible time. In the contents that in '16 will become *The Man*

Against the Sky, a somewhat baffling poem, autobiographically speaking, is *John Gorham*. Because of the unnecessary reference to "a year ago" and to the man's pretending to be "sorry when you're not," it is difficult to question the interpretation of it as a dramatic exaggeration of an actual exchange of discourtesies between Emma and Win in the fall of '09, at some moment when their tension was high to the verge of his leaving Gardiner. But, while it is not astonishing to find him accusing her of being a cat that catches a mouse "and lets him go and eats him up for fun," yet in Jane Wayland's cry—"Somewhere in me there's a woman if you know the way to find her"—there seems to be on the part of the poet a mature understanding of women such as, before 1916, he had shown no other sign of. Also, it is odd to find this dash of bitterness from Robinson when in '15 he had already formulated the high interpretation of Emma that he was going to embody in Guinevere. It would seem likely, not only that the original of the dialogue occurred during his visit in 1909, but that it was poetized soon after the event, and that Jane's desperate cry for understanding was close to a literal transcription of something Emma actually said and which Robinson had then set down without well grasping it. As such it might be taken as an account in capsule of all their lifelong advances and retreats.

This was the period when Robinson was growing in selflessness, both personally and in the ideas that would dominate his poetry from now on. The large caliber of *Old King Cole* has been mentioned. In *The Dark House* Dean's narcotic tragedy approaches mature greatness:

> There's a music yet unheard
> By the creature of the word,
> Though it matters little more
> Than a wave-wash on a shore—
> Till a Demon shuts a door.
>
> So, if he be very still
> With his Demon, and one will,
> Murmurs of it may be blown
> To my friend who is alone
> In a room that I have known.

> After that from everywhere
> Singing life will find him there;
> Then the door will open wide,
> And my friend, again outside,
> Will be living, having died.

Of the same dignity is *The Poor Relation* who

> sings and watches like a bird,
> Safe in a comfortable cage
> From which there will be no more flying.

Better known than most of Robinson's great poems is *Hillcrest*, where a man

> may by contemplation learn
> A little more than what he knew,
> And even see great oaks return
> To acorns out of which they grew.
>
> .   .   .   .   .   .
>
> And he may never dare again
> Say what awaits him, or be sure
> What sunlit labyrinth of pain
> He may not enter and endure.
>
> Who knows today from yesterday
> May learn to count no thing too strange:
> Love builds of what Time takes away,
> Till Death itself is less than Change.[10]

Great also is the end of *The Burning Book* (subtitled "The Contented Metaphysician"), portraying Robinson's best friend Burnham the mystic who, having been emptied of self, is destroying his lifework, watching its still glowing ashes:

> He has come to the end of his words,
>   And alone he rejoices
> In the choiring that silence affords
>   Of ineffable voices.
>
> To a realm that his words may not reach
>   He may lead none to find him;

An adept, and with nothing to teach,
  He leaves nothing behind him.
For the rest, he will have his release,
  And his embers, attended
By the large and unclamoring peace
  Of a dream that is ended.

Along with these affirmations of the mature Robinson in the 1916 volume there are the equally mature negations, the satires. *Cassandra*, published soon after the opening of the European War in '14, is an always valid and brilliant condemnation of patriotism for a nation whose standards are those of wealth. *The Man Against the Sky*, title poem, is one of Robinson's two major attacks on materialism, the other being the famous letter to Will Durant in 1931. It is an intellectual poem, but far advanced beyond the smartness of *Captain Craig*, which versified many notions, some Robinson's, most of them borrowed. *The Man* professes only one notion, the affirmation of some meaning in life, and the counternegation, the denial of materialistic meaninglessness.

The double epic *Merlin* and *Lancelot* was planned in the summer of 1915 [11] as a comment on the World War and the necessary destruction of nineteenth-century culture because, like Camelot, it was built on rotten foundations of self.

After finishing both poems, Robinson wrote Hagedorn, with typical evasion of the main theme, that Lancelot may, "if one insists . . . be taken as a rather distant symbol of Germany." [12] More nearly, the source of the epic was the destruction of the Robinson family, like that of Camelot, by Herman's two or more daemons of self-indulgence.

But when it came to composition, these social sources faded out of importance. Especially in *Merlin*, the autobiographical surfaces are few and unimportant. The double epic is a statement of Robinson's conclusions at forty-five about self and its relation to the good life. In the summer of 1915 the two poems were planned as a unit, *Lancelot* to carry and resolve the main theme, with *Merlin* to be "written in anticipation of" it, "to complement its various incompletenesses." [13] Robinson started *Merlin* about the

first of the year, 1916. In February, *The Man Against the Sky*
appeared and got him his first major notice. He finished *Merlin*
in the fall of '16, and wrote Isaacs that he thought it was "the
least bad thing I have done." [14] On December 22, the Unseen
Powers, through the agency of Ledoux, Isaacs, and others, all
anonymous, sent him a Christmas present in the form of notice
from the New York Trust Company that an annual sum of $1,200
was to be placed to his credit, beginning on January 1, 1917, and
possibly to be renewed for three years thereafter.[15] Robinson always considered this subsidy as a loan, and eventually paid it
all back in cash, together with manuscripts worth many times
the advances. At this time he acknowledged the gift with gratitude for its enabling him "to go on with a rather exacting piece
of literary work without worry or interruption." [16] In spite of
exhaustion from overwork on *Merlin,* he buckled down to *Lancelot* and had a bad winter—"pretty much hell," he wrote Ledoux.[17]
Meanwhile, Macmillan published *Merlin* in February, '17, a
month before the United States entered the war, and the reception was disappointing because the "so called critics" couldn't
understand it. Robinson finished *Lancelot* in the late fall of '17
and rewrote much of it in '18. Macmillan, having done badly
with *Merlin,* declined to risk another archaic extravaganza, and
it did not appear until '20.

The double epic can be read either universally or autobiographically. In the universal reading, intended by the arrange-
ment, *Merlin* comes first, presenting classical Humanism,
self-understanding, artistic self expression, a moderated form of
Robinson's early, ecstatic "idealism" and Captain Craig's "Sun,"
altogether a noble experiment in individualism, leading to the
collapse of civilization:

And there was darkness over Camelot.

Lancelot, picking up the story in chaos, presents the triumph of
Christian self-loss where Humanism had failed, the long quest
and final attainment, first by the woman and afterward by the
man, of the Grail of selflessness, the fading of Captain Craig's
hot Sun into the calm Light of Grace, and the turn of the last line
of *Merlin* into the last line of the whole epic,

. . . And in the darkness came the Light.

In the final passage of *Lancelot*, quoted earlier, if we violate the
poetry by substituting "self" for "world," we have the prose statement of the universal preachment of the double epic, that of the
meaning of the good life:

> The Voice within him said: "You are not free.
> You have come to the *self's* end, and it is best
> You are not free. Where the Light falls, death falls;
> And in the darkness comes the Light." He turned
> Again, and he rode on, under the stars
> Out of the *self*, into he knew not what,
> Until a vision chilled him and he saw,
> Now as in Camelot, long ago in the garden,
> The face of Galahad who had seen and died,
> And was alive, now in a mist of gold.
> He rode on into the dark, under the stars,
> And there were no more faces. There was nothing.
> But always in the darkness he rode on,
> Alone; and in the darkness came the Light.

This was Robinson's preachment for mankind in 1915, and he
deviated from it only a little fifteen years later in his last period.
But in the autobiographical reading of the double epic it represented only the end of his preliminary quest, the quest simply
to see the Light far off. There remained the question of what he
should do then, how he should implement the vision in his own
living. He said later, "In *Lancelot* I said what I have to say." That
is, he declared what he had *seen*. But that was not necessarily a
declaration of what personally he *was*, or of what he was going to
do. To discover those biographical matters we must turn the double
epic around. *Lancelot* becomes the preliminary statement, and
Merlin the account of what he was going to make of it. There is
no evidence that Robinson wrote even a partial draft of *Lancelot*
before he wrote *Merlin*. But, on the other hand, there is no question but that *Lancelot* was first in his mind, that *Merlin* was, in
order of conception, an afterthought of important matters that
could not be disposed of in *Lancelot*, certain "incompletenesses"

of projected *Lancelot* which, dramatically speaking, it would be well to get out of the way before the main action. In the record of Robinson's own life, the central drama of *Merlin* portrayed what he knew himself to be and the course that, having now seen the truth, he was going to follow, the way he was going to take instead of questing on to the Grail of complete self-loss and saintliness. What he called the "incompletenesses" of *Lancelot*, both the poem and the man, were the very completenesses, the realities, of Robinson himself. Although *Merlin* has nothing to do with the triangle, and Vivian in green and scarlet suggests Emma not at all, yet as presenting Robinson's own individual psychology it may be the most profoundly biographical of all his poems.

Merlin, like Robinson, is the artist whose calling is to see inwardly and to make outwardly; Lancelot is the saint whose parallel duty it is to be and to do. Merlin, like Robinson, loved the world and made Camelot and Arthur to be a "mirror" wherein men could see themselves, and at the same time "as an object lesson to prove that nothing can stand on a rotten foundation." [18] Both Merlin and Robinson knew that always "the story of the living king" is "the story of the living sin" of self, and that the same will be true of all the things men do in the outer world where the self lives, their great achievements, their works of art, their civilizations, their towers and palaces, their Camelots; all alike must vanish as part of the illusory outer world where they arose.

> "All this that was to be
> Might show to man how vain it were to wreck
> The world for self . . .
> When I began with Arthur I could see
> In each bewildered man who dots the earth
> A moment with his days a groping thought
> Of an eternal will, strangely endowed
> With merciful illusions whereby self
> Becomes the will itself and each man swells
> In fond accordance with his agency.
> Now Arthur, Modred, Lancelot, and Gawaine
> Are swollen thoughts of this eternal will
> Which have no other way to find the way

> That leads them on to their inheritance
> Than by the time-infuriating flame
> Of a wrecked empire. . . ."

Merlin, like Robinson, combined the inner prophet who could see all things, both in and out of time, with the outer maker whose compulsion was to form perfect imitations of what he saw. As the prophet he saw the Arthurs, the Modreds, the Gawaines, the early Lancelots who would "wreck the world for self," that is, the outer self; and he saw also the Galahads and the later Lancelots who would return from the outer world to the inner world of the inner self with its inner Light. As the prophet, the inner self, he perceived both the outer and the inner selves of all men, and that perception that united him to them was love. He did not desire to make them into anything else than what he saw, or to impose himself on them in any way. But as the artist, an outer self with its ordering mind, he desired to arrange all men as perceived into new and perfect units in the outer world. And among other men he "saw himself," which is to say that his inner self saw his outer self working in the outer world, and he perceived, and the outer self admitted, that his fate was to go on working there, wherefore he would not ever come to the inner and selfless Light that he had seen far off—"I shall see no grail." And as he grew old in making things with his mind he foresaw that the process would lapse into the mere play of thoughts and images for their own unimplemented and insignificant sakes, until finally these would fade, along with the world, and there would remain nothing but the outer self alone:

> "The man who sees
> May go on seeing till the immortal flame
> That lights and lures him folds him in its heart,
> And leaves of what there was of him to die
> An item of inhospitable dust
> That love and hate alike must hide away;
> Or there may still be charted for his feet
> A dimmer faring, where the touch of time
> Were like the passing of a twilight moth
> From flower to flower into oblivion,

If there were not somewhere a barren end
Of moths and flowers, and glimmering far away
Beyond a desert where the flowerless days
Are told in slow defeats and agonies,
The guiding of a nameless light that once
Had made him see too much—and has by now
Revealed in death, to the undying child
Of Lancelot, the Grail.

.   .   .   .

                   But let the man
Who saw too much, and was to drive himself
From paradise, play too lightly or too long
Among the moths and flowers, he finds at last
There is a dim way out; and he shall grope
Where pleasant shadows lead him to the plain
That has no shadow but his own behind him.

.   .   .   .

                   I see the light,
But I shall fall before I come to it . . ."

Merlin could make kings but he could not be one. He could
make Camelot, knowing it would fall through the clashing selves
of Arthur, Modred, Lancelot and Gawaine, yet he could not save
it when it was falling:

"I saw; but I was neither Fate nor God.
I saw too much; and this would be the end,
Were there to be an end. I saw myself—
A sight no other man has ever seen;
And through the dark that lay beyond myself
I saw two fires that are to light the world."

At the end, when Merlin, having returned to Merlin's Rock above
the town, sees Camelot falling, he attaches to himself Dagonet
the Fool, the prophet and the fool at last united as Robinson
always saw them in himself and in mankind. The artist-prophet
and the fool set out together toward what new work they did not
know. From Dagonet's shoulder

> the living weight
> Of Merlin's hand was lifted. They arose,
> And, saying nothing, found a groping way
> Down through the gloom together. Fiercer now,
> The wind was like a flying animal
> That beat the two of them incessantly
> With icy wings, and bit them as they went.
> The rock above them was an empty place
> Where neither seer nor fool should view again
> The stricken city. Colder blew the wind
> Across the world, and on it heavier lay
> The shadow and the burden of the night;
> And there was darkness over Camelot.

And yet that darkness was still the eternal *tabula rasa* of the artist, the blank universe in which he will start making worlds again. As Bedivere had said, there would be "another Camelot, and another King." And there were still the "two fires" of Merlin's prophecy,

> "the torch
> Of woman, who, together with the light
> That Galahad found, is yet to light the world."

And all that Robinson's Merlin saw and said and lived, Robinson himself saw and said and lived. He had seen the "time-infuriating flame" of his wrecked home and relations with Herman "lighted by the torch" of Emma, and he also knew that same torch had already driven him in sight of "the light that Galahad found." Like Merlin, he knew that if all men, so impelled, would continue on their ways toward selflessness, their combined quests would be the saving of mankind. That would be another story, not of an artist and a prophet but of a hero and a saint. That would be the story of Lancelot and Guinevere, and Robinson proceeded to offer it as the universal prescription. But for himself, he was content, like Merlin, to create man's quest without undertaking it himself, to write the play without casting himself as the hero. Like Merlin, he would tell men how to save themselves, but would not trouble about his own salvation. He would not be guilty of the "great haste . . . for your perfection" with which he had Guinevere charge Lancelot a little later. And we may wonder whether in that indifference to his own self and its grail, an indifference which he had actually achieved, he had not unconsciously already reached "the light that Galahad found" and was living by his own prescription.

In passing, it may be observed that for saturation of pure poetry *Merlin* is superior to *Lancelot,* whose aesthetic power is rather in its dramatic dialogues as such; we may wonder whether the relative lack of poetic or tropeic language in *Lancelot* may not have been due to a continuation through 1917 of the fatigue in which Robinson started it. However that may be, *Lancelot* is superior to *Merlin* in the sweep of content which is greatness. *Merlin* is a very nearly perfect work of art, an extremely rare thing in a book-length poem. *Lancelot* is uneven as art, but it takes us beyond art to the silence at the end of human experience where nothing remains to be said or symbolized. Robinson was sufficiently satisfied with it to repeat respecting it what he had already said in slightly more reserved language of *The Woman and the Wife* and of *Merlin*: ". . . it seems to me to be rather the best thing I have done." [19]

There is not a syllable in the record, in legend, or in rumor to imply that Robinson, having shown to others the way to the Light, ever considered consciously taking that course himself. Like Lancelot, he seized a last chance to go back and see Guinevere, but, unlike Lancelot, he did not ride away from her to find the Grail. In the winter of 1918/19, Emma was acting as a sort of nurse for a handicapped boy at Groton School whom she took into Boston every week to see the doctor. Early in December Robinson went up to Boston, presumably to see her, and on the fourteenth, back in New York, he reported to Burnham:

My last trip to Boston was active but not satisfactory. I don't want another like it, and from present indications I'm not going to have one. Some things die hard, but they die sooner or later. Sometimes the man dies too, but I'm glad to say that I'm not dead yet, being persuaded of the illusion that I still have things to do. [20]

This is the most likely of several possible occasions when Emma may have made him an unauthenticated offer to house him permanently in Farmingdale, without marriage. Robinson's Robinsonian reply was, "If I can't have your love, I don't want your pity." We may speculate to no purpose as to just what he meant here by "love," and what by "pity."

Five days after Robinson reported the Boston trip to Burnham, the Unseen Powers compensated him for the loss of Emma by a continuation of their assistance in the field of art, "the illusion that I still have things to do." He wrote Isaacs:

> I have just received a note from Ledoux which puts me again under great obligation to you and, as I understand (or rather don't understand) to others . . . [He gives Isaacs] my assurance of a friendship that does not change with the expiration of exceptional favors. Of course it makes all the difference with my work that things are as they are, but if they were otherwise . . . I should still be Yours invariably (you can't read that, so I'll say it again)
>
> Yours invariably
>
> E.A.R.[21]

The flat dismissal Robinson received in Boston in December of '18, doubtless with the reinforcement of other signs, put an end to his assimilation of Emma to Guinevere, with the belief that she loved him and, Héloïse-like, had refused him only for the sake of his career, his "light." From '20 through '23 Emma had a position as a house-mother in Bradford Academy in Haverhill, and they met sometimes in Boston during his migrations to and from the MacDowell Colony, spring and fall. But Emma seems always to have taken along a daughter for protection, and the meetings were only friendly and conventional. In the next volume, *The Three Taverns*, 1920, there are four triangular poems. Of these *London Bridge* seems, for both stylistic and substantial reasons, to belong to the period then twenty years past. But the other three reflected Robinson's current reinterpretations not only of Emma but of Herman also, and of her relations to him.

Nimmo was probably the earliest written of the three, having been published in *Scribner's Magazine* in 1916, the year of the appearance of *The Man Against the Sky*, the year of the composition of *Merlin* with *Lancelot* in prospect, and a year and a half before the fatal "trip to Boston." It rests, therefore, in Robinson's still undisillusionized belief that Emma loved him. The poem—one of those, like *Bokardo* and *Bewick Finzer*, that has little more than an autobiographical excuse for preservation— is of interest, as has been noticed, for the mention of the macabre element in Herman, "the devil in those eyes," and of Emma's coldness:

> The calm of women who have loved and changed.

It is important as showing a reviving respect for Herman:

> I'm painting here a better man, you say,
> Than I, the painter; and you say the truth.

And it is unique among all the triangular poems—except *Lancelot* and *Tristram*—in showing qualms on his account as the slighted husband:

> God knows if I have more than men forgive
> To tell him; but I played, and I shall pay.

Surely the obvious implication is a swagger of unfounded poetical licentiousness.

A poem that reflects Robinson's post-1918 understanding that Emma does not love him is *Rahel to Varnhagen*—again a poem that has very little reason for survival except for the personal record. It is the earliest, I think, in which the love of Herman is recognized as major, and in which the "dead hand" appears to inhibit the possibility of the new love. There is no hint of any promise to the deceased, but simply the fact that

> There is a love that ceases to be love
> In being ourselves. How, then, are we to lose it?

There is incidental identification in the fact that the widow is older than the new suitor; and the jealousy of the dead husband

suggests the future *Cavender's House.* The poem hints also that
the old love and its dead grip might be overcome by sensitive
understanding, a quality which the new candidate seems to
possess in a way that suggests Robinson. The poet's sly intentions
are revealed also in a full head-note—unique, but for two of the
late historical poems, among the 208 titles in the *Collected
Poems*—in which the author informs the gentle reader that Rahel
and Varnhagen did in course marry and live happily ever after.

Late Summer, said to record an actual evening back in late
September of 1909, presumably on one of the beaches of Capitol
Island, is the first poem in which Robinson faces and expresses
fully his new realization, not only that Emma does not love him
now, but that her love of Herman is so great that it could never
under any possible development be superseded by a new love.
It is not one of Robinson's greatest, but it is one of his most
beautiful poems, the incantation of its alcaics and assonances
being also that of the surf with its weary, universal wisdom, ad-
vancing and retreating on the beach with the alternating human
dialogue of appeal and refusal, refusal and appeal. The suitor
charges the widow with enslavement to the dead hand, the
"flimsy wraith" of her husband. Also with "pride." Also, there is
unexplained "conscience," possibly referring to the promise, or
perhaps to the feeling of infidelity, "misgivings of innocence,"
as she begins to weaken towards the new love. But most impressive of all Robinson's transitional accounts of Emma's refusal of
him is the fact that here the widow's feeling for the suitor, however genuine, is not even of the same order as her love for her
late husband. Brutally, she tells him:

> "What you believe is right for the two of us
> Makes it as right that you are not one of us."

The reference to two "two's" recalls the different duality in *Partnership* twenty-three years earlier, where "two" were to live "for
the glory of the clay" and the other "two" were to "suffer and
forgive." Here the distinction is flatly between love and its absence. To this frank exclusion from Emma's inmost sanctuary
Win has no answer:

She gazed away where shadows were covering
The whole cold ocean's healing indifference.
No ship was coming. When the darkness
Fell, she was there, and alone, still gazing.

Not long after *Late Summer* Robinson wrote, and published in 1925, *If the Lord Would Make Windows in Heaven* in which he celebrates satirically Emma's love for Herman as Win now realizes that it was in his pathetic, failing years:

She who had eyes but had not wherewithal
To see that he was doomed to his own way,
Dishonored his illusions day by day,
And year by year was more angelical.
Flaunting an injured instinct for the small,
She stifled always more than she would say;
Nursing a fear too futile to betray,
She sewed, and waited for the roof to fall.

A seer at home, she saw that his high lights
That were not shining, and were not afire,
Were such as never would be seen from there;
A saint abroad, she saw him on the heights,
And feared for him—who, if he went much higher,
Might one day not be seen from anywhere.

Also in '25 appeared the triangular *Mortmain*. It is a comment on Robinson's method of composing his narratives that before he started this poem he asked Esther Bates and others at the MacDowell Colony if they could put him on the track of a good story about the "dead hand." He had his theme in mind and was looking for some extraneous story to adjust to it. *Mortmain* is about its title and nothing else, for the deceased whose hold prevents the lady marrying an old friend was her brother. The Legend holds, nevertheless, that he was Herman, and that if in the suitor's speeches we substitute "*my* brother" for "*your* brother," and conversely in the lady's speeches, we shall have the autobiographical truth of the poem. There is only one bit of evidence of a new element in Robinson's interpretation, a suggestion that he realizes that although Emma may not love

him as she did Herman, yet she did have for him some kind of a
special feeling:

> What is it in me that you like so much,
> And love so little?

Of the five triangular poems just noticed, the important three
were published in the *Three Taverns* volume in 1920, the same
year in which *Lancelot* finally appeared. In June of that year
Robinson wrote Emma from the MacDowell Colony: "I am
haunted more than ever by the notion that there is no very good
reason why I should stay around much longer—though of course
everything will seem different when I have another spurt." [22]
And so he eased into the next year, which, from the point of view
of the worldly success he scorned, was his great watershed. In
1921 appeared the first *Collected Poems,* 165 titles and 590 pages,
and it was received by the literary world, here and abroad, with
almost universal acclaim. The next year it was granted the first
of his Pulitzer prizes, and the same year Yale made him a Doctor
of Letters, his first honorary degree. Neff says that after that he
"lived by his pen, with no further need of subsidy." [23]

In the busy year of '21 the volume *Avon's Harvest* also appeared, the title poem dealing not with the triangle but with
two sides of it. The central figure, whose name is a possible phonetic suggestion of Herman, had been a "major mediocrity" in
school to whom a young highbrow "worm" attached himself. At
first Avon merely despised him as Herman had despised little
Win. But, having found an occasion to knock him down, he felt
remorse toward him, and after remorse came fear. The intellectual haunted him through life, though absent and presently dead,
finally becoming psychologically the devil and occasioning Avon's
death through terror. The scene of his most ghastly hallucination
is on a lake in the woods, in a shack which the Legend identifies
on the back cove of Capitol Island; it was where Herman lived
some of the time during his worst period, and he may have suffered alcoholic delirium there. In passing it may be observed
that the *Avon's Harvest* volume contains the famous *Mr. Flood's
Party,* which becomes the ninth of Robinson's poems which he
assigned successively to the status of "the best," or "the least

bad," thing he had done.[24] Of the four objective poems on the list, the others being *Shiras, The Klondike,* and *The Tavern,* it is the only one with a permanent claim to greatness.

Roman Bartholow, 1923, contains Win's assistance to Herman and the passage of jealous violence which have been noticed. Otherwise, but for Emma's apparent insistence that it was auto-biographical, it would seem to be very little so. The story is Gabrielle's, who, outside of being dark and "too beautiful to live," seems to suggest Emma in no particular. She is a metropolitan society woman, less cold than empty and unawakened. Moving to the country with her husband Bartholow, she does not love either him or his friend Penn-Raven with whom she has an affair, wherefore, despairing of her capacity for love, she commits suicide. When Robinson gave Esther Bates the manuscript to type, he told her that he had had the story in mind eleven years before he went to work on it. Since we don't know when he started it, but do know that he often let a draft lie around a few years before publishing it, this eleven years might go back to the critical time at the end of 1909, and might indicate that from the beginning he had moods of doubt whether Emma ever loved anybody. Significant may be Gabrielle's inability to go along with Bartholow in the mystical adventure that oriented his life:

> I am the bridge, then, over which you pass,
> Here in the dark, to find a lighted way
> To a new region where I cannot follow.

This was Guinevere's weakness too, but with the difference that Guinevere loved Lancelot, including his mysticism, and was able to devote herself to it as part of him. After Miss Bates typed *Bartholow,* she asked Robinson whether in his next book he would have it "in for women" as much as he had before. He said, "I don't think I have it in for women any more than the world has it in for women." [25]

After *Bartholow* appeared in the spring of '23, Robinson went to England, his only trip abroad, and scarcely moved out of London.

Robinson's next book, *The Man Who Died Twice,* has nothing to do with women. It has nothing to do, except tangentially, with

the triangle. Even more than *Merlin,* probably more than any
other poem of Robinson's, this one has a following who celebrate
it as his greatest. It is supreme both in quality and quantity,
both in excellence of poetry and in sweep of content. Its theme
is the creative impulse, the experience of compulsive composition,
the relation of individual choice to what Robinson, speaking
elsewhere of himself, referred to as his "devil of poetry," what
the composer Fernando Nash here calls his "daemon":

> If I remember you
> As first you were anointed and ordained,
> There was a daemon in you, not a devil,
> Who told you then that when you heard those drums
> Of death, it would be death to follow them.
> You were to trust your daemon and to wait,
> And wait, and still to wait. You had it—once.
> You had it then—though you had not yet heard it,
> Coming as it would have to come some time,
> Blown down by choral horns out of a star
> To quench those drums of death with singing fire
> Unfelt by man before. You knew it then.
> You felt it singing down out of the sky
> When you were only a small boy at school;
> And you knew then that it was all for you,
> For you and for the world, that it was coming.

The Man Who Died Twice is perhaps as limitless in its un-
folding revelations, always new with each rereading, as a poem
can be, and a major work would be required to criticize it. Outside of its sheer poetry, its importance is as a dossier of Robinson's theological and aesthetic notions. For the present interest,
as an autobiographical statement, it records, through Fernando
Nash, Robinson's period when he believed in himself, had no
recognition, was tempted to slide off into alcoholism, and didn't.
Perhaps also it remembers Herman who, after early defeat,
failed, as Fernando failed, to "wait" and hurried off to the solace
of the bottle. Perhaps also, and unintended by Robinson, it records what might be either a conflict or a paradox in his own
nature, that between the artist and the saint, that between Merlin

and Lancelot. Through compulsive grace, Fernando achieved, not his major external composition, but personal salvation, the Grail, the Light. Yet he did accomplish the great composition inwardly; he did hear it played. Also, thereafter, instead of vanishing into some kind of selfless service, he marched around with the Salvation Army, shouting "Glory to God!" and beating "the drums of life." He did continue to practice art of a sort, an expression of the outer self, even while in grace which is the realization of the inner self and the negation of the outer. It could be that Robinson was beginning to feel, whatever he might think, that it was not necessarily true that his Merlin, or Robinson himself, even while continuing to build Camelots, could not be Lancelot also, that he could "see no grail," that art must depend on the ascendance of the outer self.

The year after its publication, '25, *The Man Who Died Twice* got Robinson his second Pulitzer prize, and in June Bowdoin College "doctored" him, as he called it. After the ceremony in Brunswick he went on up to Gardiner, made some calls, and along with Emma visited her daughter Mrs. Nivison and her husband William in their red cottage—not the original Shepherd one—on Capitol Island. In the evening Win and Emma walked out on the stony beach of the waist of the island, perhaps remembering *Late Summer*, written at least five years before. When he was back at the MacDowell Colony on June 25, Robinson wrote Burnham: "My trip to Maine was pleasant in some ways but it made me a little blue to see my relations grow old and to go over old trails." [26] A good, cryptic, Robinson understatement. Did he mean the fires were dying? Seven years later he wrote Smith more precisely: "Gardiner gave me the creeps when I saw it in 1924 [mistake for 1925] and I haven't seen it since." [27] He never did. At the end of '25 he moved to his final residence, the top floor of the house of James Fraser the sculptor, at 328 East 42nd Street.

In that summer of '25 Robinson started *Tristram*, two and perhaps three different motives coalescing to set it off. A legitimate motive certainly was that it had always been his favorite opera, and he had been planning to poetize the story for at least ten years. Another probable motive, also legitimate, was that he wanted to celebrate what he now recognized as Emma's great, lifelong love for Herman. The illegitimate motive was that he was mightily irritated at being called a "dry New England psychologist," or the equivalent. Although he had no time for the more or less Freudian sexual dogma of the twenties, nevertheless he had been badgered into wanting to announce for the public record that he had "lived" as much as the next poet. Afterwards he was much ashamed of this motive and of the consequent, spectacular success of *Tristram*. In the middle of May, '27, while the "best selling" was raging, he wrote Emma:

> Just now I'm getting a lot of unwholesome publicity over *Tristram*, which isn't any better than *Lancelot* if it is as good. But it's "all about love" and that seems to be what people want, from the aged to the young.
>
> By the way you will know from Van Doren's book that I used to read to my mother while sitting on the kitchen floor —an occupation that I don't remember.
>
> May you all prosper,
Yours always,
E.A.R.[28]

Outside of the superficial portraiture of Emma in the dark Isolt, the resemblance between the sea and cliffs of Tintagel and those of Capitol Island, the similarity of the opening scene of *Tristram* to an incident during a party in the Shepherd cottage in '91, and one or two other details to be mentioned, outside of these matters of setting, it is not easy to find autobiographical revelation in *Tristram*. In spite of the similarity in dark-haired, blue-eyed beauty, there is little in the slow languor of Isolt to suggest the intellectually busy, sprightly, and playful Emma. Especially, it seems far-fetched to identify here, as has been attempted, Robinson's definitive record of his great love. Even if we assume—what is possible—that they had an affair during the critical fall of 1909, yet Robinson's belief when he started writing *Tristram* in '25 was, and for at least five years before had been, that Emma had never loved him, that any kindness she had shown him had been the result of "pity," not of "love." Furthermore, with the dubious exception of *Roman Bartholow*, the recent autobiographical poetry had revealed his current belief that she had had a great, passionate, and irreplaceable love for Herman. If the poem involves the triangle essentially, it is as a salute to Herman and a celebration of a kind of utterly enthralling, unimaginative passion of which Win himself was incapable. If we must find Robinson in the cast, let us look first at Tristram as previously noticed in the opening, sulking scene; and from there let us jump to King Mark in his final speech on the belvedere with the harvest of the love deaths lying before him:

> Nothing in this
> Is love that I have found, nor is it in love
> That shall find me. I shall know day from night
> Until I die, but there are darknesses
> That I am never to know, by day or night;
> All which is one more weary thing to learn,
> Always too late.

The earlier, "rheumy"-eyed Mark had of course nothing to do with the poet, but here the finally generous Mark speaks for Robinson. He always presumed that the other fellow, especially if he was an opponent, knew some final secret that he did not. Greater humility could hardly be.

Robinson once said to Esther Bates, "You know this sort of thing happens. . . . People love the way Tristram and Isolt were supposed to. . . . It is not rare. . . . It happens." No doubt he believed that it did happen; but just as he was incapable of experiencing it, so he was not qualified to delineate it. Sentimental reputation to the contrary, such integrated feeling is rarely in the actual experience of artists. Poets especially are often preoccupied with sex and love, wherefore their unusual sensibility makes them specially perceptive of women's feelings and so the finest of lovers in the sense of understanding and delicacy. But, being first of all intellectuals, with their lives in their imaginations, the kind of energy that notoriously may serve either imagination or sex tends with them primarily into the former channel, leaving a subnormal rather than an abnormal capacity for Eros. The great loves of the poets, from which they get their reputations, are the absent ones, and the names of the ladies are

likely to be Beatrice, Laura, Stella, the "lady of the sonnets"—
or Emma. For sheer, honest, noble passion look to the simple
man of action of Herman's or Tristram's type, in whom the small
imaginative channel draws off no more than is necessary for
the common swagger of manly vanity and the military decisions
of the battlefield or the market, leaving the main flood of vitality
to its elementary courses.

For all Robinson's genius for projecting himself into all kinds
of people in all kinds of situations, this businessman's experience
was one which he was unqualified to portray. Wherefore, his
method of ennobling Tristram, and presumably Herman, was to
attribute to them perceptions which it would have astonished
and confused them to be told they possessed. Here is Tristram,
or Herman, ruminating in the presence of his beloved:

> The fading light
> Around them, and the shadowy room that held them—
> All these,—if they were shadows, let them be so,
> He thought. But let these two that were not shadows
> Be as they were, and live—by time no more
> Divided until time for them should cease.
> They were not made for time as others were,
> And time therefore would not be long for them
> Wherein for love to learn that in their love,
> Where fate was more than time and more than love,
> Time never was, save in their fear of it—
> Fearing, as one, to find themselves again
> Intolerably as two that were not there.

.   .   .   .

> Stronger than God,
> When all was done the god of love was fate,
> Where all was love. And this was in a darkness
> Where time was always dying and never dead,
> And where God's face was never to be seen
> To tell the few that were to lose the world
> For love how much or little they lost for it,
> Or paid with others' pain.

Thus Robinson, being Robinson, had to ennoble his erotic hero with a metaphysical perception of love such as neither Herman nor the Tristram of fiction ever enjoyed, Actually the timelessness upon which the poet here insists in such beautiful pentameters is not other than the timeless moment of orgastic realization which, though momentarily all-inclusive, is yet framed in time. In distinction, it is noticeable that in the last dozen pages of *Lancelot*, where he is dealing with true mystics, the word "time" is not once used in its metaphysical sense. And yet, albeit in far less compact rhetoric, we are made perfectly aware that Lancelot and Guinevere are truly outside of time in the realm of the timeless and selfless inner self "where death itself is less than change."

Perhaps what Robinson was doing here was to justify Emma nobly in her supposed enslavement to the dead hand. And to this end he attributed to Herman his own idealistic love for which Herman did not have the capacity. No doubt the effort was honest, the tour de force not consciously one. In order to write the honest poetry, he had to believe honestly, at least in the heat of composition, that Herman's love was as all-inclusive as he portrayed it.

Tristram, having been started in '25, represented the vanishing echo of Robinson's great period. It got him his third Pulitzer and a sum over the first two years which, with the addition of the steady returns from the *Collected Poems*, is usually guessed at $30,000. In the summer of '28 he sent Isaacs, his financial adviser, Macmillan's current statement for $14,535.88, with the marginal note, "not bad for blank verse." He now could have his once coveted respectability, and he made the appropriate gesture to confirm it. Out of the seeming independence he had established through the last ten years, he lapsed into a second anticlimax. For the last time he asked Emma to marry him, presumably by letter. This was probably in '28 when she was sixty-three and Win was approaching fifty-nine. According to report, there was no reference to the ancient promise or to her continuing bond to Herman. She turned Win down on the sensible ground that she did not think she could do him credit in the cosmopolitan literary world where he now belonged. At last Robinson had to acknowledge to himself that the play was over, that he had failed to prolong it into a happy ending. Also, this was the end of that Anticipation which he had always considered to be so large a part of his Idealism; and with Emma there had hardly been enough consummated mutuality to replace it with the Memory which might equally have served. Instead she faded into the landscape of aging every day. Their long, fond, incompleted relationship became the object of less emotionalized, more realistic scrutiny than he had given it before. If their correspondence at this time is ever uncovered, it may show some interesting revelations on Emma's part, some of which got into Win's verse a few years later. In the meantime he indulged his respectability by presenting to the Gardiner Hospital a diagnostic laboratory in memory of his brother Dean.

The end of Robinson's late attempt to revive the drama was still not yet the end of the triangle as material for his narratives. In *Cavender's House* ('29) it is Herman's jealousy again. Cavender is the typical Herman, the typical businessman, "the sort that owns and gloats." Twelve years before the story opens, suspecting his wife Laramie of infidelity with some Win who does not appear, he murdered her by pushing her off a cliff on their property, and since then he has lived in a "dark house" of self, tortured by guilt and by uncertainty as to whether she had indeed been unfaithful. Now she returns as a figment of his psyche and informs him in Robinson's mature blank verse that his problem is not to find out whether she was guilty or not but to overcome his own outer self whose possessiveness was then and still is the real cause of his discomfort.

In *The Glory of the Nightingales* ('30) the original murder theme of *The Night Before* is revived. The rich businessman has stolen the girl and in some way has caused her death. Now the wronged lover, having transcended self rather than overcoming it, proceeds to the villain's great house by the sea with the design of shooting him. The situation is neatly resolved by the villain committing suicide, leaving the true lover his palace and his fortune. A candidate for the thinnest of Robinson's stories.

A year later, in '31, comes *Matthias at the Door*, the last of Robinson's great autobiographical dramas. The sweep is still there, but the poetic and rhetorical power of *Merlin, Lancelot, The Man Who Died Twice*, and the objective *Three Taverns* and *Rembrandt to Rembrandt*, the power of the great years '13 to '25, is gone. Here is Robinson's first use of death as a central theme, perhaps because, while all his life he has had moments when he felt his work was done and there was no point in his "staying around," now he is begining to suffer his first gastronomic evidence that there actually is "something wrong." Also, here is his last elaboration in verse, perhaps his final belief, with respect to his lifelong preoccupation: the inner self and its world, the outer self and its world, and the moral significance of the latter. And here, from the point of view of the personal drama, is his summary recapitulation of the family quadrangle.

Dean Robinson, as Garth, a complete worldly failure, is Matthias's friend and the God in the Machine, here enjoying his last "glory of the unfulfilled," his last and best tribute from his youngest brother. Matthias is another version of Herman, the rich businessman who has never thought of anything but the material and superficial "realities" of life, complacent in his power and possessive of his wife in a conventionally considerate way. Timberlake, another friend of Matthias, is lean, laconic, and imaginative, has bright blue eyes that might as well be bright brown, and seems the nearest approximation of a self-portrait that Robinson ever drew. Natalie, the wife of Matthias, is a redhead who, standing in the usual place between Herman and Win, is generic Woman with little specific suggestion of Emma. The plot rises out of the situation created long ago when Matthias rescued Timberlake from a fire, in gratitude for which Timberlake, in love with Natalie, surrendered her to Matthias, and proceeded to become a world wanderer and an alcoholic. Natalie, always loving Timberlake, eventually married Matthias out of pity and because she liked him. She is now hopelessly unhappy and ready to run off with Timberlake any time. He and Garth, both neighbors, are in and out of the big house on the country estate. The "Door" is a cavernous opening in a cliff in a glen a hundred yards or so below the house. It is the entrance to Death and is flanked by vague columns with an appropriate Egyptian aura. One by one, the three intimates of Matthias go through the door in the hope of waking him out of his complacency. Garth and Natalie go by suicide, but Timberlake, always externally ineffectual, waits till his "name is called." When they are all gone, Matthias, suspecting something amiss in himself, purposes to follow them through the door, but the door won't have him.

Matthias at the Door is anticlimactic in the development of Robinson's ideas. It ignores his lifelong notion of the conflict between the inner and outer selves, and asserts instead the necessity of merging them through mutual adjustment. The problems of Matthias and Timberlake are superficially different, but fundamentally they are the same, to build an integrated personality out of both selves. Matthias, having no awakened inner self with its imagination, must die to all self and be born again as the person he has always been potentially, a fusion of an outer self working in the outer world and a rudimentary inner self whose highest vision will be of service. The ghost of Garth, returning into Matthias's consciousness when he is trying to push through the Door, recites Robinson's last message, seeming to involve a serious qualification of the quasi-Christian one spread between the contents of *The Man Against the Sky* and *The Man Who Died Twice.*

"You can not die, Matthias, till you are born.

. . . .

"There's more of you for you to find, Matthias,
Than science has found yet, or may find soon.

. . . .

You will not see it there,
Though you may find it there if a door opens.
Not this door, but another one in yourself.

. . . .

"You will go back
To build another tower—a safer one
This time, and one for many to acclaim
And to enjoy. It will be yours to build—

. . . .

> And yours to dedicate, when it has risen,
> To whom it shall serve best. . . .
> > It will be done
>
> .   .   .   .
> Out of a slumbering thought."

Here is the touch of Merlin, the artist, in every man, but it is not the great Merlin who has a powerful inner self, who sees "the light although I shall not come to it." Here the only hint of the light is a "slumbering thought," a figment of so much inner self as Matthias is capable of developing.

> "Most of us are half-born, with only self
> To cheer us with a promise of importance
> Until it is all over—in appearance—
> And one by one we're down here at this door . . .
>
> .   .   .   .
> There's a ship waiting for you; and when dawn
> Begins to let you know, you will see then
> That you are outward bound, with all your ruins
> And all your old mistakes on board with you—
> With you, and your regrets, and your possessions,
> And with yourself, and all that makes a tower."

The self here, whose function is "to cheer us" is of course the outer one with its self-preoccupation. A "tower" is not this outer self alone, or an inner self alone, but a composite of them, a person.

Matthias's deficiency was in inner development, and his problem of rebirth, as Herman's would have been had he lived, was to make his potential love, his inner objectivity, functional in the outer setting. Timberlake's original condition, like Robinson's, was opposite. He is chiefly an inner self or imagination that sees the selfless Light, but like Merlin is complicated with talent, or at least high, conscious intelligence, which is of the outer self. Throughout his life he has thought he was following his inner light, particularly in relation to Natalie and Matthias. At some early phase he thought himself unworthy of her—almost certainly an element of eighteen-year-old Win's feeling for Emma in the beginning in '88. Then, after Matthias saved his life, he believed he was following the selfless requirements of gratitude and "honor" in surrendering her to him—conceivably, this could be a reference to Win's gratitude to Herman for saving him by persuading their father to send him to Harvard, but it certainly refers to his exemplary behavior towards Emma when she was freezing to Herman, and Win was taking out his feelings in *Eros Turannos, The Clinging Vine, London Bridge,* and the rest. Robinson differed from Timberlake, apparently, in the ineptitude that made it easy for him to deny outer action, but heretofore he believed as honestly as Timberlake did that his inaction, his passivity, was selfless and right. But for dubious hints in *Lancelot* and *Tristram,* we have no evidence that before this late period Robinson ever suffered from the "dogs" of guilt that pursued Timberlake for his pusillanimous morality in abandoning Natalie to unhappiness. First they chased him into alcohol; and now, after he hears of Natalie's suicide, they tear with their teeth "the garment of [his] soul" and cause him forthwith to drink himself into pneumonia and death. Now for the first time it seems that Robinson himself may be hearing those dogs across the retrospect of his life.

Robinson in his sixty-second year is here confessing, through Timberlake, that his self-righteousness with respect to Emma has been just as much of the outer self and as indifferent to the inner as his sensuality would have been if he had courted her more aggressively early and late. As far as he himself is concerned— and this may not be intended as a universal preachment—he is concluding regretfully at this late date that action in the world is necessary to the good life, and that the outer self's criterion of self-gratification, whether in sensuous or in aesthetic terms, is, under suitable discipline, indispensable to action. What he elsewhere has called the "gleams" of the inner light, however valuable they may be for "idealism" and the materials of poetry, may be dangerous diversions from the course of true living. Says Timberlake:

> "There is no cure for self;
> There's only an occasional revelation,
> Arriving not infrequently too late.
> For me it was too early—which is granted,
> Sometimes to the elected and the damned."

Robinson's "revelations" were "early," beginning with first consciousness, and all of his life his contrapositivism has known that he was both "elected" and "damned." Now he admits the damnation, admits that the things that comprise the reality of life, not only in the outer world but in the inner world also, can be had only through outer action that involves the risk of self-centeredness, or of excess, which in each of these salutary exercises is the real "devil." Here is Timberlake's list of what is worth while— "this that I have here" is whiskey:

> "All things that are worth having are perilous,
> And have their resident devil, respectively.
> There's this that I have here, there's love, pride, art,
> Humility, ambition, pride and glory,
> The kingdom itself, which may come out all right,
> And truth. They are all very perilous,
> And admirable, so long as there is in them
> Passion that knows itself—which, if not hushed,
> Is a wise music."

In 1916 Robinson had settled for Merlin in his role of artist-prophet whose business was to see and reflect the Light for the world, but without coming to it. At most Merlin's solution was compassed within what is here called "art" and, perhaps, "the kingdom itself." Now Robinson goes farther. He seems willing to define the good life in terms of whatever the outer self considers "worth having," so long as the indulgence in it is passionate and is carried out with self-knowledge and, therefore, self-discipline. In other words, Robinson seems at last to be relaxing into complete humanism, possibly influenced by the self-expressionism which he has heard beating around him through the twenties. He is at last accepting the entire implication—originally unintended—of his *Merlin*. As suggested earlier, his indifference, *on his own account*, to the inner Light of selflessness "that Galahad saw," argued that unconsciously he had been living in it all the time. Now, fifteen years later, he seems to imply that some kind of indifference to the standard of selflessness is involved in the good life for all men, that it isn't a matter that anyone need bother about over much. In the double epic, the humanist confession of *Merlin* is followed by the Christian preachment of *Lancelot*. In *Matthias* it seems as if the humanism was not only the confession but the final and unqualified preachment as well.

This lapse from the absolute standard of the inner self and the Light is the intellectual anticlimax of the Epilogue of Robinson's drama. Implicit in it is the personal anticlimax in the form of a reappraisal of his relations with Emma from the beginning. Not that Natalie's hopeless, lifelong love for Timberlake need be taken as anything but hyperbole for the purposes of the fictional story. Robinson did not in his seventh decade return to his early delusion that Emma had always loved him alone, and that Herman had been only a passing infatuation. But what he does seem to confess through Timberlake is that the complex of his own emotions centered in Emma has been less pure than he has professed it to be in much noble poetry, that perhaps the idealistic love and high self-righteousness of the eighteen-year-old of *The Night Before* were always figments of extreme self-preoccupation, and that as such he has been dominated by them directly rather than by his love of Emma of which he thought them to be merely the virtuous sublimations. The implication is that some failure in him, some "resident devil" of self that lacked "passion that knows itself," has been responsible for his long inability to capture her, either before or after the interlude of Herman.

Robinson may well have understood before he wrote *Matthias* the resident devil in his love and in his humility, may have discovered it as the motive of Emma's final rejection of him in '27 or '28; but if so he postponed announcing the discovery until *The March of the Cameron Men*, published in the *Nicodemus* volume in '32, a year after *Matthias*. It is probably his most comprehensive autobiographical confession, both factually and essentially, and it is another of the poems which have very little claim to immortality except as bearers of the personal record. The dialogue occurs during a twilight float in a rowboat on the "lake," which is the wide Kennebec in front of the Farmingdale house. The superficial disguise is in the timing of the incident. In the poem it occurs between the husband's death and his interment, while his body is still lying yonder in the house behind the trees. Not only was this impossible because the river was frozen when Herman died the previous February, it was absurd that two people, then in their forties and both garnished with respectability, should be so impatient of courtship that they couldn't wait until the deceased was underground. Whether on the Kennebec, or by the ocean, or in the parlor, or in the garden, or upstairs in front of Win's Franklin stove, and whether it occupied, not half an hour as here, but three months, this conversation occurred in the critical fall of 1909, almost a decent year after Herman's death.

In the dialogue, involving Emma's swing at first almost to capitulation to marriage and finally back to refusal, all but one of the motives that have been attributed to her in the triangular poems of the past thirty years are touched upon and denied or qualified. The possibility of the promise to Herman is brushed aside. The notion of Emma's being overcerebral and perhaps cold, like Gabrielle in Roman Bartholow, is broached in her presentation of her final conclusion as something that she "thought." In passing she gives Robinson a dressing down on the same score, and her comment bears on the reason for her final refusal:

> "Yes, I am free—if women are ever free;
> And I am thinking—if a woman thinks.
> You men, who from your scalps down to your toes
> Are built of thought, are still debating it.
> But I'll commit myself to your misgivings,
> Your premonitions, and your still small voice,
> And tell you what I think."

The one strong motive that has been attributed to Emma in the past and that is here ignored is that of *Late Summer* and *Tristram*, that of what I called the Dissenting Account, the Isolt-like, great and exclusive passion for Herman. It is not likely that Robinson near the end of his life suffered another complete reversal in his understanding in this matter. Rather, here as in *Matthias*, the assumption that Emma now favored him provides a more dramatic setting than her love of Herman would do for his confession of his own inadequacy. Also, having made in *Tristram* his general gesture to Herman, having since been turned down by Emma on a new and common-sensible ground, and

being at an age of the cooling of passion and passionate interpretations, it is likely that he was now for the first time seeing
Emma and her problems very nearly as they were. Herman was
and remained her great love, yet she was devoted to Win and
was not beyond the possibility of capture by him if he had been
able to attack her with sufficiently appealing weapons. Among
the old accounts, he had approached the real truth in that single
cry of Jane Wayland to John Gorham, "Somewhere in me there's a
woman if you know the way to find her." And he had come nearest
to the actual account in *Rahel to Varnhagen* where the widow
was at first completely possessed by the old love but could be
and was eventually detached from its domination and reoriented
by a combination of strong ardor and subtle and patient understanding.

The story of the *Cameron Men* is that of the wife summoning
from elsewhere the doctor, an old family friend, to treat her
stricken husband who has always been a "devil" who tormented
her with "persecutions." The central drama is contained in three
lyric stanzas which the doctor composes to the tune of the old
Scottish song, a favorite in the Robinson house, which the wife
happens to be playing in the parlor when he arrives. The first
stanza recounts his arrival. In the background, he has always
loved her, but previously she has had no love "to spare" for him:

> Any tune in the world would have told him as well
>> As another of all that was there,
> For a beggar with only a story to tell
>> And a woman with nothing to spare.
> But you called, and a king who believed he was dead
>> Was alive and undying again:
> It was you, and the night, and the stars overhead,
>> And the March of the Cameron Men.

The second stanza assumes an understanding they reached,
involving in the narrative text the "careless" "lapse" of which the
doctor was later ashamed and the wife was not. It was agreed
that they would marry when the husband died:

> In your smile was a gift of ineffable things,
>> And of more than all scholars have learned.

In a palace where beggars were richer than kings
   There was more to be given than earned.
Not a murmur remained of a storm that was past,
   Or of why it had happened, or when.
You had called, and he came; and he found you at last
   In the March of the Cameron Men.

The third stanza assumes a fictional interval of absence after which the doctor returned and, in the narrative, "let [the husband] die"—an example of Robinson's old interest in euthanasia. But the crisis is in the unintended revelation of the doctor's true attitude toward the wife and the projected marriage:

When he left you again there were stars in the way
   Of his eyes, and he wandered alone
In a dream that would mock him for many a day
   With a music unheard and unknown;
Till at last he awoke, and remembered, and found
   All there was that remained of it then.
There was only the sound of the world going round,
   And the March of the Cameron Men.

If Robinson, during that period of courtship in the fall of 1909, had composed and given this stanza to Emma—for he never recited anything if he could avoid it—or if he had told her its substance, he was guilty either of lack of self-understanding or of deliberate, subtle circumlocution for the purpose of getting out of his commitment, or proposal, to marry. Almost certainly it was the former, for in spite of his perpetual self-awareness and his major sense of humor, he was throughout his life sometimes guilty of bland and humorless failure of introspection. Also, there was no impulse stronger in him than that of chivalry to women. It is not conceivable that here, any more than in the case of Mabel Moore or of the Woodland Girl long ago, he would have consciously withdrawn, even by the subtlest indirection, from an undertaking to marry.

But to Emma the real and subconscious motive was only too plain. In her account of it we seem to have her own cerebral tendency entering, the control of "thought." But it is not thought.

It is the direct, emotionalized perception of an intelligent woman on the brink of love. Incidentally, the "waiting" facial expression was one of Emma's.

> "I'll tell you what I think,"
> She said; and her calm eyes were like a child's,
> Waiting for the reward of his approval:
> "I think that when a woman and a man
> Are on their way to make of their two lives
> Deliberate and ceremonial havoc,
> There's folly in going on if one of them
> Sees what's ahead, knowing the other sees it
> And shuts his eyes. I have paid once for ruin,
> And once will do."
>
> . . . .
>
> "Is it not better to be wise tonight,
> And free tomorrow? To be wise and free
> Has always been a dream for most of us,
> And will remain a dream. Yet for a few—
> For you and me—it will be real and easy,
> If we will be ourselves. For your heart knows
> More than it lets you say—as mine did once,
> Before it let me think. His going away
> Has left a clearness where it was all fog
> While he was here. We shall see better now,
> And there will be a time for you to bless me
> That all has ended well. . . ."

The "ruin" she refers to was probably not the misery and confusion that she herself had suffered as a result of Herman's alcoholism. Rather it was the frustration of Herman's hopes—in his case financial—which had driven him to drink. Under an impulse less noble, less romantic, and more subtle than Guinevere's, she determined not to ruin Win by equivalent frustration of his vision. In that last stanza she heard the poet in him confessing unintentionally that his real "dream" was to live on alone with the sound of the world going round. The march of the Cameron Men was the march of his imagination, not, as he thought it was, a march to victory in terms of the marriage they had projected.

Emma saw in 1909, had felt, consciously or unconsciously, from the beginning in '88, what Robinson never understood in himself until some time between his proposal in '27 and the composition of this poem. She saw what had greatly confused Mabel Moore, the Woodland Girl, probably Olivia Dunbar Torrence, and perhaps others, namely that in spite of his capacity for beautiful, idealistic love, including his chivalry and apparent obliviousness to his own concerns, yet the poet in him did not want to marry her or anybody, ever—could not do so without losing his integrity. In *The Cameron Men* Emma was a great and mature woman ready to love, and, irrespective of the *practical* demands of his career, or of any promises she might have made, irrespective even of her love of Herman and its hold on her, irrespective of everything but the elementary and immediate urgings of nature, she was here responding directly to what she perceived as the deepest and most essential, not the obvious and superficial, desire of the male. She knew that it was for her, in exactly the measure she loved him or might love him, to give him what she could and still save him from the formal responsibilities and incarceration of marriage which, without his realizing it, he greatly feared.

Back in '88 when she was a girl, it had been something of this kind that Emma had felt about Win, without being able to rationalize it. Behind his puppy love and its unreal "soul music," it was not just his timid inarticulateness but his deep and unrecognized aversion to the "ceremonial havoc" of marriage, that had made it impossible for her to feel committed to him at that time; and in spite of Win's other appeals it was her basic woman's need of assurance in this respect that had made her succumb with relief to Herman's obvious desire, not to love her in beautiful abstraction, but to marry her. In the want of other evidence, we may presume that her wakening to understanding of Win had occurred in the fall of 1909 in some such fashion as he dramatized it in the poem. First, she turned him down in the same lack of comprehension that had prevented her from responding to him in '88, and that she probably still rationalized on the simple, sound ground that she did not love him enough. It was then, as he recorded in his letter to Ledoux of September thirtieth, that

he thought to give up and return to New York. Then he did or
said something—if no more than the threat of departure—which
made Emma reconsider and give him the encouragement which
caused him, as revealed in the letter to Miss Brower on October
seventh, to decide to stay on, the encouragement which in the
poem became the agreement to marry him. And then, probably in
his puzzled and puzzling reaction to the encouragement and its
prospect of marriage, she jumped to the perception, accounting
for all of their lives together, which she explained to him in the
poem with her big blue "calm eyes . . . like a child's, waiting
for the reward of his approval." She hardly expected him to understand then, but she hoped that eventually, when it was no
longer necessary for his gallantry to dictate his expressions, that
he would "bless" her for saving him. One way of explaining her
peremptory rejection of him in '18, as described in his letter to
Burnham, was that she was by then fully convinced of the cor-
rectness of her earlier observation and was growing impatient
with Win for not facing the truth, for continuing to persuade
himself that he was a respectable male and wanted what he did
not want at all.

Here of course had been Robinson's real deficiency with girls
from boyhood. It did not consist of his ineptitudes and timidities,
for those he could overcome in crisis, and even in their natural
confusion they were marks of an appealing sincerity. It was not
anything mysterious that he should do or say that would fetch
the women. His lack was simply a way of feeling towards them,
or of not feeling towards them, a state of being mixed up in his
feelings so that there was nothing clean-cut for them to take or
reject. His desire for them was normal enough. His idealism also
was healthy and genuine. But it was the conventional impulse to
marry that was false, first changing into fear and then distorting
both the desire and the idealism, denying the one and affirming
the other beyond nature, so that a woman was left confused as to
where she stood with him. Robinson was a poet, a pure seer, and
like most poets he wanted true and consecrated love, uncom-
plicated by the artificial unrealities of society. Two blocks in him
prevented his acting like the poet he was. The false block was
his lifelong conventionality, the remnant of his infantile sense of

inferiority back in Gardiner when one side of him had wanted to be like other people. The true block was his chivalry. One of the most sincere aversions of his life was to philandering and philanderers. Therefore, he must not run any chance of being one. At every rise of his temperature above casual with a woman, he must think in terms of marriage.

And marriage, as he finally learned when he was about sixty, was the one thing he did not want to think about. Back in 1909, as stated in the poem, he had been "chilled" by Emma's rejection of him, and remained chilled for almost twenty years. Then, sometime after his final dismissal in '27 or '28, perhaps as a result of Emma's explanation at that time, combined with the greater assurance which his current success with *Tristram* was giving him—sometime between '27 and the composition of *The Cameron Men* not later than '31, something that had always been vague and lofty in his idealism descended and solidified into immediate reality. In *Matthias* he confessed that for himself the good life consisted in some kind of compromise between the "gleams" of the inner light and the things that are "worth having" in the outer world. Now he carried this observation farther, into special country. He saw that his idealization of love had been honest and true, and that remaining honest and true it might have led to a love affair, or it might have led nowhere; but the one harbor to which it could never have led was marriage. He saw that his failure to win Emma, and perhaps others, had been due, not to his oral but to his spiritual inarticulateness, the fact that he had been silent or stammering in a special kind of soul music which above all other sounds the ears of women understood and required. The guilt, like that of Timberlake, that he had always felt subconsciously for not having loved anyone enough to marry them, turned out to be a function of the "resident devil" in the "perilous" calling of "art," poetry, which of all outer things he had always thought most "worth having." According to *The March of the Cameron Men*, Emma had contributed to his latest as she had to his earliest awakening. But even in '31, and so straight on to his death four years later, his chivalry could not come straight out and tell her that she had been right in seeing through his professions to the truth that he had never wanted to marry her!

Not even back in '88 and the days of the "mist all golden"! But to the limit that his reticence would permit, the poem is the "blessing" that she had prophesied that he would one day give her, his tardy acknowledgement and thanks for her lifelong understanding, her protection of him against herself and matrimony, and so for his whole career and accomplishment.

Thus the drama of Robinson's love resolved in physical anticlimax and in aesthetic victory. Spiritually, his victory, his coming to the Light, would seem to have been the surer for his having, like Merlin, ignored his own inner condition with its resident outer devil of self-concern. From his earliest days he had been almost completely impervious to that devil of devils. While holding an abstract belief in immortality he had thought of it in connection, not with himself, but with those whose lives had been less "fulfilled" than his was. When, after 1909, he saw far off the Light of the happiness that would come with the loss of self, he considered it, not as for his own enjoyment, but as something he ought to tell the unhappy world about. And finally he sought, at least for himself, no more than a disciplined, moderate enjoyment of the things of the outer world that were "worth while."

His next and last three books—the trivial *Talifer* ('33), in which he assures Emma that he does not want a highbrow wife, *Amaranth* ('34), and *King Jasper* (posthumous), both intellectual, and at least *Amaranth* rising to a fine swan song of the best poetry since *Tristram*—these his last three books add little or nothing to the personal story. For both Emma and Win the action of the drama and the confirming action of the Epilogue were ended. But for her, there remained two chores in the empty theater, two tender gestures that marked her faithful beyond the end. As throughout his life, she continued, until and after his death, to collect in a trunk mementos that started with his baby napkin-ring and included his diploma at the high-school graduation when she had sent him roses. Again, there was a matter of spirits of the undistilled sort. Starting at the time of her father's death in 1903, Emma had been interested in spiritualism, having been impressed by the information she got from a medium that his stroke had been brought on by a fall from an apple tree, to which there had been no witness. After Win's funeral in April of '35, the Frasers, with whom he had been living since '22, asked Mr. and Mrs. Nivison if they might keep a landscape of his, entitled "The Dark Hills," by his friend Franklin L. Schenck. The Nivisons of course consented. Hearing of it, Emma was distressed and consulted a medium, through whom Win's voice told her to write the Frasers for the picture, which she did, and duly received it. At another time Win told her that he "was tired and was going for a long rest." Again, according to credible rumor, she took down his copious comments on a brown paper bag which may or may not survive. Thus she became the emanuensis of his last known expression. She died on July 3, 1940.

Part III

THOUGHT'S IMPENETRABLE MAIL

> The ministering wheels
> Of anguish take us eastward, where the clouds
> Of human gloom are lost against the gleam
> That shines on Thought's impenetrable mail.
> —*Octaves*

IF philosophy is the attempt to arrive at reality by some logical system, then Robinson had no philosophy and wanted none. In his second year at Harvard he wrote Harry Smith that the only things that gave him trouble were "Logic, of which I am entirely ignorant, and German Composition, which I lack the logic . . . to put together. . . ."[1] To Gledhill he wrote that logic was "worse than hell itself." "It 'soured' me on the whole course [philosophy under Royce] . . . I do not think I was born for a philosopher."[2] In 1918, complaining to Mrs. Richards of being called an intellectual poet: ". . . Anything like a proper comprehension of [my] product . . . is . . . a matter of feeling, not of cerebration."[3] And again, from the pinnacles of success in '31, writing to a student who was doing a thesis on him: ". . . I am rather sorry to learn that you are writing about my 'philosophy'—which is mostly a statement of my inability to accept a mechanistic interpretation of the universe and of life. . . . I . . . wish that you were writing about my poetry—of which my so-called philosophy is only a small part, and probably the least important. . . ."[4]

In other words, Robinson insisted on being a poet, on being simple, sensuous, and passionate. He insisted on it not only in his method of setting down his beliefs but also in his method of arriving at them by intuition or experience, not by systematic thought.

> The soul itself must insulate the Real
> . . . .
>
> *(Octave XVII)*

The words in which he recorded "the Real" were not established tags for the reason, but sidelong hints to the imagination that knows no words:

> There are these things,
> And they are so—until we give them names,
> And harness them with words that have one meaning
> For no two men. . . .
>
> *(Roman Bartholow)*

281

What we see is not only beyond words but beyond "the cold road of knowledge" that is built of words:

> When our eyes
> Have wisdom, we see more than we remember.
> *(The Three Taverns)*

Also,

> Man's habit is to feel before he sees

.   .   .   .

> Before we see,
> . . . we suffer; and I come to you,
> At last, through many storms and through much night.
> *(The Three Taverns)*

What passed for Robinson's "philosophy," like the other content of his poetry, was what he first saw with the direct, emotionalized perception of the inner self, and afterwards put in some kind of general order, as he did his poetry, by means of outer, conscious reason. But in the expression of such generalizations, even when he seemed to make an introductory flourish of despised "logic," the concluding statement was of direct perception which had little if any relation to the systematic gesture. Writing to Mrs. Richards in '26:

> I . . . can only say again that life means everything, or it means nothing. If it means nothing, we are caught in a sorry trap. . . . I have to believe there is a little more to it than what we see now—but what that is I can't tell you.[5]

And to a student in '31:

> Nothing of an infinite nature can be proven or disproven in finite terms—meaning words—and the rest is probably a matter of one's individual ways of seeing and feeling things.[6]

If there was any "philosophy" in these and similar observations, it was in their universal scope and effort at conscious analysis, not at all in the pretense of Ramian logic that introduced them. If they happened sometimes to resemble the conclusions of systematic philosophers or theologians, such as Plato or Ramus,

Calvin or Schopenhauer, the resemblance was coincidental and none of the poet's concern.

I Idealism

Robinson always gave a genuine, though often grudging, acknowledgement to the outer, material world:

> All that we know about the world
> For certain is that it appears to be.
> > *(The Man Who Died Twice)*

Sometimes, because of his greater concern with internal rather than external life, he talks like a Solipsist:

> So let us in ourselves revere
> The self that is the universe
> > *(The Children of the Night)*

Or:

> Your world is in yourself, my friend,
> For your endurance to the end
> > *(Peace on Earth)*

Or again, Lancelot:

> Sometimes I wonder if this be the world
> We live in, or the world that lives in us.

But Robinson was no solipsist. What he meant by these passages was that the perception of truth is for the inner self. He believed both in external, material reality and in the moral necessity of objectivity. In '96 he wrote Smith approvingly of one Jones who "doesn't think that the universe is centered in himself." [7]

More effectively than by solipsism Robinson was teased throughout his life by its opposite, Pantheism, the doctrine of the loss of individual identity in pervasive God, a notion which was at diametric variance also with the individualism of his seriously espoused beliefs. In youth he seems to have been afraid of it, cautioning Gledhill in '90, "Better keep away from Spinoza

or he will have you before you know it: Pantheism is too attractive for you to tamper with." [8] There are phrases in the *Octaves*—
notably "the record of All-Soul"—and in *Captain Craig*—"God's
music has no modes"—and more dubiously in the "orient Word"
in *The Man Against the Sky*, that suggest a pantheistic interpretation, but there are few of them, and I don't know of any after
1916. In his later years Robinson would sometimes drop into a
metaphysical conversation the assertion, "I am a pantheist." But
he would do it with a smile, and his apparent object was to end a
type of discussion that bored him. Pantheism was a pleasant
mood which he no longer feared and which he knew was impervious to proof or disproof on the part of bright young logic. In so
far as his pantheism was rationalized, it was of the "orient" sort
proclaimed in the *Octaves*, associated with Emersonian Tran-
scendentalism which, while asserting the inclusive manifestations
of the Oversoul, yet left at least every individual human being
separate and responsible.

Robinson admitted his transcendental individualism, citing
The Man Against the Sky and *Matthias at the Door*,[9] but he
denied its derivation, or that of any other of his philosophical
notions, from Josiah Royce at Harvard. In typically guarded language he made the denial as his contribution to a debate about
the specific influence on him of Royce's *Spirit of Modern Philosophy*. Another denial exceeded Robinson's own by stating that
he didn't know Professor Royce at Harvard! More revelant is the
truth, namely that while he took Royce's course, entitled like the
book, he was bored with it and the teacher, once reporting to
Harry Smith, "Read Mrs. Browning . . . all through one of Prof.
Royce's lectures. . . . I get absolutely nothing from what he
says." [10] And again, "Friday afternoon I cut Prof. Royce's lecture
on Neutral Activity and went to a symphony concert in town. I
think I got more from the concert than I ever did from one of his
lectures. . . ." [11]

On the other hand, while Robinson was probably just in denying any originating influence of Royce on his "idealism," or of
Schopenhauer on his dark view of the world, yet in one of the
most passionate prose statements he ever made he set down a
striking parallelism with a passage in the *Spirit of Modern*

Philosophy, including the repetition of a word that is rare in philosophical discussion. Accepting Schopenhauer's pessimism in order to transcend it in his own idealism, Royce had written: "It is just endurance that is the essence of spirituality. Resignation, then, is indeed part of truth—resignation, that is, of any hope of a final and private *happiness* [italics added]. We resign in order to be ready to endure. But courage is the rest of truth, a hearty defiance of the whole hateful pang and agony of the will." [12] Four years after leaving Harvard, in '97, Robinson, in the letter already quoted (p. 160) wrote Smith out of his second great crisis: "I am not going crazy . . . but I am going to lose all those pleasures which are said to make up the *happiness* [italics added] of this life and I'm glad of it. I'm glad to say that I am strong enough to do without them. There is a pleasure—a joy—that is greater than all these little selfish notions and I have found the way to it through idealism." [13] Thus in his own extremity Robinson seems to recall Royce's solution of life's difficulty in the surrender of the hope of "happiness" and in the "endurance" which presently I shall call Self-Atonement. This formulation remained his doctrine and the pattern of his practice until his third great crisis in 1909. But at the same time, just as his own experience and not Schopenhauer's reasoned pessimism had led him to the renunciatory half of his determination, so the affirmative declaration was of an idealism which was altogether personal, entirely and scornfully independent of the logical demonstration upon which Royce's idealism tried to rest.

It might be inferred from Robinson's habit of contrapositives, never making a statement without jumping shortly to its opposite, that his permanent reality was in the process of thought for its own sake, the life of the mind, the mulling of ideas irrespective of their materialization. More cogent is his early aversion to carnality which may be idealistic as well as prudish, his denunciation of prostitution and his composition of *The Night Before* with its thesis of chaste love. But it was not until '96, three years after he left Harvard and the soporific influence of Royce, that he was consciously converted. He began to look dubiously on his habit of collecting stamps because "they are so obviously material and my ideas are getting to be so thoroughly ideal, that the collection of anything but wisdom often seems like going back into ignorance and barbarism." [14] In October of '96 he made his first recorded assumption of idealism as a philosophy—"I sing . . . now and then of material things (supposing they exist)." [15] In November he affirmed idealism as "the one *logical* [italics added] and satisfactory interpretation of life." [16] In December, just after his mother died, he declared unequivocally, "I am very glad to be able to stand up and say I am an idealist." [17] And in the great letter of the following March just quoted, he announced his clarified position, his renunciation of the world and his affirmation of idealism and what he called its "joy."

Even in consideration of Robinson's indifference to formal philosophy, it is still remarkable that his statements and applications of his so-called idealism show so little direct influence of the great Platonic models which he must have read—though the only references I find are to the *Apologia,* soon after his arrival in Cambridge in October, '92, one in '96 to Socrates among other high company, and a too sweeping flourish of general familiarity with Plato in early '97.[18] The beautiful arguments in the *Phaedo* for the superiority of the mind over the body and for the immortality of the soul support Robinson's position in these matters, yet he rests on his own intuitive affirmations, and for all of him Socrates might never have lived or died. In the *Symposium,* Pausanias's glorification of unilateral, unrequited love, and Socrates's famous recital of the upward progress of love from the body through thoughts, concepts, and ideas to final and desireless love and beauty, all of this is wonderfully suggestive of Robinson's own "Platonic" love of Emma and was in some ways paralleled in his own idealistic expressions in the *Octaves* and dramatized in *The Book of Annandale.* And yet, so far as I know, not a phrase, not a sequence of thought, is stolen from Plato. He declared for anticipation over present experience— "Anticipation is more than half of life" [19]—"my chief occupation nowadays is expecting." [20] Likewise for memory. Material reality is very often "humbug." We may feel uncomfortable in a situation, but afterwards we recall it as pleasant, and the memory may be more real than the current experience was.[21] Yet there is not here or anywhere in Robinson a reference to the doctrine

of the soul's reminiscence elaborated in the *Phaedo*. Unrelated to
Plato, so far as I know, was Robinson's distinction between asceticism and idealism, made in his early phase of the latter: "[I]
found myself defining asceticism (and disposing of it) as the
resistance to the material, and idealism as the denial of it." [22]

If Robinson did go through an early period of denial of the
reality of "the material," it was brief and sophistical, and its expressions should be taken rhetorically rather than literally. What
Robinson did deny with high and honest contempt was not "the
material" but the Materialism that he heard everywhere around
him, the ascription of exclusive reality to matter, the method of
materialistic science, the deification of mechanistic material Law:

> Not the faintest or the farthest whirled
> First atom of the least that ever flew
> Shall be by man defrauded of the touch
> God thrilled it with to make a dream for man
> When Science was unborn.
>
> *(Captain Craig)*

Here is the final blast of scorn at the end of *The Man Against the
Sky*:

> If there be nothing after Now,
> And we be nothing anyhow,
> And we know that,—why live?
> 'Twere sure but weaklings' vain distress
> To suffer dungeons where so many doors
> Will open on the cold eternal shores
> That look sheer down
> To the dark tideless floods of Nothingness
> Where all who know may drown.

"Know" is one of Robinson's most contemptuous words, sig-
nifying for him the rational and logical knowledge of science
which is an antonym of the intuitive "wisdom" of idealism. "The
best of life . . . is in what we do not know." Here is part of
Octave XII:

> With conscious eyes not yet sincere enough
> To pierce the glimmered cloud that fluctuates

> Between me and the glorifying light
> That screens itself with knowledge, I discern
> The searching eyes of wisdom that reach through
> The mist of shame's infirm credulity
>
> . . . .

And there is his famous letter to Will Durant who had asked him to contribute a statement of his beliefs to an anthology of such, and, incidental to the request, had implied as matter of course that materialism these days would be everybody's basic assumption:

> I told a philosopher once that all the other philosophers would have to go out of business if one of them should happen to discover the truth; and now you say, or imply, in your letter that the truth has been discovered, and that we are only the worse off, if possible, for the discovery. This is naturally a cause of some chagrin and humiliation for me, for I had heard nothing about it. It is true that we have acquired a great deal of material knowledge in recent years, but so far as knowledge of the truth itself is concerned, I cannot see that we are any nearer to it now than our less imaginative ancestors were when they cracked each other's skulls with stone hatchets, that we know any more than they knew of what happened to the soul that escaped in the process. It is easy, and just now rather fashionable, to say that there is no soul, but we do not know whether there is a soul or not. . . . The cocksureness of the modern "mechanist" means nothing to me; and I doubt if it means any more to him when he pauses really to think. His position is not entirely unlike that of an intrepid explorer standing on a promontory in a fog, looking through the newest thing in the way of glasses for an ocean that he cannot see, and shouting to his mechanistic friends behind him that he has found the end of the world.

In rejecting mechanistic materialism Robinson was not rejecting the machine age as such. "I like almost any kind of a machine," he wrote Smith in '96. "I cannot find the poetry of motion in a 'social dance' but I can see lots of it in a locomotive going about a mile a minute." [23] Also, his subjection of the material, outer world to that of the mind was in no sense the "escape" that is commonly associated with that preference. As Miss Kaplan says, he kept his "idealism in a materialistic setting." In '99 he wrote to Mason:

> I stretched out yesterday and read *Walking* [Thoreau's essay] but did not quite relish what seemed to me a sort of glorified world cowardice all through the thing. For God's sake, says the sage, let me get away into the wilderness where I shall not have a single human responsibility or the first symptom of social discipline. Let me be a pickerel or a skunk cabbage, or anything that will not have to meet the realities of civilization. There is a wholesomeness about some people that is positively unhealthy. . . .[24]

One of Robinson's qualities of mind, related to what I call his contrapositivism, was his catholicity, his necessity to see both sides. While he denied a mechanistic interpretation of the *processes* of the universe and espoused an idealistic interpretation, yet he admitted the *reality* of Matter as well as that of Idea. His idealism did not detach him from the material roundabout. He lived solidly in both worlds without any sense of inconsistency. He practiced without misgiving his inner or idealistic calling of a poet, although in expression it was an activity of the outer self in the material world and, as he confessed in *Merlin*, it stood in the way of his realization of his own inner self or idea. The ideal truth of that inner self must be expressed in material symbols. Both elements were real but idea was the dominant one. His world, like his person, was an integrated combination, matter being the surface, the limbs, the flesh, and idea the center, the essence, the life. He never took his eyes from the world and its torture of its people, and for himself accepted more of that torture, in physical, social, and mental terms, than most people face without panic and surrender. He never denied the material world. What he did do was to face it, defy it, and deny its capacity to destroy him. Miss Kaplan observes that in "retaining the egocentric predicament in a materialistic setting, he attained a form of stoicism that was distinctly more philosophic than the current literary 'realism.'" [25]

Altogether, what Robinson called his "idealism" was nothing of the sort. It made no attempt to define exclusive reality, it set up no archetypes, no ultimates. It was no more than an assertion of his preference for the life of the mind within "thought's impenetrable mail," the contemplation by his outer conscious self of his inner unconscious self whose subsensuous activity was a mood, a mood of universal clairvoyance composite of being, perceiving, and loving. This mood possessed Robinson more completely and continuously than it does most people, even most artists, and his delight in it was the "joy" of "idealism" for which he was willing to forego "all those pleasures which are said to make up the happiness of this life." Variously accoutered with the materials of outer experience, the clairvoyant mood motivated his poetry and his "philosophic" notions. Its universal love gave him his concern for all individuals. Its identity with all Being gave him his religion.

II People

The basis of Robinson's high degree of saintliness was his amazing sense of inner or spiritual identification with every separate human being. Perhaps there was a relation between this aspect of his Clairvoyant Mood and his Emersonian pantheism, the sense, as Lloyd Morris put it, "that all human beings are part of one infinite life. . . ." [1] Certainly it was the outward expression, as Professor Barnard says, of his "profound humility, which is really a sense of inescapable oneness with his fellows." [2] And his "fellows" consisted of every person who came into the sphere of his apprehension, no matter how alien or unknown. There is no anecdote nearer to the central Robinson than Hagedorn's account of an exchange with Torrence during Robinson's most destitute phase in New York:

"Do you know, one of the most terrible things is to walk alone and feel that you are receiving deadly wounds?"

"What do you mean?" asked Torrence.

"It is to go along the street and glance into the eyes of passers-by and catch a glimpse of recognition, and know that you will never see them again."

Equally profound was Hagedorn's own comment: "He was . . . measuring other's capacity for pain by his own, and marvelled how men endured." [3]

This conviction of what Barnard calls the "spiritual solidarity of mankind," this sense of the inner identity of people eclipsing their differences, is everywhere in Robinson's expressions. To Smith in '93: "There is poetry in all kinds of humanity—even in lawyers and horse-jockeys. . . ." [4] And in '94, he tells Smith that this identical essence is what is immortal: "I cannot believe that these tremendous worldly differences are to be carried on through the second Life." [5] (He is referring to differences in intelligence, not in outer circumstances.) In 1913, in reply to William Stanley Braithwaite's inquiry about his central "message": "I suppose that a part of it might be described as a faint hope of making a few of us understand our fellow creatures a little better, and to realize what a small difference there is, after all, between ourselves, as we are, and ourselves, not only as we might have been but would have been if our physical and tempermental make-up [that is, our inheritance] and our environment had been a little different." [6] Which is to assume that beneath these small differences our central selves are the same in being and loving.

> And who's of this or that estate
> We do not wholly calculate
> . . . .
>
> *(The Field of Glory)*

> If some of us were not so far behind,
> The rest of us were not so far ahead.
>
> *(Inferential)*

There could hardly be a more extreme example of Robinson's contrapositivism than the balance between this inner equalitarianism and his affirmation of inviolable external differences—

the immeasurable distances
That are between the nearest and most known
Of loving and unfathomable strangers
. . . .

(The Glory of the Nightingales)

Not only does Robinson insist on individual differences, but he seems to attach major importance to them as the bearers of private personality that must be cultivated at all costs. Barnard speaks for the consensus of enlightened criticism when he says: "It is this centering of interest on individual human beings that, even more than his style, sets Robinson apart from other poets of the twentieth century; with the exception (as so often) of Frost and the single success (*Spoon River*) of Edgar Lee Masters. Brilliant or moving portraits by other poets . . . pay allegiance first of all to abstract ideas, to the critical intellect. But Robinson's characters, in the main . . . have no other motive than mere existence." [7] Elsewhere, Professor Barnard seems to make the same distinction I wish to make, in pointing out "two basic convictions, two unwavering intuitions, in the poet himself. One is that it is only the inner life of the individual that matters . . . [and the] other guiding principle . . . is his intense perception of the distinct identity, the unique position and attributes, the existence as an end of itself, of the individual person." [8]

There is no inconsistency between Barnard's statements as intended, for as a critic he is pointing out what are perhaps Robinson's two chief literary qualities, namely his preoccupation with psychological rather than physical action, and the almost unfailing primacy of his concern for the individual over any of the abstract or general beliefs which we are considering here. Barnard's statements are true and profound. But they fail, I think, to take the final step which is to explain the line of distinction in Robinson's "unwavering intuitions" between the inner identity and the outward differences of everybody. The point is that "the distinct identity . . . the existence as an end in itself, of the individual person," that is Robinson's primary concern is precisely the inner self, with its clairvoyant mood, that is part of universal Being, seeing, and loving, and in his "basic convictions" is identical in all persons. It is this inner self to which Lloyd Morris refers in his splendid though somewhat excessive declaration for Robinson, "Humiliation is a casualty to which the human spirit is never subject." [9] The casualties strike the outer self, which includes not only the body with its passions and affections, but also "the reason [in the natural or logical sense], the will [and] the image-making power" [10] which Barnard assigns to the "inner life." Altogether the outer self comprises the continuum of traits that make up the visible personality that is perpetually assailed by the material environment and affected by it. Despite numerous misinterpreted statements of Robinson, both in prose and verse, his actual concern was for the inner self that does not exist in the environment, and his vehement pleas for respect for all outward quirks and idiosyncrasies, were only on account of their possible association with the inner self. A violation of or disrespect for them might react on the inner self also, and even identify it with the pursuit of some outward secondary devil, like morphine, alcohol, or sex for its own sake, which offered a spurious substitute for inward peace. For society to judge and condemn an entire person because of some outward foible, and so to humiliate him, was to do him a minor injustice in terms of outward society itself, but perhaps a major disservice in ruffling his still, inner reality, his clairvoyant mood. The reason that Robinson himself retained his trivial sensitiveness on the score of his supposed physical awkwardness was partly that in that field he retained a remnant of outer pride; but it was also because in his youth his non-facility in that respect humiliated him all the way to the inner reality which thereafter was never able entirely to expel the bitterness. It was from deep humiliation of this sort that Robinson, with his universal compassion, wanted to protect every human being ever born.

To return more precisely to his beliefs or convictions, his defense of all and sundry weaklings, eccentrics, and otherwise victims of the brutality of the world, and especially his devotion to "the unfulfilled," the "dead men," the failures, for all of whom his profoundly spiritual brother Dean was the prototype, were not due to any particular tenderness for their weaknesses and follies as such, their secondary devils—although it must be conceded that he always had a covert suspicion of anyone who didn't like whiskey! He broke no lance for John Evereldown's lechery, or Miniver Cheevy's or Levi's romancing, or Tasker Norcross's emptiness, or the various escapes of the "doctor of billiards" and the other failures who assembled at Calverly's. What he knew was that all these people had, even as he himself had, an inner self or reality that was more nearly pristine than that of the successful and the pious. He considered it only luck or "fate" that his own condemnation by most of Gardiner, his trials at home, and his ordeal by starvation in New York did not reduce him to the outward level of all those, just as he knew they were on the same inward level with him. He did not fight for their vices. But he fought always for their unjudged privacy in the practice of their personal eccentricities which, if society sneered at them, might turn inward into self-doubt and ruin, and back outward into the compensating vices.

Similarly, at the end of his life, in *Amaranth,* he had no special interest, whether for defense or condemnation, in the "wrong worlds," the inappropriate vocations, that most of his enormous acquaintance had chosen, beginning with the medical practice of Dean. He was concerned only that their false pursuits might have dried up their inner springs so that their essential humanity, which in some way that was beyond knowledge he believed to be identified with the central Mystery, might have desiccated and blown away. To avoid this tragedy, one of his few affirmative preachments seemed at first to require everybody to face the truth of himself—that is, look in the eyes of Amaranth—and learn to live with what he saw. But in a typical contrapositivistic reservation, he also thought it just as well that some people should remain in the dark about their faults, that they shouldn't do too much lonely brooding on themselves! Out of his most trying time at home he wrote to Smith: "Nine-tenths of the happiness in the world (if there is any) is due to man's ignorance of his own disposition. The happy people are they who never had time to think it over. It is only when I forget what an ass I am that I find life tolerable. . . ."[11] His overall attitude seemed to be that people who are so obtuse or deluded by good fortune as not to be able to understand themselves had better be left in their folly. But the elect of the imagination must look straight into the eyes of the truth.

Robinson's beliefs about mankind in groups, whether called "society," "nation," or "race," were all derivative from his inner individualism, for as a poet and interested in specific things he had no capacity for holding these cloudy, outer generalities as real. Any thought of them confused and bored him. His notions about them, therefore, were naïve and of no interest except as aspects of his individualism. "I'm well aware," he wrote to Percy MacKaye in 1920, "of my hopeless limitations when anything with 'Community' pasted on its rolls into sight." [12] Generally, he felt the "community," or any of its multiples, to be the enemy, a vast and unreal wraith that was out to strangle his hundreds of millions of individuals whom he loved and each one of whom he could see with his inner eye if he passed him on the street. They, not the community or the state, had actual existence, and the only tolerable object of politics was not to enslave or collectivize them under law but to remove the legal obstructions to their self-realization. If Robinson had ever read any Marx, he would of course have had only contempt for his politically naïve notion that you could impose virtue by violent or evil means. But he probably would have agreed with Lenin that, once you had redeemed individuals from their predatory selfishness, the essentially predatory state would likewise wither.

Most of his intuitive political perceptions were orthodox enough, being perhaps less truly intuitive than acquired from the culture of preindustrial New England that produced him. He believed in an educated aristocracy of the rural sort that knew nothing of plutocracy and was being shouted down by it and by the mobocracy that was plutocracy's concomitant:

> See not the great among you for the small,
> But hear their silence; for the few shall save
> The many, or the many are to fall—
> Still to be wrangling in a noisy grave.
>
> (Demos)

"I'm a democrat," he continued in the letter to MacKaye just cited, "in that I'm as likely to form a lifelong friendship with a coal-heaver as with a millionaire (rather more so, in fact), but there my democracy ends." To quote Barnard, he felt that wealth itself was "morally neutral; it becomes evil only when real values are sacrificed in its pursuit. . . ." [13] In a letter to Smith when he was twenty, he declared for life "Business be damned." [14] Besides the pursuit of wealth, the complacent blindness it produced in such as Matthias and Jasper was evil. Most evil of all was the reactions of jealousy, all kinds of rationalized isms and revolutions that it encouraged, and in the thirties he feared equally Russian communism and German Nazism. In '34 he wrote Mrs. Richards, referring to Sinclair Lewis's ghastly warning— apparently without having read it—: "It's all right to say it can't happen, but unfortunately it can." [15]

Wherever the cause of the individual was to be served, Robinson was a radical, but vis-à-vis the rich and the mob he was a conservative. He was for woman suffrage as a matter of course, and equally of course he was violently and criminally against Prohibition. He was not drinking when it was passed, but immediately started again—in Hagedorn's phrase, "almost as a matter of principle." He wrote Ledoux, "I don't see the independence of an alleged democracy that will accept the Eighteenth Amendment without general secession or civil war." [16] He meant it. All rational panaceas were of the devil, and this one was the quintessence of interference with the individual's freedom. Here again it is important to remember that the freedom he was concerned about was not simply the right to act outwardly as one wanted, to ruin oneself or kill oneself, though he was for those rights too if the interest of the inner self was involved. The individual whose rights he insisted on was that inner self, and the freedom he meant was the freedom to do what was consonant with the tenor of that inner self, really *the freedom to be what one is.*

It is well to preserve at least one reservation against Robinson's "unwavering intuition" of the importance of the individual. Because of his inability to reason in terms of political concepts, he failed to see that the obvious application of the individualism that he, like Emerson, insisted on, as distinguished from their equalitarianism, was producing precisely what he most despised.

For enlightened standards it was substituting the standards of the mob. And of these, the chief was the standard of power or plutocracy whose competition must end in the victory of one irresponsible plutocrat, and so tyranny. Robinson foresaw and hated the bad results, but he failed to associate them with their cause in that outward self-reliance preached by the great innocent of Concord, and by himself just as great and just as innocent.

Robinson's historical notions, like his political ones, were for the most part derived from his individualistic affirmation, but being further from that tangible center out in the chaos of amorphous cerebration, they were less consistent and intellectually respectable. Physically, the nations had no more interest for him than they did politically. His farthest adventure eastward was to England for one summer, and he spent almost all of it in London. In his own country he never went west of the Hudson River. "The rest of the country," he wrote Isaacs in '28, "means nothing to me. . . . The Grand Canyon is no doubt a grand piece of work, but I know just about how it looks." [17] In the nineties he had begun grumbling about German regimentation, and he had only contempt for any kind of nationalism. "Harvard College . . . is the object of almost the only patriotism I possess" [18]—that is, the place where he had the richest personal association. "Sometimes I wonder if it would take much to set me yelling for an absolute monarchy in this country—assuming that we haven't got one." [19] "A brain . . . that is 100% American cannot in the nature of things have many percent left over." [20] At the same time he early came "to realize that America [is] the hopper through which the whole civilization of the world is to be ground." [21] Not quite inconsistently, Robinson greatly admired Teddy Roosevelt for his attacks on big business, while in '96 he reported to Smith that he was "coming more and more to look upon [Bryan] as the greatest political figure in America since Lincoln." [22] But with the utmost inconsistency he voted for McKinley, frankly the candidate of Big Business, in '96, and wrote a campaign letter for him in 1900.

Perhaps Robinson's greatest historical blind spot was for the period that produced him, the world of peace in Europe and America between 1870 and 1914. He never swerved from his belief that it had been mankind's happiest interlude, in spite of all its brutality and degradation, which he saw and recorded. The double standard that produced the Lorraines and the Evereldowns, the spiritual emptiness that produced the Corys, the Cavenders and the Matthiases, above all the smug respectability that caused his father to ruin Dean, and the financial fashion that ruined Herman, all of these things he attributed to "the world" in general and to the "fates" of individuals, related somehow to the inscrutable "Scheme"; he refused to identify them specifically with the gigantic sham that was the whole late Victorian world. He believed until the end of his life that in this period of luxurious decadence a larger proportion of the population had been contented than during any period of comparable length in human history. At the same time he saw the evils of individual competition, wealth, and power, and the equivalent national imperialism, saw them clearly enough to make an analogy between a society motivated by them and Arthur's Camelot, which also was a superficially happy state but resting on a rotten foundation. On one side he saw the First World War as the death struggle of economic nationalism. On the other side he said that "if one insists [Lancelot] may be taken as a rather distant symbol of Germany," meaning that Germany's predatory perfidy was destroying what had been man's hope of a perfect world. (Incidentally, this remark was an instance of Robinson's sly proclivity for emphasizing an incidental theme in one of his poems while maintaining deadpan silence about the real meaning. That meaning was poetry, and not for anyone, including himself, to explain in prose—another example of his wanting to leave the spiritual or imaginative word unspoken.)

In spite of his conservatism in superficial matters and his nostalgia for the world of his youth—the gentle facet of the Victorian world that he had enjoyed with the Richardses, the Gardiners, the Ledoux, the Perrys and the rest—Robinson's steady look was always ahead, and it was not a rosy-tinted dawn that he saw. He had always feared the militaristic nationalism of Germany, and in 1913 he answered a reporter's question by saying, "Universal peace has a pleasant sound, but I don't see it.

I wish I did." [23] In 1919, on the nether side of the First World War, he wrote prophetically to Mabel Dodge Sterne: ". . . I am sure that we white folks are doing the work while some farther sighted race is waiting to show us what to do with what we have done—or maybe to exterminate us and do it themselves without our assistance or interference. Meanwhile we shall have the League of Nations to play with while Germany is getting herself and Russia together for another grand smash." [24] In 1921 he wrote Mrs. Ledoux after hearing *Tristan,* "For a few hours I fancied that our so-called civilization might not be going after all— though of course it is. The whole western world is going to be blown to pieces, asphyxiated, and starved, and then, for a few centuries we poor artists are going to have a hard time. There may not be any, in fact, for they will have either to die or to dig; and if they dig they can't compose any *Tristans,* or paint any pictures, or write any poetry." [25] His Lancelot had already said, "A played-out world, / Although that world be ours, had best be dead."

But the general note of affirmation, *The Courage to Be,* weighs heaviest in Robinson's expressions, in social as well as personal terms, and from the beginning to the end of his life. When he was twenty-two he had written Smith solemnly: "I used to think I was a kind of pessimist, but I have outgrown that idea. The world as a whole is surely growing better and better, but there is yet an enormous field for improvement." [26] Thirty-six years later, writing Edith Brower, he summarized his political attitudes and prognostications: "The socialistic dark ages are coming, and the individual is going to 'wither' as Tennyson foresaw, but he'll swell up again after a few hundred years, and knock down the whole damned business—which is description, not profanity." [27] And in '34, about a year before his death, he gave virtually the same message to Mrs. Richards: "The more I try to make a picture of this world for the next hundred years, the more I don't like it, and the gladder I am I shall be out of it. But something better will come sometime, we'll hope, in spite of human stupidity, which is a large part of destiny. . . ." [28]

III Religion

In 1930 Robinson wrote a student that there was no philosophy
in his poetry except an affirmation of an "ordered universe" and
a negation of the "general futility" that is the "basis of rational
thought." He added, "So I suppose you will have to put me down
as a mystic, if that means a man who cannot prove all his convictions to be true." [1] In '33, two years before his death, he wrote
Mrs. Richards: "As for religion in the future, I didn't say that it
wouldn't be mystical. Of course it must be that in order to be religion, but it will be free of all theological machinery." [2] Actually,
his Clairvoyant Mood was a continuous, subconscious or mystical
sense of identification with essential Being, and his "wisdom" was
that mood examining the materials of the outer world. Hagedorn
reports him as saying that a man who was destitute of the religious
sentiment was no higher than an animal.[3]

Besides the awareness of identification with generic Being,
Robinson's mysticism involved the conviction that Being is moving towards some specific and salutary resolution. In '93, about
to leave Harvard, he wrote Gledhill, "I feel that things are coming
out all right some time, but the action is slow." [4] And not long
after that, he declared in *Credo*, "I feel the coming glory of the
Light," and in *The Altar* that the flame of romantic self-immolation "burns and must burn somehow for the best." A little later,
again writing Gledhill, he said: "The universe is a great thing,
and the power of evil never put it together." [5] And twenty years
later he published *The Man Against the Sky:*

> Shall we, because Eternity records
> Too vast an answer for the time-born words
> We spell, whereof so many are dead that once
> In our capricious lexicons
> Were so alive and final, hear no more
> The Word itself, the living word
> . . . ?

The optimism is primarily cosmic, but it includes also every
separate fragment or microcosm that came under Robinson's at-

tention, including himself. And especially with regard to himself, the darker the immediate prospect, the more determined was his affirmation: "I shall keep on having the same faith in myself . . . a kind of optimistic desperation"; [6] "I don't seem to have any capacity for discouragement. . . . in my verses . . . I intend that there shall always be at least a suggestion of something wiser than hatred and something better than despair." [7] We have seen some of his powerful affirmations in the period of the family crisis of '97. Not then, or at any time, did he weaken in religious certainty, what Miss Kaplan calls his "absolutistic agnosticism" [8] —and that I wish she had called his agnostic absolutism—,his amused skepticism regarding all external experience and his fixed certainty of the reality of the inner world.

As to the nature of the divinity—"Whatever-it-is"—he so consciously affirmed, Robinson was conveniently inconsistent, shaping it to the needs of the particular passage in the particular poem. His pantheistic mood was perhaps the nearest in mystical purity to the generic affirmation of the clairvoyant mood, the least blurred by any effort at orderly analysis or synthesis. Part of it was the sense of inclusive unity, the integration of space and time "where atoms and the ages are one stuff." Later in his life the same idea is behind the statement of Garth's ghost to Matthias that "nothing is wasted." This Brahma-like unity was congenial to his early preoccupation with Buddhism and its affinities with Christianity: ". . . Nirvana and Heaven are from the idealist's point of view—which is to me the only point of view— pretty much the same thing." [9] Sometimes this unity is given the name of God, as where "God's wholeness gleams with light superlative," or where he finds

> God's parallel completeness in the vague
> And incommensurable excellence
> That equitably uncreates itself
> And makes a whirlwind of the Universe.

Again, "God" may be identified with a hot image of self-centered romanticism, as in the "gleaming of God's forge" or in "God's highways gleaming."

In most of these uses, and others like them, we feel that

Robinson's "God" is remembering the vocabulary, if not the theology, of the Congregational Sunday School from which in his boyhood he played hooky whenever he could. We are not astonished to find that in other *Octaves* than those from which the above quotations are taken, he assumes, if he does not affirm, something very like the orthodox, personal, Christian God. He is not identical with the pantheistic One, for He is outside His creation of which he keeps for our eventual perusal

> That record of All-Soul whereon God writes
> In everlasting runes the truth of Him.

And, meanwhile, we in our self-preoccupation, are

> too proud of death, and too ashamed
> Of God, to know enough to be alive.

As Robinson's notion of God is a blend between the impersonal and the personal, similarly his idea of supreme Love combines the transcended Eros of the *Symposium* and the Christian doctrine of a loving God. Sometimes the Platonic view, coinciding as it does with his own experience, is dominant, as in the Twenty-second *Octave* where "Love's complete communion is the end / Of anguish for the liberated man"; or in the Twenty-third where the wake of the ship carrying the beloved away is "Love's earnest" of "Life's all-purposeful / And all triumphant sailing" from the "crumbled wharves of time." Again, his attitude seems primarily Christian, as in *The Sage* who

> stood where Asia, crowned with ravishment,
> The curtain of Love's inner shrine had rent . . .

or in the statement of orthodox "love's revealed infinitude" in the Thirteenth *Octave*; or, late in his life, the superb affirmation of unorthodox Christianity in the finale of *A Christmas Sonnet*:

> Something is here that was not here before,
> And strangely has not yet been crucified.

But to attempt to distinguish between Platonic and Christian love in Robinson is to strain an always dubious point, for his God was compounded of both, and in most of his expressions, including all but one or two of those cited above, both ideas are present. Most typical of him are those expressions where, as in his own mystical perception, two, or even more, notions of God are fused. In the early *Sonnet,* the end of whose octet tells us that

> in love's elemental over-glow
> God's wholeness gleams with light superlative,

it would be specious to try to disentangle the Platonism, the elementary pantheism and the Christianity. Even more extremely, we find in *The Garden* that Christian Αγαπη and fundamental, unerotic idealism, are not only integrated but identical in God, wherefore every human life, leaflike, at its instance

> Outrolled itself from Thought's eternal seed,
> Love-rooted in God's garden of the mind.

As Robinson was a practitioner of the First Christian Commandment, a lover of a loving God, he was, as we have seen, all the more a practitioner of the Second. He was born to the love of his neighbor. In the realm of theory, his belief with respect to the two great commandments was single and comprehensive. He believed love was the condition of the cosmos, containing in one "over-glow" both God and the neighbor, both lover and beloved. In the instances given above, both God's love and man's love of God include also the love of all mankind. It would be possible, I think, to cite from Robinson one or more paraphrases of each of the Beatitudes. His satisfaction has been observed when, in '97, Miss Brower had persuaded him that through his verse "I possess the power of helping others, which, after all, is about the greatest thing a man, or a book, can do." [10] A month later he reports, "The fact that I have done a little spiritual good in the world is what keeps me going now." [11] In 1900 he wrote Miss Peabody: ". . . as I look back on thirty years of somewhat ridiculous existence, I find that I have helped others, and sometimes (which is the real thing, [sic] without their knowing it. And this discovery is, it seems to me, the only thing which really counts." [12] There is much preachment in *Captain Craig* about "the cursedest mean thing that crawls":

You may not ever crush him but you lose,
You may not ever shield him but you gain.

In *The Three Taverns*, Paul gives us a premonitory blast of First
Corinthians, XIII:

Many that hate
Their kind are soon to know that without love
Their faith is but the perjured name of nothing.

And near the end of Robinson's life Timberlake, in *Matthias at
the Door*, tells Matthias that we are "stairs for one another's
climbing."

Intellectually, Robinson was nearly enough disposed toward
Christianity to call it "a logical notion of human life" [13]—thus
seeming to adopt the syllogistic method which a few years before
he had dismissed as "worse than hell itself"! More consistent with
his usual vocabulary, he refers elsewhere to the "ideal truth of
Christianity," [14] and regrets that he hasn't "the stamina to be a
Christian—accepting Christ as either human or divine" [15]—meaning no doubt an orthodox Christian. Of the professing orthodox
Christians he declares flatly, "The popular misinterpretation of
Christianity makes me sick." [16] In the great letter of March, '97,
he reports that he has been flirting with Christian Science, but
has decided that for him it "will be impossible. The system is
too dependent on unsubstantial inferences. . . . It . . . will have
a tremendous power in the world; but it is only a stepping stone
to the truth. It has proved the power, however, of even a partial
recognition [of inner or spiritual reality], and thereby proved the
utter fallacy of all existing notions of religion—popular notions,
I mean." [17]

And so he swings into his favorite pastime of flogging the
materialists for the ills of mankind: "The great scholars of the
world are for the most part spiritual imbeciles, and there is where
the trouble lies. The willingness 'to be a child again' comes hard
—so hard that it will never come to many who are in the world
today. That is not what they are here for. 'The world was made
in order and the atoms march in time.' It is a damned queer time
to us who are here now. . . ." And then, as always, the affirmation: ". . . but it is all right and we are all going to hear it as

it is—when the mortal wax gets out of our ears." [18] He wrote that
to Smith in '97, in the midst of his personal ordeal. Thirty-six
years later, when he had passed his ordeals, he wrote Mrs.
Richards what might have been a continuation of the earlier
letter: "The Christian theology has so thoroughly crumbled
that I do not think of any non-Roman acquaintance to whom it
means anything. . . . The Christian ethics might have done some
good if they had ever been tried, or understood, but I'm afraid
it's too late now. There's a non-theological religion on the way,
probably to be revealed by science when science comes definitely
to the jumping-off place. It is really there now, but it isn't quite
ready to say so." [19]

Robinson neither had nor wanted a doctrine, a theology, a
religious system, any more than he wanted a philosophical system. But his race memory of the theology of his fathers appeared
in many of his attitudes and assumptions. In the twenties it was
fashionable to call him a Puritan in the derogatory sense in which
"puritanism" is still used by the more ignorant intellectuals, making it synonymous with that moralism or concern for works which
was heresy to the Puritans and equally offensive to Robinson.
The real target of the Puritan-burning that began in the twenties
was any kind of religion. If we remember the Puritans for the
antimoralistic and religious people they were, then Robinson was
indeed a bearer of their tradition in its undoctrinaire essentials.
He was the latest in that Puritan current in American poetry of
which the chief figures are Wigglesworth, Taylor, Dwight,
Bryant, Whittier, and overlapping Robinson, Emerson and Dickinson. A glance through the chief tenets of American Puritanism
will show how closely Robinson, whether intentionally or unintentionally, followed them.

At the foundation, the *Search for Truth*, in the cosmos and
in the self, both imaginatively or spiritually and intellectually,
was the cornerstone of Calvinism. And no Puritan ever carried
on the search more ruthlessly than Robinson did, calling the
object variously "Truth," "Wisdom," and "The Light."

To both the Puritans and Robinson, God was not anthropomorphic. To limited human understanding He was *Unknowable*.
In fact, as we have seen, knowledge to Robinson was a "screen"
between the distant "gleam" and the realization of the Light.

In identifying the inner self with "thought's eternal seed, / Love-rooted in God's garden of the mind," Robinson sees each human being as something very close to the Puritanical *Image of God.*

Robinson's Wordsworthian belief in the child as trailing clouds of glory, and his frequent positing of "new childhood" as the aim of life, imply a belief in something like biblical *Innocence,* not as the quality of a mythical people in a prehistoric Garden but as the starting condition of every individual life.

Similarly, Robinson took no stock in any primordial *Fall of Man.* And yet he ascribed to all men as individuals that chronic self or outer self, whether inherited or acquired, whose perpetual itch for self-aggrandizement or other self-indulgence looks very much like *Original Sin.* Merlin's statement seems to cover everybody:

> There is no man, or any woman
> For whom the story of the living king
> Is not the story of the living sin.

Robinson sometimes recalls the myth of the fall by clothing the self in ophidian features,

> the rough
> And reptile skins of us whereon we set
> The stigma of scared years . . .

His gradually changing attitude toward the outer self, with its sinfulness of self-concern and its virtue of natural reason, was part of his changing attitude towards redemption and grace, and will be discussed as part of the larger problem in a moment.

There is not evidence enough to support the view that Robinson shared the apparent inconsistency of the Puritans in holding that a Loving God could also be an *Angry God;* but there are a few passages suggesting that the orthodox view was in his mind. Captain Craig said,

> "the old
> Unswerving and inviolable price
> Gets paid: God sells himself eternally,
> But never gives a crust. . . ."

And in *The Valley of the Shadow* there were those who were indignant at "a measureless malfeasance" that had willed their misery. But it is not plain that this "malfeasance," which is uncapitalized in the text, is either God or some devil released on the world by God. The God or condition of the universe for Robinson was love, and when anyone violated that love in himself, or his belief in it, he violated his own reality and so suffered. Robinson's tragic figures, unlike those of the Old Testament and the Greek dramatists, did not suffer divine retribution for breaking literal divine laws. Many of his characters played fast and loose with the Decalogue without being called to account. As already pointed out, the most rotten stone in the "rotten foundation" of Camelot was not the adultery of Lancelot and Guinevere, but was Arthur's triple self-indulgence in violation of that love, that Αγαπη, which he professed. First, he married Guinevere when he knew she did not love him. Second, he married her, knowing she did love his friend who also loved her. Third, he condemned her to the stake, though legally, for adultery with that friend. It was for these accumulating acts of self, not for his or anybody's violation of law, that he had to pay *within himself* "the old unswerving and inviolable price."

Given everybody's "reptile skin" of self, Robinson's *Valley of the Shadow*, his "dark," his "darkness," and his "human gloom," together with his weary processions in *Twilight Song, The Town Down the River,* and the last stanza of *Eros Turannos,* all of these are obvious, retouched reproductions of the Puritan *Vale of Tears,* or *State of Reprobation,* through which corrupted mankind passes on the way to a happier country. As among two kinds of sufferers, it is to be observed that Robinson has less compassion for the more fortunate, like Matthias or the husband in *London Bridge,* who are generally the less guilty of moral misconduct but the more guilty of the most deadly kind of self-preoccupation which is self-satisfaction or complacency. His preference, and his happiest forecast for the future, is for the unfortunate, the "unfulfilled," the beaten, those "builders of new mansions in the Valley of the Shadow," who include "the dying and the blinded and the maimed." Also on his preferred list, and often identical with the beaten, are the greatest and most spirited

sinners in the world's eyes, those powerful prodigals, the Lancelots and the Tristrams, who, in Paul's phrase in *The Three
Taverns* have in their "blood the fire of time to warm eternity."
Here Robinson was accepting the doctrine of at least those greatest of Puritans, Hooker and Edwards, both of whom suspected
that great reprobation somehow deserved specially great sanctification.

As for the conduct of the passage through this Vale of Tears,
Robinson had a lifelong, though superficial, presumption in favor
of the several Puritan formulas for administering it. To the end of
his life he had a weakness for the Calvinist *Economic Virtues* of industry and public service. We have seen that through youth and
into his manhood he was continuously chewed by guilt for not
having a remunerative job, that he envied even as he condemned
the economically successful, and that he rejoiced when some
means of being socially useful, such as tutoring Mabel Moore,
fell within his proclivities and abilities. Yet the real and inner
Robinson had no time for any of this, but was close to the fundamental Christian precept of taking no thought what he should
eat or wear. When, in 1901, he was grimly lacking in both of
these supposed necessities, eating sometimes on twenty-five cents
a day and wanting both a second pair of pants and a second pair
of shoes, he wrote Mason, "I look ahead either two hours, like
the wise men of old, or at least five years." [20]

It is natural to presume that Robinson's universal equalitarianism was, like that of most Yankees, a survival of American
Puritan *Congregationalism*, the practical application of the doctrine of the equality of all before God which becomes in secular
terms the inner equality of all.

Of lesser Puritan survivals, we might find in Robinson's stylistic reversion from the Victorian "language of poetry" to the
language of common speech a revival of the *Plain Style* of the
Puritans which represented their revolt against the flowery
rhetoric of many Angelican preachers of the sixteenth and seven-
teenth centuries. More dubiously, we might argue a relation
between Robinson's common method of balanced, contrapositive
statement and the Puritan preachers' rhetorical method of *Ramian
Logic*:

"You may be right, you may be wrong," said I
                    (Captain Craig)

                    "He might have dived,
Or jumped, or he might not . . ."
                    (Ibid.)

The proper Ramian method was to present propositions in alternative pairs, usually opposites, of which the obvious falsity of one implied the truth of the other. In his verse Robinson's "disjunctions" are usually not thus aimed at demonstration but merely at a cautious inclusiveness. So it is only the balanced method that recalls the traditional use. Sometimes in his letters, as in the quotation from one to Mrs. Richards on page 282, he used the Ramian method purely.

As Robinson transferred the doctrine of the Fall and Original Sin from a myth to each individual's experience of self, so he interpreted the *Crucifixion* as symbolic of the immediate world's brutality and hatred of Love:

Tell me, O Lord—tell me, O Lord, how long
Are we to keep Christ writhing on the cross!
                    (Calvary)

In the large, Robinson's special interpretation of the *Atonement* was one of his few beliefs that might be called a doctrine. His earliest statement of it, to Smith in '97, has been quoted:

There's a good deal to live for, but a man has to go through hell really to find it out. The process is hard, but the result pays. If it didn't there would be no universe. This may sound obscure, but it isn't.[21]

In 1919 he put it even more cryptically to Mabel Dodge Sterne:

The world is a hell of a place; and if life and the universe mean anything, there is no reason to suppose that it will ever be anything else. This, as I understand it, is the true optimism.[22]

The existence of evil is a proof of the existence of good. Without negative there would be no affirmative. God must suffer if His universe and its people are to be finally perfected—

God slays himself in every leaf that flies

. . . .

(Luke Havergal)

As usual, Robinson's inclusive notion was simply a universalization of human experience. Each person must suffer if he is to win through to a resolution of his life. Beneath Robinson's theory of universal *Atonement*, his essential perception was of the necessity of individual *Self-Atonement*. Said Paul in *The Three Taverns*:

> The power that holds the world
> Away from God . . .
>
> .   .   .   .
>
> Was not, nor ever shall be a small hazard
> Enlivening the ways of easy leisure
> Or the cold road of knowledge. . . .
>
> .   .   .   .
>
> Before we see,
> . . . we suffer. . . .

The world and its havoc comprise a sort of opening act of the drama of the "Scheme," "a kind of spiritual exercise . . . by which we may, if we will, put ourselves beyond it." [23] First, we must "look life in the face without resorting to the nauseating evasions of the uncompromising 'optimist,' "—this in a letter to Richard Watson Gilder in 1908.[24] And in 1932 to Mrs. Ledoux: "Most people are so afraid of life that when they see it coming their first impulse is to get behind a tree and shut their eyes. And for some odd reason they call that impulse optimism . . ." [25] First we must face reality. Then, we must endure what we see, not resist or fight back because that would be to adopt the world's method, but non-resistantly, uncomplainingly, endure our private crucifixion in the quiet fashion that Robinson's own life illustrated so well. And finally, by some turn consonant with the Scheme which is beyond our understanding, we will "sing in the sun" of *Supremacy* and *Captain Craig*, or, better, come to the Light of *Lancelot*. There are other ways. Sometimes one person may atone for another, as Garth, Timberlake, and Natalie were all "stairs" for Matthias's "climbing," as Alcestis in *As a World Would Have It*, Guinevere in *Lancelot*, Laramie in *Cavender's House*, Emma unnamed in *The March of the Cameron Men*, indeed all loving women from the beginning of the world, in some fashion laid down their lives for their men. Then there are those who from birth enjoy the selfless Light of Natural Grace, such as most of these same loving women, or *Isaac and Archibald*, or the two brothers who gardened in "Linndale," or Lincoln who in *The Master* was "ancient at his birth," or indeed Robinson himself. But the atonement of these is more convincing when it is also sealed in suffering, as was Lincoln's and Robinson's and all the women's, when it is also Self-Atonement, along with the multitude, in the slow unremittingly burdened procession of *Twilight Song* and *The Town Down the River*.

Consideration of the *Atonement* brings us in sight of *Salvation* and, related to that, the central columns of Puritan doctrine. First there is the main issue of the Reformation, the controversy of *Faith vs. Works*, the question as to how some individuals win the benefit of the *Atonement*, and some do not. Robinson, as a good Puritan, stood consciously and articulately on the side of Faith at a time when Victorianism was recommending pink and blue propriety as the condition of admission to a pink, blue, and gilt Heaven. One of his earliest prose "sketches"—presumably lost—was on the selfishness of self-denial. His strange concern with respectability, his desire to ride both truth and the opinion of the town, comprised a violation of his general view, a sort of petty hypocrisy of his own. In his serious choices, as in his declarations, he was always on the side of Faith, the emphasis upon the individual's relation to God, rather than his conduct toward men, as the criterion of Salvation. In *The Three Taverns* Paul says that God

> holds himself away—
> Farther away than all your works and words
> Are like to fly without the wings of faith—

Also that

> the Law kills the flesh that kills the Law,
> And we are then alive. . . .

And summarily,

> I affirm
> To the last hour that faith affords alone
> The Kingdom entrance. . . .

Never did Robinson show the slightest interest in the moral law as such, even where murder was involved, as in *Cavender's House* and *The Glory of the Nightingales*. He believed in moral conduct as the expression of the generic, loving instinct of mankind, but he saw no relation between this genuine morality and legality. He respected the unique inner integrity of all individuals and he never judged anyone, in life or in fiction, for he did not know what pressures they had been under, and he did not know how he would have behaved if he had been in their place. As for sex, the chief preoccupation of the popular writers of the twenties, he took it for granted like other glandular activities, and paid attention only to the imaginative and idealistic aspects of love. With excellent irony, Barnard says that Robinson's exclusive interest was in "the thing that before the birth of psychology men could without embarrassment call the soul." He was concerned "not with what happens *to* people but with what happens *in* them." [26] From his first great poem, the *Octaves*, through his last great poem, *Matthias at the Door*, the preachment of all his work is to live by the dictates of the spirit and not those of either the flesh or the law, to live actively in the world without either deferring to it or trying to escape from it, in the language of the great orthodox Puritan John Cotton, "to live in the world as if you were in it not."

The basic reason Robinson never passed judgment on anyone, even the comfort-anesthetized rich, even the "victims of good luck," was his instinctive addiction to another central Puritan tenet, that of *Predestination*. As in all matters usually reduced to doctrine, he was undoctrinaire in his interpretation of it. Also, he was inconsistent, as indeed were most of the Puritans. But whatever relaxations in the general rule he sometimes seemed to recognize, he did not deviate from his fundamental beliefs, first, that there was some central Meaning which was working itself out in the Scheme, second, that human or natural reason can not fathom it, and, third, that man is helpless before its omnipotence. In his twenty-second year, just before he escaped to Harvard, he wrote Smith one of his typical contrapositive somersaults. He first concludes that he is to blame for having stayed at home instead of getting a respectable job. And then, "But how about the unseen powers?" The "invisible powers?" "The master of the show?" ". . . another architect behind ourselves?" [27] In the same letter he seems to refer to his brother Dean as a case of "failure where fate has been abused," presumably by act of will. But years later, in *The Dark House*, Dean is the victim of

> a closing of still shears
> On a thread made out of years.

And Paul, in *The Three Taverns*, is a "driven agent" of Christ who is being taken to Caesar because "the word / Of God would have it as you see it is." Still later, in *An Island*, Napoleon is upbraiding

> Fate, the mistress of iniquities,
> The mad Queen-spinner of all discrepancies
> . . . .

And in Robinson's final work, *King Jasper*, Zoë, who is, among other things, all knowledge, strikes the old note, curiously substituting God for Fate:

> "I don't say what God is, but it's a name
> That somehow answers us when we are driven
> To feel and think how little we have to do
> With what we are."

By the time of the composition of *The Town Down the River*, in late 1907 or early '08, Robinson had got all the way to the doctrine of *Election*—

> Long have I waited,
> Longer have I known
> That the Town would have its own,
> And the call be for the fated.

And a dozen years later Rembrandt was ordering himself to
"bow his elected head"; and Paul, always Robinson's articulate
theologian, was saying in *The Three Taverns*,

> You cannot say
> This woman or that man will be the next
> On whom it falls. . . .

Not only does Robinson talk the language of Election, but for
the elected he recognizes solid, Puritan *Compulsive Grace*, the
impossibility of escaping salvation. When the bouncing little boy
George told his old maid aunt Imogen that playing with her was
a "good game," suddenly

> The blow that she had vaguely thrust aside
> Like fright so many times had found her now.

When Lancelot was in the throes of deciding to send Guinevere
back to Arthur, he felt himself driven by external Authority—

> A power that I should not have said was mine—
> That was not mine, and is not mine—avails me
> Strangely tonight, although you are here with me
> . . . .

At the final parting, Guinevere reminds Lancelot of

> the Gleam that you must follow,
> Whether you will or not. . . .
>
> . . . there is no place
> For you save where it is that you are going.

And at the very end, when Lancelot's outer self bridles at running away, leaving Guinevere alone, Compulsive Grace takes
him—

> the Voice within him said: "You are not free.
> You have come to the world's end, and it is best
> You are not free."

Conversely, there are among Robinson's characters those, like John Evereldown and Lorraine, who seem predestined for damnation and under compulsion to carry out their fate—

> Some creatures are born fortunate, and some
> Are born to be found out and overcome,—
> Born to be slaves, to let the rest go free.

But in the main Robinson's predestinarianism didn't go that far. Till his last breath, his tortured brother Dean was for him the finest pattern of a man. He was "the pilot" who "fought so foul a gale" and had "won beyond our knowing." However cursed they might be by Fate, he could not believe that anyone was ever finally damned. It was part of his belief in the Unseen Powers that they had predestined Universal Salvation.

Seemingly inconsistent with Robinson's belief in predestination was his frequent, apparent affirmation of *Free Will* which in an early expression looks like the very heart, the instigating center, of his enormous optimism. In the definitive letter of March 15, '97, no statement was more final or more prophetic of his whole life than his proclamation of his power to overcome the world: "What I am after is the courage to see and to believe that my present life is the best thing for me, and that every man has it in his power to overcome whatever obstacles may be in his way—even that seeming obstacle we call by the name of Death." [28] Also in the verse, from the early defiance of *Dear Friends* and *Two Sonnets,* on through *Captain Craig, Sainte-Nitouche, The Three Taverns, The Man Who Died Twice, Tristram,* and down to the late statements in *Toussaint l'Ouverture* and especially *Amaranth,* seeming implications of free will are interspersed among the acknowledgments of Fate and predestiny, so that it would sometimes seem specious to try to reconcile them or to suppose either principle to have been dominant in his mind. To a casual reading he would seem to be simply another among the many first-rate minds who have preferred to rest on both horns of the great paradox rather than to weaken both by attempting a theoretical reconciliation.

Perhaps the most convincing evidence of Robinson's belief in free will to be found in the poetry is the juxtaposition Barnard makes of two of his strongest and most sympathetic characters—both artists with the greatness he felt in himself—namely the central figure in *Rembrandt to Rembrandt* and Fernando Nash in *The Man Who Died Twice*. Both are "played on" by the Unseen Powers to keep on working against poverty and neglect. Rembrandt seems to choose with the powers, endures in Robinsonian fashion, and does his finest work. Nash seems to choose for the allurements of self, gives up the struggle, sinks into the deepest dissipation, and finally in a hallucination in weakness hears, in some of Robinson's greatest poetry, the symphony he had always had in mind but had never written. As between these, among other apparent cases of free will, and Robinson's more frequent assertions of Fate, Barnard offers a "partial solution . . . by distinguishing between [external] events and actions on the one hand and [internal] states of mind on the other. Obviously a person is often involved in situations which he cannot control. . . . But how a person responds to these situations, how they affect his character—this, one may feel, *is* within his power to determine.

"Rembrandt cannot change the artistic taste of Holland, but he has his choice of yielding to it or defying it—or, like Fernando Nash, taking refuge in cynicism and debauchery. . . . Captain Craig cannot postpone his death, but he can meet it . . . with courage and a large humor." [29] So of *Old King Cole* and *The Poor Relation*. Barnard goes on rightly to include within the surrounding circumstances that Robinson recognized as fated and so limiting free will, each individual's essential traits of character, whether inherited or acquired early. He shows how Llewellyn, Reuben Bright, Vanderberg in *Sainte-Nitouche,* and especially Tristram and Isolt, make their definitive choices because they are special kinds of people, and how if they had been, as we say, conditioned differently by Fate, they would have made different choices. He quotes Robinson as admitting to an interviewer "the presence in his poetry of 'a deterministic, a fatalistic note,'" and adding, "'I suppose I do believe that we are pretty much what we are.'" [30]

I have presented Barnard's analysis because it seems to me

that up to this point it identifies Robinson's notions about freedom and determinism with those set out in the highest Puritan authority on the subject, Edwards' *Freedom of the Will*, which Robinson probably heard discussed among his early, churchgoing, Congregational neighbors. Edwards' doctrine, coming down from Hobbes and Locke, was that "a man can do as he wills," or he can "forbear"; but the will itself, which Edwards assimilates to what we call desire, is predetermined by forces outside itself. This would seem to conform to Barnard's exposition of Robinson's belief that the external and internal forces that shape desire are predetermined, but that within the limits thus set by the Unseen Powers, each individual is free to choose his own way.

I wish I could accept Professor Barnard's analysis, for it would accord with my general impression of Robinson's considerable Puritan derivation. But I am unable to find in Robinson as much evidence of belief in free will as he seems to. And I must dissent especially from his further interpretation of Robinson's belief that "character is fate." Barnard would have it that he meant something very much like the Hindu notion of Karma as continually evolving under our accumulating choices, imposing on each new choice a strong, deterministic influence from the past but leaving also a degree of free will to break the accumulated chain of influence. This goes far beyond Robinson. I find no real evidence that he carried free will even as far as Edwards did. To be sure, the *Captain Craig* volume (1902), especially the title poem itself—the Captain being a great free-willer—and *Sainte-Nitouche*, does have an aura of lightsome freedom about it which is unique in Robinson and may have been a whistle in the dark of that period of his crumbling fortunes. Also, there are evidences of a kind of wish, rather than a belief, that in the youthful matter of choosing a career "there is a choice, yes." But with these two thin exceptions, the belief set out in the letters and the poetry, the belief that kept him from judging anybody, was as absolute as Calvin's: every move and every choice a person makes, including those in Barnard's and Edwards' small, supposed free area, are predetermined in "the storehouse of his destiny," which is what he himself is and has been from infancy.

What look like professions or acts of free will in Robinson personally and in his characters who speak for him are usually assertions or acts of that individualism which represented his most passionate belief. He thought that the differences between people were slight, that in each of us there is only "a small difference . . . between ourselves, as we are, and ourselves . . . as we . . . would have been if our physical and temperamental make-up [that is, our inheritance] and our environment had been a little different." [31] As observed earlier, the inner selves of all of us are absolutely equal, in fact identical. Upon that equality there is imposed by the Unseen Powers through inheritance and environment (Robinson would never have admitted biological determinism!) the superficial distinctions of our outer selves. These differences are "small," and yet they are sufficient to base that sense of separate, inviolable personality which was Robinson's most explosive conviction. That tremendous declaration in the letter of March, 1897, was one of its explosions: "Every man has it in his power to overcome whatever obstacles may be in his way—even that seeming obstacle we call by the name of Death." This was not a declaration of belief in free choice, but an assertion of himself, his "present life," as predetermined, unique, a creation of the Unseen Powers, and so irresistible.

Likewise of the seeming assertions of freedom throughout the poetry. In Paul's numerous injunctions in *The Three Taverns*, he is only doing what he must because "I am I," and he is only trying to strengthen the faithful in the basic Robinsonian virtues of enduring and "seeing" in accordance with their separate and slightly different natures and lights. Not even excepting Captain Craig, I cannot think of a single character of Robinson's who, beyond making a mighty vaunt of freedom, did plainly address alternative courses of action, both possible for him, and make a clear, independent choice. Surely not Merlin, who foresaw Fate but insisted that he was neither Fate nor God, and incidentally said that Fate was stronger than God. Surely not Lancelot. Certainly neither Tristram nor Isolt, for all their lecturing each other trying to bolster each other's supposed freedom of action. Robinson's objection to the love philter, the "damned dose," was not that it left them predetermined, but that it left them only physically predetermined, like animals, "rabbits," without any high predestiny of idealism and loyalty.

Apparently exceptional to Robinson's predestinarianism is *Amaranth*. Writing it in '33, looking back over his life and considering how many people he had seen make wrong choices of their careers, he was not there concerning himself with whether the choices had been free or fated. But, as we shall notice presently, he probably did have a personal predilection, not an objective belief, in favor of freedom in one's choice of his calling. Most of the assorted mistaken choices in *Amaranth* may be interpreted as either predestined or as free. And yet, the one positive statement on the subject has it that Doctor Styx was "misled" into his unhappy choice by "playful fate." Wherefore, with no certain exceptions, even in *Captain Craig* or in *Amaranth*, Robinson's characters behave as they had to do from childhood. The aspect of the choice of a career that he hoped was free was the preliminary close and "sincere" self-examination in order to *see* one's predestined way and so to walk in it with a minimum of resistance and confusion from the secondary devils of the outer self. Even where the destination was apparent damnation, like King Arthur's, or Lorraine's, or John Evereldown's, it was happier to face it than to let yourself drift in "blindness"—especially as Robinson took no stock in ultimate damnation. It is your duty to strive to see clearly. There is no evidence that Robinson believed that the gift of clear introspection was not, like everything else, a gift of Fate. But here and elsewhere there is evidence that he thought that the *use* of that gift, once received, might be subject to individual will. The point will be reconsidered in a moment.

It was said earlier that Barnard made a good case for Robinson's belief in free will by contrasting his Rembrandt's decision to endure with Fernando Nash's choice of dissipation and finally starvation, bringing on the weakness in which he heard his great unwritten symphony in hallucination. The juxtaposition is excellent, for both great artists were down and out, each believed he "had it once," each addressed his self-criticism to a mirror, and the high inspiration of each—much more gloriously in Nash—was associated with liquid golden fire. The contrast of action in similar circumstances is striking, but the evidence of free choice on the part of either is weak. In the case of Rembrandt there is not a phrase of support for it; on the contrary he calls himself "elected," and "a living instrument / Played on by powers that are invisible"—Robinson's own epistolary vocabulary! The case for Fernando Nash's free will is better, for he claims it himself and takes the blame for his own downfall in colorful self-vituperation that equals anything of the kind in Shakespeare. On the other hand his friend the narrator, who talks like Robinson, takes the compassionate, deterministic view in their dialogues, and in his detached comments he informs us that both of the two contrasted rings in Fernando's circus were predestined. On the one hand he was "born"—that is, fated—to "confusions." On the other hand, in his final weakness, his reduction to selfless nothing, it was irresistible Fate that drove the great composition down through his emptied mind:

> those far sent celestial messengers
> That he had for so long a time denied
> Had found him now. He had offended them,
> And he was not forsaken. They had come,
> And in their coming had remembered only
> That they were messengers, who like himself
> Had now no choice. . . .

No free will there. That is clear, old-fashioned, Puritan Necessity. In the final passage of the poem, Robinson says of Fernando's strange composition,

> There was the nameless and authentic seal
> Of power and of ordained accomplishment—
> Which may not be infallibly forthcoming,
> Yet in this instance came.

That is a case of Robinson's humbly cautious, argumentative method, his perpetual awareness of the other side. He is not saying that in his own opinion predestination may not "infallibly" account for action. He is merely acknowledging that there may be two views of the matter.

The Man Who Died Twice is a poem of both compulsive grace and compulsive achievement, achievement in what to

Robinson was the grandest manner, the manner of symphonic composition, the only kind of art that he admitted to be grander than his own. And it was pure Robinson that the great symphony was never performed before the outer world. Until three years before the appearance of this poem, Robinson himself had enjoyed only mediocre attention. He had come to put primary value on the inner experience, the actual composition, without the expectation of an immediate outer audience. It would seem that this great poem—many call it his greatest—was another case, like that letter written twenty-seven years before, of his defiance of the world, his proclamation that his predestiny would be reached against every obstacle, including the obstacles of his own weaknesses, also fated. Finally, he said of Fernando:

> I believe
> To-day that all he told me for the truth
> Was true—as I believed him long ago
> To be the giant of his acknowledgement.
> Crippled or cursed or crucified, the giant
> Was always there, and always will be there.

That is not a shout of freedom. It is a humble, vicarious acknowledgment by one delegated by the Powers of the cosmos to do a particular job. And it is an affirmation that even beyond "that seeming obstacle we call by the name of Death" it will be done.

One of the two most important aspects of Predestination, both to the Puritans and to Robinson, was the *Calling* that is assigned to every man by the Unseen Powers. Believing, like all Yankees, in this metaphysical doctrine, Robinson found it in conflict in his own impulses with the equally Puritan principle of the *Economic Virtues*. In his twenties, as we have seen, he felt continuously guilty for not having a "regular occupation" which will "bring in the ducats instead of throwing them out all the time." [32] And yet, stronger than these scruples, and dating from even earlier, was his sense of his inescapable calling. In '93 he said, ". . . writing has been my dream ever since I was old enough to lay a plan for an air castle." [33] In '95, "I shall never be a prominent citizen and I thank God for it, but I shall be something just as good perhaps and possibly a little more permanent." [34] Later in his life he said, to Nancy Evans, "I knew from the beginning that I was in for it"; [35] and to Hagedorn, "If I could have done anything else on God's green earth I never would have written poetry. There was nothing else I could do, and I had to justify my existence." [36] Almost from the beginning, his belief in his predestined Calling outweighed his wistfulness about the Economic Virtues; for those virtues, after all, were imposed by law, while a man's calling comprised a higher duty, being imposed specifically on each individual by the Powers. There remains, however, the point raised previously, that Robinson did seem to think that the individual retains a measure of free will, not in the prescription of what his career properly is, but in the application of close self-inquiry to find out what it is, and so to avoid spending his life in the "wrong world" with most of the people in *Amaranth*. In spite of having realized that he was "in for it" from the beginning, he liked to believe that he had by introspection identified, and so had in effect "chosen," his calling as a poet against the wishes of his family, the scorn of the town, and all the practicalities. It was his sly, internal contrapositive against what he really knew. Personally, he titillated his vanity of the outer self by persuading himself, at least for periods, that he had chosen. Both instinctively and intellectually, he knew it had all been predestined from the beginning of the world.

For Robinson, as for the Puritans, the most important subject for personal Predestination or Fate was the understanding of the good life and the chances of attaining it. For both the Puritans and Robinson, the problem involved the tension between the outer self, with its combination of indulgences and reason, and the selfless inner self with its clairvoyant mood of calm watchfulness, love, and identification with the mystery of Being. For the Puritans always, and for Robinson in his great central period from 1913 through 1923, the solution was in the *State of Grace*, or, as Robinson variously called it, "wisdom," or "the Light," or "Love." For him at all times the possibility of pure Grace was complicated by the externalities involved in his calling as a poet: the use of his observations of and reactions to the outer world and its contents as materials for portrayal and comment; the use of the same, including images, words, and pencil and paper, as symbols and means for his expression; and, most important, the necessary dominance by the outer self's conscious or natural reason, if not in the inspiration then certainly in the completion of his works of art.

In terms of his beliefs with respect to the conflict between the outer self and its art and the inner self and its Grace or saintliness, Robinson's life divides into three periods. The first, running from his childhood till about 1900, the completion of *Captain Craig*, was his Selfish Period. After a transitional phase of a dozen years, the second, running from 1913 through 1923, the completion of *The Man Who Died Twice*, was his Gracious Period. The third, beginning in '27 and running to his death, was his Humanist Period. It should be born in mind that at the foundation of his attitudes and ideas in all three periods, the personality itself was from birth exceptionally selfless, that his "selfishness" never involved but a minuscule of the vanities and possessivenesses usually associated with the term.

At the height of Robinson's first period, which was for poetic purposes the nineties, he spoke of his life as "essentially selfish" and allowed that "selfishness hangs to a man like a lobster." [37] What he meant was the "joy" that he identified with his "idealism" as the life of the imagination, the sublimated orgastic ecstasy that accompanies the union of a perception by the inner, clairvoyant mood with outer, conscious reason, whether simply as a formulated "idea" or as the words that will express it. He meant the rapturous self-indulgence of the conception and composition of those early, passionate, romantic poems that look before and after and affirm what is not: the hyper-romantic recommendations of fiery self-immolation in *The Altar*, and in the "crater" in the second of *Two Sonnets;* in the affirmations of *Credo, Sainte-Nitouche;* and above all in the *Octaves:* the Sixteenth with its condemnation of

> this idiot world
> Where blood pays blood for nothing, and where life
> Pays life to madness, till at last the ports
> Of gilded helplessness be battered through
> By the still crash of salvatory steel.

And the triumphant Twenty-third that was quoted earlier.

Robinson's chief direct preachment of his early "idealism" and its "joy" was in *Captain Craig*, published in 1902 but written four, three, and two years earlier. The good Captain's "philosophy" was a potpourri of transition, swinging between the sub-sophisticated theory of human life as "God's joke" to an almost equally theoretical statement of Christian love at the other, with variously attuned way stations between. But the central message, ringing true without argumentation, is of romantic idealism and its creative joy. The Captain calls the pursuit "good courage of the Sun," the Sun being one of young Robinson's hot figures for the consummate masochistic delight of immolating the self and the cosmos together. "After time," says the Captain,

> When we have earned our spiritual ears,
>
> .   .   .   .
> Then shall at last come ringing through the sun,
> Through time, through flesh, a music that is true.
> For wisdom is that music, and all joy
> That wisdom . . .
>
> .   .   .   .
> Forget you not that he who in his work
> Would mount from these low roads of measured shame
> To tread the leagueless highway must fling first
> And fling forevermore beyond his reach
> The shackles of a slave who doubts the sun.
> There is no servitude so fraudulent
> As of a sun-shut mind; for 'tis the mind
> That makes you craven or invincible
>
> .   .   .   .

When convenient, the Captain changes his figure for the glory of the romantic quest:

> And here do I insert an urging clause
> For climbers and up-fliers of all sorts,
> Cliff-climbers and high-fliers: Phaethon,
> Bellerophon, and Icarus did each
> Go gloriously up, and each in turn
> Did famously come down—as you have read
> In poems and elsewhere; but other men

Have mounted where no fame has followed them,
And we have had no sight, no news of them,
And we have heard no crash.

After 1902, so far as I know, Robinson talks no more about
"joy" and "selfishness" and "the sun." Following his transitional,
first decade of the twentieth century, and the crisis of 1909, he
enters in 1913 his great period that lasted through the completion
of *The Man Who Died Twice* in '23. In his struggle between the
outer and inner selves, the latter came nearer than ever before or
after to breaking free from outer involvement. Sometimes in the
poetry, the clairvoyant mood almost dispenses with the symbols
of sound it uses. With the one forerunner of the end of *The Book
of Annandale*, written in 1900 after *Captain Craig* was finished,
this period after 1912 was the time of Robinson's great terminal
diminuendos. When the superficial dramas are over, their strug-
gles echo away into nothing, leaving the peace of unsymbolized,
primordial Being. In *The Dark House* the former victim of the
demon

> Will be living, having died.

The Poor Relation rests

> Safe in a comfortable cage
> From which there will be no more flying.

In *The Burning Book*, the "Contented Metaphysician," having
burned his outer life work, rests in

> the large and unclamoring peace
> Of a dream that is ended.

In *Hillcrest*, the pretensions of the materialist end in

> a sound
> No louder than the falling leaves.

The sonnet *As It Looked Then* is translucent, and its words almost vanish in

> the calm wonder of the sea—
> Calm as a quiet sky that looked to be
> Arching a world where nothing had occurred.

And there is the universal silence of death and the sea that is the resolution of *The Man Who Died Twice*. There is the silence and darkness in which The Light came to Lancelot. And just after this great period there is the silence of death and the sea and sunlight that is the end of *Tristram*.

All of this wide calm is the State of Grace, or, in Robinson's vocabulary, "The Light," or "Love," and sometimes "Wisdom." "The Light" of course means cool, universal, selfless clarity, and has nothing to do with Captain Craig's blazing, self-fulfilling "sun." Love now is Christian Αγαπη, no longer the sublimated Eros of the *Symposium* and of Robinson's self-consciously "idealistic" phase. His interchangeable use of "Light" and "Love" as synonyms for Grace recalls the same duality of interpretation on the part of the American Puritans. Some of their finest writing was on the subject of the State of Grace as renovated perception. Like Robinson, the best minds among them valued this aesthetic aspect of Regeneration as fundamental, and love as a derivative of it. Thomas Hooker, preaching in Hartford in about 1640, gave perhaps the definitive statement when he said that grace "brings a strange and sudden alteration into the world, varies the price and valew of things and persons . . . makes things appear as they be . . ." [38] About the same time his son-in-law Thomas Shepard was telling his congregation in Newtown (Cambridge) how grace makes people "see things in another manner; to tell how they cannot; it is the beginning of the light of heaven." [39] And a century later Edwards described how after his conversion "the appearance of everything was altered; there seemed to be, as it were, a calm, sweet cast, or appearance of divine glory, in almost everything." [40]

Compare these with Robinson's explanation, in a letter to Hagedorn, of his own "light that Galahad saw" as "simply the light of the Grail, interpreted universally as a spiritual realization of Things and their significance." [41] In all these statements of an ultimately perceptive simplicity or restored Innocence, it seems obvious that the outer self is lost in universal Love. Similarly, Robinson's Paul, speaking in *The Three Taverns* in 1919, holds Αγαπη to be the ultimate "measure / Of works and hope and faith"; yet the Light comes first and represents the definitive break out of reprobation. First we "feel" or "suffer," then we "see," and out of seeing finally comes love.

Whether Robinson calls Grace "the Light," or "Love," or something else, in the main his characters who reach it do so as predestined. Some of them—notably old Isaac and Archibald, Oliver and Oakes who gardened in Linndale, and the white Isolt—seem to have enjoyed Natural Grace from birth. A larger number come to regeneration through the Robinsonian self-atonement of endurance; such are Old King Cole, the Poor Relation, Aunt Imogen, Tasker Norcross, and Rembrandt. To another group grace comes more or less cataclysmically, a lightning bolt from the Unseen Powers which first prostrates the outer self, and then pours in the Light, Love or both; such are St. Paul, Fernando Nash in *The Man Who Died Twice*, and the dark Isolt.

Robinson's comprehensive statement of his belief, in his gracious period, consists of the double epic *Merlin* and *Lancelot*. Earlier the contrast was pointed out between Merlin the artist and Lancelot the saint. No matter how much Merlin "sees," he must, as a maker, remain in the outer self, while Lancelot, whose destiny is simply to be and not to make, is able to discard the outer self and rest completely in the inner. Now we may put this distinction in theological perspective. The universal significance of *Merlin* is the presentation of the Pagan, Humanistic or Self-realizing way of life, to set off the Christian or Self-losing way of Lancelot. Vivian is idealized sensuous beauty, in love not with Merlin but with her preserved adolescent image of him as the great highbrow, looking to him to understand and draw out her always enthralling and mysterious self. She is an intellectual woman seeking self-fulfillment, and a female mystic who transcends the illusion of time in the emotionally packed eternal moment. Guinevere, in contrast, is Heavenly Beauty, in love with Lancelot as he is each instant, at first blinded by passion to his mystical need but finally perceiving it and surrendering herself to it. She is a mystic, not in her own right but in her perception of his potential mysticism; she transcends time, not in the ecstatic moment which actually is framed in time, but in the truly timeless reality of Αγαπη.

Merlin is the great pagan-humanist-artist who puts the noblest agent of the outer self, the ordering mind or reason, in place of God and spirit. Through natural reason he is the architect of utopia for the outer selves of men, knowing that thus far in human history all such contrivance is based in the "living sin" of self and so is fated to fail, but hoping that his failure will be a "mirror" for some future age. He is the proto-Freudian psychologist dedicated to his own self-expression, first in the mind's perfect creation of Camelot and, when that is completed, in aestheticized sensuousness. He is the prophet who does not live either in timeless Αγαπη, or in the universal moment, or in time as daily continuity. But he lives in time as continuity running backward and especially forward beyond the perceptions of other men. He is a lover of the world as material for his own modeling of perfection, but he loves nothing in the sense of self-loss, being destined, as he knows, like Arthur to see "no grail." Lancelot, in contrast, is the Christian, the man not of intellect but of action and emotion, destined first to sin and suffer, and out of suffering to seek the Grail until he comes to the Light of self-loss, love and saintliness.

It is worth noting that neither of the two kinds of self that are portrayed in Merlin is the one associated with the joy of Robinson's youthful "idealism." That is now outgrown and forgotten. The self now condemned is that of Modred and Arthur and Gawaine that must assert itself above other selves and the world. The self that is celebrated is that of Merlin the artist and prophet who would see the Light far off but would not come to it. The self represented Robinson's humble hope of what he personally might be predestined to become. The confession of the double epic is that, while he honors self-loss and Christian Grace as the consummate human experience, he must, for himself, continue to indulge so much of the pagan outer self as must be active in the formulation of his poetry.

Aside from Robinson's personal confession there are perhaps three principal preachments in *Merlin*, all emphasizing the error of conscious self-expression, as distinguished from self-loss, as the aim of life. First, there is the social danger of self-expression in common terms, as seen in the destruction of Camelot through the conflicting selves of Arthur, Modred, Gawaine, and Lancelot before his regeneration. Second, there is the special case of this, the fate of the intellectual who "sees too much," which means that he sees early and far off the gleam of the selfless Grail, but instead of simply following it without self-concern he tries with his outer mind to apply it rationally to his own life and that of mankind, thus eschewing the possibility of reaching it. And third, there is the warning of the inadequacy of humanism to resolve the human predicament, the impossibility of man's perfecting his own condition, through his mind, his natural reason. This question, raised by Merlin, was never more critically before mankind than at this moment. Shall we continue to draw up blueprints for our own pacification, in the belief that inductive reason and rational understanding will at last overcome self, time and fate? Or may we yet try the alternative of *Lancelot*, the method of all the great religions each of which claims to speak for a Meaning and Control of the cosmos that transcend self and fate and time. We know that Merlin's humanist experiment ends with "darkness over Camelot." We do not yet know whether Lancelot's Christian one, if tried, might lead, as Robinson prophesied, through darkness to the Light.

Robinson's beliefs and preachments in his final, Humanist Period do seem to comprise apostasy from those of his preceding, Christian phase. Since his diatribe against materialism was written to Will Durant in '31, it is certain that he held scientific knowledge in as great contempt as ever as a means of sketching a workable blueprint for society. But as a basis for wisdom and the good life he now espoused *self-knowledge*. In the twilight of his life he extended to other agreeable, outer activities the same freedom, under discipline by the outer, conscious mind that he had allowed to art in *Merlin*. Although the prerequisite self-knowledge is a pagan rather than a Christian virtue, it is worth noticing that it also characterized what was perhaps the wisest of the American Puritan hedges against absolute predestination, namely Thomas Hooker's doctrine of Preparation for Grace. Under the modicum of free will allowed him for that purpose, the individual is enjoined to read and contemplate assiduously, to the end that he may acquire the self-understanding to recognize divine grace if and when it offers, and may not let it pass, leaving him in eternal and hopeless reprobation. Also, Hooker's method allowed for the *gradual* acquisition of wisdom, under his belief that grace often comes in tidbits, and that the recognition of one glimpse of the Light increases the individual's qualification to catch the next gleam when it swings by. All very much like pagan and modern healthy individual growth under increasing self-knowledge and self-expression, as distinguished from the instantaneous, entire self-loss that was requisite for earlier Robinsonian or Christian Grace.

The apostasy from quasi-Christianity to Humanism is not certain, and plenty of quotations could be taken out of context to make an argument against it. The truth probably was that Robinson, never having taken grace seriously with respect to himself, was not so much eschewing the notion of it now as concluding that the present—and hardly dissolute—comfortable life which at long last the Unseen Powers had allowed him was nothing reprehensible, was indeed worth living for its own sake. In *Tristram,* finished in '26, Isolt's state of grace was not of the full, impersonal glory of Guinevere's and Lancelot's, but it was complete self-loss and was still of Robinson's middle period. *Cavender's House* was transitional. Through the bulk of the dialogue, Cavender's subconscious, through the voice of his dead wife, is telling him he must open inner doors into self-understanding; yet when, in the final passage, peace at last comes to him, it is of the same calm, complete and irresistible fullness of the grace of Fernando Nash, or Lancelot, or the Contented Metaphysician.

It is not until *Matthias at the Door,* probably the only great work of this poetically declining period, that, as we have seen, the doctrine of self-knowledge is explicitly preached, along with the development of the whole personality rather than the loss of self. The outer self, under caution against the devils of excess and self-preoccupation, is accredited to pursue, *inter alia,* all the things which at that moment were making up Robinson's triumphantly contented existence, namely love, pride, art, humility, ambition, power and glory, and truth. (In '30 Robinson was already suffering gastronomic discomfort, and whiskey was off the list of things that were "worthwhile.") All these important matters Robinson was apparently ready at sixty to take out of the hands of the Unseen Powers and turn over to the control of his own self-understanding outer self. In the next significant poem, *Amaranth*, the touchstone of success or failure in life is still Pagan, namely the Eye of the Truth of the personality you were fated to be. The good life consists in the ability to look into that eye without dissolving into dust; and a tolerable substitute life may be found by developing a sophisticated routine which is able to avoid looking into the eye.

In his posthumous poem, *King Jasper*, Robinson characteristically leaves us guessing as to his final preachment. Zoë, here his preacher, is explicitly Knowledge, but she is a great deal more than scientific knowledge, and a great deal more than self-knowledge, although she is that incidentally. She is the kind of knowledge that is congenital in all human beings, that must always be "alone" in each one of them, and that, if ever allowed to function through all of them together, would produce a happy society. One remembers Robinson's onetime remark that Christianity might have worked "if it had ever been tried." Also, as a matter of language, mankind is now "blind" to Zoë, but sometime will have "eyes." She tells the villain, the most distorted figure in the cast, to

> let your poor, sick, stricken soul
> Suffer until it feels; and let it feel
> Until it sees. You will have died meanwhile,
> But who knows death?

That is precisely Robinson's Paul's description of the receipt of grace. It looks as though he at last were trying to reconcile the functions of the outer and inner self, of paganism and Christianity. Or perhaps acknowledging both of them in the greatest of all his contrapositives.

Zoë's dismissal of death in *King Jasper* calls attention to the remaining main column of Puritanism, namely the hope of *Immortality*, with its subdivisions of Salvation for those in Grace, and Damnation for those still in Reprobation. Robinson gave plenty of evidence of belief in some kind, albeit an unorthodox kind, of postmortal existence. One of his earliest statements on the subject is in a letter to Smith in the winter of '94 (italics added):

> . . . I . . . try to make myself believe that I am as great as anybody, or rather that I shall be when the *final examination* comes. I cannot believe that these tremendous worldly differences are to be carried on through *the second life*. I cannot conceive of eternity as an endless panorama of 'busted ambitions.' That would be hell with a vengeance. *I cannot believe that we poor devils deserve any such punishment.* Life itself is no joke to a great percentage of us, and *all things seem to point to an improvement of our condition when they are explained.* . . . *I believe in immortality—I can't help it.*[42]

Except in the sheer affirmation of the last statement, none of this conforms with the pure Puritan tradition. Even in '94 Robinson did not believe in a "final examination," a last judgment, and a permanent disposition of the "saved" and of the "damned." What he meant was the ultimate resolution of things, the end of the story, and at that vague juncture he didn't believe that a single "poor devil" was predestined for hell. Although there was no known influence on him from the late heresy of Universalism, he was instinctively a Universalist. Also, with respect to the "second life," whatever it might be it would be in some now incomprehensible or spiritual form; he never had any orthodox suspicion that

> We cherish, in the life that is to come,
> The scattered features of dead friends again.

That negation, in the *Two Sonnets,* was written early. Two years before he died, he wrote Mrs. Richards: "My notion of immortality, and I have some sort of notion, doesn't include the memory of this rather trivial—and for most people much worse than that—phase of existence." [43] Robinson's belief in immortality was simply the chief expression of his general optimism. The present phase of the Scheme of existence seemed too brutally ridiculous to be real, let alone final.

The immortality Robinson asserted may often be confused with other and more immediate expressions of his optimism.

Sometimes it is indistinguishable from the State of Grace, as in *The Dark House* where dying to the world and physical death are both metaphorically and literally one process; or again in both *Luke Havergal* and *Lancelot* where it is pointless to try to distinguish the spiritual "dark" from physical death, and present spiritual "Light" from the quality of postmortal existence.

In the large, Robinson's immortalism looks less like the Puritan's individualistic variety of it than like their *Millennialism*, the hope that originally had looked for the descent of the New Jerusalem upon this "New" England, and almost within Robinson's memory had had Millerites out on the hills at dawn in their ascension robes. Believing that things generally were bound to improve, he did not greatly concern himself with whether the improvement would come within this or some other phase of time. He was satisfied to have Bedivere foresee "another Camelot and another king," and in his own last year to prophesy to Mrs. Richards merely that "something better will come."

However, as far as individuals were concerned, there was no doubt of Robinson's belief in every single person's survival in some new, spiritual condition. In *Supremacy* "the dead men" are indeed dead to "life's little star" and are in some different "tract." At the time in his mid-twenties when each individual in his family was in some way beset, he wrote Gledhill, "I am certain . . . that this life is but one little scene in the big show." [44] In '96, three months before his mother died, he wrote Smith in a fashion that might look to grace in this life but sounds more like a prophecy of a future resolution: "All I can see to life, as an occupation, is a kind of spiritual exercise . . . by which we may, if we will, put ourselves beyond it." [45] When his mother did die, in agony after an agonizing last five years of life, there is no slightest doubt of his belief: "She has gone ahead and I am glad for her. You see I have come to look on death as a deliverance and an advancement (*vide* 'Kosmos,' 'Two Sonnets,' etc.) . . ." [46] In 1920, Paul in *The Three Taverns* tells his friends that "life will not hold all." In 1925, Robinson wrote Mrs. Richards: "If there should happen to be any next world, or any that we remember (which I am inclined to believe and hope) we shall go on somehow or other. I get no comfort out of turning into grass, and can't believe that the great Whatever-it-is would have gone to so much trouble as to make you and me (not to mention a few others) for the sake of a little ultimate hay." [47]

IV Art

For Robinson there were no essential changes in the Clairvoyant Mood according to the different areas of experience it addressed. There were merely differences in the things it reflected. In his idealism it was itself, loving, being, perceiving. In his individualism it saw and loved itself in all other people. In his religion— or what was to Robinson the same thing, mysticism—it saw and loved itself in all Being, and discovered the method of perpetuating that and all love, namely the loss of the outer self. In Art it supplied to the orderly or rational aspect of the outer mind specific perceptions of both inner and outer reality. There was, in Barnard's phrase, no essential difference between "the grace of Apollo" and "that of the Christian God." To Robinson, the predestination, or the Unseen Powers, that bestowed one likewise bestowed the other. "An artist," he wrote to Mrs. Josephine Peabody Marks in 1919, "is just a sort of living whistle through which Something blows." [1] More solemnly, he had his Rembrandt say at about the same time:

> I am but a living instrument
> Played on by powers that are invisible.

And four years later, in *The Man Who Died Twice*, his description of Fernando Nash's compulsive achievement of his symphony is also a description of the compulsive loss of self that releases the light of grace. Fernando's creative perception begins with

> a new clearness which had late begun
> To pierce forbidden chambers long obscured
> Within him . . .
>
> .   .   .   .
>
> Like shining grain,
> Long fouled and hidden by chaff and years of dust
> In a dark place, and after many seasons

Winnowed and cleaned, with sunlight falling on it,
His wits were clear again.

There came over him

A calm that all his life had been a stranger
To the confusions that were born with him . . .

and

a cool relief as if warm wings
Were in the air above him. . . .

. . . .

and a vast joy,
Which broke and swept and covered him like a sea
Of innocence.

He felt

a gratefulness
Of infinite freedom and humility.

. . . .

Hereafter it would be enough to serve,
And let the chosen shine.

Then the creative movement begins, as

another silence, like a blow
That somehow stunned him to clairvoyant awe,
Held him as if mysterious hands had bound him
With chords he could not see. Now he could hear
Those drums again, and they were coming nearer
. . . .

And so the great symphony comes down, precisely like a mystical experience.

Robinson's expressed theories about the creative arts rarely had anything but poetry in mind. He was blind to both painting and sculpture—his *Rembrandt* is a drama of fate and grace, not of art. Music was his second love after literature. Having been himself a performer on the clarinet and the saxophone, he was technically well informed and had a unique talent for reproducing the different instruments in his verse. His friend the composer Mabel Daniels says that he specially relished flutes and bassoons, but in the whole symphony reproduced in *The Man Who Died Twice* the brass and strings clearly carry their dominant place. Robinson's humility prevented him from expressing, perhaps from even entertaining, theories about music. He confessed that his love of it was impure, wholly emotional—"I care nothing for it unless it suggests something more than mental gymnastics on the part of the composer." What moved him most was the human drama implicit in anything from "Auld Lang Syne" played by a good brass band to the "Liebestod." Fernando Nash's final commitment to the bass drum may have derived from an incident Miss Daniels recounts of Robinson's standing on a New York corner listening rapt to a Salvation Army band in which the bass drummer shouted "Halleluiah!" on the off beats. He was addicted to Scottish songs and ballads, and at the MacDowell Colony sometimes invited Margaret Widdemer and others to sing them in the evening. On these occasions, or when a composer was trying out a new composition, Robinson would sit in a rocking chair absolutely silent, entirely lost in the music. He was curiously deaf to Bach, while devoted to Brahms, Verdi, and Wagner, with a corner left for Gilbert and Sullivan. An exception to his reticence in expressing musical preferences was in his always articulate dislike both of jazz and of dissonance. He prophesied that the composers of the latter were writing themselves into oblivion.

There was perhaps no field in which Robinson's duality of mind, his contrapositivist necessity to state both sides of every situation, exercised itself with more solemn conviction than in his ideas about poetry. Motivated by his love of all people, his original mission, stated in 1890—actually founding the modern tendency that jelled in 1912 after he had published four books—was to "completely knock the bottom out of the old verse-makers" with "a little reality," [2] to rescue verse from the saccharine "poetic subjects" and "poetic language" of decadent Victorianism and restore it to earthy experience and the language of common speech. Yet in art as in politics he was increasingly contemptuous of the mob who provided him with that speech. In 1908 he wrote

Mason from the Custom House: ". . . there is only a visual resemblance between verse and the other thing. For quantity (I mean size) I do not myself care a damn; but a fellow has to be dead before the public understands that a dozen titles are quite enough to string wires on that will reach through ten times as many centuries. . . ." [3] And in 1920, to MacKaye: ". . . as for the democratization of art, there ain't no such animal. Art may die, having served its purpose, but it will never be popular. . . . We poor devils of poets must face the probability that there will never be more than one person in a thousand who will know or really care anything about poetry. The few people who make the world fit to live in are comparatively negligible. . . ." [4] Apparently inconsistent also with his doctrine of common speech was his insistence on using the conventional forms of verse, his lack of sympathy with the free verse movement which, led by Amy Lowell, made a stir after 1912 on the theory that it was getting back to nature from those same Victorian affectations against which Robinson had actually led the revolt.

He did not like to be called an artist for art's sake, yet he said and did a great many things that qualified him for that esoteric company of his early period. He was suspicious of "frenzy of inspiration," thinking that it had produced "the worst poetry in the world"—but he must of course add that it had also produced "the best." [5] He spoke for his usual practice when he said, ". . . work with me means studying the ceiling and my navel for four hours and then writing down perhaps four lines—sometimes as many as seven and again none at all"; [6] but at various times he cited exceptions in poems that came rapidly and all of a piece—notably *Flammonde*. Very early, when his ideas were forming, he wrote Smith: ". . . have I the genius for selection that is the one requisite for a literary man next to an easy flow of language? . . . . I do not wholly believe in art for art's sake, but I do not believe that anything is good literature where art is wholly sacrificed to the subject matter." [7]

From this callow beginning, his insistence on art over matter grew stronger. Before anyone else had done so he was complaining of his friends' uses and the affected archaisms of Victorian "poetic language"—"lifteth" by Moody, and *o'* for *of* by Josephine

Preston Peabody. In 1900, writing from New York to Miss Peabody on her use of the word " 'sharpens' because it expresses just what you mean," he declared "what I believe to be an important fact in poetry: viz., that the word that seems to express the required meaning most clearly and concretely is very often the last word that metrical language—particularly song language—will tolerate." [8] (I remember his agonizing for years over whether "fire" was one syllable or two—"fi-yer.") About the same time Miss Peabody wrote in her diary: "E. A. Robinson exhorting me to drop 'philosophing' and twittering about infinites to write about things objective." [9] In 1914 he was still scolding her—now become Mrs. Marks—for emphasizing content over music: "The world doesn't want bread from poets, unless it is so completely disguised that they mistake it for cake; and while great poetry has nearly always an ethical value, history would seem to indicate that Apollo doesn't care a d-damn for the Uplift. . . . I don't want you to consume yourself in trying to reform the world. I don't mean to be discouraging, but you can't do it." [10] In 1932, three years before his death, he said conclusively to Nancy Evans, "Poetry must be music." [11]

Perhaps Robinson's famous obscurity could be related to this professed greater concern for sound than for meaning, or, better, for the evocation of particular words, both tropeically and phonetically, rather than for their literal significances. Certainly his crabbed condensation was one of the causes of his obscurity—he made a cliché of his own maxim, "Anything is improved by cutting." Professor Barnard in his chapter on "Barriers" makes a thorough examination of Robinson's obscurity, sometimes by overcondensation, sometimes by the opposite, garrulous circumlocution. But when he gets through he has hardly dispelled the obvious fact that here is a real fault in Robinson, a serious blemish on much of his work including some of his greatest. In his early period he was distressed by it—"Why don't they *read* me?" [12]—"One word after another!" But he was always motivated by an even greater concern for never being obvious and unimaginative. As he got older he became to a degree reconciled to his obscurity, and even made a kind of malicious fetish of it, aimed at the critics, all stupid in his opinion and comprising as a class his one enduring hatred—"If a boy or girl hasn't brains enough to do anything else, he or she is put to reviewing books." [13] In the mid twenties, reassured by his first two Pulitzer prizes, he would read a condescending complaint of his obscurity; his eyes would glitter and he would say: "Let them puzzle over that. I think it will take them about seven years to get that"—I don't know why "seven." Once he said to me with apparent seriousness, "The chances of anything being immortal depend on the length of time it takes to be understood." Granted the twinkle in this, there was candor in it too. The reference was perhaps to the fact that great poetry always has something new to give to the imagination with each rereading.

But in spite of Robinson's celebrations of craftsmanship, and in spite of his obscurity, Barnard insists on what was surely the fact, namely that his real concern was with content rather than form, "what the poet has to say rather than how he says it," language "always a medium, never an end in itself." [14] With partial inconsistency with what he had written her a little earlier, Robinson wrote Miss Peabody in 1901, "If a thing says what I meant it to say, and at the same time has rhythm and music in it, why shouldn't I use it even though I know that now and then a too conscientious critic will find fault with it?" [15] And in a famous letter to Amy Lowell he advised her, "I feel pretty confident that if you had to sacrifice one or the other you would retain that part of your poetry that had in it the good and bad solid old-fashioned human qualities. . . ." [16] We have only to remember Robinson's explanations of the Merlin-Lancelot epic as designed to show that "nothing can rest on a rotten foundation," and of his having "done his great love" and "said what I have to say" in Lancelot, to realize that he was primarily conscious of content there; and presently we shall see that he was equally so in Tristram. In fact I can't think of a poem of Robinson's, even the "jingles," that could not be denatured into a prose statement of what was probably the originating perception.

Good evidence of Robinson's primary concern with content was the fickle progress of his own judgment as to the best of his own poems. In mid-January of 1902, when he was putting the Captain Craig volume in final shape, he wrote Mrs. Richards how some time before he had "thought Shiras and The Klondike were rather the best things in the book—all of which goes to show that a fellow is not a very good judge of his own performances." [17] A month later he wrote her: "Personally I should call the woman and the wife affair the best I have ever done or am likely to do, but the next year I may throw it away." [18] It was reported to Harry Bacon Collamore that about 1910 Robinson told someone that he thought *The Tavern* was his best poem. In 1916 he wrote Lewis Isaacs that he thought *Merlin* was "the least bad thing I have done, with perhaps the exception of Ben Johnson." [19] And in '17 he wrote him that *Lancelot* seemed to him "rather the best thing that I have done." [20] In the early twenties he told Esther Bates that *Rembrandt to Rembrandt* had that honor. And some time in the late twenties he said to me, "I suppose *Mr. Flood* is the best thing I ever did." Of these nine successive favorites, *Shiras* was omitted from the very *Captain Craig* volume in which it was first preferred. *The Klondike*, while it does have a subject, man's romantic faith, is primarily a musical exercise and would fit the theory of form above content. *The Tavern* and the double sonnet *The Woman and the Wife* rate high among his dramatic sonnets, but neither has the sweep of greatness. Of the remaining five, *Ben Jonson Entertains a Man from Stratford* is a portrait of one of the world's great poets, *Merlin* is a study in humanism, *Lancelot* is an epic of progress towards Grace, *Rembrandt* is a monologue on predestination and Grace, and *Mr. Flood's Party* is a summary statement upon this mortal venture. These five are all among Robinson's great poems; but, aesthetically speaking, they are inferior to many others in saturation both of music and of pure poetry; and, with the exception of *Mr. Flood*, none is outstanding in tight dramatic construction. At least after 1915, the poet's successive preferences are for the contents, the subjects, coupled with his belief in each case that he had inscribed it poetically, that he had brought the poem off, that the motivating "message" was worth delivering and that he had delivered it.

I don't know of Robinson's ever having used in criticism the dangerous word "great"; but his late preferences for *Lancelot*, *Rembrandt*, and *Mr. Flood* tend to show a penchant for those illuminating a large, or "great," field of imaginative perception, even though, as was true at least in *Lancelot*, the saturation of poetry is relatively low. In criticizing prose, he showed a liking for greatness in this sense. In 1890 he wrote Harry Smith of *The Newcomes*, "Big thing, but a little tedious at times, like everything else that amounts to much—that is speaking of fiction and other extended works." [21] He might have said the same of most of his own long poems. During my acquaintance with him, I got the notion that he admired *Bleak House* above all other pieces of literature, in either prose or verse. He once said, "If I were put on trial of my life to reproduce *Hamlet* or *Bleak House*, I'd tackle *Hamlet*." (He'd better, his prose being what it was!)

Not only was Robinson essentially concerned with content, to an extent that caused him to be ostracized by the New Critics after 1940, he was concerned to the extent of pursuing a moral standard in his work. It was a very different moral standard from the Victorian one of sweet propriety that he was brought up to, for it was based on observation of life. It is true that necessity, predestination, was the reason he usually gave for having taken up the profession of poetry, but once he was "in for it," his conscious motive, first stated, I think, in '97 and repeated variously in his life thereafter, was a moral one: "I . . . make free to say that many of my verses [were] written with a conscious hope that they might make some despairing devil a little stronger and a little better satisfied with things." [22] Within this general motive, most of his poems were written to imply broad ethical observations, merely by portraying characters as they were, usually with dramatic development, but with no express judgment on them. In spite of all of his aesthetically orthodox condemnation of propaganda, Robinson in relaxation knew and admitted that he was an "incorrigible preacher."

Robinson's theory of poetry, like his "philosophy," like all his perceptions, was itself poetic. Which is to say that it was mysterious, and could not, in his opinion, be literally stated. As Barnard points out, he told Joyce Kilmer "that poetry has two attributes: it is 'undefinable' and it is 'eventually unmistakable.'" Here was another and very important case of his reluctance even to try to state a truth straight out. To say it in forthright, analytical prose would be to tarnish its glory. If we might rush in to use a straightforward prose term where Robinson feared to tread, we might suggest that all he meant was that poetry, and probably all truth, was a matter of imagination, "imagination" being a word that, as a synonym for spirit, is itself undefinable. Poetry was subconscious, intuitive, could not be grasped by conscious or natural reason. It was also emotional, with the generic, quiet emotion of mystical perception. In expression it could not be embodied in words literally used, this embodiment being prose. It could speak to the imagination of the reader only through tropeic uses, naming originally perceived qualities, and through musical uses which reinforced the tropes or enhanced the generic emotion of imaginative perception. Thus poetry, in Robinson's entirely unoriginal view, was musical expression of imaginative content. Whenever he came on a Miss Peabody who was leaning too far toward literal, prosaic statement, however precise, or toward tropeic but unmusical usage, he would go off on the phonetic side and declare that poetry was first of all music. But fundamentally, confronted by the contemporary sentimentalities of Riley, Field, and Bangs, he early insisted that the business of poetry was truth, and it was that insistence, that fated insistence, that compelled his life and drove him to renounce the Victorian world. It was the imaginative or literally undefinable essence of poetry, the "nimbus of what can't be said," [23] that made Robinson dubious of "conscientious" criticism. It also grounded his conviction that a poet should stand on what he had written and not try to be "his own interpreter." When, in the early nineties, Smith asked him of a new poem, "Win, what does it mean?" Win replied, "That's a hell of a question to ask a poet." [24]

If Robinson had deigned to analyze a little more prosaically his perception of what was and what was not poetry and truth, he surely would have insisted first of all on the matter of literalness, of deliberate concoction, as the quality that made both the perception of reality and the expression of it impossible. What made him pessimistic about America was not crime or corruption but banality, lack of imagination. In '21 he wrote Witter Bynner: "I am pretty well satisfied that free verse, prohibition, and moving pictures are a triumvirate from hell, armed with the devil's instructions to abolish civilization—which, by the way, has not existed, and cannot exist until the human brain undergoes many changes." [25] Which is to say that he saw free verse as a conscious attempt to make poetry according to a preconceived notion, prohibition as a comparably deliberate effort to make virtue according to a blueprint, the movies as an attempt to make art with stereotyped emotions. Similarly, his complaint of the new music was that it was consciously experimental, trying to do something literal with tones, such as lawyers, scientists, and scholars did with words, taking out of it the imaginative evocation which was reality.

Perhaps the key word with Robinson would have been "conscious," or "self-conscious." Perhaps he comes nearest to revealing his central notion of poetry in the letter to Amy Lowell in 1916, some of which has already been quoted:

. . . what seems to me the very best of your *vers libre* is almost exclusively "human" in its subject matter, and therefore substantially old-fashioned. One reason why I haven't more to say on the subject is that I have absolutely no theories. I don't care a pinfeather what form a poem is written in so long as it makes me sit up. "Imagiste" work, *per se*, taken as a theory apart from one special form, seems to me rather too *self-conscious* and exclusive to stand the test of time [italics added].[26]

There is his condemnation of Art for Art's Sake, and it would have been his condemnation of the New Criticism that ultimately condemned him. Both were self-conscious, arty, trying, like prose, to do something literal, according to a preconceived plan, fencing out the imagination. He brought against free verse the same charge that Miss Lowell brought against conventional verse, that it was contrived, artificial poetry. The language of the imagination must come out of the subconscious, no matter how much artistic scrubbing it gets afterwards. Using a vocabulary not Robinson's, it might be said that he found the contents of that subconscious to be of two sorts. Basically, there was the clairvoyant mood, and blended into it there was everything that talent and originally conscious training and experience had poured down into the subconscious memory, to lie there until ignited by the emotion of imaginative perception. As Fussell says, Robinson was a traditionalist in believing that in order to be original you must first imitate. For himself, what came up spontaneously out of the subconscious by way of prosodic impulse were native verbal talent and the traditional patterns taught him early by Dr. Schuman and Caroline Swan. For him the rhythms of prose, including the heavy prose rhythms that were free verse, would be matters of contrivance—as any of his prose shows clearly enough! Flatly Robinson accuses Miss Lowell of trying to concoct poetry out of a theory, which is impossible. And with deadly delicacy he suggests the possibility that if she and her followers were to look down into the subconscious, the reservoir of reality for poetry, they might find nothing.

The message, the sermon, of all of Robinson's poetry, as of his theory of poetry, as of all of his "philosophy," was that people ought to try to live the life of the imagination or spirit—in which we can see, though he did not, that he himself succeeded so well. It was with characteristic hope that man might reach such a state, in contrast to the immediate spectacle of society, that he wrote Bynner that civilization cannot exist "until the human brain undergoes many changes." [27] It was a typical Robinson statement, seeing the world as at once depraved, tragic, humorous, and promising. As in the other incomprehensible horrors of existence, he was sure that the current banality was in some way a preparation on the part of the Scheme for a future in which all people will live in the clairvoyant mood and its imaginative perceptions, understanding and loving each other, and understanding each other's expressions, which will all be poetry.

Part IV

WHAT TIME TAKES AWAY

Love builds of what Time takes away,
Till death itself is less than change.

—Hillcrest

WHEN I came up to E.A.'s room in New York that spring day of '26 and found him in a rage at being called a "dry New England psychologist," I was catching him at the beginning of a four or five years' apostasy which carried as incidental corollary a near lapse in our friendship. I was seeing him, at fifty-six, under his first real exposure to the third great Satanic temptation. In his youth and young manhood he had been tempted when hungry to turn stones into bread, or "ducats," by the miracle of taking a respectable job, and he had retorted to his subconscious that man does not live by bread but by poetry. Through the nineties he had been teased by the notion of casting himself down in suicide from a banal world, but he finally settled in the humble conviction that it was not for him to tamper with Fate or the Unseen Powers. Now, after two Pulitzers and a body of work some of which satisfied him, he was on a high mountain overlooking the glories of the world, and he had already succumbed a little to the vanity involved in them. He was proposing to show sophisticated mankind that he too was part of it, that he, as much as the next poet, had had his Guinevere and so knew what it was like to have an Isolt. Already he had written some or all of a draft of *Tristram*, fundamentally because he had long planned to translate his favorite opera into verse, and secondarily because he wanted to do honor to the great love of Herman and Emma. But also, in addition to these honest motives, he was aware that here at last was a theme, at once conformable to the sexy fashion of the times and obvious enough for little minds, that would probably make them "sit up" and notice him.

In September he delivered the poem to Macmillan for publication, and even before the fanfare started he was showing an interest in fame. In February he wrote Burnham: *"Captain Craig* (with paper label) sold at auction yesterday for $500. Sorry I didn't save a few." [1] The Literary Guild took *Tristram*, with 12,000 copies as a starter. They engineered a reading of it by Mrs. August Belmont, former actress, in the Little Theater, E.A. refusing to appear on the stage before the standing-room audience, but consenting to suffer in the receiving line afterwards in the lounge. The reviewers who had been unable to understand

347

his great work went into appropriate ecstasies, and his third Pulitzer prize descended. Fifty-eight thousand copies sold the first year, and it continued to sell in five, and finally four, figures a year right into the thirties and through the depression. All of E.A.'s books soared. A year or two later he once broke a profound silence by saying to me, "I understand that a copy of *The Torrent and the Night Before* sold at the Anderson Galleries yesterday for two hundred and eighty-seven dollars." [2] Pause. "I haven't got one." In his article in the *Colophon* in '30,[3] he told the world that the entire original edition of *The Torrent* had cost the author $52.

Robinson, of course, indulged in none of the common cheapness that goes with commercial glory. He refused to air his opinions on matters of which he knew nothing. Being a poor reader, he declined all invitations to perform, and he ducked Park Avenue invitations where his refusal would not hurt anyone personally. As fast as he could he paid off the ancient obligations of patronage. Superficially he was as self-effacing as ever, and women continued to describe him with the same dear old sentimentality: the "stunned, white helplessness," the "doelike questioning in his big brown eyes," the "manner of a child," [4] et cetera.

Yet, behind the white, doelike helplessness, the devil had accomplished a change. With hardly a tremor of redeeming humor, E.A. was proud, not of having money to spend, but of being a man of substance, a financier, a capitalist, somebody whom Gardiner, Maine, would recognize. At long last he had returned to the status where he was born, where he had been accustomed to hear his father and Herman talk in large terms about the market. He turned over the actual management of his affairs to Lewis Isaacs, but he liked to talk about them in a casual way, the sophisticated way of being casual about great matters. I remember my appalled incredulity one afternoon in his room when I realized that one of the world's prophets was asking my opinion on B. & O. stock, pressing his forehead with a finger as if he were thinking of something real. I gave him my learned view, that all railroads were bad buys, and a few years later he wrote to Burnham what may have been the result of my advice: "If I had bought 1,000 shares of B. & O. two months ago when it struck bottom, I could sell it now and make $6,000." [5] Again to Burnham:

"I'm hating myself for not getting some U.P. when it was down last year." [6] Esther Bates told me that at some time in the late twenties or early thirties, when he was sending help to Emma and her children, he said to Esther a little "gloatingly," "I take care of my family just as you take care of yours."

All of this by itself was no more than amusing and endearing. But in the same period there was a more serious change in attitude. It may not have occurred with his older intimates, his contemporaries, but I have confirmed it with two in the second rank of seniority. With me he grew just a touch formal, socially correct. He made conversation on trivial matters, showed less humor; his chuckle became artificial. At the same time he spoke cautiously, choosing his words with care, and he would qualify comments with, "You mustn't repeat that," or "I wouldn't want to be quoted on that." I don't think that at that time he had any particular complaint of me, but it was true that he had been improperly quoted by others. Robinson Jeffers had excerpted without permission a complimentary sentence from a perfunctory letter and used it as a blurb. E.A. trembled with fury when he told me of it.

Such violations of confidence would have hurt him any time, but not so excessively, and previously he would not have been so continuously on the watch for them. He knew I admired *Merlin,* and in June, 1930, he gave me a first edition of it. I pushed it across the table for him to inscribe, and when he pushed it back he said, "You can sell that for fifteen dollars if you want to." He was immediately flustered by the unintended affront. It was simply on his mind that everybody wanted to get something out of him.

Loud among the explosions of hauteur was an incident reported by both Hagedorn and Esther Bates. About a year after *Tristram* appeared and while its success was still booming, an attractive, middle-aged female poet at the MacDowell Colony wrote a sonnet series of which the finale was a love poem to E.A. addressed as "Tristram himself." E.A. in his fifty-ninth year, tongue-tied and lanky, to be held up against the fluent and lithe charm of young Tristram! Having received the innocent obeisance, he rose into one of his rages when sensitiveness left his face and it was bloated and unattractive. He wrote the poor woman a scathing letter and required her to destroy every copy of her generously intended effort.

In those years I assisted at another comparable performance at the Colony, this one more ridiculous and happily free of pathos. One of the painters did from memory a small full-length portrait of E.A. standing in the road that is the central artery of the Colony, clad as usual in a gray business suit, the white golf hat, and holding his stick. In all innocence the artist displayed it to the assembled geniuses one evening in Colony Hall. I saw nothing wrong with it except that it wasn't very good, but E.A. hurriedly left the company. Suspecting the occasion of this exit, I went up to his room later and found a weightier crisis than I had expected. He gave me $25 and commanded me to buy the picture. In course of due time and diplomacy I accomplished my mission, and one evening I managed to smuggle it up to his room. Holding it, he considered his bureau for a long time. At last he crystallized the idea that had been stirring, drew out the bottom drawer, and the picture proved to be about twice too large for it. Then he put it in his closet and sat down. I did not offer to destroy it for him, because I didn't want to insult the painter, even furtively, and I had no sympathy with this nonsense of E.A.'s which left me a hypocrite toward everybody. I don't know whether or not he got it down to his studio and immolated it in his fireplace. I wish it would turn up.

The basic point in all this was, I think, that at last the Unseen Powers had given E.A. a social role that was easier to enact than the graceful one he despaired of mastering, and in a slightly different way was as satisfying. Now he was a Great Man, and all that required of him was to be weighty and responsible, to bear in mind that everything he said would have an effect on others or on the world. It was a little phase of self-centeredness, quite out of keeping with the true E.A., and marking above all an incredible lapse in his sense of humor. Latterly, I have wondered whether the tension of it may not have been contributed by the fact that at some time during those years '28, '29, and '30, Emma was turning down his final offer of marriage, an offer which at last he was able to make from a platform of financial stability. It is possible that this ultimate humiliation sought to compensate itself at once in a pomposity appropriate to his new dignity and in an exacerbation of his old touchiness about his supposedly awkward and ineligible person.

But withal, this phase of top-loftiness was no more than a transient growth of thin "reptilian" skin. Almost from the start he held *Tristram* and its success in suspicion. It was in the midst of the first uproar, in May of '27, that he wrote Emma the letter already cited about the "unwholesome publicity" [7] he was getting. In July of '28, at about the time that he received his first *Tristram* statement for $15,000, he wrote Mrs. Ledoux: "Perhaps it isn't necessary that any more books by me should be written, but apparently I am so constructed that some bad habit or other is necessary for my existence, and books may be as harmless as any other." [8] One afternoon in late 1930, we were sitting in one of those long silences. With the genuine old-time gravity, half-humorous, he said, "I just heard that *Tristram* has passed a hundred thousand." Long pause, and a little rocking. "I'm not sure I like it." Some time not long after that, in response to something I had said he replied, "I wrote *Tristram* with my eye to the public." For E.A. there could be no more terrible confession. About this time he wrote Mrs. Richards of his plan to give a laboratory to the Gardiner Hospital, and his old humility concludes the letter:

I thought it well and right to make some sort of memorial in the Gardiner Hospital to my brother, Dean, who drew unlucky cards for the game of living. I can't see wherein he could have been different, and I am glad to build a small monument to what he really was. His infirmities had nothing to do with his self, or with his real mind and character. He knew more when he was twenty years old than I shall ever know. [9]

By '30 or '31 E.A. had emerged from his four or five years' passage of pomposity. From that time, in his attitude toward the world and in his conduct toward his friends generally, he was his old objective and humorous inner self, now adorned with the new outer self-assurance of his final mildly hedonistic phase that he announced through Timberlake in *Matthias at the Door*. At least two and probably three factors contributed to this relatively comfortable twilight of his life. For one thing, he had now done something which assured him henceforth of being somebody wherever he went, even Gardiner—no more nincompoop, no more "no good," awkward "long Robinson." Another thing was financial assurance; it was unlikely that he would ever again go hungry or need to borrow two dollars from a waiter. Both of these bases of self-assurance are apparent in a letter to Mrs. Richards in March of '31 in which he adds two items to Timberlake's catalogue of things that are "worth having":

> This reminds me that in my approaching age I am able to make a fairly good living out of poetry that only a few people can understand. There is something a little comic in this, and it doesn't mean anything particular except that I can have a lobster or a baked apple if I want it. The only really important thing is what people are saying about my books one hundred years from now. By that time they should be beginning to read them, and perhaps by that time I shan't mind so much if they pronounce "harassed" as if it rhymed with "aghast. . . ." [10]

A third factor contributory to his late relaxation was probably the fact that Emma, in turning him down latterly, had persuaded him at last that he had never wanted to marry her or anyone, as he proceeded to admit in *The March of the Cameron Men*. It was about this time that he said to Carty Ranck, "If I had married in those days I never would have written a line of poetry." Whichever "those days" may have been, the implication was the same. In spite of the probably epistolary overture and refusal in the late twenties, the better view is that E.A. did not see Emma again after he went up to be "doctored" at Bowdoin in '25. She moved in with Ruth Nivison, her eldest daughter, in Ruth's Gardiner house in '30, and on the first of that year E.A. had declined Ruth's invitation to come and live there too. In November he thanked Emma for some apples which "took me back into the past—where as a rule I don't go." [11] In '31 she sold the Farmingdale house, and in October E.A. wrote her that he was not interested in the house at Head Tide where he had been born and which Ruth was thinking of buying.[12] There is no doubt that in matters of companionship he had grown away from Emma and the girls, though he was forever writing Emma about buying the latter dinners and miscellanies in Boston and New York, and he contributed to the education and musical training of Ruth's boys.[13] Marie, the middle and more philosophical niece, once said to him, "Now you don't belong to us any more, Uncle Win. You belong to the world." To which E.A. replied in his traditional mode, "I don't think the world is much disturbed about it."

Through '30 and '31 he often spoke to me of the nieces— though I don't recall his ever having revealed that they had a mother! The four of them were certainly his dearest association emotionally, and it is not surprising that he left them what money he had instead of giving it to the MacDowell Colony as had been expected. They were the family his affection had fixed on without having to pay the price of matrimony.

After *Tristram*, the lyric power of E.A.'s poetry declined, with a vanishing echo in *Matthias*. He continued to write about the triangle; four of his seven last, long, title poems treated aspects of it directly, and a fifth volume contained *The March of the Cameron Men* and *Annandale Again*. He continued to turn out his blank verse stories annually because, being now in his sixties he had written steadily all his life, and it was an exercise as natural and necessary to him as any bodily function. Shortly before his death he said to me, "I can turn these things out once a year as long as they want me to." In May of '34, just before he went up to the Colony for the last time, he wrote Mason: "I expect to 'do' another book. Apparently the habit is incurable but there is never much left of me when the frost comes." [14] That book turned out to be *King Jasper*. It was the one that finished him.

Although E.A.'s little tour of self-conscious grandeur ended for me, as for his other friends, in '30 or '31, yet a little later something like the stiffness of it revived toward me. It was not until many years later that I learned that E.A.'s puzzling attitude toward me during those last years had to do with my second wife whom I married late in '29. Her beauty was of the Raphael Madonna sort which I think was Emma's in her youth. Also, she frequently displayed a kind of lightsome eagerness which may have touched E.A.'s memories. And for incidental virtue, she soon became a good, rich, Yankee cook.

It was through her that I learned the significance of the big box of presentation copies that E.A. kept by his door at Frasers'. When we were leaving after the first time I brought her to show her to him, he stood beside the box in what I recognized as the throes of hesitation under an impulse to act. Presently he gave his little leap of decision, leaned down, took up a book—any book— handed it to my wife, and said, "I'd like to give you a book." "Oh, thank you, Mr. Robinson," said she, "I'll be very careful of it and return it soon." Quickly he stuck up both hands in horrified deprecation. "No, no," he said, "don't bring it back." The book turned out to be Floyd Dell's *Love in Greenwich Village,* duly inscribed to E.A. No aspersion on Mr. Dell or the particular fine book.

In due course, my wife learned how to make a kind of Brown Betty that seemed to rate high by E.A.'s gustatory standards. She used to give it to him in a large bowl, and he would shovel it down gluttonously, looking up frequently to lick his lips, and so long as he had two or three big helpings of that he wanted little else for dinner. One night after one of these orgies we took him to the melodrama *Shanghai Gesture,* for he liked thrillers. We walked back from the theater along Forty-second Street, and at Fifth Avenue we would part, he to proceed eastward to the Frasers', almost at Tudor City, we to take a bus down to the Village. When we reached the corner we all stopped and stood silent. The light went green, but E.A. did not cross. It went red again, and he continued to stand looking upward, keeping on his small felt hat. It changed again, and he stood fixed through the second green light and on through the succeeding red one. When it went green the third time I said, "Come on, E.A.," led him across the street and started him toward home. Afterwards I wondered whether he wasn't trying, by way of thanking us for the evening, to think up something specially nice to say to my wife about the Brown Betty. Several times he told me that he "liked" her, which was maximal praise. In letters and in inscribing our books he used her nickname. So far as I know, that was a unique sign of acceptance.

In what must have been late '32 I began to recognize the resumption of E.A.'s former self-consciousness with me. I attributed it to the probability that he was bored with my treatise on poetry, just out, and was unable to tell me so. Or perhaps that he was disturbed that my publishers, having eased me into prose, had started me on another book in that questionable medium. For no matter what cause, I couldn't seem to make him easy. All the familiar mannerisms were there—the pouting lips, the chuckle, the forehead multiwrinkled in wild surmise. Yet they were all performed behind a film of artifice. Mildly troubled, I left New York to live permanently in the country without having broken whatever the ice was.

Years after E.A.'s death, in fact recently, a mutual friend told me that E.A. was distressed because he thought I was "treating my wife badly." For years I had discussed all intimate matters with him, and had continued to do so during the two years since my marriage. Now for the first time his combined chivalry and conventionality went into action in the premises. He had observed that some confidence I had given him was ungallant—as it undoubtedly was. Under the code of the '90's, whose shadow always hung over E.A., there wasn't much that a man couldn't *do* with impunity if he held his tongue about it. But talking was a different matter. One of the strongest taboos was upon discussing one's wife with even one's closest friends—especially if E.A. "liked" her! This was one of those cases where his humility prevented him from criticizing a friend's conduct of which he disapproved. The humility was a great virtue, but sometimes it was hard to distinguish it from timidity which was a fault. Here it almost ended a friendship on a false note that could have been talked out. And in at least one other case the consequences of the same timidity were grave beyond redemption.

Besides its motivation in timidity with his friends, the strange tragedy of Carty Ranck was related to another curious flaw in E.A.'s personal relations, a flaw also related to his "skin [being] put on inside out." Because of the danger of uncongenial tensions between some of his amazingly miscellaneous acquaintances, he seemed deliberately to keep them apart, or rather in small circles which were congenial within themselves. Wherefore, there existed in those latter days, as there survives somewhat to this day, these compartmented groups, each of which had good reason to suspect that it alone represented the inmost discipleship, and was alone accredited to protect him against the uncomprehending, insensitive and obviously predatory rest. For present purposes it is necessary to mention only two of these committees on the well-being of E.A.'s soul.

In my time the dominant New York group centered around two moderately wealthy and cultivated families, both highly respectable in the late Victorian sense which E.A. admired. Both were extraordinarily protective, which is to say possessive, of him. Lewis Isaacs had started life as a musician, developed into a lawyer, and from the beginning of the indispensable patronage in 1913 was E.A.'s financial backlog and eventually his executor. Also, he had a genius for keeping E.A. at ease in mixed company, even drawing him into talk, and through the winters he habitually took him to the opera and entertained him in his apartment with the recorded music of the world. Louis Ledoux had an early choice to make between being a professional tennis player and a professional poet, and he chose the latter. At one time E.A. thought he had great promise as a dramatist. He had a famously charming wife whom E.A. addressed in letters as "Jean"; she rated high in the triumvirate of his closest female friends, the others being Miss Brower and Mrs. Richards. The Ledoux' entertained E.A. for long visits in their big house up the Hudson, and Ledoux became the literary executor. Hermann Hagedorn was younger and only superficially a member of this group, which is to say he was in comfortable means and had Victorian prejudices and a habit of entertaining E.A. in his house in Westport. Otherwise he was qualified as the biographer of E.A.'s spectacular patron, Teddy Roosevelt, was sensitive to E.A.'s sensitivity, and as the official biographer attempted honestly to subserve his own predilections to the inner and different perceptions of his subject. More than any other coterie of Robinson's friends, the Isaacses and the Ledoux', though not Hagedorn, were intolerant of the rest. Perhaps the most remarkable instance of the barriers E.A. erected between his friends was that revealed by Ledoux, who stated that until after Robinson's death he never heard of the three nieces in Gardiner.

Another important group, emotionally the closest of any to

E.A. after the family, was the remnant of his acquaintance in the years of trial by hunger in the late nineties and first years of the twentieth century. There was an outer circle of these whom I did not know. In the inner circle was preeminently George Burnham, and close to him, though coming in at a later period, was Carty Ranck. The other members of this central group were the MacKayes, whom I knew slightly, and the Torrences, whom I knew well. In so far as I was attached to any group, it was to this one, and because of my relative ignorance of the other groups, together with my youthful arrogance, I enjoyed the delusion that my gang was of the highest status, wherefore I was the inside man after Burnham and Ridgely and Percy! After E.A. died I was amazed at the herds of devotees who everywhere sprang up out of the bushes. I pled for days with Ridgely to do the official biography, never doubting that if it didn't go to him if would come to me!

The tragedy of Carty Ranck rested, of course, fundamentally in his own dichotomies, between an outer boorishness and a curious, limited, inner perceptiveness that saw and loved, as he saw few other things, the reality of E.A.; between banal perceptions and humor and a distinguished prose style; between the dramatist who was a failure and the special-article writer who had done one of the first sound appreciations of Robinson. In his life work of Boswellizing him, it was said that by the mid-thirties he had accumulated notes two feet deep, on 8½- x 11-inch paper. He seemed to like me, and I liked him.

E.A.'s direct contribution to the tragedy was in his inability to hurt Carty by showing doubt of his talent, his failure to stop the Boswellizing at the outset, although he knew about it early, failing to pay any attention to it until Carty was gone in it beyond return. Until *Tristram* E.A. simply didn't take the notion of a biography seriously, and even after *Tristram* he was for some time averse to having one. In the late twenties I saw the seriousness of the situation. I realized that while Carty had almost twenty years of material which no one else could duplicate, he would not be able to make of it much more than a collection of facts. Meanwhile, his failure as a playwright was becoming complete. He was getting more nervous, tending to snort in breathing, frequently laughing aloud without occasion, and his always bulging, watery eyes were tending into blindness. I saw a light, and once when he and I were dining together at the Brunswick in Boston, I began talking about starting to Boswellize E.A. myself, having in mind to work towards some kind of collaboration. A few days after that I was in New Haven and had a note from Carty. He wrote me in his role of a Kentucky mountaineer, putting me on notice that he was going to shoot me on sight. Some time later in Peterborough I told E.A., and he rocked in slow, prolonged agitation. Finally, he said simply, "I've got to do something about Ranck." In September, '30, he wrote Burnham about him: "He has been in a very nervous condition during the past two or three weeks, and I can't help worrying about him. If he doesn't have something in the way of success before long, I'm wondering what will happen." [15] In '32 E.A. dedicated *Nicodemus* to Carty, and it must have been at about that time that, according to the family legend, he authorized him to do the biography under Burnham's supervision.

That would have been the solution if only the commission had been reduced to writing, for E.A.'s executors were bound to reject Ranck if they could legally. When E.A. died they could not overlook Burnham for bearer, but they neglected Ranck. Burnham got him in, and then they both made enough uproar to get me in. Carty was a friend. Soon after the funeral, he reported to Isaacs and Ledoux with his bales of paper. He was abruptly spurned, and the official biography was assigned to Hagedorn. During the rest of '35 and part of '36 Carty lived with Burnham at Head Tide and worked on his unauthorized project. He did not like the country, and presently was rooming in Leonia, New Jersey. Since that time I have had only sporadic news of him: his rheumy eyes went totally blind; he did a turn in an insane asylum; he destroyed his notes and tentative copy. I am certain of none of this. At this writing I have been unable to discover him or his one known relative. My most recent rumor, by way of a credible intermediary, is that he is dead. He was absolutely true to E.A. Some of E.A. disappears with him, absolutely.

Next to Ranck, or along with him, the object of E.A.'s greatest worry in the last years was Burnham. Early in the depression

a case of flu lost him his job of ticket agent in Newton. He could
have had it back, but when he reported, the hiring authority said
it would mean firing the poor fellow who had replaced him, who
had a family to support. So Burnham didn't go back, and for
some time had no means of support. In February, '31, E.A. wrote
him from New York, "I agree with Ranck in wishing you had an
overcoat, but we might as well ask you to buy a pair of riding
breeches." [16] He enclosed a little money. The following July he
was sending him a little more, and now it appeared that the
"Contented Metaphysician" was not entirely contented with himself. E.A. said: "There is something wrong in your philosophy
if it doesn't tell you that you have done all that a man should do,
and more than most men would try to do. Your last twenty years
or so make me feel as if I had been sitting on the fence and
watching the procession go by. . . ." [17] In August he begs Burnham not to go "back to the office," and tells him that he can always send him money. From the hospital in the winter of '35 he
wrote Marie, who was a trained nurse in Boston, to see that Burnham got proper medical treatment for the stumps of his legs that
were then bothering him. [18] After E.A. died, the family and executors put Burnham in charge of the collection of Robinsoniana
then being assembled under Mrs. Nivison's direction in "Robinson
House" in Head Tide. There he lived off and on for five and a
half years. I last saw Burnham at Presbyterian Hospital, New
York, where he reported for treatment of cigar smoker's cancer
of the mouth. In August, 1940, his nephews moved him in an
ambulance to Hartford, where he died shortly in a nursing home.
It was coincidence that Emma and Burnham, the two principal
relics of E.A., died within two months of each other.

In the depth of the depression in the early thirties, when E.A.
was getting concerned about Burnham and Ranck, he had begun
to feel the shadow looming over himself. He had always felt it
near in metaphysical terms, representing fate, and whenever in
the past he had thought his work was done, he had expected it
to fall. In 1905 he had written Harry Smith his doubt as to
whether he should "remain" in the world—"The best of me is on
paper." [19] And in '20, at the height of his great period, he wrote
Emma that he saw "no very good reason why I should stay

around much longer." [20] Now, after '30 and his restful commitment to the semihedonistic world of things "worth having," he felt the shadow rising in physical reality. For years, at least since '25, most of his letters to Burnham had contained complaints of intestinal discomfort and he was always asking the metaphysician to send him some nostrum he had just heard of—agar, or sal hepatica, or some kind of meal.[21] Some say that, in spite of his vast capacity for liquor, he always suffered from hangovers. Certainly by '31 they were getting worse, and Mrs. MacDowell asked me not to encourage him to drink any more. In '32 the doctors proscribed whiskey and put him on ale, in which he found no virtue except as providing a glass to hold in his hand. In June he wrote Mrs. Richards: "Perhaps I am lucky to be on the way out, so to speak. On the whole I have been pretty fortunate, but I shouldn't care to go through it again." [22] He must end affirmatively—"Apparently I have an invisible public of hardy perennials who are not afraid of long things in blank verse." About this time he came into the friendship and partial care of Merrill Moore, the Boston doctor-poet who wrote hundreds of sonnets while waiting at red lights on the way to his calls. On his or other official orders, E.A. went on the wagon for good. In June, '34, he wrote Burnham from the Colony, "Slow dying is a sort of obsession with me." [23] Talking to Esther Bates about *King Jasper*, then in process, he suddenly stopped, put his hand on his back and said the one word, "Pain." Late that summer, when Mrs. MacDowell was making her routine calls, they stood at the door of his studio and looked at distant Monadnock through the trees. E.A. said, "I rather think the old fellow will miss me when I am gone." [24]

Meanwhile, through '33 and '34, being seldom in either New York or the Colony, I saw E.A. rarely, and settled into the assumption that he was no longer my actual friend. I was merely one of the more or less promising youngsters whom he had encouraged and whom, therefore, he would not let down. I conceived that, if he ever thought of the matter, he must wonder whether he hadn't been wrong in the beginning in advising me to quit law for poetry—and, busy on my second prose book, I sometimes entertained the same doubt. On the three or four occasions when I saw him in this period, we didn't get for long beneath the level of making conversation, which was easy to do because of our large mutual acquaintance, mutual interests and mutual sense of humor.

Nevertheless, he did me favors when appropriate, and occasionally there were moments of the old, usually silent mutuality. When I asked him to write me for publication an acknowledgment of my dedication of my epic to him, he complied with a little statement which for him was hyperbolical. One day I came into his room in New York and found him sitting as usual beside his round table with his back to the door, and he failed to greet me. Something important. I sat down as usual in the second rocker between the guest bed and the second window. E.A. had a letter in his hand, one page. He seemed to be reading it over and over. I don't think he rocked any. Perhaps his rocking days were over. He laid the letter on the table, didn't look at me, and presently said, "I'm afraid Frost is a jealous man." There was pain on E.A.'s face which may have been physical, but also may not have been. He could not understand a poet being small. He could ignore it in others, but not in his peers. Perhaps that was why Jeffers' probably innocent little malfeasance had so enraged him in the touchy period which was now past. Now he was only hurt and confused. He did not tell me the contents of the letter. Frost, of course, was notoriously a sly one. E.A. didn't say anything for a very long time. I fetched him back by telling him they were trying to get me to do a historical novel. He pressed a finger to his forehead, then looked up and away and said in the tone of the recent two years of formality, "I don't see any reason why you shouldn't write a good novel." The door that had opened a crack had closed again. I returned to my conviction that he had surrendered any large expectations he might once have had for me.

Until now I had not suspected there was anything worse wrong with him than some kind of intestinal complaint that alcohol made worse, and I'd known plenty of people in that minor dilemma. I was probably too egocentric to notice till it was forced on me what others seem to have been observing for months. Without knowing when his birthday was I called up and invited him out to dinner, either on the very day, December 22, or within a few days after it, for by early January he wasn't at Frasers'. When I came in, he wasn't at all himself, kept hopping up and taking something from one spot and putting it in another. Possibly he was packing. He said he was off his feed, couldn't eat much for dinner, wouldn't be much of a companion. Once he paused in his activity, looked down at me and said with slow profundity, "I'm sixty-five years old." I wondered if he wanted to get rid of me, but he didn't take a lead in that direction. Presently he sat down, put a whole hand up to his forehead and said, "They're making me go into the hospital next week for an examination. Doesn't amount to a damn." He got up again, made another pointless adjustment in the room and came back to his chair slowly. He didn't look at me, but, still standing, he put both hands up on his back and said with slow emphasis, "There's something wrong." All my blood stopped.

I think he felt the shock his understatement gave me, and from that moment any doubts of my work or disapproval of my conduct were forgotten, superficial matters. We were back in the intimacy of '25 and '26, of '30 and '31; only now it was deeper because we both knew that in the silence we were in the presence of the final mystery of the Scheme. He went into his bedroom, came out, and paused as usual in front of his bureau. Ever since I had known him, and for much longer, he had a scraggly old hairbrush, wooden, probably varnished once, the bristles worn concave by having time out of mind been thrust in exactly the same arc over precisely the same curve of the same increasingly naked head. It was one of the worldly gestures he had learned to make, and like all such he made it with a special, delicate grace of his own. I watched him doing it now, and all of a sudden heard myself blurting out, "E.A., give me that brush." He turned, and his big brown eyes looked at me with an expression in which delicate surprise and amusement resolved into equally delicate understanding and affection. He considered the brush, and set it down on the bureau where it belonged. He went into the bedroom again, and came back with his latest picture, duly inscribed. He handed it to me with no comment, then looked around, embarrassed. He had a piece of white cloth in his hand, and presently he thrust it at me, saying, "You can have this if you want it." It was one of his nicely initialed handkerchiefs. That was the last time I saw E.A. in his room at Frasers'.

That winter of '34–'35 my wife and I spent with her family in Rye. Early in January I learned that E.A. had returned from his checkup. Then, in the middle of the month, I read in the paper that he was in New York Hospital. I wrote him and asked if I might come in, and in a few days he wrote back, first apologizing for his delay in answering me:

> . . . I have been a pretty sick dog and have been overhauled until I'm rather tired of it. The doctors think they will have me going again before long, but I shall wobble for some time. Of course I should be glad to see you, but don't come in from Rye. Just now I'm not worth the trip, but your friendly thoughts are very valuable.
>
> . . . For some reason writing, even a scrap like this, is a mighty task. Tell Nannette that I hope she will be well soon.

That was longer than most of his notes to me, and I could feel the effort in it; so I hurried in. Isaacs was in charge, and I don't think he told me the truth then—if he knew it himself. E.A. did not look unusually pale. Our talk was not self-conscious and I don't remember any of it. The dark prescience that had struck me a month before faded out. He had a fine room high up, with a handsome view down on Welfare Island and over Long Island and the Bronx into Westchester. When Ridgely Torrence had congratulated him on the view, he had said he didn't like to look out the window because it reminded him of the wretched, lonely old men down there on Welfare Island in their dingy, crowded quarters, while here he was, enjoying every comfort and attention. His reaction recalls the similar letter to Harry Smith in '92 from the hospital in Boston where he had just had his ear opened up, and he allowed that "I ought not to complain when I think of those in the house who are so much worse off than I am." [25] It was during one of those early visits of Ridgely's to the hospital that E.A. told him that what had saved his life in the old days was that he never took a drink before six o'clock.[26]

About this time Ruth Nivison, the senior niece, came down from Gardiner as emissary of her mother and Laura Richards, bringing twenty-five dollars from the latter for flowers or any other purpose. Having provided the flowers, Mrs. Nivison was embarrassed by the balance of the money, and E.A. performed one of his last acts of courtesy by telling her to accept it and give Mrs. Richards his thanks. As a highly experienced graduate nurse, Mrs. Nivison had brought down her uniform and wanted to serve. But her services were refused, and someone in authority, presumably Isaacs, sent her home to Gardiner.

It must have been in the middle of March that I read in the paper that E.A. had been operated on, and I went in again. That was the operation in which they found they couldn't remove the cancer without killing him straightaway, so they sewed it up in him. When I came up to his floor, I found many of his friends drifting around in hospital silence, tending to assemble in the floral solarium to await their turns. Isaacs told me the truth then, cautioned me not to give E.A. an inkling, and said everybody was limited to ten minutes. He went in with me, and spent my first two or three minutes confirming some changes E.A. wanted made in Esther Bates's typescript of *King Jasper*. He was already so weak that reading tired him, and Isaacs, Ledoux, and Ridgely were taking turns reading to him for his corrections. When Isaacs went out, he left the typescript on the bed. The nurse also left, as she did for every caller.

The great change was already at work, and the image of E.A. from then on remains unforgettable. He was propped up, and his face was the color of the big pillow behind it, as if there were nothing of him but the great eyes, unusually black, shining out of the whiteness. I didn't understand him as well then as I do now. I admired him for sticking to work when he must have known he was dying, but it did not occur to me that here at the end he was Merlin, going on building his Camelots, indifferent to his last mortal chance at selflessness and Grace, and Lancelot's orthodox Salvation. I did not realize then that here at last was the humility outliving everything but aesthetic integrity, the humility that did not think itself worth the self-assertion of riding on alone through the dark towards self-loss and human perfection. I did not consider then the saintliness purer than Lancelot's, purer than that of any man he had fictionized, the saintliness that as a matter of course put his calling above his private interest, wanting to tell others of the Light he had seen far off rather than to concern himself about coming to it as Lancelot had done. I did know of his belief in immortality, but I didn't know then that he thought of it only objectively, in terms of suffering mankind and their prospects, and would have considered it a mighty piece of disqualifying selfishness if, standing on the threshold, he had worried about the next step Fate had for him alone. I knew intimately six of the people who stood that long last watch with E.A., and they all said that he never once broached the subject of death or immortality or any related consideration. I think that I already understood his predestinationism, his certainty that all things with him were going as they were intended to, that all the lines were pulling together in compliance with the Scheme.

That afternoon, the next to the last that I clearly remember with him, he mentioned *King Jasper*, but more than anything he spoke of what he was planning to do next—my only experience with him of that kind of advance confidence—and he said he hoped he could go up to the Colony earlier than usual in the spring. The falseness of this made me intensely uncomfortable. It seemed to me either that in this whistling in the dark he was failing to face the fact of death or, what would have been even more petty, that he was trying to trick me into revealing something I might know of his physical prospects. For most of eleven years, I had been accustomed to sit with him in silences of more than ten minutes, silences warm with the certainty that our minds were turning in the same slow vortex around the same central truth. Now the center around which we were turning was death and eternity, the final question, yet it seemed that we were prevented from letting ourselves be drawn into it, even in silence, by something like evasive fear in E.A. On the other hand, this may have been the last case of his not wanting to violate the truth by addressing it directly, even in silence. But I saw none of that then. Outside of admiring E.A. for working up to the end, I got only frustration out of that call, and presently was impatient for the nurse to come in and let me get outdoors with Ridgely and have a drink.

Soon after that we moved into New York in order to be nearby, and Carty, and presently Burnham, came down from Boston and took their meals with us. Toward the end three or four of us ran a roster by which one of us, duly supplied with telephone numbers, spent the night with others of the faithful, among the flowers and the full moonlight in the solarium. I hesitate to name those watchers for I am sure to forget some of them. My little group included Elizabeth Sparhawk-Jones and Carty. I was not there at the end, and Elizabeth called me.

During that last week, between Friday, March 29, and April 5, 1935, at two o'clock in the morning, there were a number of memorable final partings. Among the old friends, Ridgely Torrence was probably the one whose companionship had been most continuously salted with humor. Ridgely and E.A. were both tall and lean, and seem to have required vests with eleven buttons instead of the ten that had been orthodox in the nineties when they were young. When Ridgely last saw E.A., he was too near coma to speak. But he was able to lift his hand, and what might have been the last gesture of that long first finger was to reach up and, starting at the top, to go through the motion of counting the buttons downward, slow one after one.

Elizabeth Sparhawk-Jones, the only one of the women who admitted frankly that she loved E.A., was not permitted to see him. She sent in a rambler rose by the nurse who hung it on the head of his bed, and he opened his eyes, looked up, and said, "Pretty." Immediately after he died, the nurse let her in, and she knelt and prayed. She planted the rose cutting near her home in Westtown, and it flourished.

When Leonora Speyer was leaving after her last call, she stood at the foot of the bed and said, "E.A., I have always loved you." He stared at her with the great eyes, and said hoarsely, "Amazing woman." At the door she looked back. His eyes were still on her and she could not move until he lowered them.

Harold Latham had been his editor at Macmillan for about twenty years, beginning with *The Man Against the Sky*, and the parting with him filled five days of that week. On Friday, March 29, E.A. told him that he had a little more to do on the typescript *of King Jasper,* and he promised to have it for him the following

Wednesday, which would be April 3. Outside in the hall, the nurse told Latham that she doubted that he would see him again, that E.A. was sinking rapidly. When he told her of the appointment next Wednesday, she said she would keep him informed. On Monday the first E.A. sank into coma, and on Tuesday the nurse phoned Latham, told him of it and said there would be no point in his coming up the next day. But on Wednesday morning E.A. came out of the coma and called for him. Both the nurse and one of the doctors told Latham it was the most striking case they ever saw of the power of the subconscious in a dying person. Robinson had had in mind to deliver that copy on that day, and the determination was strong enough to push him all the way back up into consciousness. Latham reached E.A.'s room an hour after he called for him. He smiled when Latham entered, picked up the typescript off the bed, and handed it to him. "Here it is," he said. "Take it now." Then he added, "And thank you, Latham —thank you for everything."

The last time I saw E.A. was during that week, for the night watch was already established. It was probably Saturday or Sunday, for the typescript of *Jasper* was still on the bed and he was not in coma. But there was a great internal change, the beginning of the relaxation out of outer consciousness. When I was alone with him sitting in a chair at the foot of the bed, there were the same great eyes staring out of the vast pillow, but now I felt ultimately comfortable. There was no tension, nothing remotely like fencing between us. In the silence he was telling me that he knew, and I was telling him that I knew he knew, and we both knew he was ready. We sat through a timelessness of a minute or two, I waiting as usual for E.A. to comment out of our mutual meditation. As if we had been back in his room or in his studio, he broke the silence, his voice faint in sound but clear and strong in conviction. He said, "I never could have done *anything* but write poetry." It was the last articulate thing he said to me.

I had heard that before, and it had meant the only thing in E.A. I didn't respect, the old wistfulness to be one of the respectable boys back in Gardiner. I might have thought now that it was a remarkable thing that that small shadow of inferiority should come down to disfigure the simplicity of death that otherwise I knew he was meeting easily, as something "less than change." But instead, I remember very clearly hearing with a sense of grandeur this final pronouncement of his life-long little cliché. I don't know that I understood then my sense of gratification, of consummation, but I do now. He was summing up, making his last declaration that he had done his work to the best of his ability; he had fulfilled his predestined calling; he had kept the faith. It didn't make any difference whether or not it had been something that Gardiner would admire. It was his, it had been assigned by the Powers to him and to no other. And through sixty-five years of concentration he had carried out his commission and finished it.

He was telling me, if I might come to understand it, that this and nothing other was what he had to do, that he could not have done *anything* else, that he never could have *been* in any detail different from what he *was*. That meant more than his not having been a banker or a lawyer. It meant also that he couldn't in the way of predestiny have ever acquired the social ease he had coveted so long. It meant that he could not ever have married Emma or the Woodland Girl or Olivia or anyone else, that he could not have lived in a house and had children of his own to love, that he could not have experienced lifelong love in any form except as an idea. Perhaps he was confessing that his one great mistake had been to have fancied at one time that he might have cherished his love permanently in the frame of the flesh as other men do. Instead, it had been his commission to experience it in the ideal world and to transcribe it as the love of Alcestis and of Vanderberg, of Lancelot and Guinevere, of Tristram and the two Isolts, and of Natalie. Except in the foolish dream of respectability and marriage he had been true, through the child-hood years when he wondered why he was born, through the early years when idealism meant self-indulgence, through the great years of Merlin the prophet and Lancelot the saint, and finally through the recent years when the harmless indulgence of the mature outer self had evinced the peak of selflessness, the loss of concern even for the disposition of the inner. Now at the end, he was going farther beyond the dark than Lancelot had, but without thinking of himself as questing at all.

And besides this boast that he had kept the faith, the boast before the court of his own last self-judgment, there were certainly other and objective meanings that were perhaps the actual motives of this final statement, meanings involving his concern for any other person who might be present. One thing he was probably doing was to tell me to search the wells of my own introspection and see my own calling clearly. He was telling me that his calling was not mine, that the fact that he couldn't have done anything but poetry didn't mean that my calling might not be to prose. He was telling me out of his last absolute humility, that it was not for him and his trivial opinions to settle what only another inner self could know. He was telling me that I the other person was everything, and that he himself did not matter at all.

What I saw as we continued to look at each other in silence was that humility in a new magnitude that made it the image and explanation of things and all that anyone needs to know. The last flurries of the outer self, even the clamors of the devil of perfection in poetry, together with the shadows and storms of the outer world, had all subsided and left only the whiteness, the pure white pillow, the Light that is Nothing and is Everything. There remained only the Light whose work is simply to be and to see and to love, and out of seeing and loving to provide the material for the separate seconds and bodies and poems of time. I saw God in man in the eyes shining black out of white that were also the blazing black eyes of the Byzantine Christ shining out of the mosaics of gold. I saw the selfless Light that was white and gold, and within it the eyes of a man who had come into time and had seen the outer world and loved it and now would return.

I sat there with E.A. who was Being in man, as every man is at first till the outer self wakes and chooses the outer world. For two or three minutes we sat there in the last silence while our eyes said to each other the simple Word that is everything mankind can say. We sat there in eternity that was not entirely uncovered by vanishing time, for besides our inner selves our outer bodies were sitting there breathing and seeing. The outer world was not yet all gone, and we saw it still in each other with the inner sight whose seeing of things discordant is compassion and smiles. We were out of time, but we smiled in time, and the nurse came in and I rose and picked up his hand. His weakness did not try to lift it, but it still was a symbol in flesh and it gave me a final, fluttering squeeze. He stuck out his lips as he always did before he said something absurd. I knew he was making a joke about death, and I smiled and I knew he was smiling inside. I said, "Good-bye, E.A." He moved his lips unintelligibly, indifferently, as if he were saying good-bye knowing he'd see me again in the morning.

COMMENT ON SOURCES

Until very recently, and in some part still, all of the sources on which a full biography of Robinson might rest have not been available to any one person. The reasons for this restriction on the material derive from a combination of Robinson's own qualities.

Fundamental was his social helplessness, real enough, though exaggerated by some of his more tender friends. Its pertinent aspect here was his discomfort in the presence of more than one person at a time, or at most two or three who were intimate among themselves and did not pull his extreme responsiveness in different directions. The result was the partition of his large acquaintance into small groups who scarcely knew each other, as mentioned on page 34 and discussed on pages 355–57, groups that were suspicious of each other and not prone to cooperate in a mutual project of fitting together the complete mozaic of Robinson's record. In consequence, most of the dozen or so books on Robinson are either criticism or letters, or they are slim memoirs setting down the observations of one friend. Each of the two full-length biographies was handicapped by the denial to the respective authors of access to one or more of the correspondences or to the unpublished, intimate knowledge of friends outside his particular circle. At this late date I have been refused help by the chief survivor of what might be called the New York executive group, originally containing the two executors. But recently the bulk of the sources, especially the indispensable family records and mementos, have been opened to research.

A second reason for the concealment of important facts about Robinson has been that many of his friends, including the members both of the New York executive group and the family group, wore the velvet of Victorian genteelness which required that no spade should be known as a spade, but should be disguised by some other epithet assigned to it by current respectability. Up to date this blushing and pompous hypocrisy has successfully hidden the essentials of Robinson's personal life. Prominent among the disguises thrown over him has been his reputation for

lifelong celibacy, accounting for such strange allusions as that of
Professor Neff to his "thwarted sexuality," and the succeeding
statement that "requited passion lay outside his experience." [1]
The prudishness reached its reduction to hilarity in two cases of
Robinson's simple realism in his letters. In July, 1925, complaining to Laura Richards of the "fool potion, or philtre," in the
classical story of *Tristram*, he wrote, "Men and women can make
trouble enough for themselves without being denatured and
turned into rabbits." [2] In the *Selected Letters* "rabbits" has been
purified into "robots." [3] On September 30, 1909, writing Louis
Ledoux from Gardiner, where he was staying with his sister-in-
law, he referred to his three nieces to whom he was devoted:
"The kids coming home from school make me feel blue and old." [4]
His normal colloquialism with his friends was too much for some
pious scribe who not only corrected the wicked word but made
further and unaccountable changes. In Hagedorn the offensive
sentence becomes "The lads coming home from school make me
feel like an old man." [5] In neither of these passages can the change
be excused by Robinson's difficult handwriting.

Finally, a partial justification for the reluctance of Robinson's
friends to reveal anything true about him has been their knowledge of his own extreme reticence, to the verge of secretiveness.
As Richard Cary said, "In 1913 he chilled a reporter from the
Post with, 'I have nothing to say about myself. My poems speak
for themselves.'" [6] Until late in his life he claimed that he wanted
no biography, although he knew that his friend Carty Ranck had
been Boswellizing him, probably from that same year of 1913,
and ultimately he seems to have authorized Ranck's project under
certain limitations. To this day, though most of the personal
sources are generously open, each of Robinson's surviving intimates, including this writer, suffers guilt in sensibly giving to
history the secrets of a great man.

In my attempt, not at a biography but at a more complete portrait than has yet been offered, I have relied chiefly on five among
the many sources, one of them secondary, one primary and well
known, two primary and not, to my knowledge, used before,
and one primary and tapped heretofore only lightly.

My principal secondary source has been Hagedorn's biography, whose chronology I have followed except where some other source is indicated. Since Robinson's letters to his friend Harry DeForest Smith are the most personally revealing of any of the five major correspondences, I have made very numerous use of them, mostly from Denham Sutcliffe's edition, partly from unpublished originals in Houghton Library, Harvard.

In the matter of finances, it would seem from the lack of references elsewhere that I am the first to have consulted the archives of the Court of Probate and the County Clerk of Kennebec County, Maine, and thence to elicit particulars not before published respecting, *inter alia*, the loss of the family fortune, the venture of the drugstore and Robinson's connection with it, and in New York his decline into penury.

The major new source I have had opened to me, at least in part, is a body of almost entirely undocumented evidence, chiefly relating to Mrs. Herman Robinson, the poet's sister-in-law, which I have called the "Legend of Emma," broaching it in the *Preface*, and discussing it further on pages 203 and 204. Allegedly it derives from Mrs. Robinson's recollections as recounted by her between Robinson's death in 1935 and her own in 1940. And thence it descends by word of mouth through two separate channels which I call respectively the "Orthodox Account" and the "Dissenting Account," each of which has its surviving custodian. All transmissions of it may be taken to have aimed at veracity, and many of its items are confirmed by other evidence. At the same time, having been verbal only, it is undoubtedly tinctured by the wishful fantasies, wishful recollections, and wishful ratiocinations of at least three people through the thirty years since Robinson's death. But in spite of the uncertainty hanging over this material, it is yet far too voluminous, too intimate, and in the main too consistent with itself and with the well-founded evidence to be ignored. A very little that seems fantastic I have omitted. Most of it I have qualified as "unlikely," "likely," "improbable," "probable," "possible," "apparent," and so on. Sometimes, I have drawn my own tentative inferences, labeling them. A few items, strongly supported from other sources, I have stated as facts. For the time being, a special shadow upon this congeries of evidence is that, except for its original source in the confidences of Mrs. Herman Robinson, it must remain anonymous. I shall deposit among my papers in the Yale University Library a sealed statement of the names of the witnesses through whom, in so far as I know of them, the legend reached me; and I shall leave instructions that this document may be opened on my order, on that of my literary executor, or after the lapse of a certain number of years. I have indicated this Legend of Emma, or in abbreviation simply "The Legend," by capital letters, in order to distinguish it from the also anonymous, miscellaneous sources which I call sometimes the "family legend" or "family report," or simply "the legend" or "report." These sources also will be explained in my papers and will eventually be available.

My fifth principal source, hardly touched heretofore for biographical purposes, has been the poetry itself. A considerable part of the "Legend of Emma" consists of biographical interpretation of much of it on the part of people who knew Robinson and his personal story well. Though they were little qualified as scholars or critics, perhaps they saw the revelations the more clearly for that. Following these interpretations as leads, and adding a few related ones of my own, I have identified forty of the items in the *Collected Poems* as autobiographical in some significant respect. The number of titles is not impressive among the total of 208 in the collected volume, the others comprising 27 that might be called intellectual poems and 141 that seem dominantly objective-dramatic. But if we consider the actual quantity of verse in these categories, the autobiographical division, dealing always with some aspect of the triangle of Robinson's love life and including most of the long poems, becomes larger than the others combined. As I have interpreted them, there are nineteen short poems, eleven of medium length, and ten of book length dealing with the triangle or two or one of its members, comprising 899 pages of the 1488 in the *Collected* volume. Of the balance, 224 pages are of chiefly intellectual verse and 365 are dramatic-objective. In those 899 pages, it seems to me, more profoundly than in the letters, and with respect to love more literally, is the confession of Robinson's life.

ACKNOWLEDGMENTS

Any work which presumes to associate Robinson with his poetry must start with the *Collected Poems* (The Macmillan Company, any edition after 1935), and with Charles Beecher Hogan's *A Bibliography of Edwin Arlington Robinson* (Yale University Press, 1936). For the copious use I have made of these sources, the former without citation, I am gratefully beholden to the respective publishers and to Mr. Hogan. Among the volumes reproduced in the *Collected Poems*, Charles Scribner's Sons held until recently the copyright of *The Children of the Night*, and still hold the copyright of *The Town Down the River*. I wish to thank them for permission to quote: from *The Children of the Night*, *The Miracle* entire, and excerpts from *Calvary*, *The Garden*, *Luke Havergal*, *The Night Before*, five of the *Octaves* complete, with four lines each from three more, *Sonnet*, and *Two Sonnets;* and from *The Town Down the River*, *Exit* entire, and an excerpt from *For a Dead Lady*.

For most of the chronology in the biographical part of the book, and for numerous anecdotes, I have drawn heavily on Hermann Hagedorn's *Edwin Arlington Robinson* (The Macmillan Company, 1938). My use of it has been so continuous that, except in direct quotations, for the use of which I am grateful to Mr. Hagedorn and The Macmillan Company, I have not given particular citations in the notes. Generally, an assertion in Part Two not referred to any other source comes either from Hagedorn or from the anonymous "Legend of Emma."

Some items not found in Hagedorn I have taken from Emery Neff's *Edwin Arlington Robinson* (American Men of Letters Series, William Sloane Associates, 1948), and for permission to make these references and quotations I wish to thank Professor Neff and William Morrow and Company who now control the copyright. I have made very extensive use of the two excellent memoirs, Laura E. Richards' *E.A.R.* and Esther Willard Bates's *Edwin Arlington Robinson and His Manuscripts*. For permission to quote considerably from them I am beholden to John Richards, to Miss Bates, and to the respective publishers, the Harvard University Press and the Colby College Library. I also wish to thank Rollo Walter Brown and Appleton-Century for permission to quote from his memoir, *Next Door to a Poet* (1937).

Undoubtedly Robinson's most revealing correspondence was that with Harry DeForest Smith, and with the kind permission of Harvard University Press and Denham Sutcliffe I have quoted voluminously from the latter's very full collection of the letters, published as *Untriangulated Stars* by Harvard in 1947. Very useful also has been *Selected Letters of Edwin Arlington Robinson* from which The Macmillan Company has permitted me to quote largely.

Of the notable critical works, I have made little use of those of Lloyd Morris, Mark Van Doren and Charles Cestae, but have referred often to Ellsworth Barnard's *Edwin Arlington Robinson —A Critical Study* (The Macmillan Company, 1953). While maintaining the critical approach, yet upon a topical outline Professor Barnard builds from the poetry and some of the sources by far the most perspicacious portrait of Robinson the person that has yet appeared. Thanks to Professor Barnard and Macmillan, I have cited several of his conclusions, often with quotation. A work of intellectual criticism which I found useful in relation to some of Robinson's academic experience at Harvard, is Estelle Kaplan's *Philosophy in the Poetry of Edwin Arlington Robinson,* and for permission to quote from this book I am indebted to Miss Kaplan and the Columbia University Press. For the local history of Gardiner, Maine, Robinson's home town, I used chiefly *The Gardiner Story* (The City of Gardiner, 1949).

Of periodicals, I have quoted from the *Colophon,* December, 1930, Robinson's own "The First Seven Years"; from the *Bookman,* November, 1932, Nancy Evans, "Edwin Arlington Robinson"; from *The Virginia Quarterly Review,* Winter, 1937, "Early Letters of Edwin Arlington Robinson: First Series," edited by Daniel Gregory Mason, and Spring, 1937, "Edwin Arlington Robinson to Daniel Gregory Mason," edited by Daniel Gregory Mason; and from the *Radcliffe Quarterly,* November, 1962, Mabel Daniels, "Edwin Arlington Robinson—A Musical Memoir." The *Colophon* and the *Bookman* being no more, my thanks go to the editors of *The Virginia Quarterly Review* and of the *Radcliffe*

Quarterly for permission to make these quotations. I have made use, without quotation, of David S. Nivison's "Does It Matter How Annandale Went Out" and Richard Cary's "Robinson's Notes to His Nieces," both in the *Colby Library Quarterly* for December, 1960.

My thanks are also due to the Colby Library and its staff, and especially to Professor Richard Cary, Curator of Rare Books and Manuscripts, for permission to quote from Robinson's letters to Laura Richards, George Burnham, Emma Shepherd Robinson, and others, and to Professor Cary particularly for answers to specific questions regarding material in the Edith Brower correspondence which is in his custody. I am grateful to the Princeton Library, and especially to Alexander P. Clark, Curator of Manuscripts, for permission to quote from Robinson's letters to Ridgely Torrence and others; also to W. H. Bond, Curator of Manuscripts of Houghton Library, Harvard, and to his staff for their courtesy in giving me access to Robinson's unpublished correspondences with Laura Richards, Arthur Gledhill, Harry DeForest Smith, Louis and Jean Ledoux, and others, and to Rosalind Richards' record of interviews with many of Robinson's friends. Most helpful has been Donald Gallup, Curator of the Collection of American Literature in the Yale University Library, in supplying me with copies and facsimiles of early Robinson publications. Dean Kendrick and Registrar Helen B. Johnson of Bowdoin kindly supplied me with important information respecting the academic career of Dr. Horace Dean Robinson. The staffs of the Probate Court and the County Clerk's Office of Kennebec County, Maine, were considerate in providing me with the testamentary and real estate documents of the Robinson family, as was the County Clerk of Wiscasset County with respect to the Robinson-Shepherd property on Capitol Island.

Always courteous and indispensably helpful has been Mrs. William Nivison, Robinson's niece and latterly his executor, in giving me access to the houseful of Robinsoniana in Robinson House, at Head Tide, Maine, in answering barrages of questions by mail, in supplying me with four of the pictures used, in giving me scores of permissions to quote unpublished material, and in supplying me personally with much information. Voluminous and generous also was the contribution of the late Rosalind Richards, daughter of Laura Richards, not only in permitting me to quote from her interviews with many of Robinson's friends deposited in Houghton Library, Harvard, but in composing for me an invaluable biographical study of Robinson's friend and patron John Hays Gardiner, together with accounts of Maine culture and of the Emerson family. Indispensable also has been the kindness of Harry Bacon Collamore in supplying me with four pictures of Robinson.

Of the anecdotes given me personally by mutual friends, those provided by Esther Bates, in addition to the contents of her book, are by far the most numerous, and their implicit comments upon Robinson's character are in several respects the most penetrating. Also indispensable, and comparable in richness, have been the contributions of Nancy Byrd Turner and Elizabeth Sparhawk-Jones, both, like Miss Bates, Robinson's companions during many of his twenty-four years at the MacDowell Colony. Among the most important contributions by Robinson's surviving friends has been the anecdote given me by Boris Todrin which clarifies the much rumored Dunbar-Robinson-Torrence triangle. Hermann Hagedorn most generously amplified some of the material in his biography, and Harold Latham, for twenty years Robinson's editor, has added some details to Hagedorn's account of his dramatic final parting with him.

High among those who have provided me with important material is John H. Labbie, City Clerk of Gardiner, who went far afield to supply me with material from old newspapers and other obscure local sources. Mrs. Benjamin W. Jackson kindly confirmed some details of the sale to her husband of the drugstore previously rented to the Robinsons. Useful items of personal information about Robinson were given me by Evelyn Hooker Davis and by Emma Shepherd Day. Professor Edwin Fussell provided his uniquely qualified opinion on some points respecting Robinson's early verse, and directed me to other valuable material. Lyman Leathers clarified the date and other details respecting the marriage of Olivia Dunbar to Ridgely Torrence. Professor Lawrence R. Thompson kindly directed me to some invaluable letters.

Finally, my greatest gratitude is due to my wife for reading all of the manuscript in process; and afterwards to Ellsworth Barnard, Esther Bates, Granville Hicks, Harry Staley and Anita Witten for reading parts of it and making valuable comments. And always on the firing line has been Patricia McManus, that perfect typist, in patience, perspicuousness, and execution, who is every writer's dream.

C.P.S.

A GLOSSARY OF WRITERS AND ARTISTS
MENTIONED IN THE TEXT

Anderson, Tennessee. Sculptor, former wife of Sherwood. Friend of Harriet Monroe, Eunice Tietjens, and the others of the group that founded *Poetry* in Chicago in 1912. Showed talent for sculpture, especially caricature, and appeared in several exhibitions in the mid-twenties. She never reached self-supporting status, sank into extreme poverty in Chicago, and was found dead in her room. Text, pp. 9, 23, 35.

Baker, George Pierce (1866–1935). Famous teacher of dramatic writing in the "47 Workshop" (English 47) at Harvard and afterwards at Yale. Author of standard textbook, *Dramatic Technique*. Text, p. 37.

Bates, Esther (1884–   ). Dramatist and novelist. About thirty plays acted and published, notably *Be Your Age* and *The Wing is on the Bird*. Teacher of playwriting at Boston University and Head of the Department of English at Rhode Island School of Design. Author of juvenile novels. For six years columnist on the *Providence Journal*. At present engaged in compiling her columns for book publication. MacDowell Colonist. After 1913 typed most of Robinson's verse. For references, see Index.

Beach, Amy Marcy (Mrs. H. H.) (1867–1944). "Most celebrated of American women composers. . . . she made her public debut as a pianist at sixteen." (*Reader's Encyclopedia*, William Rose Benét, ed.) Her chief work, *Gaelic Symphony*. MacDowell Colonist. Text, p. 15.

Benét, Stephen Vincent (1898–1943). Poet and fiction writer. *John Brown's Body*, Pulitzer prize, 1928. Text, p. x.

Benét, William Rose (1883–1950). Poet and critic. Eleven books of poetry, including *The Falconer of God* and *The Dust Which is God* (Pulitzer Prize, 1942). For many years critical columnist of "The Phoenix Nest," *Saturday Review of Literature*. Editor of three anthologies. Husband of Elinor Wylie and editor of her works. Also husband of Marjorie Flack, children's book writer. MacDowell Colonist. Text, pp. x, 11, 14, 15, 16.

Betts, Craven Longstreth. A Nova Scotian descendant of Tories who fled from Boston. An effusive sonneteer, blank versifier, and reciter of poetry. One of Titus Munson Coan's bohemian crowd of the nineties, who comprised Robinson's first friends in New York. *Dionysus in Doubt* dedicated to him. For references, see Index.

Bodenheim, Maxwell (1892–1954). Vital, bohemian, pugilistic, unwashed and excellent poet and novelist. At least six books of verse and five novels. MacDowell Colonist. He was murdered. Text, p. 38.

Braithwaite, William Stanley (1878–1962). Grandson of British Admiral Braithwaite who retired to Barbados as Governor and married a Negro. Was for many years literary editor of the *Boston Transcript*, editor of the Brimmer Press, and for about twenty years the compiler of *Braithwaite's Anthology*, the annual of magazine verse. Was the discoverer of many of the principal poets of the twenties. Left Boston because his wife was not suitably received, and taught in Howard University until his retirement. Greatly respected and loved by most poets of the twenties and thirties, and variously honored by the Poetry Society of America. Text, pp. 35, 37, 236.

Brower, Edith (1884–1931). Essayist, short-story writer and poet. Fan letter on Robinson's first book started lifelong correspondence. Text, pp. 152, 158, 163, 226, 275, 299, 303.

Brown, Rollo Walter (1880–   ). Essayist, lecturer and teacher at Harvard and elsewhere. Text, pp. 20, 238.

Burnham, George. Not a literary figure, but a lifelong philosophical influence on Robinson. *Merlin* dedicated to him. After Robinson's death, curator of Robinson House, Head Tide. For references, see Index.

Calkins, Clinch. Poet, dramatist, story writer, and sociologist. Text, p. 43.

Coan, Titus Munson. A New York manuscript doctor and dandy of the nineties. After seeing Robinson's first book, invited him to call on him. Robinson declined to be doctored, but he liked Coan, who introduced him to his first literary association in the city. Text, p. 175.

Cohen, Rose. Talented writer of magazine fiction and author of a successful autobiography, *Out of the Shadow*, recounting her rise from immigrant poverty on the East Side of New York to substantial literary success. In the late twenties her market shrank, and patronage which had helped her before deserted her. She concealed her straits from her many friends and died tragically. Text, pp. 15, 23.

Colum, Mary (1887–1957). Irish-American critic of classical disposition and large influence during the twenties and thirties. Also a short-story writer of distinction. Her principal critical work is *From These Roots* (1937), and her autobiography is *Life and the Dream* (1947). Wife of Padraic Colum. MacDowell Colonist. Text, p. 9.

Colum, Padraic (1881–   ). Irish-American playwright and poet, associate in the Irish National Theater of A.E., Yeats, and Lady Gregory. Many plays, stories, books of verse and Irish folklore. MacDowell Colonist. Text, p. 9.

Daniels, Mabel (1878–   ). Composer, distinguished especially for choral compositions. Steady MacDowell Colonist. Text, pp. 5, 11, 15, 336.

Day, Frederick Lansing. Playwright, graduate of G. P. Baker's 47 Workshop. Author of many plays produced in little theaters. Mac-Dowell Colonist. Text, p. 23.

Dodge, Mabel (1879–   ). Greenwich Village and Taos, N.M. Patroness of the arts. Visited the Harry Taylors with whom Robinson was living on Staten Island in their haunted castle. On a second visit encountered the ghost and fled between midnight and dawn. (Hagedorn, 281). Text, p. 299.

Dunbar, Olivia Howard. Successful short-story writer of the early twentieth century. Member of the literary group at the Hotel Judson, Washington Square, and persistently mentioned with Robinson in gossip. Married Ridgely Torrence in 1914 and sacrificed her career to him. After his death in 1950 staged readings of his work in order to arrest its decline in popularity. MacDowell Colonist. Text, pp. 55–6, 219, 238–40.

Duncan, Isadora (1878–1927). American dancer. Text, pp. 55, 219.

Erskine, John (1879–1951). Distinguished English teacher at Columbia. Great personal charm. Insignificant poet, and president of the Poetry Society of America. Wearied of the critics' condescension and turned to popular, pseudosophisticated, pseudohistorical novels, notably *The Private Life of Helen of Troy* (1925). Amateur musician. Director of the Juilliard Foundation and of the MacDowell Colony. Text, p. 3.

Fillmore, Parker (1878–1944). Teacher, banker, and after 1910, prolific novelist and short story writer. MacDowell Colonist and director of the Edward MacDowell Association. Close friend of Robinson. Text, p. 3.

Fraser, James Earle (1876–1953). Sculptor of portrait busts, including Grant and Theodore Roosevelt, and of many civic memorials. Robinson's host, on West 8th Street in New York City from 1922 to 1925, and on East 42d from 1925 until Robinson's death. Text, pp. 26, 29, 208, 238, 258, 278, 362.

Frost, Robert (1875–1963). Text, pp. x, xiv, 3, 4, 221, 361.

Gardiner, John Hays (1864–1913). English professor at Harvard, editor and director of the *Harvard Bulletin*. Much beloved. He and his cousin Laura Richards were Robinson's two most important early patrons. Guaranteed *Captain Craig* and left Robinson a legacy at a critical time. Text, pp. 165–8, 182, 184, 207, 211, 236–8, 240.

Gorman, Herbert (1893–1954). Critic and biographer, notably of Joyce. MacDowell Colonist. Text, p. 48.

Gorman, Jean (Wright). Wife of Herbert Gorman, afterwards of Carl Van Doren. Much envied in Greenwich Village and at the MacDowell Colony for having a dressing allowance not applicable to her or her husband's necessities. Text, p. 48.

Hagedorn, Hermann (1882–   ). Poet. Friend and editor of Theodore Roosevelt. Friend, patron, and official biographer of Robinson (*Edwin Arlington Robinson*, Macmillan, 1938). Text, pp. xv, 19, 236, 237, 356.

Hapgood, Hutchins (1869–1944). Teacher at Harvard and Chicago, novelist and essayist. Acquaintance of Robinson's at Harvard. Personally popular in the literary world of the twenties and thirties. Text, p. 119.

Hapgood, Norman (1868–1937). Critic, editor, and biographer. Acquaintance of Robinson's at Harvard. Text, p. 119.

Heyward, Dorothy (1890–1961). Wife of DuBose Heyward. Playwright. Graduate 47 Workshop. Among her plays, dramatizations of her husband's *Porgy* and *Mamba's Daughters,* collaboration in *South Pacific,* and her own *Set My People Free,* all Broadway productions. Handicapped by arthritis. Text, pp. 10, 11, 23.

Heyward, DuBose (1885–1940). Poet (*Skylines and Horizons,* 1924) and novelist (including *Porgy,* 1925, and *Mamba's Daughters,* 1929). Handicapped by polio. Text, pp. 10, 11, 23, 25.

Holden, Raymond Peckham (1894–   ). Poet (inter alia, *Collected Poems,* 1946, and *The Reminding Salt,* 1964). Novelist, naturalist, and author of many scientific books for young people. Text, p. x.

Isaacs, Lewis Montefiore (1877–1944). Lawyer and amateur musician. Friend, leading patron, financial adviser and executor of Robinson. *Lancelot* dedicated to him. Treasurer of the Edward MacDowell Association. Text, pp. 237, 244, 251, 262, 297, 340, 348, 363, 364.

Jeffers, Robinson (1887–1962). Text, pp. x, 349.

Latham, Harold. Robinson's editor at the Macmillan Company. Text, pp. 366–7.

Ledoux, Jean. Wife of Louis Ledoux. Text, pp. 76, 299, 300, 351.

Ledoux, Louis (1880–1948). Poet and authority on Japanese art. Member of the Judson Hotel group. Friend, leading patron, and literary executor of Robinson. For references, see Index.

Lee, Muna (1895–   ). Former wife of Luis Muñoz Marín, Governor of Puerto Rico. Poet (*Lyric* prize, 1915), including much Spanish-English and English-Spanish translation. MacDowell Colonist. Director of National Activities, U.S. National Woman's Party; Associate Assistant, Division of Cultural Relations, Department of State; and many other international activities. Text, pp. 23, 25.

Louis, Alfred H. Anglo-Jewish, Cambridge-educated, prophetic-bearded man of letters, poet, pianist, lawyer, student of government, and philosopher, with a unique presence, at once magnificent and delicate. He had been blocked by Gladstone from nomination for Parliament by the Liberal Party, and latterly was impoverished in New York, ragged, unwashed, and eating what he could pick up.

Moody successful with the plays *The Great Divide* (1906) and *The Faith Healer* (1909), but his most pretentious verse dramas were never produced. *Cavender's House* dedicated to his memory. Text, pp. 42, 121–2, 187, 219.

Moore, Douglas (1893–). Composer, his many works including the operas *Giants in the Earth* (1950) and *The Ballad of Baby Doe* (1955). Pulitzer prize, 1951. Chairman Department of Music, Columbia. MacDowell Colonist. Director of the Edward MacDowell Association. Text, pp. 23, 25.

Moore, Dr. Merrill. Psychiatrist and poet. Wrote many sonnets, one of his books, *M*, containing a thousand. A late friend of Robinson. America." Text, p. 360.

Morris, Lloyd (1893–1954). Critic and biographer: *The Rebellious Puritan* (1927), biography of Hawthorne; *The Poetry of Edwin Arlington Robinson* (1923), the first critical work on Robinson. MacDowell Colonist. Text, pp. 3, 4, 8, 11, 13, 14.

Nazimova (1879–1945). Actress. Member of the Judson Hotel group. Text, p. 219.

Neff, Emery (1892–). English professor at Columbia and biographer of Robinson (*Edwin Arlington Robinson*, American Men of Letters Series, Sloane, 1948). Text, p. xv.

Norton, Charles Eliot (1827–1908). Founder of *The Nation*. Professor of Literature at Harvard. "By all odds the greatest man in America." Text, p. 114.

Noyes, Alfred (1880–1958). English poet, popular in America before the First World War. Text, p. 238.

Patterson, Frances. Moving picture critic. MacDowell Colonist. President of the MacDowell Colonists. Text, pp. 11, 12.

Peabody, Josephine Preston (1874–1922). Poet and dramatist. Her *The Piper* won the 1910 verse play contest of the Shakespeare Memorial Theatre at Stratford-on-Avon. Friend of Robinson in his second Cambridge period and his early New York period. Text, pp. 184, 211, 303, 334, 338, 339.

Phelps, William Lyon (1865–1945). English professor at Yale, popular lecturer and critic. At Harvard when Robinson was there. Text, p. 119.

Ranck, Edwin Carty (born in the late 1880's and died about 1950). Journalist and unsuccessful dramatist. Graduate of G. P. Baker's 47 Workshop. Close friend of Robinson, who dedicated *Nicodemus* to him. Spent most of his life after 1913 preparing to write Robinson's biography, but failed to finish it. For references, see Index.

Reynard, Grant (1887–). Successful artist. Many one-man shows and prizes. MacDowell Colonist. Text, pp. 11, 14, 15, 16.

Richards, Laura (1850–1943). Successful author of children's books and Pulitzer prize biographer of her mother, Julia Ward Howe. Robinson's first major patron, close friend and one of his principal, lifelong correspondents. For references, see Index.

Roosevelt, Theodore. President. Discovered Robinson through his son Kermit who learned of him from his English instructor at Groton School, Henry Richards, son of Laura Richards. Supported Robinson by government patronage in the form of nominal employment in the Custom House, 1905–09, and wrote laudatory criticism of his work. *The Town Down the River* dedicated to him. Text, pp. 216, 220, 224.

Rorty, James (1892–   ). Major poet and social critic. Work in ecology forthcoming. Text, pp. x, 386.

Rourke, Constance (1885–1941). Biographer, historian, and critic, especially of American humor. Her books include *Trumpets of Jubilee* (1927), *Davy Crockett* (1934), *Audubon* (1936) and *The Roots of American Culture* (1942). MacDowell Colonist. Text, pp. 11, 23.

Santayana, George (1863–1952). Poet and philosopher. Graduate student and instructor at Harvard during Robinson's residence there. Text, p. 119.

Schauffler, Robert Haven (1876–   ). Poet and musical biographer. Husband of Margaret Widdemer (div.). MacDowell Colonist. Text, p. 23.

Schenck, Franklin L. Painter whom Robinson admired. Text, p. 278.

Sinclair, May (1870–1947). Member of the Judson Hotel group. Text, p. 219.

Sparhawk-Jones, Elizabeth. Painter, late in receiving recognition and one-man shows. Devoted to Robinson, and after his death did a series of impressionistic representations of phases of his life. Text, pp. 37, 48, 53, 180, 366.

Speyer, Leonora (1872–1956). Violinist and poet. Married the German-born banker Sir Edgar Speyer. Their house in London was mobbed during World War I, Sir Edgar renounced his baronetcy and came to America. Mrs. Speyer won the Pulitzer prize for *Fiddler's Farewell* (1927), and many other prizes. Taught poetry at Columbia. MacDowell Colonist. Entertained many literary people, especially poets, and especially Robinson, at her house on Washington Square. Text, pp. 5, 6, 11, 53, 366.

Stedman, Clarence (1833–1908). Journalist, poet, critic, anthologist, stock broker, and patron. Recognized Robinson early, was the first to anthologize him (1900), and became his friend. Text, pp. 186, 187.

Stork, Charles Wharton (1881–   ). Poet, translator of Scandinavian poetry, founder and editor of *Contemporary Verse*, important among the poetry magazines of the twenties. Text, p. 38.

Taylor, Henry. Painter who married the former Mrs. Davidge, Robinson's patron. Text, p. 236.

Todrin, Boris (1915–   ). Poet and novelist. His poetry was greatly admired by Robinson. Text, pp. 386, 404.

Torrence, Ridgely (1875–1950). Excellent minor poet, his best work *Hesperides* (1925) which Robinson expected to win the Pulitzer prize. Got the Shelley Memorial Award in 1941. Wrote plays about and for Negroes, hoping for the foundation of a Negro theater. Poetry editor of the *New Republic*, 1920–1934. Member of the Judson Hotel group. MacDowell Colonist. Intimate friend of Robinson, who dedicated *Matthias at the Door* to him. For references, see Index.

Torrence, Olivia Dunbar. See Dunbar.

Turner, Nancy Byrd (1880–   ). Poet and short story writer. Winner of the Golden Rose poetry prize. MacDowell Colonist. Text, pp. 5, 14, 38, 46, 47, 49, 51, 54, 134.

Widdemer, Margaret (1890–   ). Popular poet and novelist. MacDowell Colonist. Text, pp. 23, 25, 336.

Wilder, Thornton (1897–   ). Novelist and dramatist. Pultizer prizes for *Our Town* (1938) and *The Skin of Our Teeth* (1942). MacDowell Colonist and director of the Edward MacDowell Association. Text, pp. 10, 11, 14, 23.

Wylie, Elinor (1885–1928). Considered by many the best woman poet of the twenties: *Black Armour* (1923), *Trivial Breath* (1928), and *Angels and Earthly Creatures* (1928). Wife of William Rose Benét. MacDowell Colonist. Text, pp. 11, 20.

A SUMMARY OF CHIEF EVENTS
IN ROBINSON'S LIFE

May 30, 1857.	Birth of brother Horace Dean.
January 6, 1865.	Birth of brother Herman Edward.
April 19, 1865.	Birth of Emma Loehen Shepherd.
December 22, 1869.	Birth of E. A. R., at Head Tide, Maine.
September, 1870.	Family moves to Gardiner, Maine.
School year 1881–82.	Clip on the ear by a teacher starts life-long mastoid infection.
1883–84.	Dr. Schuman begins teaching him prosody.
Winter, 1888.	Meets Emma Shepherd.
February 12. 1890.	Marriage of Emma and Herman.
March 3, 1890.	First publication, the sonnet *Thalia*, in local paper.
Summer, 1891.	Completion of the cottage on Capitol Island, Boothbay Harbor.
September, 1891.	Entered Harvard as special student.
July, 1892.	Death of father, Edward Robinson.
1893.	Financial panic. Beginning of decline of the family estate.
June, 1893.	Concluded work at Harvard. Began "farming" the family's two acres in Gardiner, while writing verse and some prose systematically. Here during the next four years completed the contents of *The Torrent and the Night Before* and *The Children of the Night*.
Winter and spring, 1894.	Engagement and its collapse.
1895 and '96.	Continuing decline of family fortune.
November, 1896.	Death of mother, Mary Palmer Robinson. Private publication of *The Torrent and the Night Before*. Emma and Herman move into the family house.
1897.	Year of tension with Emma and Herman. Beginning of friendship with Laura Richards and Hays Gardiner. "The Quadruped."
Late summer or early fall, 1897.	Break with Herman. Final departure from the house. Settlement in Winthrop, across the Kennebec from Gardiner.
November, 1897.	To New York.

December, 1897.	Vanity publication of *The Children of the Night*.
Spring, 1898.	To Cambridge.
Summer, 1898.	Back to Winthrop. "The girl of the woodland walks."
Winter and spring, 1899.	Secretarial employment in University Hall, Harvard.
September, 1899.	Death of Dean. Permanent return to New York.
Winter, 1899–1900.	Several poems in Stedman's anthology.
Summer, 1900.	"Last smash" of the family estate; diminishing allowance from it.
November, 1901.	Last reported receipt of money from the estate. Absolute pennilessness. Begins years of borrowing.
October, 1902.	Publication of *Captain Craig*, guaranteed by Mrs. Richards and Hays Gardiner.
1903.	Sale of the family house by Herman. No evidence that E. A. R. shared in proceeds. Death of Emma's father and depletion of his estate. Herman to Capitol Island. Emma remains in her family house and begins supporting her mother and her children by sewing.
Fall, 1903–August, 1904.	Employment as timekeeper in New York subway construction.
January–June, 1905.	Employment in advertising in Boston.
July, 1905.	Begins employment New York Custom House as sinecure provided by President Theodore Roosevelt. Congenial association in Hotel Judson, Washington Square.
Fall, 1905.	Publication by Scribner's of new edition of *The Children of the Night* under pressure from Roosevelt. Unsuccessful experiments with drama.
February, 1909.	Death of Herman in Boston City Hospital.
March, 1909.	Quit Custom House job.
September, 1909.	To Gardiner "for an indefinite stay." Emma refuses to marry him.
December, 1909.	Returns to New York.
October, 1910.	*The Town Down the River*, first independent, commercial publication.
1910–1913.	More unsuccessful attempts at remunerative writing of plays and novels.

1911. First visit to the MacDowell Colony, Peterborough, New Hampshire, where he went every summer thenceforth till the end of his life.

1913–23. Great period, comprising the volumes *The Man Against the Sky* (1916), *Merlin* (1917), *Lancelot* (1920), *The Three Taverns* (1920), *Avon's Harvest* (1921), *Collected Poems* (1921)—Pulitzer prize, *Roman Bartholow* (1923), *The Man Who Died Twice* (1924)—second Pulitzer prize. Paid most of his debts.

December, 1918. Emma again refuses to marry him. Resulting determination.

1922. Honorary degree from Yale.

1923. Visit to England.

1925. Honorary degree from Bowdoin. Last visit to Gardiner.

1927. *Tristram*: best seller, third Pulitzer prize. Paid last debts and accumulated a reserve. Final refusal of Emma to marry him.

1929–35. Publication of a book a year, including *Matthias at the Door* (1931) and *Amaranth* (1934).

April 5, 1935. Death in the New York Hospital.

NOTES

Sources referred to only once, or more than once in close proximity, are fully cited as they appear. All others are referred to by the following abbreviations:

Barnard: Ellsworth Barnard, *Edwin Arlington Robinson—A Critical Study* (New York, Macmillan, 1952).

Bates: Esther Willard Bates, *Edwin Arlington Robinson and His Manuscripts* (Waterville, Maine, Colby College Library, 1944).

Brown: Rollo Walter Brown, *Next Door to a Poet* (New York, D. Appleton-Century, 1937).

Colby: Unpublished letter in Colby Library.

Colby Quarterly: Colby Library Quarterly.

Colophon: "The First Seven Years," *Colophon*, Part IV, Dec., 1930.

Evans: Nancy Evans, "Edwin Arlington Robinson," *Bookman*, Nov., 1932.

Gardiner Story: The Gardiner Story (City of Gardiner, 1949).

Hagedorn: Hermann Hagedorn, *Edwin Arlington Robinson—A Biography* (New York, Macmillan, 1938).

Harvard: Unpublished letter in Houghton Library, Harvard.

Kaplan: Estelle Kaplan, *Philosophy in the Poetry of Edwin Arlington Robinson* (New York, Columbia University Press, 1940).

Labbie: John H. Labbie, City Clerk of Gardiner, Me.

Letters: Selected Letters of Edwin Arlington Robinson, ed. Ridgely Torrence (New York, Macmillan, 1940).

Morris: Lloyd Morris, *The Poetry of Edwin Arlington Robinson* (New York, George H. Doran, 1923)—as quoted in *Barnard*.

Neff: Emery Neff, *Edwin Arlington Robinson* (American Men of Letters Series, New York, William Sloane Associates, 1948).

Princeton: Unpublished letter in Princeton Library.

L. Richards: Laura Richards, *E.A.R.* (Cambridge, Harvard University Press, 1936).

R. Richards: Rosalind Richards, Record of statements by friends of Robinson, in Houghton Library, Harvard.

Sutcliffe: *Untriangulated Stars: Letters of Edwin Arlington Robinson to Harry DeForest Smith, 1890–1905*, ed. Denham Sutcliffe (Cambridge, Harvard University Press, 1947).

Virginia Quarterly, Winter, 1937: *Virginia Quarterly Review*, Winter, 1937, "Early Letters of Edwin Arlington Robinson, edited by Daniel Gregory Mason."

Virginia Quarterly, Spring, 1937: *Virginia Quarterly Review*, Spring, 1937, "Letters of Edwin Arlington Robinson to Daniel Gregory Mason, edited by Daniel Gregory Mason."

PREFACE

1. Leon Edel, *Literary Biography* (Toronto, University of Toronto Press, 1957), pp. 82–3.
2. Hagedorn, supra, and The Legend of Emma, pages 203–4 and 373–4.
3. Pp. 110–12.

PART ONE

1. Robinson's friend Daniel Gregory Mason wrote of his hands that they seemed "made not to grasp objects—saws or hammers, hardly even pens . . ." (Hagedorn, p. 149). Yet these same hands had done most of the heavy work around the family's big house from his boyhood until he left home in his twenty-eighth year. (See p. 107, and thereafter in Part Two, *passim.*)
2. Sutcliffe, p. 152.
3. Quoted by Mabel Daniels, "Edwin Arlington Robinson—a Musical Memoir," *Radcliffe Quarterly*, November, 1962.
4. Brown, page 19.
5. Robinson was universally accredited with this piece of self-description and it is supposed that he expressed it to Ridgely Torrence during his lowest period in 1902–3. I have not been able to verify the rumor.
6. Hagedorn, p. 351.
7. Bates, p. 28.
8. *Letters*, p. 48.
9. *Ibid.*, pp. 137–38.
10. This incident occurred much later than the period 1924–27, probably in '31 or '32. It is given here as an important revelation of character, in several respects.
11. Colby.
12. Quoted by Mabel Daniels, "Edwin Arlington Robinson—a Musical Memoir," *Radcliffe Quarterly*, November, 1962.
13. Hagedorn, p. 83.
14. Sutcliffe, p. 107.
15. *Ibid.*, p. 284.
16. *Letters*, p. 155.
17. *Virginia Quarterly*, Spring, 1937, pp. 239–40.
18. *Ibid.*
19. *Letters*, p. 135.
20. *Virginia Quarterly*, Winter, 1937, pp. 57–58.
21. Recollection of Esther Bates.
22. *Ibid.*
23. Hagedorn, p. 297.
24. Carty Ranck reported that this entourage comprised the *Veteran Sirens*. Because the poem was written before 1916, and because of Robinson's gallantry, the slur seems doubtful.
25. The probably true account of the relation between Robinson and Olivia Dunbar is set out on pp. 238–9.
26. In the summer of '25 Robinson, starting to work on *Tristram*, had written Mrs. Louis Ledoux much the same impatient sentiments that he

expressed to me in the spring of '26: "The key and color of the thing are altogether different from those of *Merlin* and *Lancelot* and may cause some readers to suspect that I'm getting a little tired of hearing too much about my New England reticence." (*Letters*, p. 146.)

PART TWO

PROLOGUE

1. Sutcliffe, p. 300.
2. *Letters*, p. 89.
3. Sutcliffe, p. 269.
4. *Letters*, p. 103.
5. Bates, p. 5.
6. James Barstow, *My Tilbury Town* (privately printed, 1939), p. 7.
7. *Gardiner Story*.
8. Mrs. Allen, in R. Richards.
9. Hagedorn, p. 10.
10. *Colophon*.
11. Laura Lewis Macumber, in R. Richards.
12. *Ibid*.

ACT I

1. Sutcliffe, p. 300.
2. Neff, p. 4.
3. *Letters*, p. 91.
4. The model of Eben Flood was not one of these early rustic acquaintances, although he was a distant cousin. Much later Harry DeForest Smith's father directed Robinson's attention to him.
5. Sutcliffe, p. 112.
6. Hagedorn, p. 155.
7. *Letters*, p. 9, letter to Arthur R. Gledhill.
8. Leonard Barnard, in R. Richards.
9. Caroline Swan, in R. Richards.
10. *Ibid*.
11. L. Richards, p. 25.
12. Hagedorn, p. 32.
13. *Ibid*., 59.
14. It is difficult to identify the generous "man Flammonde" with the forthcoming Herman of *Eros Turannos, The Clinging Vine*, and *London Bridge*. But the family legend holds that his nature shriveled after his failure. A shred of identification may be found in Flammonde's being "taken on / By friends not easy to be won," a possible reference to Herman's acquaintance with Henry Richards before the rest of the family knew him. Another straw may be Flammonde's concern for the education of the young man who had in him "the rare seed / Of learning," possibly referring to Herman's part in Win's going to Harvard. More suggestive is Robinson's statement (*Letters*, 104) that "Flammonde is the man who sees but cannot do for himself, 'others he saved. . . .'"; such a dichotomy might be consistent with what we know of Herman. In 1932 Robinson said that *Flam-*

monde came to him complete while he was in a movie theater (Evans, p. 677), and because of his earlier impecuniousness this was likely to have been after 1905. Because the poem was first published in the *Outlook* in 1915, it was presumably written not long before that date. This dating makes the casting of Herman more plausible, because generally after 1909 Win treated him with compassion in his poetry. The prominent location of the poem at the opening of *The Man Against the Sky* volume, 1916, together with Robinson's original intention to make it the title poem, an honor which its smattering of banality scarcely merits, is the kind of salute that Robinson would tend to give his unfortunate brother. Altogether, *Flammonde* may be taken tentatively as the partial portrait the legend claims it to be.

15. Harvard.
16. *Ibid.*
17. *Kennebec Reporter*, Feb. 15, 1890.
18. David S. Nivison, *Colby Quarterly*, December, 1960, p. 175.
19. Hagedorn, p. 57.
20. *Colophon.*
21. Harvard, July 24, 1890.
22. *Ibid.*, Sept. 27, 1890.
23. Sutcliffe, p. 3.
24. *Ibid.*, p. 14.
25. *Ibid.*, p. 8.
26. Harvard.
27. Sutcliffe, p. 9.
28. *Ibid.*, pp. 9–10.
29. *Ibid.*, p. 21.
30. *Ibid.*, p. 18.
31. Harvard, March 20, 1891.
32. Sutcliffe, pp. 20–21.
33. *Ibid.*, p. 21.
34. *Ibid.*, p. 22.
35. Deed in Wiscasset County Clerk's Office.
36. Harvard, Aug. 10, 1891.
37. Several factors point, though inconclusively, to the completion of the cottage, Herman's and Emma's entry, and the housewarming, in mid-August. For Win to have been there it must have been early in July, before he went to Boston, which was unlikely because of the time necessary for building, or after July 28 when he returned. Also, Herman's swing in August to the support of Win's Harvard ambitions is some evidence that he was not there earlier.
38. Sutcliffe, pp. 23–24.
39. *Ibid.*, p. 25.

ACT II

1. Harvard, to Arthur Gledhill, Oct. 11, 1891, and May 22, 1892.
2. Sutcliffe, p. 76.
3. Hagedorn, p. 78.
4. Sutcliffe, p. 40.
5. Harvard, to Harry DeForest Smith, Feb. 3, 1892 (mistakenly written "1891").

6. *Ibid.*, Feb. 7, 1892.

7. *Ibid.*, May 15, 1892.

8. *Ibid.* Mrs. William Nivison, Robinson's niece and executor, naturally regrets what seems to me the necessity of recording this brief passage in his life, so normal in its beginning for any young man in the nineties, and so typical in its conclusion of Robinson's special nobility. Generously, Mrs. Nivison first wrote me tentative permission to quote passages from the letter in question and from another letter of similar purport. Subsequently she wrote me that, while still deploring any reference to this phase of her uncle's life, she yet preferred quotation of the passage to paraphrase; and at the same time she forbade any other quotation from the letters in this field. On hearing of the original correspondence between Mrs. Nivison and me, William A. Jackson, eminent head of Houghton Library, Harvard, which has custody of the letters, encouraged her to withdraw the tentative permission she had given me, which she did. He also suggested that she refuse me permission to quote from all and sundry inoffensive letters of Robinson if I persisted in making any reference to the experiences recorded in the letters whose quotation he had prevented. Mrs. Nivison did not adopt this suggestion. Upon my later notifying Mr. Jackson of her subsequent preference for quotation over paraphrase, he denied, through his agent, the library's permission to quote—I having originally signed an undertaking not to quote without the library's permission.

The account of the controverted letter given here is an objective summary of its pertinent contents, being neither quotation nor paraphrase, and failing therefore to reproduce Robinson's eloquence or otherwise to record his strong feelings in the premises. A copy of the quotation in question, together with quotations from other letters to Smith during the same period, and together with my correspondence with Mrs. Nivison and Mr. Jackson, will be deposited among my papers in the Beinicke Library of Yale University, to be made available at some future time when their publication will not embarrass any person now living, and when Harvard's prohibition of their publication will have expired. It is my belief that, in view of Mr. Jackson's censorious posture, this is what Robinson would have desired.

9. *Ibid.*, March 13, 1892.

10. *Ibid.*, June 5, 1892.

11. Sutcliffe, pp. 83–84.

12. *Ibid.*, p. 49.

13. *Ibid.*, p. 67.

14. *Ibid.*, p. 46.

15. Hagedorn, p. 68.

16. Sutcliffe, p. 44.

17. *Ibid.*, pp. 57–58.

18. Hagedorn, p. 83.

19. Sutcliffe, p. 48.

20. *Ibid.*, p. 60.

21. *Ibid.*

22. *Ibid.*, p. 80.

23. *Ibid.*, p. 53.

24. Hagedorn, pp. 82–83.

25. Sutcliffe, p. 76.

26. *Ibid.*, p. 102.

27. *Ibid.*, p. 31.
28. *Ibid.*, p. 66.
29. *Ibid.*, pp. 86–87.
30. *Ibid.*, p. 126.
31. *Ibid.*, p. 61.
32. *Ibid.*, p. 40.
33. *Ibid.*, p. 73.
34. *Ibid.*
35. *Ibid.*, p. 47.
36. *Ibid.*, p. 61.
37. *Ibid.*, p. 53.
38. Hagedorn, p. 83.
39. Harvard, March 13, 1892.
40. Sutcliffe, p. 37.
41. *Ibid.*, pp. 102–103.

ACT III

1. Sutcliffe, p. 107.
2. *Colby Quarterly*, Dec., 1960, David S. Nivison, "How Annandale Went Out," p. 181.
3. Hagedorn, p. 85.
4. Sutcliffe, p. 117.
5. *Ibid.*, p. 152.
6. Harvard, Oct. 28, 1893.
7. Sutcliffe, p. 113.
8. *Ibid.*, p. 131.
9. *Ibid.*, pp. 135–36.
10. *Ibid.*, p. 148.
11. The *Sonnet* finding "God's wholeness" in "love's elemental overglow" was probably not written before '94 nor later than '95. It is probably Emma's, but might have drawn something from Mabel Moore.
12. Sutcliffe, pp. 159–60.
13. *Ibid.*, p. 163.
14. *Ibid.*, pp. 149–50.
15. *Ibid.*, pp. 153–57.
16. *Ibid.*, p. 161.
17. *Letters*, p. 13.
18. Sutcliffe, p. 273.
19. *Ibid.*, p. 289.
20. *The Miracle*, in the form given here, was first published in September, '94, in *The Globe*, Chicago and Philadelphia. In *The Torrent and the Night Before*, "love" is substituted for "Faith" in the last line.
21. Sutcliffe, p. 170.
22. *Ibid.*, p. 186.
23. *Ibid.*, p. 211.
24. *Ibid.*, p. 215.
25. *Ibid.*, p. 219.
26. *Ibid.*, p. 228.
27. *Ibid.*, p. 227.

28. *Ibid.*, p. 230.
29. *Ibid.*, p. 234.
30. *Ibid.*, p. 239.
31. *Ibid.*, p. 241.
32. *Ibid.*, p. 244.
33. *Ibid.*, p. 247.
34. *Ibid.*, p. 246.
35. *Ibid.*, p. 249.
36. *Colophon.*
37. Sutcliffe, p. 254.
38. *Ibid.*, pp. 259–60.
39. *Ibid.*, p. 261.
40. *Ibid.*, p. 166.
41. *The Dark House* is usually interpreted as Robinson's confession of his own alcoholism, which in fact never existed except in his friends' apprehension over his enormous capacity. Whenever he thought he was drinking too much for the good of his work, he stopped easily and rode on the water wagon for many months. The Legend assigns *The Dark House* to Dean, which seems to me reasonable on all scores.
42. Robinson himself reported that he wrote the first twenty-four lines of what he first called "George Annandale" in New York on January 13, '98. This does not necessarily vitiate the Legend. After the funeral he may well have gone upstairs to the death chamber, experienced some of the feelings of the poem, and even conceived a few tentative lines.
43. Sutcliffe, pp. 264–65.
44. R. Richards.
45. Sutcliffe, pp. 267–68.
46. *Ibid.*, p. 277.
47. *Ibid.*, p. 270.
48. *Ibid.*, pp. 273–74.
49. This is from an excellent source outside the legend, who also wishes to remain anonymous.
50. The biographies and biographical sketches of Robinson to date state that in one fashion or another the family bought the drugstore. One school holds that Edward Robinson bought it, which would have made the purchase not later than '92. Another school holds that in '97 Win heroically put the last of his inheritance into the purchase "in order to give his brothers another chance." The latter account is nearer the truth but it is still very far from it. The investment was the modest one of $2,700 made out of the estate of about $15,000 in which Win had a third interest. It was in the stock of the store only, and the real estate itself was never purchased. The records of the County Clerk of Kennebec County show that one Henry Johnson got title to the premises from his father in 1881, that he held them until 1918 when he died leaving them to his wife, that in 1919 she sold them to Benjamin W. Jackson who was then occupying them as a drugstore and who was the same Jackson who in July of 1901 had bought the stock of the store from the estate of Dean Robinson. In short, the title of Johnson was continuous from 1881 to 1919, the premises being operated as a drugstore under successive leases, first to F. M. Noyes from some uncertain date until '97, then to the Robinsons from '97 to 1901, and there-

after to Jackson until he bought the premises and continued to operate the drugstore there well into living memory.

51. *Gardiner Story.*

52. Harvard.

53. R. Richards.

54. *Ibid.*

55. In September, '96, Robinson had indicated in a letter to Smith (Sutcliffe, p. 253) that he had been experimenting with "Lucretius Octaves."

56. Richard Cary, "E.A. Robinson as Soothsayer," *Colby Quarterly*, June, 1963, p. 237. See also Sutcliffe, p. 283.

57. Sutcliffe, p. 278.

58. Professor Cary, basing his opinion on the correspondence with Edith Brower, presumes that the composition of the *Octaves* continued through May.

59. Sutcliffe, p. 281.

60. *Ibid.*, pp. 280–81.

61. *Ibid.*, p. 282.

62. *Ibid.*

63. L. Richards, p. 49.

64. Sutcliffe, p. 284.

65. For the personal material on Hays Gardiner I am especially grateful for an account of him written for me by his cousin the late Rosalind Richards; also for the obituary account of him in the *Harvard Bulletin* for May 21, 1913, which she sent me.

66. Sutcliffe, p. 286.

67. R. Richards, dictated by Laura Richards.

68. *Ibid., et seq.*

69. *Ibid.*

70. *Ibid.*

71. Sutcliffe, p. 285.

72. *Ibid.*, p. 287.

73. Neff, pp. 95–96, citing R. Richards.

74. *The Admirable Discourses of Bernard Palissy*, translated by Auriele la Rocque (Urbana, University of Illinois Press, 1957, p. 198ff).

75. A fair example of Robinson's bland disingenuousness about his "objectivity" is his note on this poem for Sanders and Nelson's *Chief Modern Poets of England and America* (New York, Macmillan, 1949 ed., p. 495): "Partnership was published under the title 'The Wife of Palissy' . . . In a misguided moment I changed it—with some notion, I suppose, of giving the poem a more general application. It is (or was) obviously one of Palissy's porcelains. Now it can be almost anything"—such as a manuscript one has labored on, is about to send off to the publisher, and shows in triumph to one's girl!

76. For the financial records, see pp. 206–09ff, and Note 37.

ACT IV

1. Sutcliffe, p. 293.

2. Harvard, letter to Smith, Jan. 5, 1898.

3. Bates, p. 14.

4. Hagedorn, p. 143.

5. Sutcliffe, p. 297.

6. *Ibid.*, p. 298.

7. *Ibid.*, p. 297.

8. Neff, p. 97.

9. *Ibid.*

10. Hagedorn, p. 153, and Neff, p. 101.

11. Sutcliffe, p. 299.

12. Harvard, letter to James Barstow, July 1, 1899.

13. *Virginia Quarterly*, Winter, 1937, pp. 54–55.

14. *Ibid.*, p. 56.

15. *Letters*, p. 22.

16. Sutcliffe, p. 301.

17. *Colby Quarterly*, December, 1960, David S. Nivison, "How Annandale Went Out," pp. 179–84.

18. Record by Laura Richards, June 29, 1939, Harvard.

19. Hagedorn, p. 156.

20. *Ibid.*, p. 163.

21. *Ibid.*, p. 164.

22. Sutcliffe, p. 305.

23. *Virginia Quarterly*, Winter, 1937, p. 61.

24. *Ibid.*, p. 66.

25. *Ibid.*, pp. 67–68.

26. *Virginia Quarterly*, Spring, 1937, p. 236.

27. Hagedorn, p. 180.

28. *Ibid.*, p. 181.

29. *Virginia Quarterly*, Winter, 1937, p. 69. According to the family legend, the last of Herman's investments to collapse was the Jasper Mine, which inspired the title of Robinson's posthumous *King Jasper*.

30. Neff, p. 106.

31. *Virginia Quarterly*, Winter, 1937, p. 67.

32. *Letters*, p. 50.

33. There is a cryptographic school that holds that Robinson aimed at phonetic resemblances between the names of his characters and their models in the family. "The Book of Annandale" is one of the best exhibits: "Annandale" is suggestive of "Robinson"—or why not "Arlington"? "M" dominates in both "Emma" and "Damaris," while the latter virtually elides into a two-syllable word; "Argan" does very neatly as a cipher for Herman, "Miriam" for Mary, Robinson's mother. Other points for this argument are "Avon" for Herman, "Penn-Raven" for Edwin, Roman Bartholow for Herman Robinson, and all the trisyllables Cavender, Nightingale, Timberlake, and Talifer, all supposedly suggesting "Robinson." Or perhaps either "Robinson" or "Arlington"—a reminder of a remark he once made, that his whole name sounded like a tin pan falling down the cellar stairs. Some doubt falls on the cryptographic theory when we recall that most of his principal female characters after Damaris—namely Vivian, Guinevere, Gabrielle, Laramie, Agatha, and Natalie—also bear melodious trisyllabic names with accent on the *antepenult*, always easy to handle in iambic verse.

34. Hagedorn, p. 184.

35. Neff, p.106.
36. *Virginia Quarterly*, Spring, 1937, p. 232.
37. It would seem that a useful paper, based on more research than has here been attempted, might be written on the Robinson estate and its bearing on the poet's economy, in Gardiner, Cambridge, and New York, during the years 1897–1904. But for the $600 Hagedorn allows him (Hagedorn, p. 126) out of the estate when he left Gardiner in late '97, the absurd job in Harvard in '99, and the more absurd job in the New York subway construction in 1903–04, the biographies and sketches leave him from the outset to the mercy of God, friends who don't collect rent, friends who buy him meals, waiters who lend him $2, and an occasional garbage can. This charming image of the starving poet is surely exaggerated. None of these pathetic symptoms appear till the spring of 1901, and the reasonable assumption is that from early '97 through 1900, Robinson had enough from the estate to live in respectable poverty that was a good way short of destitution. For a young man of modest habits and bohemian association at the end of the nineties, this could have been as little as seven or eight hundred a year. From Robinson's reference (page 187 of the text) to "the last smash in my western real estate," the effects of which he was feeling by September, 1900, it would seem highly probable that during the preceding four years he had been getting some such support out of the estate, presumably by the sale of western lands the records of which, doubtless buried in county clerks offices from Minnesota to Oklahoma, have not been unearthed.

On the question of the amount and method of administration of the estate of Mary E. Robinson, formerly that of Edward Robinson, there are two sets of inconclusive though pertinent figures available, one among the papers of the family, the other in the archives of the Kennebec County Probate Court.

Among the family items there is, under date of February 13, 1897, a Bill of Sale of drugstore stock by F. M. Noyes to Horace Dean Robinson for $2,700 (not paid for till the following July, as shown below); there is, under date of March 26, 1897, a cancelled note of Herman E. Robinson to the Maine Trust and Banking Company for $670, endorsed by Horace Dean Robinson, then administrator; there is, under date of April 1, 1897, a cancelled note of "H. D. Robinson & Co.," to the bank for $400; there is, as of July 20, 1897 a cancelled note to the bank of Herman E. Robinson as administrator for $400; and, under date of January 1, 1898, there is a note of Herman E. Robinson to the bank for $400.

In the probate records, the appraisal, probably as part of the final accounting, of the estate of Mary E. Robinson, on January 21, 1901, is in summary as follows:

Real Estate:

Homestead on Lincoln Ave., Gardiner	$2,500.
1 Block 4 Lot 7 Kings addition	Unknown value
Exposition lot	Unknown value
2 lots in Windom addition	85.33
24 lots in Boardman's addition	Unknown value
2 lots in Cottage City	Unknown value
	$2,585.33 2,585.33

Personality:

50 shares L.A.W.P. stock	$3,000.
20 shares Merchants National Bank Stock .	1,000.
1 bond City of McPherson, Kansas, par 1,000	970.
1 bond Arkansas City, Kansas, par 1,000 .	970.
1 bond Coolidge Township, Kansas, par 1,000	Unknown value
Notes of Herman E. Robinson in the amount of $5,800	Unknown value
10 shares Madison Woolen Company $800 —sold	800.
Mortgages on Preble and Keene property, Gardiner, Me., sold by H.D. Robinson in July, '97, and put in drugstore stock	2,700.
	$9,440.

$9,440.00

$12,025.33

In the personalty, the item of Herman's $5,800 of worthless notes can be disregarded as probably representing old borrowings from his mother, or even from his father, when they were alive. For Herman as administrator to have borrowed personally from the estate would have been criminal, and no such suggestion has ever been included in the charges against him. Likewise we may ignore the $2,700 item of the drugstore stock, which had been bought for Dean and belonged to him. The amount of liquid personalty in the estate, as of January, 1901, becomes $6,740. Since no further accounting of this sum appears, since there is no evidence that any of it reached Win, and since there is no basis for felonious suspicions against Herman, it may be presumed that it went into some legitimate disposition of the estate, either administration, distribution, or payment of debts. Allowing for Herman's peripatetic habits of administration, $6,000 would seem a moderate estimate of value of the estate, outside of the house, that disappeared between January, 1901, and early 1903 when there was nothing left.

Since the family papers show borrowing on the part of the estate of at least $1,070, and probably $1,470, for the year 1897 alone, it would seem likely that this was a method of effecting distribution in anticipation of the irregular sales of the western lands. Wherefore, a reasonable explanation of the disappearance of the $6,000, more or less, could be that at the time of the accounting in January, 1901, the bank held notes in some such amount, covering advances to Herman and Win during the past three years. Considering that we know, from the family papers, of advances to Dean, on account of the drugstore, of $2,700 for the stock, and further $400, presumably also out of the estate, since we know of advances to Dean totaling $3,100 early in 1897, after which the drugstore presumably carried him, $6,000 would be such an amount as we might reasonably expect to have been divided between Herman and Win thereafter, until the accounting in 1901. This would have given Win about $750 a year, which was enough. For the care of Herman and his family we are left to our guesses between western lands Herman owned personally and the previously enjoyed largess of Emma's father.

38. Dean's administrator, appointed February 2, 1901, made his "First and Final Account" on the Fourth Monday of December, 1904. It shows property collected as follows:

July 27, 1901—Sale of drugstore stock to B. W. and
          J. R. Jackson $2,400.00
July 27, 1901—November 5, 1903, miscellaneous items
          totaling   257.87
                                              $2,657.87

Out of this amount there were payments "except to heirs,"
between May 10, 1900, and April 2, 1902, of   1,086.57
                                              $1,571.30

This balance was distributed evenly between Win and Herman, as follows:

To Win		To Herman	
8/15/01	$100.00	10/25/01	$500.00
8/30/01	275.00		
id.	125.00		
1/ 3/02	60.00	2/24/02	100.00
3/25/02	133.25	4/ 2/02	95.01
4/ 1/02	40.00	id.	53.10
4/ 3/02	14.86	11/ 5/02	37.54
11/ 5/02	25.00		
id.	12.54		
	$785.65		$785.65 1,571.30
			$0,000.00

39. Colby, March 9, 1902.

40. Photostat of *Mss.* in Colby Library, initialed and dated in Robinson's hand, April 2, 1901.

41. *Virginia Quarterly*, Spring, 1937, p. 236.

42. See Note 38, above.

43. *Virginia Quarterly*, Spring, 1937, p. 237.

44. Hagedorn, p. 186.

45. Neff, p. 141.

46. Daniel Gregory Mason, *Music in My Time* (New York, Macmillan, 1938), p. 127.

47. *Letters*, p. 53.

48. *Ibid.*

49. Hagedorn, p. 207.

50. *Ibid.*, p. 208.

51. *Letters*, pp. 53–54.

52. The family legend dates this incident "about 1905." It must have occurred at some time between Robinson's emergence from the subway in August, 1904, and his departure for Boston in January, 1905.

53. Although *Bokardo* was not published till 1915, it was probably written much earlier, because Robinson generally did not flay Herman in verse after 1909.

54. Emma put it in the Legend that the gruesome sonnet *En Passant* referred to Herman during the years "1906–1909." But it suits so nicely

Win's coming "out of his . . . grave" at this time to take care of Herman,
that it is tempting to attribute the basis of it to the events of late '04 and
the first half of '05. More than *Bokardo*, it is transmuted into a fictitious
form, and so was presumably written very much later, possibly not long
before its publication in 1924:

> I should have glanced and passed him, naturally,
> But his designs and mine were opposite;
> He spoke, and having temporized a bit,
> He said that he was going to the sea:
> "I've watched on highways for so long," said he,
> "That I'll go down there to be sure of it."
> And all at once his famished eyes were lit
> With a wrong light—or so it seemed to me.
>
> That evening there was talk along the shore
> Of one who shot a stranger, saying first:
> "You should have come when called. This afternoon
> A gentleman unknown to me before,
> With deference always due to souls accurst,
> Came out of his own grave—and not too soon."

Here, as elsewhere, is Herman's fiendish "kink" that found full expression, at
about the probable time of the composition of this, in *Avon's Harvest*.

ACT V

1. The legend contains a vague generality that Win visited Herman *at
some time* on Capitol, but it is clear that he did not visit Gardiner at this
period. Since the Boston boat put in at Boothbay Harbor, not far from
Capitol, Robinson might have gone up there and back without undertaking the other thirty miles up to his home town.

2. Hagedorn, p. 236.

3. MacKaye celebrated the restaurant and the company in *Uriel*
(Boston, Houghton Mifflin, 1912) written in honor of Moody after his death
in 1910. In the poem MacKaye devotes a stanza to Robinson's compassion
for suffering humanity, perhaps the first published recognition of this his
central quality.

4. *Letters*, p. 61.

5. *Ibid.*, pp. 61–62.

6. *Ibid.*, p. 62.

7. Sutcliffe, p. 308. Actually, the correspondence continues until 1932.

8. Hagedorn, p. 222.

9. *Ibid.*

10. There are no clear dates of Herman's coming down with tuberculosis, and of his going to Boston for treatment. He died early in 1909, and
Neff (p. 151) says he was ill two years.

11. Hagedorn, p. 252.

12. Harvard. The Ledoux correspondence began a little earlier than
1909 and lasted till Robinson's death in '35. It involved both Mr. and Mrs.
Ledoux, and I believe she was the only female correspondent Robinson ever
addressed personally by her Christian name. The double correspondence
was the sixth and youngest of his great ones, the others being, in order of

seniority, those with Gledhill, Smith, Edith Brower, Laura Richards, and Mason.

13. Hagedorn, p. 252.

14. Harvard. (Commodore Peary had discovered the North Pole the previous April, had returned safely in August, and I have not found what new craziness he was up to in September.)

15. *Ibid.*, Sept. 13, 1916.

16. Hagedorn, p. 255. Two days later on October 9, he wrote Ridgely Torrence in the cryptic, allegorical vein that was their practice with each other. The "Mrs. D" referred to is probably Mrs. Dunbar, the mother of their mutual friend Olivia in whom Robinson was supposed to have an interest and whom Torrence eventually married. Mrs. Dunbar was often on Monhegan Island in Boothbay Harbor, in sight from Capitol Island: "Dear T— . . . I was glad to hear yesterday from Mrs. D that you have caught a fish. I hope that means that you are to have at least a better fed winter than I can see for myself. But as I expect to do the work the coming year that I have not done in the past four years, I shall not have time to worry about grub. . . ." (Princeton.)

17. Pages 57-58.

EPILOGUE

1. Bates, p. 22.

2. Colby, August 7, 1912.

3. *Letters*, pp. 79-80.

4. Colby, March 23, 1913.

5. Harvard, June 7, 1913.

6. R. Richards.

7. Brown, p. 69.

8. The account of this episode and its results was given me by Boris Todrin as given to him by Ridgely in the frankness of friendship and cups not long before his death. The rumored affair between Olivia and Robinson is most dubious. If it ever occurred, it would have been before Robinson's visit to Gardiner in late 1909, for I take as credible Ridgely's statement to me that following that debacle Robinson "took the veil." I also tend to accredit Ridgely's bawdy guffaw when I asked him whether E.A. always lived celibate. Text, p. 57.

9. Princeton.

10. Santayana was a graduate student at Harvard when Robinson was there. In *Poetry and Religion,* published in 1900 (Scribner), speaking of the experience of saints, he said (p. 87): ". . . redemption was actually accomplished and the soul was lifted above the condition of life, so that death itself could bring but a slight and unessential change of environment."

11. *Letters*, p. 87.

12. *Ibid.*, p. 112.

13. *Ibid.*, p. 113.

14. Hagedorn, p. 319.

15. Neff, p. 192.

16. *Ibid.*, p. 193.

17. Hagedorn, p. 319.

18. *Letters,* p. 112.
19. *Ibid.,* p. 106.
20. Colby, Dec. 14, 1918.
21. *Letters,* p. 114.
22. Colby, June 3, 1920.
23. Neff, p. 207.
24. Robinson said to me, "I suppose Mr. Flood is the best thing I have done."
25. Bates, p. 12.
26. Colby.
27. Harvard, June 16, 1932.
28. Colby, May 18, 1927.

PART THREE

1. Sutcliffe, p. 80.
2. Hagedorn, p. 78.
3. *Letters,* p. 111.
4. *Ibid.,* pp. 165–66.
5. Harvard, Aug. 20, 1926, quoted in Barnard, p. 297.
6. *Letters,* pp. 165–66.

I

7. Sutcliffe, p. 267.
8. Kaplan, p. 5.
9. Nancy Evans, "Record of an Interview," *The Bookman,* Nov., 1932, p. 679.
10. Sutcliffe, p. 87.
11. *Ibid.,* p. 88.
12. Kaplan, p. 29.
13. Sutcliffe, pp. 279–80.
14. Edwin S. Fussell, *The Literary Background of a Traditional Poet* (Berkeley, University of California Press, 1954).
15. Kaplan, p. 11.
16. Sutcliffe, p. 263.
17. *Ibid.,* p. 264.
18. *Ibid.,* pp. 70, 263, and 274.
19. *Ibid.,* p. 239.
20. Harvard, to Smith, April 24, 1892.
21. *Ibid.,* March 13, 1892.
22. Sutcliffe, p. 264.
23. *Ibid.,* p. 253.
24. *Yale Review,* June, 1936, pp. 860–64.
25. Kaplan, p. 31.

II

1. Morris, p. 38, cited in Kaplan, p. 25.
2. Barnard, p. 178.
3. Hagedorn, p. 198.

4. Sutcliffe, p. 108.
5. *Ibid.*, p. 130.
6. Hagedorn, p. 286.
7. Barnard, p. 121.
8. *Ibid.*, pp. 158–59.
9. Morris, p. 71, cited in Barnard, p. 206.
10. Barnard, pp. 158–59.
11. Sutcliffe, p. 285.
12. *Letters*, p. 121.
13. Barnard, p. 235.
14. Sutcliffe, p. 4.
15. *Letters*, p. 175
16. Hagedorn, pp. 332–33.
17. *Letters*, p. 158
18. Sutcliffe, p. 216
19. *Letters*, p. 115.
20. *Ibid.*, p. 128.
21. Sutcliffe, p. 251.
22. *Ibid.*, p. 261.
23. Hagedorn, p. 285.
24. *Letters*, p. 115.
25. *Ibid.*, p. 124.
26. Sutcliffe, p. 53.
27. *Colby Quarterly*, June, 1963, Richard Cary, "E. A. Robinson as Soothsayer," p. 242.
28. *Letters*, p. 175.

III

1. *Letters*, p. 160.
2. *Ibid.*, p. 170.
3. Hagedorn, p. 72.
4. *Ibid.*, p. 83.
5. *Ibid.*, p. 91.
6. Sutcliffe, p. 244.
7. *Ibid.*, p. 247.
8. Kaplan, p. 32.
9. Sutcliffe, p. 274.
10. *Ibid.*, p. 281.
11. *Ibid.*, p. 286.
12. Harvard, Sept. 14, 1900, quoted in Barnard, p. 246.
13. Sutcliffe, p. 260.
14. *Ibid.*, p. 288.
15. *Letters*, p. 13.
16. Sutcliffe, p. 270.
17. *Ibid.*, 280.
18. *Ibid.*
19. *Letters*, p. 169.
20. Hagedorn, p. 186.
21. Sutcliffe, p. 285.

22. *Letters,* p. 115.
23. Sutcliffe, p. 252.
24. *Letters,* p. 65.
25. *Ibid.,* p. 168.
26. Barnard, p. 149.
27. Sutcliffe, p. 24.
28. *Ibid.,* p. 279.
29. Barnard, pp. 227–28.
30. Karl Schriftgiesser, "An American Poet Speaks His Mind," *Boston Evening Transcript,* Nov. 4, 1933, Book Section, p. 1, quoted in Barnard, p. 229.
31. Hagedorn, p. 286.
32. *Letters,* p. 9.
33. *Ibid.*
34. *Ibid.,* pp. 11–12.
35. Evans, p. 676, quoted in Barnard, p. 9.
36. Hagedorn, p. 89.
37. *Letters,* p. 13.
38. *The Application of Redemption,* p. 55.
39. *Works,* John A. Albro ed., Boston, 1953, p. 235.
40. *Representative Selections,* Faust & Johnson (New York, American Writers Series, American Book Company, 1935).
41. *Letters,* p. 113.
42. Sutcliffe, pp. 130–31.
43. *Letters,* pp. 170–71.
44. Hagedorn, p. 91.
45. Sutcliffe, p. 252.
46. *Ibid.,* p. 264.
47. *Letters,* p. 142.

IV

1. Harvard, to Josephine Peabody Marks, Nov. 17, 1919, quoted by Barnard, p. 12.
2. Sutcliffe, p. 4.
3. *Letters,* p. 64.
4. *Ibid.,* p. 121.
5. *Ibid.,* p. 103.
6. *Ibid.,* p. 63.
7. Sutcliffe, pp. 115–16.
8. Neff, pp. 108–9.
9. *Ibid.,* p. 109.
10. *Letters,* pp. 81–82.
11. Evans, p. 676, quoted in Barnard, p. 17.
12. Hagedorn, p. 298.
13. *Letters,* p. 106.
14. Barnard, p. 15, and p. 54.
15. *Letters,* p. 40.
16. *Ibid.,* pp. 93–94.
17. *Ibid.,* p. 48.
18. *Ibid.,* p. 50.

19. Hagedorn, p. 319.
20. *Letters*, p. 106.
21. Sutcliffe, p. 5.
22. *Ibid.*, p. 273.
23. Barnard, p. 28, quoting Joyce Kilmer, *Literature in the Making* (New York, Harper, 1917), p. 269.
24. Hagedorn, p. 101.
25. *Letters*, p. 128.
26. *Ibid.*, p. 93.
27. *Ibid.*, p. 128.

PART FOUR

1. Colby, Feb. 3, 1927.
2. I do not vouch for my memory of figures.
3. *Colophon.*
4. Hagedorn, p. 352.
5. Colby, August 7, 1932.
6. *Ibid.*, July 4, 1933.
7. Page 259.
8. *Letters*, p. 156.
9. Letter to Laura Richards in October, 1930; also Hagedorn, p. 155.
10. Colby, March, 1931.
11. *Colby Quarterly*, Dec. 1960, Richard Cary, "Robinson's Notes to His Nieces," p. 200.
12. Colby, Oct. 23, 1931.
13. *Colby Quarterly*, Dec. 1960, Richard Cary, pp. 196–7.
14. *Virginia Quarterly*, Spring, 1937.
15. Colby, Sept. 9, 1930.
16. *Ibid.*, Feb. 15, 1931.
17. *Ibid.*, July 31, 1931.
18. Hagedorn, p. 376.
19. Sutcliffe, p. 308.
20. Colby, June 3, 1920.
21. *Ibid.*, June 30, 1925, Jan. 21, 28, Aug. 8, 1931, *et al.*
22. *Ibid.*, June, 1932.
23. *Ibid.*, June 20, 1933.
24. Hagedorn, p. 371.
25. Sutcliffe, p. 73.
26. Hagedorn, p. 376.

Comment on Sources

1. Neff, p. 224.
2. Hagedorn, p. 341.
3. *Letters*, p. 145.
4. Harvard, Sept. 30, 1909.
5. Hagedorn, p. 252.
6. *Colby Quarterly*, Dec., 1960, Richard Cary, "Robinson's Notes to His Nieces," p. 167.

PERSONAL INDEX

Except where it is possible to quote a familiar phrase of Robinson's, no attempt is made to distinguish in the Index between his attitudes and the author's interpretations of them. Because of the considerable use that has been made of letters of Daniel Gregory Mason and Harry DeForest Smith, and the mostly uniform sources of them respectively, as given in the Notes, those quotations derived from these uniform sources are not cited individually in the Index, but general reference is made, in the case of Mason to the entries of *Virginia Quarterly Review* in the Notes, and in the case of Smith to the entries of "Sutcliffe." The names of persons mentioned in the Comment on Sources, the Acknowledgments, and the Notes are omitted from the Index unless there is some close relationship with Robinson.

INDEX OF TITLES